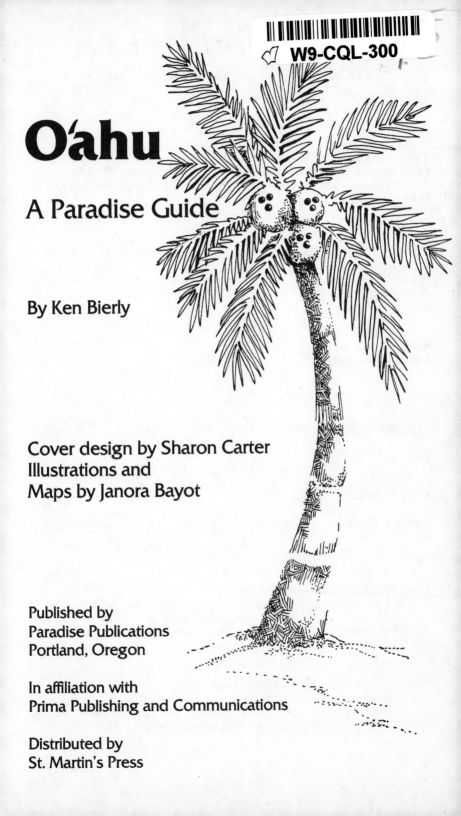

W9-CQL-300

# O'ahu

## A Paradise Guide

By Ken Bierly

Cover design by Sharon Carter
Illustrations and
Maps by Janora Bayot

Published by
Paradise Publications
Portland, Oregon

In affiliation with
Prima Publishing and Communications

Distributed by
St. Martin's Press

# "O'AHU: KAHI O KA HUI 'ANA"
# (O'ahu: The Gathering Place)

This book is dedicated with affecftion and gratitude to our hosts and hostesses, the people of Hawaii, past present and future - whose tradition of Aloha offers a beacon of hope to our weary world, and makes Hawaii Nei the loveliest spot on Earth.

Paradise Publications
8110 S.W. Wareham
Portland, OR 97223
(503) 246-1555

First edition: June 1989

ISSN 1042-8038

Printed in U.S.A.

COVER DESIGN: Sharon Carter
Sharon Carter received her BA in fine arts in 1972 from the University of Texas. Currently a resident on the Big Island of Hawaii, she is involved in a variety of freelance multi-media activities including cartooning and weaving, and has been featured in a number of exhibitions.

PEN & INK SKETCHES and MAPS: Janora Bayot
Janora Bayot is a freelance artist living in Portland, Oregon. In addition to working for six years with the Vancouver Columbian newspaper, she has worked on behalf of animal agencies. She especially enjoys cartooning.

# ACKNOWLEDGEMENTS

As the list of people I interviewed grew longer and longer, it became impossible for me to list each of these generous people for you. So let me acknowledge all at once the people I have omitted. This book is written in part by each of them. To the bellhop who took an extra moment to describe the hotel, the tired traveler who shared a favorite restaurant with me, the local resident who pointed out a sight that no visitor should miss, to every one of you who offered input - this is your book. Please accept my thanks, and those of the reader, for breathing life and aloha into these pages. Whatever enjoyment and assistance this book brings to its owners is largely due to your generosity and willingness to share your beloved island with new friends.

This book is dedicated to you the reader, for sharing your aloha; and to every person who helped with this book's conception, gestation and birth, including:

My family - Mom and Dad, Pam, Brandy, Becky, Jamie, Kendall, Travis, Deede, Lenore, Lucille, Dick and Fran, and John; Greg, Christie, Maren and Jeff; Linda, Jan, Judy and Sharon; Leilani, Kilohana and Imaka; Montez and Mr. Pollock at HAL; Jo Garner; Lindy Boyes and the HVB; Rod and Lynette Tam; Lydia and Bill Maioho; Rudy Mitchell; Ma Pahinui, Bla and all the Pahinui family; Nancy Brown; Ron and Donna Kats; Evie Warner and Al Davis; students and staff of Kahala and Nuuanu Elementary Schools; June Gutmanis; Keo, his family and staff; Don and Jeanie Blum and Barbi; Dr. Art King, Jr.; Jay Larrin; Mahaka Sons of Niihau; KCCN; Father Claude DuTeil; Vicki McDaniel; Kehau and Bruce Yap; Marilyn Allen; Mason Altiery; Tricia Atkinson; Marge Awai; Michael Tongg; Paul Naki and the King's Guard; Al Harrington, Jay Pomaika'i Thomas, and Yvette; Melody Ball; Mary L. Bishop and Mr. & Mrs. Larry Ogle; Willie Blanco; Smiley; Lea; Helen Gibbons; Doug Taylor; Robert Miller; Dennis, Sheryl and Esther at Book People; David Brodis; Jay Dowsett; Andy Engilis; Dean Konia, Allan, Julie, The Honolulu Skylark, and all the folks at KQMQ; Elizabeth Lau and Pops; Cecilia Lindo; Rick Evans and Ivy; Tom Farley, Frank Fasi, Gloria Fiedler; Marylou Foley; Reverend Pujitani; Mike Egami, Stacey, and Mai Murakami; Jon Madsen; Cal A.; Kaleo; Maxine & Paula; Joan, Brian, Patsy Mink, Kimi & volunteers; Kent; Patty Thompson; Scotty; Lani Von; Elder Patterson; Jeanne Park; Terry Rollman, and Lori Howard; Peter Moon & the Band; Ken Phillips; Piilani Lua Plemer; Bob Leinau; Chef Poesch Siegfried; Clara & Gloria; Mike Foley; Senator Hiram Fong & family; Dr. Raymond, Lorri T. and Rebecca W; Clint Marantz; Mary Mast; Sherri Rigg & family; Carl Rossetti; Jackie & Herb Ward; Michael Winchatz; Sue Marsh; Judy Neal; Sue Kodani; Mick Riegel; Moku; Les Babb; Jim & Carol Zukemura and all budding magicians; Darek Sato and Holly; Ralph Seewald Jr.; Phil Sammer; Sergio!; Allan B. Shaw; Hooipo DeCambra; Barbara Sheehan, Vicki and Lisa; Michael Slackman; Noelani Cashman; Louise Cavanaugh; Norm & Doris Chula; Robbie Jean Ostrowski; Scottish Scotty; Bill Waters; Kaviko; Phoebe; Steve Mirashiro; Brian Klum & Lisa; Fred Sammis; Lynn Cook; Harriet Robinson; Kent McCoud; Bill at Ala Wai; Rhoda; Romona; Willie & Sharla; Carolyn Corn; Barbara Brunson, Jo, Dave Erdman & Jeff Hendrix at Tropical; Denis Courtois; Rick Cox, Ph.A.; Robert Cravalho; Lillian Cunningham; Evelyn Dennis; Jim Doney; Gordon Dougherty; Diane Stant; Ken Steitz; Joleen Takahaski; Mitchell Tanaka; Bruce

Ulrich; Kim; Mr. Nakamatsu; Dorothy Smith; Louis Russell; Mr. Chong; Mary & David & the Opera; Elton Murata; Mari; JoAnne & Keith Vieira; Cynthia Min; Bruce McEwan; Pege Miller; Lane Muraoka; Agnes Orlando; Ron Panzo; Mary Muirhead; Julie Franko; Marge Garza; Rev. Richard N. Gaspar; Pam Gentry; Mitsue Goya; Dana & Barbara Gray & the crew, especially Lisa & Kaycee; Sue Hansen; Paula Helfrisch and Sandy; Curtis Carlsmith; Anna May Kaanehe; Alvin Katahara; Robin Rich; Jeanne Camp; Tom Liu; Calvin & Cecilia Wong; Peter at Waikiki Plaza, Marilyn J. Cole; Doug Okada; Clyde Shimota; Glen Nakamura; Charles St. Sure; Bruce Nishamoto; Donna Jung; Fred Diamond; Herb & Verna Calvert; Marilyne Cole; Joyce Matsumoto; Louise Fujioka; Jan Pang; Merle M. Tokunaga; Mr. & Mrs. Willie Clay; Carl at Huevos; Ahi & family; Jeton; Kern Rogerson & Sal Ricca; Rance at the Pagoda; Randy Lee & staff; Elton & Mark at the Third Floor, Lea; Cindy at the Garment Factory; Frances and Jay at Pat's; Howard at Crouching Lion; Toshiko McCash; Shirley and Davenport; Melvin K. Inatsuka; Reverend Nagao and Andrea; Dave Evans; Samiko; Judy Kawahara; Joyce Oblow; Brent Ness; Don Ho & his cast; Glen Koons; Darlene Martin; John McLaughlin; Mililani Trask; Will Kyselka; Tony Huynh; Lauri and Walter Kawamoto's sister; Donna-Marie Muhlenforth; Deborah Pope; Al Danzer; Margaret Naai; Fast Eddie & wife; Beverly Fetig; Rory and Lance Fairly; Vera Rose; Bryan Lukas; Betty Okubo; Jeff & Grace Warmouth Koreyasu; Auntie Marie; Paul Atkins & Gracie Niska Atkins; Betty Lupenui; Commander Gary Schrout; Larry Ing; Jim Pavelle; Sherry Higa; Joan Aanavi; Andre DuBay; Sandra Frewer; Charlotte Clark; Bob Smolenski; Bernard at the Jubilee; Jackie at the Garden Bar; Alvin at the JR: William Panttaja; John Springsteen; Ann in Rod's office; Helen Berg; Marilyn Cole; Adriana; Elizabeth White; Irving Kukanaka; Bob Moberg; Jill Keegan; Ann Marie & Elton Murata; Marty Diamond, Caz, Joe Lungrin, Wally Martin, Keith, and all the Vietnam Vets; Bruce Burkland; John Landovsky; Georgina Surles; The Junior Company of the Hawaii State Ballet; Benji Marantz; R.M. Keahi Allen and all dancers at the Fifteenth Annual King Kamehameha Hula Competition; Sam Min and Nikki; Dr. Masaura Hanai and Chantelle; Momi and Donna at Miramar; Joe Tasso; Jean Magoffin; Alvarene & Nancy; Carol Sakagawa; Nani at Mikiala's; Folks at Heart to Heart Floral & Gifts; Steve Allen Silvanus; Donna Smith; Likly Tanaka; Clifford Biscardy; Floyd Fitzgerald; Jan Brenner; David Eskaran & Wright Bowman; Jim Patterson; Ken Coffey; Patrick J. Birmingham; Adam Susapaia; Lee Hooker; Mary C. Murphy; Lincoln J. Stokes; Jadine; Lt. Ed Awakuni; Bill Fredrickson; Durwin Tanimoto; Maria Zimmer; Jack at the Perfumery; Keiko Kishimoto; Victor Tamamoto; Rosie & Chuck Jenkins and Jeanie; Alice Guild; Bruce Ulrich; Mona Roblin; Peter Borrier; Sieni Cai; Joshua Agsalud; Frank Black; Captain Conner; Sergeants Edward Douglas and Onaga; Tiona at McCaw; Haunani; Gard Kaaloa and Josephine; Connie Crosby; Miriam Pahulehua; Tony at SOSC; Doreen at Outrigger; Paul; Josie; Mille Fuginaga; Eddie and Al at Marie's; William Lillis & Jeff; Bill Wise; Alma Cabebe; Dr. Judith Timbers; Peter F. Henze; Laurie Rodarty; Carolyn Tanaka; and Anne Ramos; Mom Kenyon; Dorothy; Annie and Susan.

*Aloha au ia oe.*

## MAYOR'S MESSAGE

Aloha. I am pleased to welcome you to the Island of Oahu.

Since their settlement in the 1100s by Polynesian voyagers, the Hawaiian Islands have served as a haven for ethnic groups from throughout the world. These groups have intermingled with the Hawaiians to form a society of mutual trust and understanding that is unparalleled in the history of other cultures.

While we have breathtaking scenery and pleasant weather year-round, what truly sets us apart are our people who generously share the spirit of aloha with their neighbors and others who come to our shores. It is my wish, therefore, that during your visit, you will make a point of getting to know us personally.

On behalf of the people of the City and County of Honolulu, I wish you a pleasant and relaxing stay on our island and express the hope that you will take our aloha with you when you leave.

FRANK F. FASI, Mayor
City and County of Honolulu

## AINAHAU

*Na ka wai lukini wai anuhea o ka rose*
*E hoʻope nei ka liko o na pua.*
*Na ka manu pikake manu hulu melemele*
*Na kahiko is o kuʻu home.*

*Na ka makani aheahe i pa mai makai*
*I lawe mai k ke onaona lipoa,*
*E hoʻoipo hoʻonipo me ke ʻala kuʻu home,*
*Kuʻu home, kuʻu home i ka ʻiuʻiu.*

*Nani wale kuʻu home ʻAinahau i ka ʻiu,*
*I ka holunape a ka lau o ka niu,*
*I ka uluwehiwehi i ke ʻala o na pua,*
*Kuʻu home, kuʻu home i ka ʻiu ʻiu.*

## COOL LAND

*O the fragrance of the flowers with their*
                    *beauty all about,*
*And the colors blending like a huge palette,*
*For the view in all directions, with the*
                    *sea a gorgeous blue,*
*Is a picture that I'll never forget.*

*From the sea come gentle breezes*
*While we watch the glistening foam,*
*And the birds add a color all their own-*
*So much beauty, so much pleasure, in a scene*
                    *beyond compare.*
*Ainahau, Ainahau, my loved home, far away!*

*O my home, my loved home,*
                    *Ainahau, Ainahau.*
*With the palm leaves gently swaying,*
*And the verdant beauty and fragrant flowers,*
*Ainahau, my loved home far away.*

-Song about the place near what is now
the Princess Kaiuluani Hotel in the
Waikiki Beach area.

Reprinted from Samuel H. Elberet and Noelani Mahoe, *Na Mele o Hawaiʻi Nei*.
© 1970 University of Hawaii Press.

# FOREWORD

Greetings, and congratulations on your choice of *O'AHU, A Paradise Guide*. My name is Ken Bierly and I have the privilege of serving as your personal travel guide while you plan and take your vacation to Hawaii's Main Island of O'ahu.

This book is the fourth in an outstanding series of successful travel guides by Paradise Publications. The Paradise Guide Series was created by two dedicated traveler-author-publishers named Greg and Christie Stilson. If you've visited Maui you know them through their first-of-its kind personalized guidebook to Maui, *MAUI: A Paradise Guide*, published originally in 1984 and now in its fourth edition.

Since writing that first guidebook, Greg and Christie, as publishers, have invited other writer-travelers to create guidebooks to each of the other Hawaiian Islands. In 1987 Kauai residents Don and Bea Donohugh wrote the widely acclaimed *KAUAI: A Paradise Guide*. *HAWAII: The Big Island, A Paradise Guide* by Big Island resident John Penisten is a new release for 1989.

A Paradise Guide to the main island of O'ahu remained to be written. Since 80% of the population of Hawaii resides on O'ahu, and since most hotels, restaurants and tourist attractions in Hawaii are also to be found there, the creation of an O'ahu guidebook with the high standards of the other Paradise Guides posed a considerable challenge. In early 1987, Christie and Greg invited this writer to undertake that challenge.

The result is the book you hold in your hands - a book of love letters to you from the most enchanting, varied, mysterious, friendly, exciting, addicting, island one can imagine - O'ahu. This book, like the original Paradise Guide to Maui, is written from a tourist perspective. As a resident of Oregon, an educator-writer-traveler, who fell in love with O'ahu on my first trip there, I was excited to spend time exploring O'ahu from top to bottom in order to bring you its best and most interesting aspects.

As part of the research for this book, I toured hotels and condominiums, stayed at bed and breakfast homes, ate in restaurants, both famous and brand new, rented cars, took tours, sampled souvenirs and listened to advice from both locals and tourists in compiling the information presented here.

The following pages are packed full of information from thousands of these sources, and you are the beneficiary of their, and my, desire to help make your trip to O'ahu a memorable one.

Inside you'll find hundreds of places to dine and stay, sights to visit and things to do. As you read our brief descriptions you can tell by the ★ which ones we feel are your best choices. By planning ahead you save money, time and energy. This book is specially designed to make your planning fun and easy.

Need to know about the weather on O'ahu? Looking for the phone number of the Hawaii Visitor's Bureau? Want to find out which annual cultural events are on the O'ahu calendar? Consult our Index or Table of Contents, flip to the page, and there it is.

Concise descriptions of attractions and transportation options are included so you can pre-plan your priorities. If you decide to visit these attractions independently the accompanying maps and tips will make your visit especially interesting. Interested in shopping; we tell you where the biggest and best shopping centers are located, as well as how and when to get there and back.

As an introduction to out-of-the-way places and fascinating people we reveal where to find hidden O'ahu; the secret, the interesting and little known places, and the special people who are the real secret of O'ahu.

You have purchased our services through this guidebook; therefore our allegiance and loyalty are exclusively to you, since we sell no advertising and have no financial arrangement with any travel, tour or vacation companies. We bring you complete and unbiased information about O'ahu's accommodations, restaurants, tours, attractions and activities. Our sole responsibility is to provide you with the most objective and complete information possible, and to help you make choices that best suit you and your vacation needs.

Save this book as a memento which will remind you of your vacation as you reread favorite items, and it will introduce family and friends to your favorite vacation spot when you lend *O'AHU, A Paradise Guide* to them - or better yet, when you give them a gift of their very own copy!

So as you, the reader, begin your travels through this book and across O'ahu, I hope you will keep one thought in mind. By visiting O'ahu you become an honorary member of Hawaii's "Ohana" - its extended family. With this new honorary family membership will come many advantages. You will be invited to share some of the most beautiful and unique sights, sounds, tastes, and people in the world. You will be offered new experiences, new friendships, and new understandings. You will be accepted as you are, and welcomed with sincere affection.

Your vacation, and your life, will be enhanced and enriched to the degree that you can share this aloha with those who freely offer it to you. For this is the most powerful, the most lasting, and the truest gift of Hawaii.

Aloha,

Ken Bierly

# TABLE OF CONTENTS

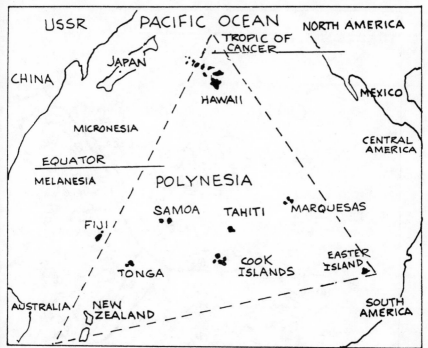

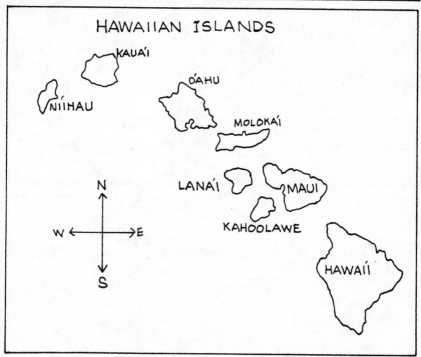

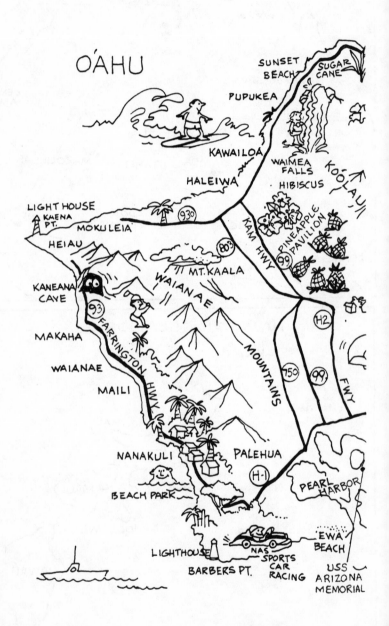

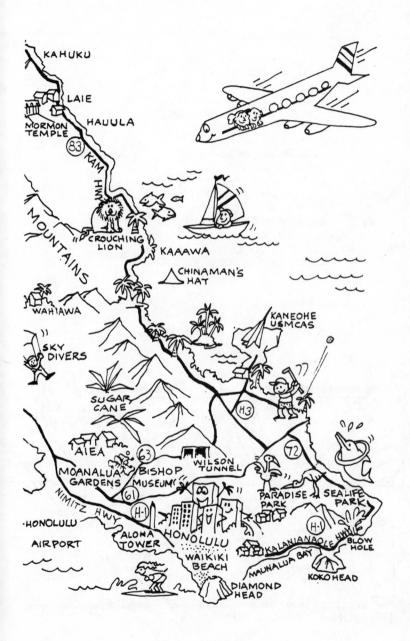

*"...when you are in that blessed retreat,*
*you are safe from the turmoil of life;*
*you drowse your days away in a long*
            *deep dream of peace;*
*the past is a forgotten thing,*
*the present is heaven,*
*the future you can leave to take*
            *care of itself.*
*You are the center of the Pacific Ocean;*
*you are miles from the world;*
*as far as you can see, on any hand,*
*the crested billows wall the horizon,*
*and beyond this barrier the wide universe*
            *is but a foreign land to you,*
*and barren of interest."*

*Mark Twain, 1872*

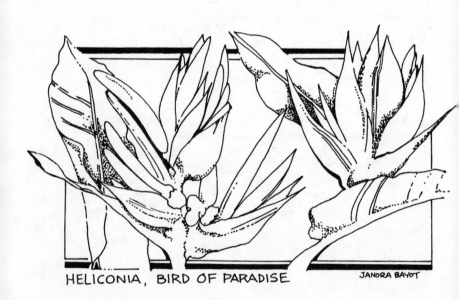

HELICONIA, BIRD OF PARADISE            JANORA BAYOT

# INTRODUCTION

## *O'AHU, THREE ISLANDS IN ONE*
## *(Hawaii's Best Kept Secret)*

The Island of O'ahu is really three islands in one. Waikiki, surrounded almost completely by water, is an island onto itself - a self contained community with more hotels, restaurants, shops and entertainment than all the other Hawaiian islands combined.

Honolulu is O'ahu's second "island." Often described as America's most beautiful city, Honolulu surprises the visitor with its open spaces, its parks, and its languid charm. Protected by mountains and sea, Honolulu has a flavor all together different from Waikiki. Near to, but separate from the tourist bustle, metropolitan Honolulu is a loose confederation of distinct neighborhoods, each with its own flavor, history and identity. The city pulses with slower rhythms than Waikiki; a lower frequency. And at night, it becomes a tropical wonderland.

Rural O'ahu is the third island-within-an-island. If you were blindfolded, lifted by helicopter off Waikiki and told you were being flown to an outer island, but were in fact set down somewhere in rural O'ahu, you would believe that you had been transported to a neighbor island. Think of almost any feature of an outer island - waterfalls, rural churches, deserted beaches, green rolling hills, small mill towns lazing in the sun - you can see them all in rural O'ahu.

Why, then, do so many visitors to O'ahu assume that Waikiki is the only place to stay, and that the attractions outside Waikiki should only be visited on a packaged tour? The reason is simple. Millions of dollars have been spent to make Waikiki into a tourist heaven, with luxurious hotels, fine restaurants, exclusive and bargain shops, and world-class entertainment. Waikiki is a classic example of an adult playground created by a healthy American free-enterprise system.

And Waikiki is *very* exciting. It's where the action is. It's where the wine, women (or men), and song flow almost 24 hours a day. For decades it has been the in-thing to vacation on Waikiki. For past generations of tourists, Waikiki *was* O'ahu, and for many Waikiki was Hawaii. But during the last 25 years, tourists began to look for an option. They discovered Maui, then Kaua'i, and more recently the Big Island and Moloka'i. They flew directly to these outer island getaways, stayed, played, got tan, swam and relaxed.

Yet for many of these outer island vacationers, something was still missing. That something often was easy access to the Disneyland atmosphere of Waikiki and so, recently the akamai (smart) tourist has been returning to O'ahu. The Main Island has become the current secret of the insider - the traveler-in-the-know has begun to rediscover O'ahu's three distinct environments.

Many of these sophisticated trend setters now book accommodations outside Waikiki, either in their favorite ethnic neighborhood of metro Honolulu, or in one of the hidden oases dotting O'ahu's magnificent coastline. Other veteran O'ahu visitors continue to stay at their favorite places in the heart of Waikiki's throbbing excitement, but leave Waikiki often, to explore glorious O'ahu in search of the bucolic settings it offers to those who know where to look.

So, in order to help you get the very most from your vacation, we have played Alice and followed this new white-rabbit breed of traveler around O'ahu in order to see where they disappear to, and now bring their secrets to you. As a result, you'll find many of O'ahu's scintillating and still-untrampled places and adventures sprinkled throughout this guidebook. So go ahead and take the tour of Honolulu you've been planning (perhaps on a re-creation of the trolleys that clanged around the city at the turn of the century) and let yourself be taken with a group to Hanauma Bay to snorkel.

But then - break the velvet bonds of Waikiki and explore the rest of O'ahu. Get lost, eat snake fillet, see how sugar is milled, sample fresh shrimp right out of an aquafarm tank, or bathe in a secluded cove. You'll find yourself in a magic land on the other side of the Waikiki looking glass, and you'll be among that lucky and growing class of traveler who can say of their O'ahu vacation, "We came in search of the hidden islands of Hawaii, and we have found them - right here on O'ahu."

# GENERAL INFORMATION

## *PERSONAL BESTS*

Best Hotel (money no object): Halekulani, Royal Hawaiian or Sheraton Moana Surfrider

Best Hotel Getaway (money no object): Kahala Hilton

Best Moderate Hotel: Princess Kaiulani

Best Resort: Hilton Hawaiian Village

Best Condo: Marine Surf Waikiki or Waikiki Beach Condominiums

Best Restaurants: Hearty breakfast - Eggs 'n Things or Michel's at the Colony Surf. Island style Lunch - Burgerland or Separate Tables. Slow, Elegant Dinner - The Third Floor or Keo's Thai Cuisine

Best Ice Cream: Bubbies, at 1010 University Avenue, Honolulu

Best Shopping: Fong's Plantation Gift Shop and Ala Moana Center

Best Pub: Rose and Crown

Best Brunch: Captain's Table at the Holiday Inn Waikiki, or Kahala Hilton Hotel

Best View: Outside - Nuuani Pali; Inside: Windows on Hawaii, Top of Waikiki or Hanohano Room in Sheraton Waikiki Hotel

Best Salad Bar: Sizzler and Chuck's Steak House. Also excellent Chinese vegetarian dishes at Five Spices on Ewa Road

Best Sunset View: Jameson's by the Sea, Hale'iwa

Best Sunrise View: Lanikai Beach, Kailua

Best Parade: Aloha Week Parade

Best Attractions for Kids: Zoo, beaches, Honolulu Aquarium, and a hike up Diamond Head Crater

Most Spectacular grounds: Hilton Hawaiian Village

Best Souvenirs: Woolworth's Waikiki

Best Luaus: Paradise Cove and Chuck Machado's

Best Beaches: #1 Waikiki - #2 Hanauma Bay, #3 Kailua Beach Park, #4 Hale'iwa Beach Park, #5 Pokai Bay Beach Park

Best Pizza: Sbarro in Makai Market at Ala Moana Center

Best Pizza for kids: Chuck E. Cheese or Show Biz Pizza

Best Golf Course: Sheraton Makaha Resort and Country Club (hotel side course)

Best Radio: Hawaiian - KCCN AM 1420. General and Top 10 - KQMQ AM 690 and 93 FM. Easy Listening - KUMU AM 1500 and FM 94.7

Best Darts: Brandy's Grill, in the Stadium Mall near Aloha Stadium

Best Show: Al Harrington, King's Guard at King's Village or Royal Hawaiian Band Concert

Best Dancing: Younger - Studebakers. Older - Del Courtney at the Royal Hawaiian Hotel

Best Singing Group: Makaha Sons of Niihau

Best Department Stores: Liberty House and Shirokiya

Most Sacred Places: Punchbowl Cemetary, Arizona and Utah Memorials, Royal Mausoleum

Most Romantic Evening: To walk in the moonlight at Waimea Falls Park; To swim at Waikiki at night during a luau or concert on the beach; To drive Tantalus; To enjoy dinner and cocktails in a private grass hut for two at the Tahitian Lanai Restaurant at the Waikikian Hotel or a candlelight dinner for two at Michel's in Colony Surf; To luxuriate with breakfast in bed in the main building at the Royal Hawaiian Hotel; A bento for two at night on Sans Souci Beach.

Best Magic Shop: Zuke's Magic and Jokes, 1516 Auld Lane, Honolulu

# EXPERIENCE OʻAHU !

To enrich your Oʻahu vacation, see and do things that are unique to Hawaii. Search out those sights and adventures you can find nowhere else, then experience them first hand.

Hawaii is rich with history. Don't miss the opportunity to experience it at the many sights around Oʻahu; The Iolani Palace, Queen Emma's Summer Palace, and the Bishop Museum. See the magnificent feathered capes of the kings, a life size sperm whale or King Kalakaua's crown. Watch the ancient Hawaiian hula dances and enjoy island music. Visit a reconstructed heiau. Listen to the Hawaiian language spoken between the local people. Stand on Pier 7 and gaze down on the *Hokuleʻa*, a recreation of an ancient Polynesian voyaging canoe. Take a ride in a double hulled canoe.

Eat Hawaiian food. Go to a luau. Try at least five things: fresh fruit such as pineapple, mango, papaya, bananas, and guava; fresh fish cooked Island style; fresh island vegetables including Manoa lettuce, Maui (Kula) onions, fresh Waimanalo corn on the cob, sweet potatoes with bright purple insides; poi eaten in combinations with a salty food such as fish; and desserts such as haupia (coconut custard). Try breadfruit chips, shave ice and a plate lunch.

Explore Oʻahu beyond Waikiki. Gaze across pineapple and sugarcane fields in the central plain and stand on the Nuuanu Pali. Visit the 1800 acre Waimea Falls Park, and see the ruins of a chief's house, or try your hand at ancient Hawaiian games. Explore tropical gardens with some of the rarest and most beautiful plants in the world, and view the huge surf on the North Shore. Enjoy an outer island experience at one of the Leeward Coast or North Shore resorts.

Meet Oʻahu residents. Learning about today's Hawaiians and some of their values and unqiue aspects of their culture will offer insights that no tour can, and you might make some new friends.

Seek out Hawaiian music. It has been said that pure Hawaiian culture still lives in its music and dance. Kihoolu, or slack key guitar, is a style of play that reflects the essence of Hawaii. There have been many artists of slack key guitar, one of the greatest, and my personal favorite is the revered Gabby Pahinui, whose music *is* Hawaii. If you're in Honolulu during the annual Kani-Kapila (playing together or jam session) in the late fall, get a ticket! Visit the House of Music in Ala Moana Center and find other slack key guitar music. This is Hawaii, pure and simple. For anyone who loves Hawaii, musicians like the Pahinui Family, Peter Moon, The Makaha Sons of Niihau, Raymond Kane, Atta Issacs, Sonny Chillingworth, and others are cultural treasures to be supported, celebrated, enjoyed and cherished.

Enjoy the Asian cultures in Hawaii. Hawaii has seen, and will continue to see, wave after wave of visitors and cultural influences wash over the islands from many parts of the world. One of Hawaii's magical powers has been her ability to absorb these waves, transform and make them a positive part of the Island's rainbow culture. As visitors to Hawaii today, we have the enviable chance to touch the culture of Japan, China, Korea, Thailand, and other parts of Asia, and to experience their foods, dress, holidays, language, and most importantly, to share the knowledge they have accumulated over thousands of years. These are venerable cultures with many things to teach us; and our fresh, strong young culture has much to offer them.

Plan a neighbor Island trip. To experience Hawaii you must see each island, with its own unique flavor, cultural heritage, and lifestyle. While you're visiting Oʻahu is the perfect time to read the companion guides to Maui, Kauaʻi, and the Big Island, and perhaps take a cruise or flightseeing tour to one or more of these neighbor islands. You don't want to miss an eruption of the volcano on the Big Island, if it's happening during your visit. On Kauaʻi, journey down Hawaii's only river, see Waimea Canyon and the Fern Grotto. And only on Maui can you see the whaling capital of Lahaina, Hawaii's capital city of a century and a half ago, and Halekala, the world's largest dormant volcano.

Be sure to check our Calendar of Events to see what special events, celebrations, and contests are taking place on Oʻahu during your visit. You won't want to miss a moon walk at Waimea Falls, the Bon Odori Festivals, or the Hawaiian Islands Tall Ships Parade.

While this guidebook is filled with hundreds of valuable and important things to do, realize that island time moves at a different pace than mainland time. Put your clock or alarm clock in your suitcase and leave it there. Give yourself an extra hour to get things done. Relax! After all you have entered the "island time zone" where anything that is late is still on time and it comes with your ticket! Polynesian paralysis may be one of the most enjoyable phenomena you will experience on the island.

Splurge! Save some time and money to treat yourself while on Oʻahu. Eat at a fine restaurant. Buy yourself that coral necklace you saw in Duke's Lane. Take that helicopter tour you've dreamed of.

JANORA BAYOT

# HAWAIIAN GEOGRAPHY

While you're still at home dreaming of a vacation in Hawaii, one of the first things you want to do is get a picture in your mind of just what the Island of O'ahu looks like and where it fits into the chain of Islands that makes up our fiftieth State of Hawaii. To do this let's take an imaginary flight high over the State. Our reference maps for this air tour are the ones on the previous pages.

We'll start sixty or seventy miles up, directly above O'ahu. Looking down you can clearly see that the Hawaiian Islands lie at the northern tip of a triangle extending westward to Samoa and New Zealand, and eastward past Tahiti and the Marquesas to Easter Island. This triangle encompasses the thousands of islands known collectively as Polynesia, sharing not only locality, but many aspects of their culture, language, religion, food and physical characteristics. From up here it's easy to see the broad route our ancestors probably took to reach Hawaii: starting from Asia, moving for centuries across Samoa, Tonga, west to Tahiti and the Marquesas, then northward to Hawaii. From sixty miles up it's also apparent that the famous statement is true - Hawaii is the most isolated archipelago in the world.

Descending to only several miles high, we see the eight major Hawaiian Islands laid out below us. What we call Hawaii (eight major islands) is only the south-eastern tip of a 1600 mile chain of islands stretching from the Big Island of Hawaii to Kure Atoll, (northwestern-most of the Midway Islands). Called the Leewards, these are the oldest of the Hawaiian Islands, some estimates say as old as 25 - 35 million years. All Leewards, except the five Midway Islands, are part of the City and County of Honolulu, and only two are permanently inhabited by humans (Midway and Kure). The rest constitute the Hawaiian Islands National Wildlife Refuge, providing a habitat for 18 species of seabirds, turtles, the rare monk seal, and several species of land birds found nowhere else on earth. You can see how the volcanoes create land (Hawaii, the island closest to the hot spot, is the largest and tallest) which is then gradually eroded until very little is left above the surface (as with most of the Leeward Islands.)

Of the eight major Hawaiian Islands, the youngest and largest is the Big Island of *Hawai'i*, containing about two-thirds of Hawaii's total land mass. The Big Island is famous for its Kona (protected) coast resorts, its orchids, Kona coffee, macadamia nuts, the towering volcanoes of Mona Kea and Mona Loa, and as the birthplace of Kamehameha I, the first King of all Hawaii.

Next in the chain is a cluster of four islands, Maui, Moloka'i, Lana'i, and tiny Kaho'olawe. *Kaho'olawe* is currently uninhabited and is used by the U.S. Military for target practice. A group called Protect Kaho'olawe Ohana is trying to stop the bombing and wants the Island returned to local use under the stewardship of native Hawaiians, who consider it sacred land.

*Maui*, the second largest of the Hawaiian Islands, was (like O'ahu) formed when two shield volcanoes erupted and formed a central connecting valley. Lahaina,

21

early capital of Hawaii and whaling capital of the Pacific in the mid 1800's, is Maui's most famous town. Maui has recently become one of Hawaii's most popular vacation Islands.

Nearby *Lana'i*, the Pineapple Island, was a Mormon farming community in the mid 1800's, before being sold to the Dole Company in 1922. Privately owned Lana'i, is still a pineapple plantation with employees living in a planned community known as Lana'i City. Sightseeing is permitted and a short hunting season is an annual event. A new hunting lodge and a beachfront resort have brought Lana'i more fully into the modern tourist era.

*Moloka'i*, fourth island in this cluster, is a long narrow island made up of lava from three separate shield volcanos. It is still an old fashioned piece of Hawaii, and is home to the Moloka'i Ranch, second largest cattle ranch in the State (after Parker Ranch on the Big Island). Moloka'i's best known landmark is the old leper colony at Kalaupapa. Although there is now a cure, a few patients have chosen to remain at the compound. Visitors can take a plane, helicopter, or ride a mule down the steep precipice which isolates Kalaupapa from the rest of the Island. This historical spot is well described in Michener's novel *Hawaii*.

*O'ahu*, third largest island in the chain, is made of lava from the eruptions of shield volcanoes on two separate islands which formed a central connecting plateau. Diamond Head, Punchbowl, and other volcanic cones on O'ahu were formed more recently as a result of eruptive explosions. Today nearly 80% of the State's residents live on O'ahu. Honolulu is the state capital and business center of Hawaii. Military bases occupy one-fourth of O'ahu's land area. And Honolulu International Airport is one of the busiest in the country, accommodating more than four million visitors each year. O'ahu also has extensive sugar and pineapple plantations in the northern and central areas of the Island.

*Kaua'i* is the oldest of the eight major Islands. Erosions over millions of years have carved the spectacular Waimea Canyon, nearly 3,000 feet deep and fourteen miles across. Also on Kaua'i are the famous Na Pali Coast and Hanalei Valley, where parts of many movies have been filmed, including *South Pacific*, *Blue Hawaii* and *King Kong*.

*Ni'ihau*, the "Forbidden Island", is the second smallest after Kahoolawe. Purchased by the Sinclair family in the 1860's. Ni'ihau is now operated as a sheep and cattle ranch by their descendents, the Robinson family. The rural lifestyle and Hawaiian language of long ago are still very much in use on Ni'ihau, which is open to visitors only by (rare) invitation, in a courageous effort to protect the island and its 200 inhabitants from encroachment by modern "civilization." If you can't go there, you can take a piece of Ni'ihau home. Ni'ihau shell leis are beautiful, delicate and expensive pieces of artwork that can be purchased in selected O'ahu stores.

Descending to only a few thousand feet directly over O'ahu we get a perfect view of the entire island. I cannot help comparing its shape to that of a boar's head. Kaena Point and Kahuku Point are the two pointed ears. Mokapu Point, jutting out on the south side of Kaneohe Bay, forms its snout, Pearl Harbor is its snarling mouth, showing bared teeth, and Barbers Point forms the point of its jaw. Some say O'ahu resembles a wolf's or a dog's head more than a boar.

To the west is the older Waianae Mountain Range with the highest spot on the Island, Mt. Kaala, at 4,050 feet above sea level. Running down the boar's head from its forehead to its snout, on the east, is the younger volcanic mountain range, the Ko'olaus. And there between the two mountain ranges you can see the central O'ahu Valley lowland, the result of volcanic flows from the two mountain ranges which met and united the two islands into one.

O'ahu has four coastlines; North Shore (between the boar's two ears); the Windward Side (from Kahuku Point to Makapuu Point, at the southern tip of the boar's snout); the Waianae Coast (the boar's jaw, from Barbers Point to Kaena Point); and the Southern Coast, made up of the Pearl Harbor area (the boar's tusks) and Metropolitan Honolulu, including Waikiki (the underside of the boar's snout).

Since the prevailing winds blowing across the Island are from northwest to southeast, the rainfall pattern creates three distinct environments. The Windward O'ahu coast is lush and green, with towering ferns and tropical plants creating a jungle atmosphere. Waterfalls cascade down velvet green canyons, and a rainbow seems to be never more than a few hours away. The Central Valley is temperate, with ample rain and thick green ground cover, lower vegetation and lower humidity. One could mistake these rolling hills and valleys for parts of Kentucky or the valleys of western Oregon and Washington.

Looking across to the leeward side, where deep valleys lie between the crescent-shaped Waianae Mt. Range and the sea, the land is often brown, with sparse low vegetation and seemingly little rainfall. The sun is hotter here somehow, and the mountains feel hot and dry above the rocky plain jutting to the sea.

The lowland plain stretching from Barbers Point across the Ewa area and down across the Honolulu City lowlands to Diamond Head is built entirely on a coral bench, once submerged and part of the shallow reef that surrounded the island. It was this accessible coral shelf that provided the raw material for many early (and some modern) Honolulu buildings - a classic example being Kawaiahao Church, built in 1842. You can also see clearly the major highways: H-1 running through Honolulu to the Barbers Point area; H-2 running up into the Central Valley; and H-3, a short spur, going into Kailua. It is still impossible to drive completely around the Island, since a short stretch across Kaena Point has never been completed.

Of course you can see Honolulu down there between Diamond Head and Pearl Harbor. Hale'iwa (between the boar's ears) is the most famous North Shore town, Kailua is the Windward Side's favorite vacation spot, and Waianae is probably the busiest part of the Leeward Coast. Some of O'ahu's best deep-sea charter fishing can be found in the deep waters off the Waianae Coast.

And there, just next to Pearl Harbor, on the water, is Honolulu International Airport - our next stop. Take her down, captain, and make it slow so we can see the Harbor close up. Now where on O'ahu shall we have our imaginary dinner?

# O'AHU'S LIVING HISTORY

I remember being surprised on my first visit to Italy when I discovered that there was very little connection between the ancient and the modern cities of Rome. Modern Romans seemed to want to live their own lives and leave ancient Rome to the tourists.

Not so in Hawaii - history here is a living, breathing, vitally important aspect of modern life. In fact, you can literally re-live Hawaiian history by visiting a few of its spectacular sites and by listening to the Hawaiian people as they bring their history alive through stories and legends. Let's go back in time to recapture some of the major periods in Hawaii's glorious and tragic past.

The story of Hawaii can be told in three basic parts; The Ancient Times, The Monarchy, and The Modern Era.

## The Ancient Times
Ten million years ago a tiny piece of volcanic rock, no bigger than a pea, broke the surface of the sea and grew to be an Island called O'ahu. It is on top of that mountain peak, more than three miles above the bottom of the ocean, that we now vacation on at Waikiki, Kailua, or Makaha.

The Hawaiian Islands are actually a 1600 mile chain of volcanic mountains stretching across the middle of the Northern Pacific Ocean. Each of these mountains is made of the cooled magma spewed up from the earth's interior through an opening, called a "hot spot," in the ocean floor. The gradual north-western shift of the ocean floor has carried these mountains further and further away from the hot spot, which even today continues its endless building.

You can go to the Big Island and see this mountain-building process close up. You can watch as the liquid earth creates new land at the ocean's edge. In fact, scientists say that a brand new island, yet submerged, is today forming to the south of the Big Island. A name befitting its heritage has already been given to this about-to-be-born Island. Its name is Lo'ihi, meaning long, tall, or prolonged in time. Films of this incredible undersea lava eruption have recently been made.

But you don't have to travel to the Big Island of Hawaii to see this ancient process. You can see its effects all around you on O'ahu. The two mountain ranges on either side of O'ahu, the Waianae and the Koolau, were once two boiling lava caldrons (on two separate islands) spewing red-hot liquid rock from the split on the ocean floor three miles below. Gradually, they formed one island: O'ahu. The landmarks all around the Island, including Diamond Head, Punchbowl, Koko Head, Koko Crater, the Salt Lake, Aliamanu and Makalapa Cones, were all formed in a much more recent period of volcanic activity (100,000 to 250,000 years ago) along three east-west lines - one running through Salt Lake, Punchbowl and Round Top, another connecting Koko Head, Koko Crater and on out to Rabbit (Manana) Island off the windward coast, and a third connecting Diamond Head, Kaimuki Cone and several other cones in a direct line across the Koolau Mountains.

In the beginning, then, there was rock. Rainwater gradually eroded the mountains and made soil. Birds dropped seeds into the soil, and long, long, years later the Islands had developed a flora and fauna.

How and when did humans first come to these Islands? Our best guess is that our species came by voyaging canoes from the South. From islands in the Marquesas Group in about 500 A.D. came fierce, tattooed natives in huge, 60 - 80 ft., long double-hulled canoes. They settled in Hawaii, became peaceful, and learned to cultivate the land and sea. Then again in the 12th century A.D. a migration of warriors came to Hawaii and conquered the settlers. They were from Tahiti, so gradually Hawaiian and Tahitian customs became one. After that second major influx, the population of Hawaii became isolated and stable for at least 500 years.

Amazing as it seems, in downtown Honolulu today, you can stand next to one of the same type of craft that brought these first humans to Hawaii 15 centuries ago. The place is Pier 7, on the dock at the new Hawaii Maritime Center next to the *Falls of Clyde* berth. The ship is a faithful re-creation of an ancient Polynesian voyaging canoe - accurate in almost every detail, and built with ancient craftsmanship. Her name is the *Hokule'a* - Star of Gladness. Her name comes from the star Hokule'a (Arcturus) which can be seen directly over Hawaii at night, and which was used by ancient navigators to spot the islands on voyages from Tahiti.

You'll be filled with amazement as you stand on the seawall above *Hokule'a's* berth and realize that you are looking at one of the great vessels in the history of mankind, similar in scope to the Apollo spacecraft that first took humans to the moon. The *Hokule'a* and her crew in 1976 successfully re-created a trip between Hawaii and Tahiti, almost 3,000 miles, using ancient methods of seamanship and navigation, in order to prove that such ancient planned migrations were possible. The *Hokule'a* has since made numerous voyages, and will make more in the future. Between trips, you can see this living piece of history moored in Honolulu's harbor.

Two stops remain on our tour of ancient Hawaii. First, what was life like in old Hawaii, centuries ago? Everyday life involved worship, hard work, and a well developed social hierarchy.

The land was divided into pie-shaped sections, widening out from points high in the mountains across the valleys and into broad sections of the reef in the ocean. Each section, called an ahupua'a (ahu means alter, pua'a is a pig). Carved wooden pigs' heads on altars of stone marked the boundaries of each section of land, which provided the needs of the residents who lived in it. Each ahupua'a had a sub-chief. A group of these land sections made up a moku, or district. On O'ahu the ancient districts can still be seen in modern legislative and judicial boundaries. The seven Moku on O'ahu included Kona (now called Honolulu), Ewa, Waianae (Leeward), Waialua (North Shore), Ko'olau Loa and Ko'olau Poko (Windward), and Wahiawa (Central Oahu). Each moku had a district chief, often responsible to a high chief who ruled the entire side or sometimes the entire island. No ancient chief was powerful enough to rule all the islands.

Within each ahupua'a the classes were well defined. First came the alii (the royalty), determined by ancestry. These rulers were assisted by the kahunas, powerful priests who kept the Gods and were experts in medicine, astronomy and government. Then came the commoners, called maka'ainana. These were the planters, fishermen, craftsmen, soldiers, and parents. At the bottom of the social scale were the outcasts, (kauwa) similar to the untouchables in India. These wretched slaves lived alone and provided the human sacrifices which the pagan religion demanded.

You can still see this social system in Hawaii today at Waimea Falls Park, an 1,800 acre privately owned park in an ancient valley ahupua'a on O'ahu's North Shore. Historians have brought back to life an ancient Hawaiian village on the actual site where it first existed centuries ago. Here you can see what the ahupua'a section looked like, walk or ride a tram among ancient plants and animals, visit a re-creation of an age-old Hawaiian home and grass buildings, and even participate in the same games and dances you would have seen for millennia in Old Hawaii. Waimea Falls Park is a living museum you should see. Also, once a year in the fall, Waimea Falls Park re-creates the Makahiki Festival, a yearly tradition in old Hawaii to honor Lono, God of Fertility and the harvest. Song, dance, feasting, games, and ancient hula is there for you.

Our last stop on this journey to ancient Hawaii takes us up to O'ahu's Leeward Coast, to another beautiful valley - Makaha. There, near the modern Sheraton Makaha Resort, is probably the best preserved and reconstructed ancient temple (called a heiau) in all Hawaii.

Kaneaki Heiau was originally dedicated to Lono and was the domain solely of ancient male ali'i (royalty) and kahunas (priests). The heiau is a huge rectangular area bounded by stone walls and divided into sections inside. A small city of carved idols, wicker towers, and two thatched huts are arranged in the inner courtyard of the temple. The thatched huts were used by the kahunas for meditation and storage of ceremonial drums.

Offerings, usually of food wrapped in ti leaves, were laid at the center altar in front of two oracle towers of woven branches. Thousands of worshippers from this Makaha ahupua'a would hold festive harvest ceremonies at Kaneaki Heiau during the fall Makihiki celebrations in honor of Lono each year. Standing at this ancient site you can almost see the colorful banners and huge crowds dancing and chanting to the sacred drums as kahuna dedicate offerings inside the temple. Heiau ruins are found on every island in Hawaii, and were a central part of the ancient Hawaiian religion and social culture.

## The Hawaiian Monarchy

By visiting two places on modern O'ahu, we can get a rare glimpse back into the glorious days when Hawaii was an independent kingdom and there was one supreme ruler over all the islands.

One man and his followers unified Hawaii, and we can meet him at the Bishop Museum in Honolulu. His name is King Kamehameha I (Kamehameha means "solitary one"). He lived from about 1758 to 1819, and during his lifetime he fought numerous wars until in 1795 his armies supposedly forced Oʻahu defenders up the Nuuanu Valley and over the Pali (cliff) precipice to their deaths. With this victory, Kamehameha became what no one had been before him -the undisputed monarch of Hawaii.

In the Bishop Museum you can see his portrait, painted from life, and many of his personal belongings - his incredible feathered cape, his ceremonial spear, gifts given to him, and some of his implements of war.

Our second stop to visit Kamehameha is northeast of Honolulu at the Nuuanu Pali, where legend says that in 1795 Kamehameha had several of his own warriors leap to their deaths to persuade reluctant warriors on the opposing side to accept their fate and do the same. Human bones have been recovered below the Pali, suggesting that this famous spot is in fact the location where Kamehameha first realized that he was King of all Hawaii.

After Kamehameha's death, a succession of six kings and one queen followed him as monarchs of Hawaii. You will see their names everywhere - on streets, buildings, and memorials. You can feel their presence especially strongly at several places on Oʻahu. One such place is at Kawaiahao Church in Honolulu, where portraits of these Hawaiian monarchs line the balcony, where many of them were married or baptized, and where one, Lunalilio (Kamehameha IV) is buried. If you attend services here (offered in Hawaiian and English) on a sunny Sunday morning, you can sense their royal presence through the honor and devotion accorded to them by today's congregation.

---

DID YOU KNOW...that in 1864 King Kamehameha IV offered to sell all the land between Honolulu and Diamond Head (including all of Waikiki) for $10,000 and was refused? The gutsy woman who turned down the King's offer was Mrs. Eliza Sinclair, who had come to Hawaii from New Zealand to start a ranch. She found the offered Oʻahu land too arid - so she bought the Island of Niʻihau instead. Today the real estate she refused would sell for $1,000,000 per acre or more.

---

Almost across the street stands the greatest single living monument to the Monarchy, the Iolani Palace. Every Hawaiian monarch had a palace and they all led to this one, built by King Kalakaua in 1882. Walk across the palace grounds; listen to a concert at the Coronation Stand, played by the Royal Hawaiian Band, Fridays at noontime. Tour the palace and hear the tragic and glorious stories of Hawaiian royalty, lovingly told by the tour guides who are their descendants or the descendants of their loyal subjects.

While you are inside this one-and-only royal palace in the United States, recall that the century of the Hawaiian Monarchy witnessed cataclysmic changes that thrust the islands out of their ancient culture and into the modern world. During this one century, Hawaii underwent the sandalwood tree export to China (early

1800's), the growth and decline of whaling (mid 1800's), and the sugar industry that brought wave after wave of immigrants to Hawaii (mid 1800's on).

This wrenching century ended abruptly on January 17, 1893 when a bloodless coup deposed Queen Liliuokalani, the proud Hawaiian monarchy ceased to exist, and Hawaii became a republic, headed by American businessman Sanford B. Dole. After less than a decade, in 1898, Hawaii was annexed as a Territory of the United States, a status it retained until it became our 50th state in 1959. Although this transformation period was considered a tragedy and loss of national identity by a majority of Hawaiians, the economic and political affiliation with the United States allowed Hawaii to develop a stable, modern government as it entered the twentieth century.

## Hawaii's Modern Era

Since becoming a State on August 21, 1959, Hawaii has enjoyed a renaissance of cultural awareness and economic prosperity. Today the people of the "Aloha State" continue to keep alive the identity and pride of this ancient and unique island culture.

Visit the beautiful new Dole Cannery Square in Honolulu and realize, as you watch pineapples being cored, sliced and canned, that it was this process, this machinery, and people like these who brought Hawaii into the twentieth century. A new invention - a machine to core pineapple - created a new industry.

Visit the Waipahu Cultural Garden Park near the Oahu Sugar Mill, and watch the fascinating 10-minute slide-tape presentation, telling the story of the sugar industry in Hawaii and the people who made it work. Or take the walking tour through the Kahuku Sugar Mill, and remember that most of today's Hawaiians have ancestors who came here to work the sugarcane.

### Sugar: The Plant that Built Hawaii

Many people take sugar for granted - we use it every day, it is plentiful and inexpensive. But did you know that sugar was once so rare that it was presented to kings and queens in jewel-studded boxes?

28

Sugar from sugarcane has been grown on Hawaii since ancient times. Captain James Cook on his Voyage of Discovery in 1778 saw sugarcane plantations on the Hawaiian Islands. The first commercially successful plantation harvested two tons of raw sugar from 50 acres in 1837 on the island of Kaua'i. By the 1850's the fledgling industry had reached O'ahu, Maui, and The Big Island.

These first sugar planters faced a series of seemingly insurmountable obstacles. First, there were not enough workers. The native Hawaiian population had been decimated by diseases introduced by western sailors. The solution was to have Chinese laborers shipped to Hawaii, first in 1852, under contract to help raise and process sugarcane. This initial wave of immigrants was followed by many others from all over the world, including Japanese, Filipinos, Russians, Puerto Ricans, Portuguese, Koreans, Spanish, Germans, and South Pacific Islanders. More came from Norway, Austria, and even the southern United States. The descendants of these sugarcane workers today constitute a large part of the rainbow mix of cultures, races and religions in Hawaii.

A second major problem was a supply of water. Sugarcane is a grass, and grasses need water. Lots of it. There was plenty of water available, but not where it was needed. It was not until 1856 that the first irrigation ditch was dug; and not until 1879 that a sailor-turned-planter dug the first artesian well in Ewa on O'ahu. By the turn of the century sugar planters discovered that each island stores rainwater in a "lens" or lava rock reservoir atop the salt sea-water permeating the island. Today about 110,000 of Hawaii's 185,000 acres of sugarcane are irrigated.

The final problem was economic. Once the sugarcane was grown and sugar extracted and milled from it, where in the world could this sugar be sold? Two major events helped create a stable market for Hawaiian sugar: 1) The 1876 Treaty of Reciprocity with the U.S.A., which traded a duty-free status for Hawaiian sugar in return for a U.S. naval station at O'ahu's Pearl Harbor; and 2) the annexation of Hawaii by the United States in 1898.

In many ways the story of sugar is the story of Modern Hawaii, since no other economic activity did more to create the social and economic fabric of our 50th state.

**From cuttings to crystals:** Sugarcane is grown from cuttings, tended for two years, then harvested when the cane reaches its peak sugar content. After flash burning of the ripe cane fields to burn off dry stalks (the cane is unharmed because of its 75% moisture content and tough outer shell), giant tractor-cranes cut the cane at ground level and load it on large trailers for the trip to a local sugar mill. Nearly 9 million tons of Hawaiian sugarcane are harvested and processed each year in one of Hawaii's sugar mills.

**At the mill:** After being washed and cleaned, the cane is milled between huge rollers to remove the juice, which is then heated and filtered to remove impurities. After evaporators and vacuum pans reduce the juice to a heavy syrup and crystals, centrifuges spin the mixture to remove the molasses and wash the raw sugar crystals. The raw sugar is then bagged and shipped to the mainland refinery in San Francisco where it is transformed into the many sugar products we use every day: granulated sugar; powdered sugar; brown sugar; cubes; molasses; and sugar syrups for baked beans, sugar cured hams and butterscotch. This refinery also produces sugars for such industrial uses as ice cream, soft drinks, and candy, as well as canned, frozen and prepared foods. A small refinery in Aiea, a suburb of Honolulu, produces enough granulated and other refined sugar products to the meet Hawaii's needs.

**You can see the story of sugar:** A visit to the Waipahu Cultural Garden Park is a must on your O'ahu tour itinerary. You can see the developing re-creation of a Sugar Plantation Village, artifacts and displays of early sugar plantation life, stories and old photos of the many cultures and ethnic groups brought to Hawaii to work sugar, and a scale model showing a complete turn of the century plantation community, just the way the village will look when completed (see the WHAT TO SEE chapter for further information). Taking the self-guided tour at the Kahuku Sugar Mill is another way to step back into Hawaii's history. Having ceased production a few years ago, this mill is still intact, so you can see close up how the cane was processed. A free self-guiding tour brochure explains each part of the process. A modern shopping and dining area has been created in and around the Kahuku Mill, so you can spend a fascinating morning or afternoon enjoying the history of sugar in Hawaii!

*NOTE:* This information was prepared with the help of the Hawaiian Sugar Planters Association, a cooperative non-profit association dedicated to protecting, maintaining and improving Hawaii's sugar industry. They invite your inquiries: PO Box 1057, Aiea, Hawaii 96701.

Other forces besides industry have helped shape modern Hawaii - one such force can be seen at the Fort DeRussy Army Museum in Waikiki. Curators have done an outstanding job re-creating the feel of a World War I and II gun battery, the sights and sounds of a "Barefoot Bar" during the Vietnam War, and the military weaponry of both ancient and modern Hawaii.

So as you tour O'ahu, and stand at such monuments as those described in this historical journey, pause to reflect that you are visiting a place where people are living their lives and building their future on the foundation of a proud past.

'ILIMA

# TODAY'S O'AHU

**Size and Population:** O'ahu is Hawaii's third largest island, with a total land area of approximately 608 square miles. It is home to nearly one million people. The island hosts more than four million visitors each year, and has 209 miles of coastline.

**Nicknames:** O'ahu has been called "The Gathering Place", perhaps because it was once the meeting ground for all of Hawaii's island kings (in fact, the peninsula of Mokapu near Kailua, which today is the site of a U.S. Marine Corps Base, was once the off-limits meeting place of King Kamehameha I and his island chiefs. This ground is still considered sacred by many Hawaiians). O'ahu has also been called "The Capital Island", referring to the fact that the State Capital has been located in Honolulu since King Kamehameha III moved it there from Lahaina (Maui) in the 1840's. Possibly the most popular of O'ahu's nicknames is "The Main Island", reflecting the fact that although the population of Hawaii is an extended family living on seven different islands, the family's main house, its headquarters, is without a doubt, O'ahu.

**O'ahu as part of Hawaii:** O'ahu (including all the Leeward Islands Northwest of Kaua'i) is one of four counties in the State of Hawaii. Its official name is the City and County of Honolulu. The other three counties of Hawaii include: The County of Kaua'i (Kaua'i and Niihau); the County of Maui (Maui, Lanai, Moloka'i, and Kahoolawe); and the County of Hawaii (The Big Island). Interestingly, an additional area (at the leper colony on Moloka'i) termed Kalawao County is administered separately by the Hawaii State Department of Health.

**Hawaii's State Flower:** The Hibiscus can be seen in hedges and borders throughout O'ahu. All eight islands have a flower or plant emblem except Niihau, which has a seashell. O'ahu's emblem is the Ilima, a shrub with yellow-orange flowers containing fine petals an inch or so across. An Ilima lei is strung through the center of the flower and takes many hours of work. The beautiful O'ahu girl on our front cover wears orange Ilima blossoms in a colorful display of her pride and love for her home island of O'ahu.

**Hawaii's State Bird:** The Nene (nay-nay) is an endangered species related to the goose. Once plentiful in Hawaii, they can now be seen in the Honolulu Zoo and Waimea Falls Park. An effort is underway to raise Nene and release them to join the wild flock.

**Hawaii State Marine Animal:** The Humpback Whale can be seen during the winter months off O'ahu as they complete their migration to winter quarters in Hawaiian waters.

**Hawaii State Fish:** The Humuhumunukunukuapua'a (Humu-humu-nuku-nuku-a-pu-A-a) or trigger fish is Hawaii's State Fish.

**Hawaii's State Nickname:** "The Aloha State", was designated in Honolulu on April 23, 1959 by the last Territorial Legislature in preparation for Statehood.

**The State Flag:** Flown just below the U.S. flag at all public buildings on O'ahu, it consists of eight white, red and blue horizontal stripes representing the eight major Hawaiian Islands, with the British Union Jack in the upper left corner. Since the flag was designed prior to 1816 for King Kamehameha I, the inclusion of the Union Jack is thought to reflect Kamehameha's appreciation of Great Britain's protection of the islands against the threat of hostile foreign invasion.

**The State Motto:** "UA MAU KE EA O'KA AINA I KA PONO", means "The life of the land is perpetuated in righteousness." These words were spoken by King Kamehameha III in Kawaiahao Church on July 31, 1843 after the monarchy was briefly usurped by an overzealous British admiral.

**Hawaii's State Anthem:** "Hawaii Ponoi", was co-written by King Kalakaua and Royal Hawaiian Band Director Henry Berger. You can hear it and many other pieces performed by the same band in concert at Iolani Palace on Fridays at noon or at the Queen Kapiolani Park Bandstand.

---

DO YOU KNOW...about Hawaii's anti-smoking laws? Smoking is banned in all public restrooms, elevators, museums, libraries, art galleries and in the public areas of hospitals, clinics, doctors' and dentists' offices. You cannot light up either in most stores and financial institutions. In restaurants seating 50 or more, no-smoking areas must be set up. Smoking is also banned in all State and County buildings including airports, community centers, auditoriums, and meeting rooms.

---

**Climate and weather:** Hawaii's climate is so wonderful all year round that the ancient Hawaiians had no word for weather! O'ahu, and all of Hawaii, has only two seasons: summer, between May and October; and winter (if it can be called that!) from November through April. Winter brings slightly cooler temperatures, a bit more rain and more frequent interruptions in the comforting tradewinds. Summer brings warmer, drier weather and more regular tradewinds. The National Weather Service tells us that the temperature in Honolulu varies only seven degrees Fahrenheit (4 degrees Celsius) between summer and winter. And there is an average difference of about 12 degrees Fahrenheit (7 degrees Celsius) between night and day temperatures. The average O'ahu summer temperatures will be around 79 degrees; 72 degrees in winter.

Average rainfall for all Hawaiian Islands is about 70 inches per year, whereas in Waikiki the average annual rainfall is only 27 inches per year. And get this - the average year round water temperature at Waikiki Beach is 80 degrees, just slightly cooler than an indoor heated swimming pool! So you can expect the forecast on O'ahu, whenever you arrive, to be delightfully mild, semi-tropical with balmy tradewinds and low relative humidity (50 - 60%). And thanks to occasional warm showers in mauka (mountain) areas, you're bound to see at least one rainbow while you're there!

*SAFETY FIRST:* There are a few simple steps you can take to make sure that your vacation on O'ahu is calm and comfortable. The Hawaiian Visitors Bureau printed an excellent pamphlet in 1978 (no longer in print) which has helped thousands of visitors. Its suggestions are still worthwhile:

1. Take the sun in small doses. Limit your exposure to direct sun to fifteen minutes a day at first, increased 15 minutes each day thereafter.

2. Swim where it is safe. Even though most Hawaiian waters are warm and safe, all beaches and swimming pools can be dangerous at certain times. So please consult a lifeguard before you swim, and heed all posted signs and warnings.

3. Take good care of your valuables. A locked car may not be safe; nor should you leave valuables on the beach while you swim. An in-room safe is your best bet, or a hotel safe deposit box. Please observe all normal precautions regarding your personal safety, as well as that of your belongings. Tourists are tempted to act in such a casual fashion that they may make themselves vulnerable. So relax - but only after assuring that your valuables are properly protected from loss. One last tip - leave your room key at your hotel desk every time you go out!

4. Stay on well lit, well traveled streets. This applies both at night and daytime. Keep your purse close to your body. And remember that you're under no obligation to stop for people who accost you on the street. If you're not interested, do not pause.

5. Put litter where it belongs. If we all work together we can make sure Hawaii will be as beautiful on your next trip, and someday on your grandchildren's first trip, as it is today. If you can't find a receptacle for your trash, improvise!

We're all minorities in Hawaii, and we live in reasonable harmony in large part because of the Hawaiian tradition of Aloha - love, generosity and respect for people, for the land and water, and for Hawaii. We hope you can feel it, and will share it with us. We want you to know that you're invited to take as much Aloha as you can carry home with you! (Thanks to the nice folks at the Hawaii Visitors Bureau for these tips!)

---

DID YOU KNOW...that the Hawaii Visitors Bureau has a special visitor satisfaction specialist to "offer a sympathetic ear and a helping hand to visitors with problems or complaints during their stay in Hawaii?" Call (808) 923-1811.

---

# IMPORTANT PHONE NUMBERS

American Red Cross ............................... 734-2101
The Bus ......................................... 531-1611
Child Protective Services ......................... 942-5877
Directory assistance (interisland) .................. 1-555-1212
Directory assistance (local) ....................... 1-411
Emergency (no deposit needed) ..................... 911
Hawaii Visitors Bureau .......................... 923-1811
Life Guard ...................................... 922-3888
Medical Hotline ................................. 926-4777
Operator Assistance ................................. 0
Parks & Recreation .............................. 527-6060
Passport Information ............................. 541-1919
Poison Control .................................. 941-4411
Police (non-emergency) .......................... 943-3111
Suicide & Crisis Control ......................... 521-4555
Surf Report ..................................... 538-7131
Time of Day .................................... 983-3211
Volcano Hotline ................................. 967-7977
Weather forecast ....................... 833-2849 or 836-0212

# O'AHU'S PEOPLE AND LANGUAGE

"Living on isolated islands, we cherish our diversities. For we have come from many places and in many different ways to this enormous yet intimate chamber of summer." From *The Hawaiians*. When I first visited O'ahu, I wondered if it was perhaps my imagination that people in Hawaii were really more friendly than people anywhere else. But as I watched, listened and asked, I eventually became convinced that Aloha - that intangible feeling of generosity, respect for each human being, willingness to go out of your way to help someone else, and true affection for other people - that genuine Aloha is alive and strong here.

In order to get the most enjoyment from your vacation, you must realize that you are a person with aloha too. You bring to the island something the people who live here value and respect: your unique point-of-view, your special talent, and your one-of-a-kind personality. By finding the hidden treasure of Hawaii, its people, and meeting them face to face, you share your aloha. And when you do, all the flowers, buildings, music, food, warm nights, all the miracles that exist in Hawaii will become even more enjoyable.

Here are several short cuts to help you meet and get to know the people of Hawaii. Be respectful of people's rights, privacy and space. Go out of your way to be courteous and helpful. If you are going 20 miles per hour in your rental car in a 45 mile hour zone because you can't read the map, pull over and let the line of cars behind you pass. You'll see the map better, and the locals trying to get home from work will appreciate your consideration.

Realize that Hawaiian citizens are people of great pride. This Island is their home and we as visitors can learn from talking and listening to Hawaiian residents. If you ask, they'll be glad to tell you the meaning of a word, the story of their part of the island, or which bus stops at your destination. Hawaiians love to "talk story," and will likely respond with the same courtesy and friendliness with which you approach them.

Greet and speak with the people you meet. Perhaps in New York City it is not accepted to converse with a salesperson or ask a bellhop about his family, but in Hawaii it is a grand tradition to take an interest in people and find out about what is important to them.

Be willing to share part of yourself with the people you meet. Inquire about their interests and activities, and tell them about your own. After all, Hawaii is a meeting place of East and West. So, by communicating your values and expertise, as well as showing an interest in others, you enter into a dialogue which enhances both participants, and allows you both to find new understanding and pleasure in your similarities and your differences.

Another good way to get to know people is to know something about them before you meet. You can show Hawaiian residents that you're interested and respectful of their culture by showing them tthat you've taken the trouble to learn something about them, their lifestyle and their language.

Here are some common words and phrases in daily use on Oʻahu. If you learn what they mean, you will feel more comfortable about meeting kamaainas, and talking with them. If you can say a word or two of greeting, your new friends will be delighted and willing to help you learn more!

# PRONUNCIATION GUIDE TO HAWAIIAN WORDS

The alphabet consists of five vowels (a, e, i, o, u) and seven consonants (h, k, l, m, n, p, w), often accompainied by a glottal stop. This is a "catch" in the voice, similar to the sound in the middle of "oh-oh" in English, and represents the omission of a hard consonant. In print it is indicated by a hamzah ('), or reversed apostrophe.

Every syllable and every word ends with a vowel, giving the language a musical sound. The accent in each word usually falls on the next-to-last syllable. The diphthongs, ei, eu, oi, ou, ai, ae, ao, and au, are all stressed on the first letter. The one exception is iu, in which the stress is even. The second vowel is always pronounced - not lost, as with diphthongs in English. All letters are pronounced! Consonants are pronounced much as they are in English, and the vowels as follows:

| | | |
|---|---|---|
| A as in father | E as in let | I as in marine |
| O as in over | U as in rule | OO as in boot |

# PLACE NAMES AND DIRECTIONS

Familiarity with a few place names and directions will help in reading maps and asking directions, so practice a little and you'll catch on in no time.


Ainahau (Ina-HOW) cool land of breezes

Ala wai (AH-la-y) means freshwater bay. Name of Waikiki canal and Boulevard

Diamondhead (As it looks) Toward Diamond Head Crater

Ewa (EH-va) Toward Eva (a town between Pearl Harbor and the Leeward Coast)

Hale'iwa (Ha-lay-EE-va) means house of the Iwa (frigate) bird. Surfing town on North Shore

Hawaii (Ha-WA-ee or Ha-VA-ee) a name taken from the land of our ancestors (ancient meaning lost)

Honolulu (Ho-no-LU-lu) means fair haven or sheltered harbor

Ka'a'awa (Ka-a-AH-va) the aawa wrasse fish

Kahuku (Ka-HOO-ku) means the project. Town on Northern Windward Side, site of Sugar Mill

Kailua (Ki-LU-a) means two ocean currents. A town and beach on O'ahu's windward side

Kalakaua (Ka-LA-ka-wa) means day of battle. Waikiki's major Avenue, named for the last King of Hawaii, David Kalakaua, who reigned from 1874 until his death in 1891

Kaneohe (Ka-nay-O-hay) means slim bamboo man. Windward side town near Kaulua

Ko'olau (KO-o-lao) Mountain range on O'ahu (meaning on the windward side)

Kuhio (Ku-HEE-yo) major avenue and mall in Waikiki named for royal Prince Jonah Kuhio Kalanianaole (1871 to 1922) who served as a territorial delegate from Hawaii to the U.S. Congress for twenty years.

Laie (La-EE-a) means leaf of the ie plant. Town on Northern Windward Side; site of Polynesian Cultural Center, Morman Temple, and Brigham Young University of Hawaii

Makai (Ma-KI) Toward the sea

Mauka (MAO-ka) Toward the mountains

Nvvanu (New-u-AH-new) cool heights

O'ahu (Oh-AH-hu) The Main Island (ancient meaning lost)

Pokai (PO-kai) night of the supreme one

Wahiawa (Wa-HEE-a-wa) means landing or roaring place. Town in Central O'ahu famous for its Royal Birthing Stones

Waianae (WI-a-ni) means mullet (fish) waters. Name of town on the leeward coast, and one of O'ahu's mountain ranges

Waikiki (Wi-kee-kee) means spurting water (from the three streams that empty into the ocean here)

Waimea (Wi-MAY-a) means reddish water. A famous bay and area on O'ahu's North Shore

Waipahu (Wi-PA-hu) means gushing water. Town in Ewa District near Pearl Harbor, known for its still operational sugar mill

# COMMON HAWAIIAN WORDS AND PHRASES

aina (I-na) the land

akamai (AH-kah-my) smart or clever

ali'i (ah-LEE-ee) Hawaiian chief or member of royal class

aloha au ia oe (ah-LOW-ha ow-eea-oay) I love you

auwe (OW-ay) alas!, oh

halakahiki (ha-la-ka-HEE-kee) pineapple

hale (HA-lay) house

hana (HA-na) work, activity

haole (HOW-lee) caucasian, tourist

hauoli la hanau (how-O-lee la ha-NOW) Happy Birthday

hauoli makahiki hou (How-O-lee ma-ka-HEE-kee-HO) Happy New Year

haupia (How-PEE-a) coconut custard served at luaus

Hawaii Nei (Ha-WA-ee Nay) All islands of Hawaii

he'e (HAY-ay) octopus

heiau (HAY-ow) ancient Hawaiian temple composed of an outdoor platform and low walls made of fitted stone

ho'olaulea (HO-o-lau-LAY-a) Hawaiian picnic, outing or party

huli huli (HU-lee HU-lee) barbecue, as huli huli chicken

hula (HOO-lah) the dance of Hawaii

Humuhumunukunukuapua'a (Humu-humu-nuku-nuku-a-pu-AH-a) Hawaii's State Fish. Like most Hawaiian words, this one looks impossible to pronounce until you break it into syllables (often starting with a consonant and ending with a vowel) and be sure to pronounce each letter. You can have fun with friends if you learn this word, then rattle it off as though everyone knows it!

imu (E-mu) A pit filled with hot rocks, leaves and meat, fish, taro, potatoes, corn or whatever food is to be steamed for a luau.

kahuna (kah-HOO-nah) a teacher, priest or other trained person of old Hawaii endowed with skills and often supernatural powers.

kalua (ka-lu-a) any meat roasted in an imu. Most often Kalua pig

kama'aina (ka-ma-INA) literally "a child of the land" - a native Hawaiian or old timer

kane (KA-nay) man (often seen on men's room door)

kapu (KA-pu) forbidden, tabu, off limits. In ancient Hawaii many things were Kapu: women eating with men; standing on the King's shadow; or going any places the King said was kapu. Some kapus were punishable by death.

kapuna (ka-PU-na) grandparent. Many Hawaiian schools have programs in which kapuna regularly teach students Hawaiian culture, language, and crafts.

kaukau (COW-cow) chow, food

keiki (KAY-kee) child, kid

ko (ko) sugar cane

kokua (ko-KU-a) help, assistance

kona wind (KO-na) warm, moist wind from the South, which usually covers the leeward coasts of Hawaiian Islands with hot, sticky weather, especially during summer months.

kukui (ku-KU-ee) candlenut tree; Hawaii's State Tree

lanai (la-NI) patio; deck; porch; veranda

lau lau (lau-lau) a traditional Hawaiian dish of meat and potatoes wrapped in Taro and ti leaves and steamed

lei (lay) traditional Hawaiian garland usually of shells, flowers or yarn given at any festive occasion

limu (LEE-mu) edible seaweed traditionally gathered from Hawaii's beaches.

lomi lomi (LO-mee-LO-mee) literally "massage", often referring to a luau dish of raw salmon chunks "massaged" with onion, tomato, and spices

luau (LU-ow) traditional Hawaiian feast; specifically the tender Taro tops eaten at such celebrations

lua (lu-a) bathroom

mahalo (ma-HA-lo) thanks. Mahalo nui means thanks a lot; mahalo a nui loa is thank you very much

makai (ma-KAEE) toward the sea

malihini (ma-la-HEE-nee) stranger; recent arrival

mauka (MAU-ka) toward the mountains

mele kalikimaka (ME-lay ka-lee-kee-MA-ka) Merry Christmas!

mana (MA-na) a person's personal power; spirit; energy

menehune (may-ne-HU-nay) ancient Hawaiian elf or race of little people who first arrived in the islands and built the oldest structures.

moana (mo-AH-na) ocean

mu'u mu'u (MU-u-MU-u) long gown of "mother hubbard" style introduced by missionaries and widely used today. Often mispronounced as mu-mu, which means to be silent or blunt!

niu (NEE-u) coconut

ohana (o-HA-na) family; extended family; sense of belonging to a group

ono (O-no) good, delicious. Often pronounced as onolicious

opihi (o-PEE-hee) ocean limpets; served raw as a delicacy. Very expensive!

paniolo (pa-nee-O-lo) Hawaiian cowboy. Derivation of "Espaniola" - the name applied to early Mexican cowboys imported to teach horsemanship to the Hawaiians

pau (POW) finished; through

pau hana (pow HA-na) finished work. Time to relax!

pilau (pee-lau) stinking; bad smell, rotten

pilikia (pee-lee-KEE-a) trouble; difficulty

poi (poee) staple of Hawaiian diet; purplish paste made by mixing pulp of Taro root with water. Tourists often try poi alone and dislike it; Hawaiians often combine bland poi with salty foods, which results in a tasty combination. Try some!

puka (PU-ka) hole

pupus (PU-puz) hors d'oeuvres; appetizers

pupule (pu-PU-lay) crazy; nuts; acting crazy

tapa (TA-pa) traditional Polynesian paper-cloth again being made in Hawaii

tutu (TU-tu) grandmother; term of affection

ukulele (oo-ku-LAY-lay) literally dancing or jumping (lele) flea (uku). A well-known and very popular instrument imported from Portugal and modified by Hawaiian musicians.

wahine (wa-HEE-nay) woman, girl

wai (wi) fresh water

# PIDGIN - HAWAIIAN STYLE

A good example of unique Hawaiian language styles is pidgin. Much has been said and written about this language form. In fact, the Hawaiian State Board of Education once outlawed the use of Pidgin during instruction in all Hawaiian schools. And yet, at least from a linguistic point of view, Pidgin is a very important dialect and is used as a mark of group solidarity and as a code to exclude unwanted individuals. Interestingly enough, Pidgin was developed by plantation supervisors as a way to communicate with workers from many different language bases. Pidgin has constantly changed, absorbed various words and patterns, and today is used by most Hawaiian residents to one degree or another. If you are interested in learning more about Pidgin, you might start with the very popular paperback book *Pidgin to Da Max* by Doug Simonson.

Pidgin is wonderful to listen to - it has a distinctive flow, rhythm, and sound. The best advice to the non-pidgin speaker is to listen to it, learn what some words and phrases mean, but avoid trying to use it. Most attempts are unsuccessful, and can alienate you from the very people you are trying to get to know. Here is a sampling of some common Pidgin words and expressions:

an'den? - A sign of boredom. Similar to so..now what?
ass why - That's why. Often used at the ending of any statement, especially an explanation
Baddah you? - You want to do something about it? A challenge
Brah - Brother. As in "Howzit, brah."
Bummahs - variation of bummer, bum deal
Bus you up - Bust you up. Break your face
Chicken skin - goosebumps
cockaroach - to steal or rip-off. Usually small items like cookies or car keys.
da kine - a basic phrase used in Pidgin for anything and everything. "Is this da kine you wanted to take to da kine tonight?" Meaning is often deduced from syntax.
hana hou - Again, one more time
howzit - Pidgin greeting, like "How you doing?" or "What's happening"
kay den - Okay, then. Enough, already
laydahs - Later for you. See you later. I've had it.
li'dat - Like that. I told her off. Li'dat
like beef? - Want to argue about it? Like to step outside?
local style - How they do it in Hawaii
make A - to make an ass of oneself
minors - "No beeg ting"; Nothing to worry about
mo' bettah - better. It's better that...
o'wat - Or what? This phrase is often added to a question.
shaka - name of hand signal with thumb and little finger extended. Means howdy, howzit, I'm cool.
some ono - good "Dat some ono da kine, eh, Brah?"
talk story - shoot the breeze; have a conversation
to da max - To the maximum; all the way; the most
wadascoops - What's up? What's going on?

39

# ANNUAL O'AHU EVENTS

As you plan which time of year you wish to visit O'ahu, you'll want to check this listing of special annual events. Here are cultural and sporting events, special festivals, holidays, and competitions. You'll enjoy your visit more if you can time it so you can participate in one or more of these special days. Someone once said "the best way to get to know the people of Hawaii is to join us in our celebrations." You're invited! We've left specific dates out for events which vary from year to year, so check local newspapers, TV, and free tourist literature for current events and call the numbers below for more information.

## JANUARY

Queen Emma Museum Open House. Honolulu. 595-6291
Chinese New Year Celebration
Cherry Blossom Festival (January to April): Japanese cultural celebration with song contest, concert, coronation ball. 945-3545
Hula Bowl: annual classic college all-star game at Aloha Stadium in Honolulu
Honolulu Symphony
Narcissus Festival (January to March)
Chinese New Year Celebration: lanterns, dragons, and fireworks. 533-3181
Robert Burns Night: Scottish celebration of poet's birth, Ilikai Hotel. 988-7872
NFL Pro Bowl (late January or early February). Aloha Stadium. 488-7731

## FEBRUARY

Humpback Whale Month: sightings, lectures. Sea Life Park. 259-7933
NFL Pro Bowl Football Game. Aloha Stadium. 488-7731
Hawaiian Open Golf Tournament. Waialae Country Club. 836-0060
Lei Queen Competition Ala Moana Beach Park. 521-9815
Great Aloha 8-mile run from Aloha Tower to Aloha Stadium. Charity for various schools. 732-2835 or 735-6092
Moon walks: One hour guided tours of Waimea Falls Park by moonlight (every month). 638-8511
Hawaii Opera Theater Season opens. 521-6537 or 537-6191
Punahou School Carnival: rides, crafts and best malasadas anywhere - by Julie Franko! 944-5754
Buffalo's Big Board Surfing Classic: Makaha Beach. 696-3878
Hale'iwa Sea Spree: four day event, surfing, bicycle race, canoe races

## MARCH

World's Greatest Garage & Plant Sale. Blaisdell Center. 531-1662
Honolulu Academy of Arts: visiting artists, workshops, seminars. 538-3693
Hawaiian Song Festival and Song Composing Contest. Kapiolani Park Bandstand. 521-9815
11th: Emerald Ball in honor of St. Patrick: dinner and dancing
17th: Parade and St. Patrick's Day Festivities
19th: Polo Club Season opens: every Sunday until August. Mokuleia. 533-2890
26th: Prince Kuhio Day: festival and State holiday celebration. 546-7573
Highland Games (late March or early April): gathering of the clans, food, dancing, pipe bands at Fort DeRussy. 523-5050

## APRIL

Buddha Day (on the closest Sunday to April 8th): celebrates the birth of Buddha. 538-3805

Easter Sunday: sunrise service at Punchbowl. 531-4888

Bud Lite Tin Man Biathalon: Ala Moana Beach Park. 926-5755

Carole Kai International Bed Race and Parade: charity fundraiser. 735-6092

Annual Hawaiian Festival of Music competition with groups from Hawaii and mainland. Waikiki Shell. 637-6566

Iolani School Carnival: kid's rides, food, fund raiser. 949-5355

Aloha Basketball Classic. Top college seniors in charity games. 527-5400

## MAY

1st: Lei Day: pageants, school festivals and entertainment. 521-9815

2nd: Leis placed on royal graves. Royal Mausoleum. 521-9815

Pacific Handcrafters Guild Spring Fair. Ala Moana Park. 538-7227

5th: Japanese Boy's Day: watch for flying paper carp

7th: Bill Cratty Dance Theater: dance/theater extravaganza. Castle Theater, Windward Community College, Kaneohe. 235-7433

Mother's Day (Kapuna Wahine Day): Moms free at Sea Life Park and Waimea Falls Park with kids. 259-7933

Filipino Fiesta (all month): celebration of Filipino culture with great food, dances, music

Hawaii State Fair (late May to early June): exhibits, food booths, entertainment. Aloha Stadium. 488-7731 or 536-5492

Annual Festival of the Pacific (Late May): athletic tournaments, music, songs, dances of multi-ethnic Pacific cultures. 395-7063

30th: Memorial Day Services. Punchbowl. 541-1430

## JUNE

National Zoo and Aquarium month: lectures and special tours throughout the month. Sea Life Park. 259-7933. Family entertainment each Wednesday night at Honolulu Zoo. 524-1400

Annual "Gotcha" Pro Surf Championships: water & beach events. Sandy Beach

11th: King Kamehameha Day: State holiday, statue draped with leis

Mission Houses Museum Fancy Fair: homemade food, entertainment. 531-0481

19th: Father's (Kupuna Kane) Day: Sea Life Park, dads free with kids. 259-7933

Annual Hawaiian Festival of Music: repeat of April competition, wide variety of music. Waikiki Shell

Annual King Kamehameha Traditional Hula and Chant competition. Brigham Young University, Laie

Bon Odori Annual Japanese Festival, held between June and August. 595-2556

---

DID YOU KNOW...that the hula was a religious ritual in ancient Hawaii? The hula's movements, and the words of the accompanying chants, were considered to be a method of communicating with God. Many Hawaiians have become serious students of both ancient and modern hula, and dance at hula festivals throughout the year.

---

## JULY

1st-10th: State Farm Fair, petting zoo, exhibits, rides. McKinley H.S. 848-2074

3rd: Band concert and fireworks. Kailua Beach Park. 261-2727

4th: Parade in Kailua. 261-2727

4th: Hawaiian Islands Tall Ships Parade: ships sail from Koko Head to Sand Island and back. Don't miss this one!

16th: Prince Lot Hula Festival at Moanalua Gardens. 839-5334

Tin Man Triathalon: swim, bike and run. Waikiki-Diamond Head. 533-4262

Pan Am Clipper Cup Series: big race around the State

Trans-Pacific Yacht Race from LA to Honolulu on odd-numbered years

Pacific Handcrafter's Summer Fair. Thomas Square, Honolulu

31st: Annual Ukulele Festival. Honolulu Kapiolani Park Bandstand. 487-6010

Bon Odori (Buddhist Festival of Souls) late July to early August: Bon dances and lantern ceremony. 637-4382

## AUGUST

Samoan Flag Day: parade, dances, singing, flag raising. Keehi Lagoon Park. 545-7451

Hula Festival: hula halaus (schools) perform the first part of the month. Kapiolani Park Bandstand. 521-9815

Honolulu Zoo Day: kids and adults get to look close up at the animals. 524-1400

Biennial World Spring Championships: outrigger canoe sprint and marathon races. Keehi Lagoon. 326-1011

19th: Admission Day: State holiday, celebrating Hawaii's admission as a State

Hawaiian Open State Tennis Championships. Honolulu. Prizes

Floating Lantern Ceremony (late Aug): part of Obon Festival. Thousands of colored paper lanterns afloat on Ala Wai Canal, each lit with candle. 595-2556

Queen Liliuokalani Keiki (kids) Hula Competition: ancient and modern hula, boys and girls ages 6-12. Kamehameha Schools gym. 521-6905

## SEPTEMBER

Grandparents' (Makua Kane & Makuahine) Day: grandparents get in free with children at Sea Life Park 259-7933 and Waimea Falls Park 638-8511

Waikiki Rough Water Swim: covering two miles of open ocean - open to all. Sans Souci to Duke Kahanamoku Beach

Waimea Falls Park Aloha Week Festival: crafts, exhibits, entertainment. 638-8511

Annual Parade of Homes (late Sept. to early Oct. wknds): sponsored by Building Industry Association. Tour some amazing O'ahu residences. 847-4666

A Special Day at Queen Emma's Summer Palace. 595-6291

Annual Moloka'i to O'ahu Canoe Race for Women (Men's race is in October): A big event!

16th to 25th: Aloha Week Festival: huge celebrations with canoe races, street parties (ho'olaule'a), parade, stage shows, fun! 944-8857

Annual Okinawan Festival (late in month): dances, exhibits, dance contest. 546-8119

Chinese Moon Festival Celebration: stage show, music, food booths. 533-3181

## OCTOBER

Makahiki Festival: re-creation of ancient harvest celebration with games, music, hula competition, dancing, feasting. Waimea Falls Park. 638-8511

Pacific Handcrafters Guild Fall Fair: crafts from some of Hawaii's best artists. Ala Moana Park. 538-7227

Bank of Hawaii Molokai Hoe (Men's Moloka'i to O'ahu Canoe Race): finish at Hilton Hawaiian Village Beach. 525-5476

Compadres South Pacific Chile Exposition Cookoff with prizes: a "hot event"

Octoberfest: oompa bands and lots of beer. Budweiser warehouse, 99-8771 Iwaena St., Honolulu

Annual Orchid Plant and Flower Show. Blaisdell Center. 527-5400

Steinlager Hawaiian Canoe and Kayak Championships: one and three person canoes, K-1's, kayaks, and surf skis. 682-5233

Sunday - Bishop Museum Festival: arts, crafts and tours. 847-3511

31st: Halloween - This is a grand night in Hawaii - parties, dances, superb costumes. A treat for the whole family!

## NOVEMBER

Ho'olaule'a in Waianae: put on by military. Entertainers, food, music, all day event. 438-9761

Pearl Harbor Aloha Festival: a fair with rides, games, music, food and the Al Harrington show. 471-0818

11th: Veterans' Day parade and national holiday. 949-1140

Nuuanu YMCA Turkey Swim at Ala Moana Beach Park. 536-3556 ext.217

Hawaiian Pro Surfing Championships & Men's Masters (late Nov.- early Dec.) dates based on waves. TV coverage and big prize money. 926-0611

Artists of Hawaii Annual Exhibition: showcases some of Hawaii's best contemporary artists. Honolulu Academy of Arts. 538-3693

Mission Houses Museum Christmas Fair: crafts, food, books, gifts. 531-0481

International Film Festival (late Nov. to early Dec.): featuring award-winning film-makers' creations from Asia and USA. Films shown throughout O'ahu. 944-7200

## DECEMBER

Triple Crown of Surfing: top pro surfers. Dates based on waves. North Shore

Pacific Handcrafters Guild Christmas Fair. Thomas Square. 538-7227

Kanehohe Christmas Parade featuring the Royal Hawaiian Band: floats, and (of course) Santa. 235-4543

Hawaii International Film Festival: (continued from November)

Honolulu Marathon: thousands of entrants, AAU certified event

Kailua Christmas Parade: a small parade that's fun to watch. 10 a.m. at Kailua Intermediate School. 261-2727

Kamehameha Schools Christmas Concert. Blaisdell Center. 842-8211

Honolulu Marathon and Wheelchair Marathon: very popular races. 734-7200

Annual Rainbow Classic (invitational collegiate basketball). Blaisdell Center Arena. 948-7523

Aloha Bowl: college football game. Aloha Stadium

31st: New Year's Eve: another big party night in the Islands.

# *BRIDES AND GROOMS*

The Hawaiian Islands are certainly among the most romantic spots on earth, so it is no surprise that Hawaii has become the honeymoon capital of America.

According to "Modern Bride" magazine in 1987, more than 13.5% of their readers honeymoon in the islands. Add that to the 200,000 Japanese honeymooners yearly, and you can see why, with a total of more than 516,000 honeymooners per year, seven pages in the Hawaii Yellow Pages book are devoted to wedding services and items.

So if you're planning to wed or honeymoon on O'ahu, here are some very important things you should know. Most of these preparations should be made before you go.

The State of Hawaii requires a premarital exam only for the bride-to-be. A doctor must sign a form for a rubella screen test. This test can be done in Hawaii, but it takes time to get results. Check with your physician. An information packet on getting married in Hawaii is available from the State of Hawaii Department of Health, 1250 Punchbowl St., Honolulu, HI 96813 (808-548-6479). The packet also contains information on license and procedures. Only a Hawaiian marriage license is valid in the State of Hawaii. Man and woman must be present and over 18 years of age, with birth certificate or valid driver's license if under 20 years old. There is no waiting period, but the couple must wed within 30 days of obtaining a license.

Marriages can be performed in churches, synagogues, or temples, outside in such places as Waimea Falls Park, in a hotel or restaurant, in a cave, on the beach, under water or in the air. Two very unique locales are the Top of Leahi (Diamond Head Crater), a permit is required from State Parks Dept., PO Box 621, Honolulu, HI 96809 (808-548-7455), and on the *Falls of Clyde*, a century-old antique sailing ship moored at Pier 7. Up to 700 guests. Contact Joan Aanavi, Hawaii Maritime Center, Pier 7, Honolulu Harbor, Honolulu, HI 96813 (808-523-6151).

Unless you live in Hawaii, the services of a wedding planner will greatly simplify arrangements. Several of the bigger agencies are:

A Hawaiian Wedding Experience, P.O. Box 8670, Honolulu, HI 96830 (808-926-6689); Exclusive Wedding Service, 2020 Algaroba, Honolulu, HI 96826 (808-946-7905); Waimea Falls Park, 59-864 Kam. Hwy., Waimea Bay, HI 96712 (808-638-8511); The Royal Banquet, 799 Kapahulu Avenue, Honolulu, HI 96816 (808-735-6428); Haiku Gardens, 46-336 Haiku Rd., Honolulu, HI 96744 (808-247-6671).

Even more couples come to O'ahu to honeymoon than to be married, so many hotel chains offer specials to honeymoon couples. For example, the Kahala Hilton Hotel offers a "Honeymoon in Paradise" package that includes breakfast in bed. Turtle Bay Hilton on the North Shore also offers a honeymoon package.

Check with your travel agent to see if the hotels you've fallen in love with in the accommodations chapter have a honeymoon arrangement. And they may be willing to make special arrangements for your wedding if you plan to honeymoon at the same hotel.

A number of tour companies also offers honeymoon packages which feature substantial savings. Pleasant Hawaiian Holidays, for example, offers an amazing 7-night stay at the Hilton Hawaiian Village starting at a total cost slightly over $1,000. MTI Vacations offers couples the chance to create their own Custom Honeymoon Delight Tour with 3-night minimum stay at a choice of hotels and condos with room and rental car upgrades, free champagne, free gift basket, honeymoon photo, $10 gift certificate and a free pineapple. These tours usually include air travel, rental auto and lodging. Check with your travel agent for current packages and rates.

# TRAVELING WITH CHILDREN

O'ahu will be a wonderland for your children. There are so many things to see and do, and for those kids who live in a cold climate, being able to play, eat, read and swim outside while in Hawaii will seem magical to them.

Before your visit is the perfect time to plan a basic itinerary for your children. You can involve them in the planning, and take time to make decisions now that will afford everyone in your party the maximum comfort and freedom during your trip. Here are tips, suggestions, ideas, and activities for you and your children to read and choose from. No matter how your travel plans shape up, your trip to O'ahu will be more interesting and enjoyable with kids along.

## BEFORE YOUR VISIT

Review the selections in the accommodations chapter with the kids in mind. What kind of transportation will you use on O'ahu? If you're planning to stay in Waikiki and use public transportation, write (or invite your kids to) for an O'ahu bus pamphlet. (A good one costs $1.99 and is available from CP International, Ltd., 79-154 Guff Bay Ct., Bermuda Dunes, CA 92201. Ask for "The Bus Guide: 89 Edition.") Then plan to stay in a place that is near the bus route.

Choose a place to stay that has activities for kids. A pool is a priority, especially if a lifeguard is on duty. An apartment or suite with a bedroom that can be closed off is an investment in peace and quiet. For a family, a place with cooking facilities comes in very handy, not only for meals, but also for snacks and beverages.

Look for a place near the attractions you and your children enjoy. Are you hikers or bicyclists? Then accommodations outside Honolulu near trails and wilderness areas might suit you best. If the Zoo and Aquarium are top attractions for your family, check the lodgings on the diamondhead side of Waikiki. (See the WHERE TO STAY chapter)

Your children will enjoy their trip much more if they know something about O'ahu and the Hawaiian Islands. A birthday, Christmas or Hanukkah present from Hawaii would surprise, delight and help acquaint your child with your upcoming vacation. The Bishop Museum's "Shop Pacifica" (1344 Kalihi Street, Honolulu, HI 96819, 847-1433) has a marvelous selection of educational gifts for kids of all ages. The following are some examples. Hawaiian calendars for your kitchen have photos and special events list. *Lets Count In Hawaiian* ($2.50) is a coloring and activity book from Island Heritage. *Polynesian Crafts Step By Step* ($4.50) is a great book to take with you on your trip or give after you return. It tells in detail how to make the Maori Poi Balls you'll see at the Polynesian Cultural Center, how to weave coconut leaf creations and much more. *How To Make Your Own Hawaiian Musical Instruments* offers a challenge to older kids, and makes a good present before you go, since they'll be able to find the materials they need more easily in Hawaii. *Legends Of O'ahu* as told by Lani Goose, has a book and read-along cassette to assist listener/readers with correct pronunciation of commonly-used Hawaiian words, and will introduce everyone to Hawaii's traditional folklore.

*The Hawaii Puzzle Book*, Bess Press, PO Box 22388, Honolulu, HI 96822, is a fun way for kids to learn about Hawaii during their trip. This collection of puzzles, brainteasers and games will fit in a pocket and help stretch a mind.

Kids love animals. Write the Honolulu Advertiser, 605 Kapiolani Blvd., Honolulu, HI 96813, for a copy of their *Wildlife Of Hawaii* ($3.95) containing drawings and short stories about Hawaii's fish, birds, plants, reptiles, even the house gecko and Bufo (giant toad)! This great book will help your kids learn what creatures to look for when they arrive in Honolulu.

*My Travels In Hawaii* is a blue paperback ($2.95) published by Hav'in Fun and available from Paradise Publications (see the back of this guide for the address). This is a great activity book to do as a family or to give kids for the plane trip over. It has information and games about each island, surfing, volcanoes, the hula, and plenty of room to create a trip scrapbook.

Another resource for families is *Hawaii For You And The Family* by Mitchell & Shifflette (1979, Hancock House, 12008 1st Avenue South, Seattle, WA 98168). Check it out from your library or use an inter-library loan if the publisher can't provide it for you. It has tons of good information on each island, even a section on Natural History. A valuable resource when traveling with youngsters.

Be sure to write the Hawaii Visitors Bureau at Waikiki Business Plaza, 2270 Kalakaua Avenue, Suite 801, Honolulu, HI 96815 (808-923-1811). Request information for families and kids. Also ask for recent copies of their excellent newsletter, "He Kukini." It's done with short articles and upbeat graphics that kids really enjoy. It also has a calendar of events and cartoons.

*The Waikiki Beach Press* is a newspaper published weekly and distributed on airlines, in airports, hotels and street stands in Waikiki. You can write and request back copies (and perhaps subscribe too): Hawaii Press Newspapers, Inc., 2110 N. Nimitz Hwy., Honolulu, HI 96819 (808-848-1414).

Want a no-tears way to help your child learn the essentials of Hawaiian history? Give them a handsome deck (in its own protective case) of Hawaiian Heritage Playing Cards. Each card in the pack illustrates a scene from Hawaiian history, from Captain Cook's visit in 1778, through the monarchy to the annexation of the Islands by the United States in 1898. A thoughtful gift for a birthday or Christmas before your vacation. Available from Hawaiian Heritage Playing Card Co., PO Box 25907, Honolulu, HI 96825.

## DURING YOUR VISIT

When in transit, your kids will benefit from a few simple arrangements you can make for them, or help them to make.

Hawaii requires that children under the age of four be in an approved child restraint or seat belt while riding in a vehicle. Rentals arranged with your car are subject to availability and their quality is uneven at best, so bringing your own is a good idea. Check with the Federal Aviation Administration (202-426-8374), regarding use of carseats on your aircraft. Also, Hawaii State Law requires anyone in the front passenger seat of any moving vehicle to be buckled in.

Pack a carry-on travel kit for each child (they might want to help decide on contents), including an extra swim suit, sunglasses, chewing gum (helps with cabin pressure on ears), juice-in-a-box, snacks, playing cards, a book or two, a blank book for journal and sketches, a favorite toy and game.

If you have infants or very young children with you, pack baby supplies, medicine, clothing and diapers in a carry-on bag, in the unlikely event you are separated from your luggage. Having your baby nurse or drink from a bottle during take-off and landing helps equalize ear pressure.

O'ahu has numerous medical facilities and hospitals for children, including the Kapiolani Medical Center for Women and Children; 1319 Punahou St., Honolulu (947-8511). Look for others in the phone book yellow pages under hospitals. Also, under community services in the very front of the yellow pages book are such listings as Poison Center (941-4411), and the American Red Cross (734-2101).

The walk from airplane to transportation can be long, so you might want to bring a baby-carrier, rent a luggage cart, or request assistance from your airline desk.

Sun is especially hard on children's skin, so buy a lotion for them which contains PABA (para-amino-benzoic acid) with a high sun factor and apply an hour or so *before* exposure. Many parents mistakenly believe that water filters out harmful rays; not so. Burning rays can penetrate at least three feet into the water. Remember, too, that the sun is hottest between 10 a.m. and 3 p.m., so cover up or avoid those hours. Start children off gradually in the sun, 15 to 20 minutes at first, and full sun block is worth considering for kids, especially for the first day or two.

O'ahu is a big place, so if you'll make a nametag for each child and attach it to shoelace, wristwatch or belt, it will give them, and you, a sense of security. Include their name and home address and number, plus the address and phone of your local accommodations on O'ahu. It takes just a second, and is worth it.

Give each child enough money to call you in an emergency, and include on their luggage or personal nametag any medicine they take and the name, address and phone number of a contact person at home. Discuss with older children your strategies for emergencies and separations.

Many of the sights and attractions described in the WHAT TO SEE and WHAT TO DO chapters will also be of interest to youngsters. Examples: The Honolulu Zoo and Waikiki Aquarium are sure winners; the Flea Market held on Wednesdays and weekends at Aloha Stadium has tons of interesting items (including fresh coconuts); kite flying in Queen Kapiolani Park; and a trip through the free Whaling Museum at Sea Life Park.

Check out the souvenirs at Woolworth's Waikiki, 2224 Kalakaua Avenue (923-2331), on the second floor. One of the best selections and prices in town.

## AFTER YOUR VISIT

Before you leave O'ahu, try to have at least one roll of film (shot by the kids if possible) developed. Kids and you can notate each photo on the back so you'll remember names, dates and events. If kids have a small tape recorder they can make an end-of-trip recording or audio letter to their class or someone at home. The plane is a perfect place to write those postcards you didn't write on O'ahu, and to color the illustrations in this guidebook!

You and your kids can have fun making a list together of places on O'ahu you'd like to visit next trip, and people you want to keep in touch with or see again. If your child has found a pen pal in Hawaii, encourage correspondence. Perhaps their friendship will lead to a vacation visit from your Hawaiian friends.

If you'll involve your child(ren) in the documenting and enjoyment of the visit after your return, you'll enhance their enjoyment too. And perhaps you can all plan a return trip together!

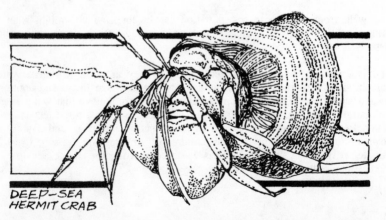

DEEP-SEA
HERMIT CRAB

# SPECIAL INFORMATION FOR HANDICAPPED TRAVELERS

Many resources exist which you'll want to know about before leaving on your O'ahu vacation. Here are some.

Your airline will make special arrangements for you if you contact them as far in advance as possible and tell them your needs. Free bus passes are available, but you must apply in advance. (808-524-4626). An excellent resource is the *Handicapped Traveler's Guide*, available from the Commission on the Handicapped, Old Federal Building, 335 Merchant St., #215, Honolulu, HI 96813 (808-548-7606). The Hawaii Visitors Bureau offers a *Pictorial Aloha Guide to Honolulu for Handicapped Travelers*. Request this and other materials specific to your needs from the HVB at Suite 801, Waikiki Business Plaza, 2270 Kalakaua Ave., Honolulu, HI 96815. Also request the HVB's current year Accommodations Guide and Restaurant Guide, which include facilities that accommodate wheelchairs and offer other handicapped services.

Regarding transportation, Handi-Van offers free curb-to-curb service, with arrangements 24 hours in advance. Contact them for details, before your visit, at 650 S. King St., Honolulu 96813 (808-524-4626). Handi Cabs of the Pacific, at 50 South Beretania St., 524-3866, has vans with ramps and will arrange special tours. Contact them in advance. Avis Rent-a-Car, (808-836-5511), will rent cars with hand controls, with one week's notice.

Several sources to help you locate nurses, nurses aides, or companions:

Hawaii Center for Independent Living, 677 Ala Moana Blvd., Rm. 615 Honolulu, HI 96813  (808-6537-1941)
Handicapped Commission, 335 Merchant St., Rm. 353 Honolulu, HI 96813 (808-548-7606)
Voluntary Action Center, 200 N. Vineyard Blvd., Rm. 603 Honolulu, HI 96817 (808-536-7234)

And two travel agents who specialize in travel for handicapped persons are:

Flying Wheels Travel, 148 West Bridge St., Box 382, Owatoma, MN 55060
Evergreen Travel Service, 19505 L 44th Avenue West, Lynnwood, WN 98036

The Library for the Blind and Physically Handicapped, at 402 Kapahulu Ave., Honolulu, HI 96815 (808-732-7767) provides assistance for anyone needing special library materials and services, including people with deafness or hearing impairment, mental retardation, serious emotional disturbance, learning disabilities or speech impairments.

Gallaudet University Center on Deafness opened at the University of Hawaii's Kapiolani Community College in 1988. Located at 4303 Diamond Head Rd., Honolulu, HI 96816 (808-734-9210).

Most of the restaurants in the WHERE TO EAT chapter are wheelchair accessible. We suggest that you call ahead to find out if entry, elevators, and restrooms are accessible. In many cases restaurant management will be glad to make special arrangements in advance of your visit.

Two additional pamphlets you'll want to send for: "Access Travel" from the U.S. Printing Office, Washington, D.C. 20402 (small fee); and a brochure from The Society for the Advancement of Travel for the Handicapped, 26 Court Street, Brooklyn, NY 11242. (718-858-5483). And please let us know which places are most accommodating to your special needs so we can pass your recommendations along to others.

# *ESPECIALLY FOR SENIORS*

A number of specials and discounts are available for seniors. Here are some of the best.

Free bus passes are available for those 65 years of age and older. Apply three weeks before your 65th birthday or six weeks before arrival, to 725 Kapiolani Blvd., Honolulu HI 96814 (808-531-7066). Photo and proof of age are required.

The Elderhostel, 100 Boylston St., Suite 200, Boston, MA 02116 offers noncredit courses at Hawaii Loa College for those 60 years and older. Fees include course, room and board.

Many restaurants on O'ahu offer substantial discounts to senior citizens, including such bargains as Early Bird Specials for diners arriving at slower hours. Check with individual restaurants and look for specials in the free tourist booklets listed in this chapter. Hotels and condominiums also will quote discounted prices to seniors upon request. Many such discounts are not listed in the brochures or on rate cards, so be sure to inquire.

Your travel agent will be helpful in locating accommodations which may offer senior discounts. Also ask your travel agent about the benefits of joining a discount travel club. One such club is Vacations to Go, 41 Sutter St., Suite 1041, San Francisco, CA 94104 (415-982-8336, or toll free 1-800-624-7338). Members pay a small annual fee to become eligible to get short-notice discounts for unsold seats on usually high priced tours. Membership in Vacations to Go includes the entire household family for one year. If you're retired and can go on fairly short notice, such a club could afford you considerable savings.

Possibly the best source of information on senior citizen discounts is the Yellow Pages. Those advertisers, in every category, who offer discounts to seniors are identified with a white star in a black circle in their ad. At a glance you can find discounted hotels, restaurants, retail stores, and more. If you can locate a phone center or library near your home that has Hawaii Yellow Pages, you've got a source that will allow you to locate discounted places all over O'ahu before your visit. If not, be sure to check "the book" as soon as you arrive!

# FIRMING UP YOUR PLANS

Vacationers who get the most enjoyment from each travel dollar are often those who do the most pre-planning before their trip begins. So as your personal vacation guide and private consultant, I can help you most, through the information within the pages of this book, if you will read this Part One in the comfort of your living room months before you get on the plane.

Once you arrive in Honolulu you will find yourself standing in a maze of choices, decisions, opportunities and alternatives, all competing for your time and attention. Especially on O'ahu, where there are so many choices at every step, a special kind of confusion can set in which sometimes leads to an overwhelming desire to sit on the bed in your hotel room and watch TV. The medicine to prevent this vacation paralysis is simply to start using this guidebook at home before your trip, carry it with you when you travel, refer to it on O'ahu, and follow its suggestions before, during and after your visit.

Before you begin to make detailed plans and decisions about your vacation, take time to consider your expectations and wishes. If all were possible, what would your dream vacation be like? As you contemplate your dream vacation, browse through these pages to find items that stimulate your interest. You might discover a hotel that would be the perfect setting for your second honeymoon, or a restaurant with an atmosphere you were searching for in your vision of the perfect evening.

Soon you will begin to realize that you do in fact have certain expectations for your O'ahu getaway, and you'll be able to identify some, if not all, of them. Keeping this list in mind you can now designing your vacation to come as close as possible to your list of dreams. This creative process of getting in touch with your innermost desires and designing the various aspects of your vacation plans to fit them, is perhaps the most important part, and the most often overlooked of your pre-visit planning. So dream away and build your vacation around them.

## GETTING INSIDE INFORMATION

Have you ever been somewhere on vacation and discovered that the couple you met in the lobby of your hotel was staying there on a package deal for one-half the cost you were paying? Or have you ever returned home and found out your favorite entertainer had done a show at your vacation spot while you were there, but you missed it because you didn't know about it? You can avoid this kind of frustrating experience by getting hold of a few important kinds of information before you leave for vacation.

Here is a list of suggestions; browse and take your pick. Remember that a dollar or two invested in information now can yield significant savings during your trip. Not to mention more fun! If you have older children, they can join in the sending-away-for-stuff game and thoroughly enjoy it. Chances are good that you'll all be pleasantly surprised by the bargains and bonuses you discover. Happy hunting!

*Firming Your Plans*

Buy a video tape portrait of Hawaii. A videotape is the perfect companion to *O'ahu, A Paradise Guide*. After reviewing many videos, I am convinced that "Forever Hawaii" is the very best. It is available thorough Video Releasing Company, 1370 Kapiolani Blvd., Suite 101A, Honolulu, HI 96814 (808-941-3399). Created by premier video artists John and Sheila Dobovan in 1985.

Review the annual events listed in our "Annual O'ahu Events" calendar in this chapter. Then write or call for more information about the events you'd like to attend during your vacation on O'ahu. You can plan your accommodations and vacation dates with the information you'll receive.

After reading the WHERE TO STAY chapter call (often there's a toll-free 800 number) or write a selection of hotels, condos, and bed and breakfast places for a current brochure, tariff card, pictures of the accommodations and amenities. This information will help you narrow down your choices, and will prepare you to work with your travel agent to make your final decisions.

The Hawaii Visitors Bureau (HVB) exists to assist you at all stages of your vacation including the all important planning phase. Write them at 2270 Kalakaua Avenue, Honolulu, HI 96815 (808-923-1811). Explain your plans and interests, request a current copy of their excellent twice-a-year newspaper, *He Kukini*, and be sure to ask for specific information for any special category of traveler you fit into, such as physically impaired, senior citizen, honeymooners, tour group, family with children, religious orientation, or special interest (such as golf, sewing or archaeology). They'll be glad to send you a packet of up-to-date material.

The Hawaii Visitors Bureau also has regional offices on the mainland:
HVB, 441 Lexington Ave., Rm 1407, New York, NY 10017 (212-986-99203)
HVB, 1511 K St. N.W., Suite 415, Washington, D.C. 20005 (202-393-6752)
HVB, 180 N. Michigan Ave. #1031, Chicago, IL 60601 (312-236-0632)
HVB, Central Plaza, 3440 Wilshire Blvd., Rm 502, Los Angeles, CA 90010 (213-385-5301)
HVB, 50 California St., #450, San Francisco, CA 94111 (415-392-8173)

Ask them also for the current HVB Accommodations and Dining Guides. Thankfully, all HVB information is free.

There are a number of monthly magazines containing special articles and information for travelers to Hawaii. One such is *Aloha* Magazine, published bi-monthly by Davick Publications, Suite 640, 828 Fort Street Mall, Honolulu, HI 96813-4377. Call Hawaii toll-free to subscribe: 1-800-367-5134. Back issues are also available from: *Aloha*, Box 3260, Honolulu, HI 96801 for $6.00 each.

Be sure to write Paradise Publications for a complimentary copy of the companion newsletter for this O'ahu guide. The quarterly *THE O'AHU UPDATE* has information on all that is new, and in the news, on O'ahu. Please send a self-addressed, stamped, long (legal size) envelope to Paradise Publications, Newsletter Department, 8110 S.W. Wareham, Portland, OR 97223. Yearly subscription is only $6.

Another good bi-monthly magazine is *Hawaii - Gateway to the Pacific*, published by Fancy Publications, P.O. Box 6050, Mission Viejo, CA 92690. (714-855-8222). Back issues, also available, contain such interesting articles as "O'ahu's Beaches," "Waikiki Today," and "Insiders' Honolulu."

For a monthly magazine specifically attuned to O'ahu, you might subscribe to *Honolulu* magazine, established in 1888, and published by Honolulu Publishing Company, 36 Merchant Street, Honolulu, HI 96813 (808-524-7400). Sections include: About Town, Politics, Sports, Modern and Classical Music, and Honolulu Dining Directory. This is an upscale publication with yearly restaurant awards (Hale 'Aina) and a feature called "Sour Poi Awards," containing hilarious short news items about O'ahu comings and goings. A good read.

It's expensive (about $70 monthly for daily and Sunday; $20 a month for Sunday only) but you can have the Honolulu daily (Star-Bulletin or Advertiser) and Sunday edition (Star and Advertiser) sent to you. These dailies contain sections on Restaurants, Entertainment, Sports, and Classified, with information on Rentals. Contact the Hawaii Newspaper Agency, Circulation Department, P.O. Box 3350, Honolulu, HI 96801.

When you arrive on O'ahu you will notice the display racks everywhere containing free tourist booklets and newspapers. You can't miss them. These free publications are funded by the advertisers and are very limited in scope, but are still good sources of all sorts of information. Below is a listing of the major titles. If you contact them they may be able to send you several copies to review. Lots of discounts and freebies are included in their pages too.

*Waikiki Beach Press* is a free travel weekly newspaper published by Hawaii Press Newspapers, 2100 N. Nimitz Hwy., Honolulu, HI 96819 (808-848-1414). It contains features such as "Notable women of Hawaii" and "Iolani Palace," a section on Travel, Dining, Entertainment, and Shopping, a featured menu each week and a section with tips for travelers.

*This Week, O'ahu* is a long, slender booklet published weekly by Hagadone Hawaii, 715 S. King St., Suite 325, Honolulu, HI 96813 (808-526-1702). The sections in this popular free booklet include, shopping, touring, activities, and dining, all specific to the week of publication. Freebies and discount coupons.

*Spotlight O'ahu* is another popular long and slim booklet (205 pages) published weekly by Spotlight Hawaii Publishing at 532 Cummins Street, Honolulu, HI 96814-3399 (808-524-8404). Their masthead states that the subscription rate is $45 per year, with individual copies available on request at $2.50 per copy in advance. Their format is similar to This Week's with maps, Calendar, Savings (a page of coupons and discounts), Dining, Entertainment, Cruises, Sightseeing, Sports and Shopping. Printed (as most are) in 4-color, this publication is fun to read, especially in your home at your leisure before your visit.

*Key to the Island* is a TV Guide-sized 80-page freebie for tourists published monthly by Adams Media Group, Inc., 1376 Kapiolani Blvd., Suite 204, Honolulu, HI 96814 (808-942-5127). Sections include Key Facts at Your

Fingertips, Transportation, Sightseeing, Things To Do, Royal Hawaiian Shopping Center, Dining/Luaus/Nightlife, feature articles, Shopping, Calendar of Events and maps.

*Guide to O'ahu* is a weekly, 96 page 8" x 11" tourist freebie published by Guide Magazines, 1314 King St., Suite 520, Honolulu, HI 96814 (808-521-5019). Sections include: Activities, Calendar of events, Dining and Entertainment, Features, Helpful Information, Maps, Shopping, Sightseeing and Television Listings. A good publication with large, detailed maps and easy-to-use format.

*Freebies and Discounts* by This Week Magazine is a small 4" x 5" booklet containing coupons for free and discount offers to tours, car rentals, buffets, dinner cruises and photo services. Contact This Week Magazine (see above).

*Remember as you use these free publications that they only publish information on places that pay them to do so. So don't expect to get a balanced picture or a complete listing of what's available, but they're still fun.*

# WHY CONSULT A TRAVEL AGENT ?

Years ago, most travelers put their vacation plans in the hands of a travel agent. Today more and more vacationers enjoy researching and making their own travel arrangements. With the help from a full service guidebook like ours you can review choices and make direct contacts with hotels or condos, bed and breakfast places, restaurants and tour companies.

Remember two things; Travel agents are very helpful with some arrangements (especially flight packages) if you know or can locate one you trust. Secondly, travel agents make their living from commissions paid by the businesses they represent. This means that while there is no charge to you, your travel agent deals with only a portion of the businesses in the travel spectrum.

So in today's travel market, whether you get help from a travel agent or not, you are the primary agent of your own travel arrangements, and you should consider yourself the person in charge. If you choose to consult a travel agent, use them as another resource within the overall plan that you create and control. A good travel agent has the contacts to find you the lowest air fares, best airlines, most convenient flight times and connections, best seats, make sure you have boarding passes, and generally make sure your air transportation is the way you like it. They also have access to up-to-the-minute quotes on airfares, hotel and condo rates, and special packages on such items as auto rentals.

Whether you consult a travel agent or make your own travel arrangements, you'll want to follow these suggestions as you prepare for your vacation.

Read your guidebook. Become familiar with O'ahu and Hawaii. Plan ahead. Give yourself as much time as possible. Firming up your plans more than a year ahead is not too far in advance if you're going at peak times (mid-December through March, and mid June through August). Many Christmas and Spring vacation bookings are made 12 months or more ahead. Decide how much money you wish to spend for your vacation. This will help you to choose options and alternatives. Decide how long you'll stay on Oʻahu. Will you visit any other Hawaiian Islands? Send away for information you've read about in this guide and review it before you meet with your travel agent. Visit your local library; read about Hawaii and Oʻahu. Search travel magazines for interesting articles about Oʻahu. Prioritize your vacation wishes and expectations. What do you want from your vacation - a tan, romance, great food, adventure, new friends, or a better understanding of the culture and history of Oʻahu? Make a list and decide what's most important to you and your fellow travelers.

## BON VOYAGE!

As the date of your vacation approaches, you will feel most relaxed and comfortable about your trip if your travel plans are confirmed, if your home is prepared for your departure, and if your packing is organized. Put these items on your departure checklist.

_____ Each child has a flight-pack of things to do on the plane.

_____ Arrangements have been made for a friend or relative to check on the house and they have an address and phone where you can be reached in case of an emergency.

_____ Plants, pets, and people for whom you are responsible have been taken care of.

_____ Mail and newspaper are being picked up or held until your return.

_____ A few lights have been left on (or on timers), and the thermostat has been turned down.

_____ All doors, windows and other entrances to the house have been secured.

_____ You have mailing addresses of friends and relatives you want to send post cards to.

_____ Everyone in your travel group has medications, accessories (glasses), and luggage they plan to take.

_____ Each bag, purse, and suitcase is labelled with name, home address and place you can be reached on Oʻahu.

_____ Young children have a similar label attached to their clothing or printed in indelible ink on their arm.

_____ Checked to see that all appropriate stove burners, electrical cords, and pilot lights (gas water heater) have been removed or secured.

_____ You've made a last minute call to Hawaii to confirm your reservations and you have called your airline to confirm your flight number, time, gate, and check in time.

Remember, if you're traveling from a very cold area during the winter your heavy outerwear will be unnecessary in Hawaii. Leave coats, etc. in the car if you've driven or are being driven to the airport. To be most safe, take the keys to the car you left parked at the airport with you to Hawaii, or better yet, leave your car with a friend who will meet your plane when you return. If you do leave your car in long-term parking, be sure to record the parking space number and to arrive at least an hour and a half before your flight to allow ample time for parking, possible shuttle transportation and check-in.

# WHAT TO PACK

There are three key ideas to keep in mind as you decide what to pack: 1) travel light; 2) cool and casual; 3) leave room to bring home more than you take.

What should you leave at home? Raincoat, formal wear, cold weather wear and office or school wear. What is essential to bring? Beachwear including your suit, sunglasses and lotion with PABA, shorts, walking shoes and warm weather casual wear. For women, a muumuu or a light skirt. For men one tie and a light jacket if you plan to attend a more formal evening dinner or night spots. If you are a sports person and plan to play - bring dress appropriate to your sport. And remember that you can find reasonably priced clothing on O'ahu.

Pack an empty flexible suitcase or lightweight nylon duffle bag inside your luggage; it will come in handy as a clothes hamper during your trip and can be packed to leave room in your suitcase for souvenirs on your return trip. Divide your medication and other essentials into two parts and carry one part with you on the plane in the unlikely event that you are separated from your luggage. Be sure to label each piece of luggage with your home and island vacation address and phone number.

# GETTING THERE

Be sure to consider a trip package which includes airfare, hotel and rental car. Your travel agent can arrange such a package at considerable savings.

Competition between the airlines is stiff with rapidly changing air fares and various ticketing requirements and restrictions. If you don't plan on making your own airline bookings, a good travel agent, along with their computer, can put you in touch with the best options for you. There are presently nine major American air carriers serving Honolulu International Airport from several mainland U.S. cities. Telephone numbers are as follows:

AIR AMERICA - Reservations 1-800-247-2475, in Hawaii 1-808-833-4433
AMERICAN - Reservations 1-800-433-7300, Hawaii 1-808-526-0044
CONTINENTAL - Reservations 1-800-525-0280, Hawaii 1-808-836-7730
DELTA AIR LINES - Reservations 1-800-221-1212, Hawaii 1-808-955-7211
HAWAIIAN - Reservations 1-800-367-5320
NORTHWEST - Reservations 1-800-225-2525
PAN AM - Reservations 1-800-221-1111
TWA - Reservations 1-800-221-2000
UNITED AIRLINES - There is no central 800 number; but rather one for each area of the U.S. See the Yellow Pages in your area. In Honolulu, the number for reservations and information is 1-808-547-2211. United Airlines is the dominant air carrier to Hawaii with about half of all traffic.

If you are planning a trip to the outer islands, there are several options as well. You should also inquire about are the special inter-island, airfare-room-car packages, that both Hawaiian and Aloha offer. These vary from season to season but are almost always a bargain for short stays on the neighbor islands compared to purchasing each item separately. Contact the inter-island carriers for information as follows:

ALOHA AIRLINES - 1-800-367-5250; in Honolulu, 1-808-836-1111.
HAWAIIAN AIRLINES - 1-800-367-5320; in Honolulu, 537-5100.
ALOHA ISLAND AIR (Owned by Aloha Airlines) - This small commuter-tourist airline (formerly known as Princeville Airways) flys Dehaviland Twin Otters between Honolulu and the neighbor islands. Their number is 1-800-652-6541; in Honolulu, 1-808-833-9555.

Have you considered a cruise to Hawaii? They can be a unique part of your vacation experience. Two ships, the *S.S. Constitution* and the *S.S. Independence* cruise inter-Island. But once a year each ship makes one crossing to the mainland (in Nov. and Dec.). For information on these cruises contact American Hawaii Cruises, 550 Kearny St., San Francisco, CA 94108 (800-227-3666).

---

DID YOU KNOW...there is an agency which will help match you up with a traveling companion for "double occupancy" cabins on a cruise to Hawaii? Many people prefer to choose their cabinmate, rather than being randomly assigned by the cruise line. For more information on this interesting concept, contact Partners-in-Travel, PO Box 491145, Los Angeles, CA 90049.

---

Ask your travel agent about other cruise alternatives, including P & O Lines, Royal Cruise Line, Naru Pacific Line, Holland America Line, and Society Expeditions. The *Monterrey* also cruises inter-island, it is currently owned/run by Aloha Pacific Cruises, (800-544-6442), 1350 Old Bay Shore Hwy. #400, One Bay Plaza, Burlingame, CA 94010. Cunard runs the Queen Elizabeth II, and is making two crossings from Ensenada to Hawaii in 1989. Contact Cunard at 555 Fifth Avenue, NY NY 10017 (212-880-7301). You can also book passage on a freighter, if you have time to spare and want a memorable experience. Contact: Freighter Club of America, Box 12693, Salem, Oregon.

Major tour companies (some of which buy tickets and rooms in huge lots and re-sell them at discount prices) often have excellent packages. You might want to send for information, or ask your travel agent for brochures. A few are: MTI Vacations, 1220 Kensington, Oak Brook, IL 60521. Pleasant Hawaiian Holidays, 2404 Townsgate Rd., West Lake Vlg, CA 91361. Creative Leisure, PO Box 7777, Itasco, IL 60143-7777. Others you can ask your travel agent about include: Classic Hawaii, United Vacations, American Express, Haddon Tours, Student Travel Network, Nature Expeditions International, Sun Trips, Pacific Out-door Adventures, and Hawaiian Holidays.

# GETTING AROUND

The walk from your arrival gate to the baggage claim area in the Honolulu International Airport can seem endless, especially if you're carrying luggage or are helping tired kids. Plan to rent a luggage cart or two (kids can ride on one without luggage) for the trip from plane to transportation. Each cart costs a dollar and is well worth it.

Arrange your transportation from the airport to your lodgings and back prior to your trip. If you're renting a car, a shuttle to the pick-up point will be available if required. If you're using public transportation, forget the City Bus, unless you have no luggage or backpack (not allowed on the Bus!) The Gray Line Airporter (834-1033) outside the baggage claim area will take you to Waikiki for $5 per person. Shuttles such as the Airport Motorcoach (926-4747), E.M. Airport Shuttle Services (942-2177), and Waikiki Airport Express (949-5249) also appear regularly outside the baggage claim area, and cost $5 for each adult, $2.50 each child 6-12 years old. Extra charge for wheelchairs, bikes and surfboards. Very few resorts provide airport pick-up and those that due often charge a fee. Check with your hotel.

Taxicabs are available at the airport, most major hotels, or by phone. City regulated fees should total about $15 from the airport to Waikiki - a 10 mile trip. If you have a group the cabfare is low and not having to wait for a shuttle is a luxury. Almost any ride within Waikiki will cost $5 - $10 with tip. Major taxi companies include: Charlie's (833-3411); Aloha State Cab, Inc. (847-3566) who also have handicapped facilities; Americabs (521-6680 or 531-9999); State Independent Drivers Association - SIDA (836-0011); and Century Cab (528-4655) offering senior citizen discounts.

Want to go in style, try a limo! It's expensive ($40-150), but what a way to go. Silver Cloud Limousine Service (524-7999) will transport you in a Silver Cloud Rolls seating four for $100, or in a bigger, more elegant Phantom VI Rolls Royce which seats 7 for $120, major credit cards accepted. Americabs Limousine Service (521-6880 or 531-9999) will transport you in a stretch Cadillac seating 7 for just under $40. Five Star Limousine (545-1500) charges a flat rate of $100 for hotel to Airport in a stretch Lincoln Continental, and $150 flat rate for a stretch Rolls Royce. They require two days advance notice.

The current fad (I wonder who creates these?) is to rent a car for only a day or two during a week's stay on O'ahu. The thinking is that since Waikiki is already overcrowded with vehicles and short on parking, public transportation is the way to go for everything except a quick car tour of the island. My experience is that a rental car is a very handy and convenient thing to have on O'ahu no matter where you stay or how long you visit. I like to feel independent, be able to come and go on my own timetable, and be assured of some degree of privacy no matter where I am. For my family and me, then, it is worth the extra cost to have access to a car. I've found that most hotels and condos do have paid parking available for only a few dollars per day, and that even in Waikiki a car saves loads of time and offers comfort and mobility.

Anyone who realizes that many of O'ahu's treasures lie outside the boundaries of Waikiki will find an automobile a daily essential. A trip from Waikiki to Ala Moana Center (10 blocks) can take one half hour by bus; but by car - five minutes. For a family with children the space and privacy a car provides is alone worth the rental price. And for a person or group that likes to explore secret places in the city, in the recesses of Waikiki, and in the rural countryside, a car is necessary equipment.

Many package tours to Hawaii purchased through your travel agency will include a rental car as part of the fixed cost. Take it. Make sure you have a car during your entire stay on O'ahu, and that you can pick it up at, and return it to, the Airport. A shuttle ride to the pick-up point is an acceptable alternative, but do not arrange for a downtown or Waikiki pick-up unless a complimentary company shuttle will take you from and to the Airport.

Some rental car companies are national chains while others are local. They all have a variety of cars available at a variety of rates, with special low-season, weekly discounts, or holiday package deals. You can check out the following list and contact them yourself (many have toll free numbers) or you can have your travel agent do it. Don't overlook packages that include your rental car with your airlines or accommodations.

The daily rental rate for a compact or subcompact is from $20-36. Some agencies offer a special weekly rate of $99. For a mid-size sedan, the daily rate range is from $26-$40, some weekly rates as low as $149. Seven passenger vans have a daily rate ranging $50-$60, weekly rates are $209 and up. Various luxury cars and convertibles are also available and they command premium rental rates. Four wheel drive vehicles are available from some agencies. No mileage charge for any model. Gas in Hawaii ranges from $.32-.40 cents per liter/$1.20-1.50 per gallon. Prices do not include insurance (optional) which runs an additional $5 - $10 per day plus sales tax (4%). Several major rental companies have announced plans for rental rate increases during the next year (this is reported to be a result of fewer people purchasing their insurance coverage). Be sure and check with your car insurance agent before you leave to learn just what coverage you have. Hawaii is a no-fault State. Car rental agencies have certain requirements. Most require a minimum age of 21 to 25 and a major credit card or a deposit to hold your reservation.

## RENTAL CAR COMPANIES:
ALAMO RENT A CAR  1-800-327-9633
AVIS RENT A CAR  1-800-831-8000
BUDGET RENT A CAR  1-800-527-0700
DOLLAR RENT A CAR  1-800-342-7398
HERTZ RENT A CAR  1-800-654-3131
HONOLULU RENT A CAR  (808) 941-9099
NATIONAL CAR RENTAL  1-800-227-7368
ROBERT'S HAWAII RENT A CAR  (808) 947-3939
SEARS  (808) 922-3805, 1-800-527-0700
THRIFTY  (808) 833-0046, 1-800-367-2277
TROPICAL RENT A CAR  (808) 836-1041, 1-800-367-5140

*Getting Around*

Most hotels and condominiums in Waikiki have parking facilities, however, there is a small daily charge. If you are traveling from outside Waikiki for a day, public parking facilities are available at rates beginning at $1.50 per hour. Lots can be found behind Woolworth's, near the Queen Kapiolani Hotel, at the Royal Hawaiian Shopping Center, and on Kuhio near the Marine Surf.

Travel time from the Honolulu International Airport to your accommodations is brief, except during rush hour traffic. To Waikiki 30 minutes, to Sheraton Makaha Resort (leeward coast) 30 minutes, Windward Oʻahu or the North Shore 45 minutes to one hour. Tip! If you are driving a rental car, a short cut to Waikiki (except at am and pm rush hours) is to take the Lunalilio Freeway (H-1), exit at University Avenue, take a U-turn and head Makai on University, take a right onto Kapiolani Blvd, then a left onto Kalakaua and straight ahead into Waikiki. If you have a rental car or taxi, try it. If you get lost, just head downhill toward the ocean, and enjoy the view of the city.

The bus system on Oʻahu is one of the best in the country, with routes everywhere, a good safety record, and discounts for special groups such as students and seniors. However, if you do decide to use public transportation, remember you may lose in privacy, convenience and time what you may gain in savings. Send for the current year's edition of *The Bus Guide*, published by C.P. International Ltd., 79-154 Buff Bay Court, Bermuda Dunes, CA 92201. Or call for Bus Schedule Information directly, as well as for the pamphlets they have available at (808-531-1611). *The Bus Guide* is convenient for tourists because it has brief descriptions of sights, shopping centers, hotels, and tips on how to tour the island by bus for $1.20. Each description has directions as to which bus to take, where to catch it, and how to transfer, if necessary. A handy reference. Be sure to have the correct change in coins. Drivers are not permitted, for instance, to accept three dollar bills for five 60 cent fares. Also avoid The Bus during rush hours 7-9am and 4-6pm on weekdays. In fact, it's wise to avoid driving or riding anywhere at those hours - traffic in metropolitan Honolulu at rush hour is often bumper to bumper - especially on the freeways! And the Pali or Likelike Highways, forget it. No smoking, drinking, or eating is permitted on The Bus, and baggage must be lap held or fit under the seat. Bathing suits must be dry, and no surfboards are allowed.

Pedicabs (open-air bicycle rickshaws) were a Waikiki institution before the City Council outlawed them on Kuhio and Kalakaua. You still see a few, but at least for now they are more of a curiosity than a viable transportation alternative.

Mopeds have recently become very popular touring vehicles for younger tourists, who would be shocked to discover how many serious accidents these motorbikes cause each year. Mopeds are fun and trendy, but they are hard to see in traffic and can be a red flag to some young motorists looking for excitement. Please ask the dealers what safety precautions are recommended, and follow them. You and your family want your vacation to be safe and enjoyable.

Carry a Honolulu city map with you on the plane, or buy one at the Airport when you arrive. You'll be able to identify your route into Waikiki and points of interest along the way.

# WHERE TO STAY

Before you begin booking your accommodations, we suggest that you review this chapter to decide what part of O'ahu you want to make your headquarters, what type of lodgings you prefer (hotel with no kitchen; hotel-condo with kitchen plus hotel services, condominium with full apartments, bed and breakfast, private home rental or trade, hostel, YMCA/YWCA, or University housing are all options), and what price range best fits into your vacation budget (lodgings range from $20 to thousands of dollars per night; with the greatest number in the $40 - $100 bracket).

As you read our description of each lodging, refer to the Accommodations map (#2) to locate each property and see where it is in relation to the rest of Waikiki, Honolulu and rural O'ahu.

Since more than 90% of the places to stay on O'ahu are located in Waikiki, by far most of O'ahu's visitors stay there. And chances are that Waikiki is the place you'll decide to stay, too. But don't let that probability stop you from taking a good hard look at the accommodations sprinkled around O'ahu's rural and rustic coast. They are usually lower priced, almost always secluded, and virtually every one is within an hour's easy drive of Waikiki.

You might want to make a checklist of characteristics you want in your accommodations, then use your list to identify the places you are most interested in. For instance, do you want to be on the beach? Do you need a kitchen or a separate bedroom? Is an oceanfront important to you? Do you require daily maid service? Do you want to stay in a building with restaurants, shops or a travel desk? Would you like to be near a bus stop, major shopping center or children's attraction such as the Zoo or the Polynesian Cultural Center? Would you prefer a wetter (windward), moderate (central O'ahu, Honolulu and Waikiki) or drier (leeward) climate? Want to be near a famous golf course? Or be able to take a tennis lesson at your hotel? These are things to consider while choosing your favorite two or three places to stay. And remember, you don't have to make all your choices alone. We'll help with information and suggestions as to which places are best bets.

Accommodations that are well located, are reasonably clean and secure, offer comfortable amenities, have a friendly staff, and in general deliver very good quality for your dollar are identified as a best bet with a star ★. We suggest that you give careful consideration to these properties.

We have divided O'ahu into nine regions, with all accommodations listed first in an alphabetical index for easy reference, then in groups according to each of the nine geographic areas. Quick referral to the accommodations maps will allow you to determine the island location of each property. If you wish to refer to a more detailed map of one of the nine O'ahu regions, turn to the regional touring maps in the "Exploring O'ahu" section of the WHAT TO SEE chapter. These maps will allow you to pinpoint the location of each accommodation in rural O'ahu and determine its relation to points of interest in its vicinity.

We've tried to offer you the most information in the briefest space. In each listing you will find the property's address and phone number plus rental agents (if any) who handle the booking of reservations. Prices, although current at press time, are subject to change without notice. As island visitors ourselves, we felt it was important to include the actual prices in addition to the four basic price range categories: Inexpensive, up to $75; Moderate, $75 - $125; Expensive, $125 - $200; and Deluxe, more than $200. Remember, although prices are current at the time of printing, a slight increase should be expected (4-7% per year). Also, prices listed do not include the 9.43% sales tax (Hawaii State Tax and Hawaii Hotel Tax), and that parking is usually available at the hotels for a small daily charge.

In general, there are two "seasons" for accommodations on O'ahu. High season lasts from mid December until mid April. During this peak time, prices for lodgings can include a surcharge of 5% to 20% or more. Availability is also less. Off season extends from mid April to mid December, except that summer, from mid June to late August, is also a busy family vacation time and therefore is also considered "high season" by some establishments. Some resorts are moving to a flat, year round rate. So if your vacation dates are flexible, you might want to consider visiting in the less crowded, less expensive periods - late November to early December, April to early June, and September to October. Ironically, these are some of the best weather months (especially in the autumn).

We do suggest that you write or call each property you're interested in, and request both a recent brochure and tariff card with the hotel rates for the time of year you plan to visit.

For the sake of space, we have made use of some abbreviations. All listings are condominiums unless specified as a "(hotel)". All condominiums have kitchens, T.V.'s. and pools unless otherwise specified. The size of the units are abbreviated as studio (S BR), one bedroom (1 BR), two bedroom (2 BR) and three bedroom (3 BR), and quality as, (std.) standard, (mod.) moderate, (dlx.) deluxe, and (PH) penthouse. The number in parenthesis refers to the number of people who can occupy the unit for the price listed. Occasionally we have a listing such as (2, max 5). This means that the price is for two people, but there are enough beds for a maximum of five people to occupy the unit. The description will tell you how much it will be for additional persons over two, e.g. each additional person $6/night. Some facilities consider an infant as an extra person, others will allow children free up to a specified age. The abbreviations (o.f.), (g.v.), and (o.v.) refer to oceanfront, gardenview and oceanview units. The prices are listed with a slash dividing them. The first price listed is the high season rate, the second price is the low season rate. Those with a flat yearly rate will show only one rate.

Condos are abundant, and the prices and facilities they offer can be quite varied. As we described above we have indicated our own personal preferences by the use of a ★. We feel these are best buys or special in some way. However, it is impossible for us to view all the units within a complex and since condominiums are privately owned, each unit can vary in its furnishings and its condition.

For longer than one week, a condo unit with a kitchen or kitchenette can result in significant savings on your food bill. While this will give you more space than a hotel room and at a lower price, you may give up some resort amenities (shops, restaurants, maid service, etc.) There are several large chain grocery stores around the island with fairly competitive prices, although most things at the store will run slightly higher than on the mainland. (See the "Dining In" section of the WHERE TO EAT chapter).

There is a growing trend to offer only limited maid service in the condominiums, perhaps only on check out or once a week. Additional maid service is usually available for an extra charge. Rooms without telephones or color televisions usually have lower prices and a few condominiums do not have pools. A few words of caution: condominium units within one complex can differ greatly and, if a phone is important to you, ask! More complexes are adding phone service to their rooms, however there are still many that have only a courtesy phone or a pay phone at the office. Some may add 50 - 75 cents per in-room local call, others have no extra charge. Some units have washers and dryers in the rooms, while others do not.

Travel agents will be able to book your stay in O'ahu hotels and also in most condominiums. If you prefer to make your own reservation, we have listed the various contacts for each condominium and endeavored to quote the best price generally available. Rates vary between rental agents, so check all those listed for a particular condominium. We have indicated toll free 800 numbers when available. Numbers listed without an area code are local Hawaiian numbers and need to be prefixed with (808) if calling from the mainland. You might also check the classified ads in your local newspaper for owners offering their units, which may be a better bargain.

Condominiums require a deposit, usually equivalent to one or two night's stay, to secure your reservation and insure your room rate from price increases. Some charge higher deposits during winter or Christmas holidays. Generally a 30 day notice of cancellation is needed to receive a full refund. Most require payment in full either 30 days prior to arrival or upon arrival and a great many do not accept credit cards. The usual minimum condo stay is 3 nights with some requiring one week in winter. Christmas holidays may have steeper restrictions with minimum stays as long as two weeks, payments 90 days in advance and heavy cancellation penalties. It is not uncommon to book as much as two years in advance for the Christmas season.

Weekly and monthly discounts are often available. Room rates quoted are generally for two. Additional persons run $8-10 per night per person with the exception of the luxury resorts and hotels where it may run as much as $25-35 extra. Many complexes can arrange for crib rentals. Some hotels offer a Family Plan in which children under a specified age stay free when in the same room occupied by accompanying adults and using existing bedding. Each accommodation offering this plan will be identified "Family Plan" in our listings.

We have tried to give the lowest rates available which might be offered through the hotel or condo office, so check with all agents listed as well as the office. When contacting condominium complexes by mail, be sure to address your correspondence to the attention of the manager.

> DID YOU KNOW...that you can rent a home on a long-term basis in Hawaii from a service called "World-Wide Home Rental Guide," which puts you in direct contact with homeowners? Published twice per year, the cost is $9 for 1 year, $15 for two. To list an ad costs $35. Contact Stan Cohen, World-Wide Home Rental Guide, 142 Lincoln Avenue, Suite 652, Santa Fe, NM 87501 (505) 988-5188.

Choosing a place to stay is one of the most important vacation decisions you'll make. Now, before your visit, in the calm of your own living room, is the time to enjoy trying each place on for size, and having fun deciding which one fits you best. Good hunting!

GINGER &
ANTHURIUMS

# ACCOMMODATIONS INDEX

# *EWA WAIKIKI*

The Ewa (western) end of Waikiki, especially the area known as the Hobron Lane District (Ala Moana Blvd. to Ala Wai Blvd. to Kalakaua Ave.), is Hawaii's most densely populated area. There are at least 10 giant condominiums in this section of Waikiki, so prices are often lower and rooms plentiful.

Many visitors prefer this area because it is close to the Ala Moana Shopping Center and somewhat less hectic than mid Waikiki.

Notice that the prices are lower and bargains better on the fringe of Waikiki as you move away from the beach. Also, note that beachfront accommodations on the extreme Ewa and diamondhead sides of Waikiki seem to offer more reasonable rates.

Ambassador Hotel of Waikiki
Big Surf Condo-apartments
Discovery Bay
Hale Koa Hotel ★
Hawaii Dynasty Hotel
Hawaiian Colony Hotel
Hawaiian Monarch
Hilton Hawaiian Village ★
The Ilikai ★
Inn On The Park

Maile Court ★
Outrigger Ala Wai Terrace
Outrigger Hobron Hotel
Waikiki Gateway Hotel
Waikiki Marina Hotel
Waikiki Parkside
Waikiki Plaza Hotel
Waikiki Seiwa ★
Waikikian On The Beach ★

**AMBASSADOR HOTEL OF WAIKIKI**    *Inexpensive*
2040 Kuhio Ave., Honolulu, HI 96815 (941-7777). Try the deluxe studios with kitchenette, or the one bedroom suites with full kitchen. Corner suites offer better views. Pool and sundeck, restaurant and lounge one floor above street level. Coffee shop. *S BR std. $46, sup. $50, dlx. w/kit' net $54; suites w/kit. $80.*

**BIG SURF CONDO-APARTMENTS**    *Inexpensive*
1690 Ala Moana Blvd., Honolulu, HI 96815 (946-6525). This small, clean, 44 unit condo apartment building is a bargain for singles and students. No air conditioning or pool; TV available. Some refrigerator and cooking facilities available. The front desk folks are very friendly.
*S BR $30, 1 BR m.v. $45-75, o.v. $45-75*

**DISCOVERY BAY**    *Expensive*
1778 Ala Moana Blvd., Honolulu, HI 96814. Agents: Hawaiiana Resorts, Inc., (941-3307). This upscale condo is in twin 42-story towers on the corner of Ala Moana Boulevard and Hobron Lane. Amenities include full kitchen, washer-dryer in your condo unit, cable TV and central air conditioning. Building complex contains stores and dining, including award-winning Bon Appetit Restaurant, McDonald's and even a Bank of Hawaii outlet. One block from beach and marina. Close to Ala Moana Shopping Center.
*1 BR m.v. $105, o.v. $121; 2 BR m.v. $158, o.v. $191*

**HALE KOA HOTEL**  ★   *Inexpensive*
2055 Kalia Road, Honolulu, HI 96815. (955-0555), 1-800-367-6027. You may have heard about the beautiful military hotel on the beach at Waikiki. It's the Hale (house of) Koa (the warrior), built in 1975 and open only to active and retired military (and some federal government) personnel and their dependents. Although a 200-400 room expansion plan for the Hale Koa is before Congress, the hotel as is fills up fast so make reservations months in advance if possible. This hotel costs the taxpayer nothing; it was funded entirely with nonappropriated funds - monies generated by profits from military clubs and exchanges worldwide. Hale Koa has more than 400 first-class guest rooms, featuring lanais that look over ocean or mountains. Excellent restaurants, weekly luau on the beach, special entertainment, and some of the best beach in Hawaii. The hotel even provides a golf shuttle to O'ahu's best military golf courses! The hotel is a part of the Armed Services Recreation Center at Fort DeRussy. If you qualify (write the hotel if you're not sure) you'll never forget your stay at the Hale Koa. *Most rooms max-4 same rate, single occupancy deduct $2. Family Plan.*
*S BR std. $29-50, sup. $35-60, par. o.v. $40-70, o.v. $45-75, o.f. $56-82*

**HAWAII DYNASTY HOTEL**    *Inexpensive-Moderate*
1830 Ala Moana Blvd., Honolulu, HI 96815 (955-1111), US: 1-800-421-6662, Calif: 1-800-352-6686, Canada: 1-800-448-5970, In Hawaii: 1-800-362-8530. Set back from the street, this hotel is convenient and comfortable. The Chinese Dynasty Restaurant is on the street level. Location is close to Ala Moana Shopping Center. Pool is one of the largest in Waikiki. Family Plan.
*S BR std. $45/40, dlx. $50/45, sup. $55/50, Deluxe Suite $135/130*
*S BR std. Gov't/military rate $39, Kamaaina-airline rate $36*

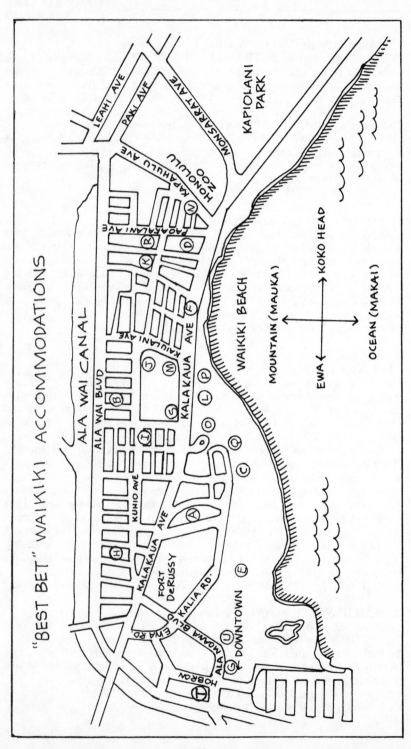

"BEST BET" WAIKIKI ACCOMMODATIONS

(A) THE BREAKERS

(B) 444 NAHUA

(C) HALEKULANI

(D) HAWAIIAN REGENT

(E) HILTON HAWAIIAN VILLAGE

(F) HYATT REGENCY

(G) THE ILIKAI

(H) MAILE

(I) MARINE SURF HOTEL

(J) MIRAMAR AT WAIKIKI

(K) OUTRIGGER PRINCE KUHIO

(L) OUTRIGGER WAIKIKI

(M) PRINCESS KAIULANI

(N) QUEEN KAPIOLANI

(O) ROYAL HAWAIIAN HOTEL

(P) SHERATON MOANA SURFRIDER

(Q) SHERATON WAIKIKI

(R) WAIKIKI BANYAN

(S) WAIKIKI BEACHCOMBER

(T) WAIKIKI SEIWA

(U) WAIKIKIAN ON THE BEACH

69

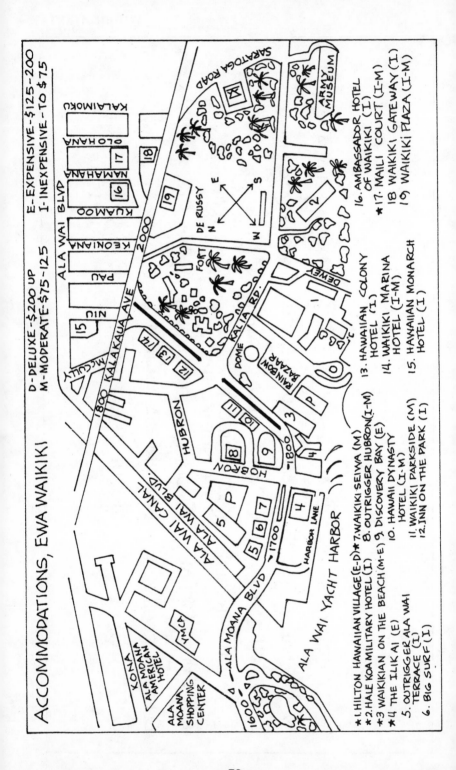

# ACCOMMODATIONS, EWA WAIKIKI

D - DELUXE - $200 UP          E - EXPENSIVE - $125-200
M - MODERATE - $75-125        I - INEXPENSIVE - TO $75

★ 1. HILTON HAWAIIAN VILLAGE (E-D)
★ 2. HALE KOA MILITARY HOTEL (I)
★ 3. WAIKIKIAN ON THE BEACH (M-E)
4. THE ILIKAI (E)
5. OUTRIGGER ALA WAI TERRACE (I)
6. BIG SURF (I)
★ 7. WAIKIKI SEIWA (M)
8. OUTRIGGER HUBRON (I-M)
9. DISCOVERY BAY (E)
10. HAWAII DYNASTY HOTEL (I-M)
11. WAIKIKI PARKSIDE (M)
12. INN ON THE PARK (I)
13. HAWAIIAN COLONY HOTEL (I)
14. WAIKIKI MARINA HOTEL (I-M)
15. HAWAIIAN MONARCH HOTEL (I)
16. AMBASSADOR HOTEL OF WAIKIKI (I)
★ 17. MAILI COURT (I-M)
18. WAIKIKI GATEWAY (I)
19. WAIKIKI PLAZA (I-M)

70

**HAWAIIAN COLONY HOTEL**   *Inexpensive*
1946 Ala Moana Blvd., Honolulu, HI 96815 (955-0040). This set back, secluded
hotel has a small, delightful courtyard, natural wood doors and a former swimming pool now containing koi and arched by a Japanese bridge. Only 1 1/2 short
blocks to the beach and recently renovated.
*S BR $41.57/day (double) $249.43/week*


**HAWAIIAN MONARCH (ASTON) (hotel)**   *Inexpensive*
444 Niu Street, Honolulu, HI 96815 (949-3911), US: 1-800-922-7866 or 1-800-
367-5124, Canada: 1-800-423-8733 ext. 250, In Hawaii: 1-800-342-1551.
Conveniently located next to Jack-in-the Box Restaurant, this hotel is easy to get
in and out of by car. Superior rooms have twins or queens; deluxe have twins/-
queens/kings. Be sure to request your preference, as well as floor and gar-
den/city/mountain/or ocean view. Units were refurbished in 1987.
*S BR sup. $45-65, dlx. $51-71 (no kitchen)*


**HILTON HAWAIIAN VILLAGE**  ★  **(hotel)**   *Expensive-Deluxe*
2005 Kalia Road, Honolulu, HI 96815-1999 (949-4321). Agent: 1-800-HIL-
TONS. This is a world-class resort; you could spend your entire O‘ahu vacation
happily here without ever leaving the grounds. O‘ahu has a number of oases in
which a person can have an outer-island experience without leaving O‘ahu.
Turtle Bay on North Shore, Sheraton Makaha Resort on the Leeward Coast, and
several small beachfront properties on the Windward Side are major examples.
The Hilton Hawaiian Village is such an oasis right in the midst of Waikiki. It
has its own post office. It has the only private dock in Waikiki. It has 2,600
rooms; three pools and a great stretch of beach; its own catamaran; the stellar
Don Ho Show in the world's first geodesic dome; 34 rooms especially designed
for guests with special needs; computer-compatible phones (in the Ali‘i Tower);
more than 100 shops and boutiques; complete audio visual services; the largest
meeting, convention, and banquet facilities in Hawaii; 22 acres of nightclubs,
discos, dining, and enjoyment. A city within a city - an adult's Disneyland.
Before you decide where to stay on O‘ahu, send for a brochure on this one and
compare prices. It's worth a good, long, hard look.
*S BR $139-295, 1 BR $370-$780, 2 BR $625-2,550*


**THE ILIKAI**  ★  **(hotel)**   *Expensive*
177 Ala Wai Blvd., Honolulu, HI 96815 (949-3811) 1-800-FORTHEI or 1-800-
367-8434. The Ilikai has been a Waikiki landmark for years; you may have seen
it in scenes of "Hawaii Five-O" or "Magnum PI." In fact, the Harbor View Suite
in the Yacht Harbor Building was once used as Steve McGarrett's office in
"Hawaii Five-O." Today the Ilikai is known as Waikiki's only complete tennis
resort. It features six hard-surface courts (including a lighted stadium court), ball
machines, hitting alleys, and two full-time tennis pros available for clinics and
private lessons. Also famous are the Ilikai's huge guest rooms - some as large as
600 square feet. The Ilikai is actually a complex of three buildings - the Tower
Building, the Yacht Harbor Building, and the Ilikai Marina across the street, for
longer stays. About 300 units have full or executive kitchens.

Ilikai means "surface of the sea." Whether you stay at the Ilikai or not, walk through its open-air mall overlooking the beach, Duke Kahanamaku Lagoon and the Ala Wai Marina. Perhaps take lunch at Pier 7, outside at Centre Court, or dinner at the Ilikai Yacht Club Restaurant. After you've seen the wide range of shops on the Ilikai mall, it's nearly dusk and you're just in time for the famous Ilikai sunset torchlighting ceremony. The Ilikai has observed this ancient Hawaiian custom for more than 20 years at its mall - a conch blower sounds his single note to the north, east, south, and west, heralding the coming of night, as flame bearers light the torches. Performed Tuesday through Saturday, the ceremony is conducted regularly on Oʻahu only at the Ilikai. Centre Court is a perfect vantage point.

The Ilikai hotel complex has much to offer, even a putting green and shuffleboard court. And do not miss the ride in the exterior glass elevator to the Top of the I Restaurant and Annabelle's, a popular night and dancing spot. And if you're a tennis buff write the hotel for dates of the annual Nissan-Hawaii tennis championships, held at the hotel. * Full or executive kitchen.
*Yacht Harbor Bldg.    S BR std. $100, mod. $120, sup. $140*
*Tower Bldg. *          S BR std. $150, mod. $160, sup. $170., dlx. $180*
*Suites: 1 BR o.v. $220, 2 BR w/kit. m.v. $290, o.v. $360*

**INN ON THE PARK**   *Inexpensive*
1920 Ala Moana Blvd., Honolulu, HI 96815 (946-8355), 1-800-225-1347. This condominium hotel is a sleeper. Its lobby has recently undergone extensive renovation, and the fifth floor pool deck is very well decorated with a stunning view of Fort DeRussy and the Waikiki skyline. No charge for kids using same room & same beds. *S BR std. m.v. $55, sup. o.v. $65, dlx. kit' net $70*

**MAILE COURT**  ★   *Inexpensive-Moderate*
2058 Kuhio Ave., Honolulu, HI 96815 (947-2828). Agent: Colony Resorts, Inc. 1-800-367-6046. Good location for getting in and out of Waikiki by car. Newly redone lobby. Excellent kamaaina rates and specials. Small rooms. Great views from higher floors. One bedroom corner units with kitchenettes recommended.
*With kit' net: S BR sup. $75, dlx $85, 1 BR  $130, Suite $150*
*Hotel RM w/frig. sup. $65, dlx. $75*

**OUTRIGGER ALA WAI TERRACE**   *Inexpensive*
1547 Ala Wai Blvd., Honolulu, HI 96815 (949-7384). US/Canada: 1-800-367-5170. This is a low budget accommodation, recommended primarily for single males and students. Located next to Ala Wai Canal; convenient to Ala Moana Shopping Center. Tower suites are preferable to garden rooms. Guests have use of the Outrigger Hobron swimming pool across Hobron Lane.
*S BR tower $60-70/50-60, g.v. $40/35, 1 BR g.v. $45/40*

**OUTRIGGER HOBRON HOTEL**   *Inexpensive-Moderate*
343 Hobron Lane, Honolulu, HI 96815 (942-7777), 1-800-367-5170. Clean, small rooms. Nice pool - secluded. Well landscaped entrance with fountains and pools. Refrigerator in each room. No kitchen facilities.
*S BR std. $60/40, mod. $65/50, mod. w/kit' net $70/55, dlx. $75/60*
*Suite (1-4) w/kit' net $90/90*

**WAIKIKI GATEWAY HOTEL**   *Inexpensive*
2070 Kalakaua Ave., Honolulu, HI 96815 (955-3741). Agent: Aston Hotels & Resorts. US: 1-800-367-5124. Canada: 1-800-423-8733 ext. 250. In Hawaii: 1-800-342-1551. This hotel is distinctive because of its shape (described as looking like a Mayan pyramid) and location at the delta of Kalakaua and Kuhio Avenues. Also famous as the home of Nick's Fishmarket, one of Waikiki's highly rated restaurants. One source has stated that rooms get smaller on higher of the building's 16 floors. Eight deluxe units have waterbeds.
*Superior $39-65, dlx. $49-75*

**WAIKIKI MARINA HOTEL**   *Inexpensive-Moderate*
1956 Ala Moana Blvd., Honolulu, HI 96815 (955-0714), 1-800-367-6070. This hotel is located near the Sizzler Restaurant and Eggs n' Things Restaurant is around the corner. Bar under the pool features magicians and large screen TV.
*S BR no kit' net $36-64, w/kit $41-69, 1 BR w/kit $60-110*

**WAIKIKI PARKSIDE**   *Moderate*
1850 Ala Moana Blvd., Honolulu, HI 96815 (955-1567), 1-800-255-3050. In HI: 943-0339. This 250 room 18 year old hotel is located next to the popular 24 hour Wailana Coffee Shop and near the Ala Moana Shopping Center. Recently renovated rooms. Amenities include a restaurant, two lounges, secured parking, meeting rooms, and recreation facilities.
*S BR single $65/double $95, 1 BR suite $150, PH $150 no kitchens*

**WAIKIKI PLAZA HOTEL**   *Inexpensive-Moderate*
2045 Kalakaua Ave., Honolulu, HI 96815. (808) 955-6363, US: 1-800-367-8047 ext. 101. Canada: 1-800-423-8733 ext. 101-3413. Extra person $12. Friendly hotel with spacious open cocktail area on mezzanine. Good dinner show featuring the Alii's in the Plaza Showroom. Two blocks from Fort DeRussy beach. Large, comfortable pool and deck. *S BR std. $58, sup. $66, dlx. $88*

**WAIKIKI SEIWA**   ★   *Moderate*
1700 Ala Moana Blvd., Honolulu, HI 96815 (942-7722), 1-800-942-7722. One of Waikiki's most beautiful buildings and a favorite of mine. Each of the 160 condominium studios has a complete kitchen. Rooms are nicely appointed and furnished, smallish but creatively shaped, with wonderful views. The building is set back from the street and luxuriously landscaped. If you're security conscious this is your spot - each guest gets a code to open the security gate. Pool, jacuzzi and tennis court complete this elegant property. Complimentary parking, and the ride on the exterior glass elevator alone is worth the price. Hawaiian koa wood in the lobby; marble from Italy; sauna and BBQ's. Laundry on third floor. You've got to see this one to believe it. One of Waikiki's best.
*Std. $70/60, mod. $90/80, sup. $110/100, club $130/120*

**WAIKIKIAN ON THE BEACH (ASTON)**   ★   *Moderate-Expensive*
1811 Ala Moana Blvd., Honolulu, HI 96815 (949-5331), 1-800-367-5124. Agent: Aston Hotels & Resorts - US 1-800-367-5124, Canada 1-800-423-8733 ext. 250, in Hawaii 1-800-342-1551. One of the best buys on Waikiki. This unique hotel-condo is old time Honolulu, the only garden torchlight setting of its kind where rooms in one wing overlook a tropical jungle setting. A-frame lobby

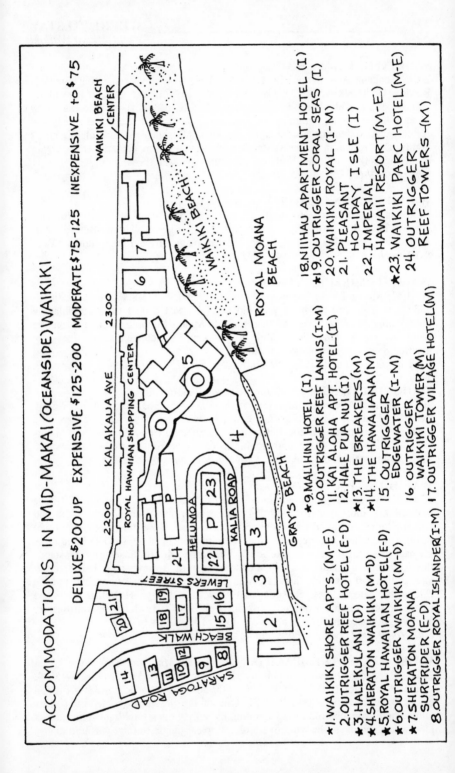

ACCOMMODATIONS IN MID-MAKAI (OCEANSIDE) WAIKIKI

DELUXE $200 UP    EXPENSIVE $125-200    MODERATE $75-125    INEXPENSIVE to $75

★1. WAIKIKI SHORE APTS. (M-E)
2. OUTRIGGER REEF HOTEL (E-D)
★3. HALEKULANI (D)
★4. SHERATON WAIKIKI (M-D)
★5. ROYAL HAWAIIAN HOTEL (E-D)
★6. OUTRIGGER WAIKIKI (M-D)
★7. SHERATON MOANA SURFRIDER (E-D)
8. OUTRIGGER ROYAL ISLANDER (I-M)

★9. MALIHINI HOTEL (I)
10. OUTRIGGER REEF LANAIS (I-M)
11. KAI ALOHA APT. HOTEL (I)
12. HALE PUA NUI (I)
★13. THE BREAKERS (M)
★14. THE HAWAIIANA (M)
15. OUTRIGGER EDGEWATER (I-M)
16. OUTRIGGER WAIKIKI TOWER (M)
17. OUTRIGGER VILLAGE HOTEL (M)

18. NIIHAU APARTMENT HOTEL (I)
★19. OUTRIGGER CORAL SEAS (I)
20. WAIKIKI ROYAL (I-M)
21. PLEASANT HOLIDAY ISLE (I)
22. IMPERIAL HAWAII RESORT (M-E)
★23. WAIKIKI PARC HOTEL (M-E)
24. OUTRIGGER REEF TOWERS (M)

leads to a jungle path with rooms on either side, ending at the Tahitian Lanai restaurant and Papeete Bar. Under a banyan tree near the lobby each Tuesday is a free mai tai party. The Papeete Bar is famous for its friendly sing-along atmosphere; and the eggs benedict at the Tahitian Lanai restaurant are world famous! Good service too; a great place to stay. Manager Darek Sato and staff are some of the best. This good-location hotel is a place where you can still experience old Hawaii. I was also amazed at the variety of rooms - from traditional Hawaiian (even with the lauhala floor mats used by the ancients) to modern Oriental or upscale Waikiki. Let Darek know what you're looking for - he'll arrange it for you. This is one of my very favorite places to stay.
*S BR sup. $69-89, dlx. $79-99, new wing $99-119*
*1 BR (max 4) suite $115-135, PH $160-180*

# MID-MAKAI WAIKIKI

This small area, mid Waikiki from Kalakaua Avenue to the ocean, is the heart of Waikiki. This is the hub of activity, where hotels command the highest rates and where most tourists would prefer to be if they could afford it. Fact is, many tourists *can* afford to lodge here but don't realize it. Most hotels on our list which are located in this prime mid-Waikiki beach area are in the Inexpensive to Moderate range. This section of Waikiki is made up of two basic divisions - hotels directly on the beach and hotels near the beach in the densely populated area between Saratoga Road and Royal Hawaiian Avenue, from Kalakaua Avenue to Kalia Road. Most major happenings in Waikiki are within comfortable walking distance of these hotels. Here are the oldest, and most prestigious, tourist accommodations in Hawaii.

| | |
|---|---|
| The Breakers ★ | Outrigger Reef Towers |
| Hale Pua Nui | Outrigger Royal Islander |
| Halekulani ★ | Outrigger Waikiki Hotel ★ |
| The Hawaiiana Hotel ★ | Outrigger Village Hotel |
| Imperial Hawaii Resort | Outrigger Waikiki Tower |
| Kai Aloha Apartment Hotel | Pleasant Holiday Isle |
| Malihini Hotel ★ | Sheraton Moana Surfrider ★ |
| Niihau Apartment Hotel | Sheraton Royal Hawaiian Hotel ★ |
| Outrigger Coral Seas ★ | Sheraton Waikiki Hotel ★ |
| Outrigger Edgewater | Waikiki Park Hotel ★ |
| Outrigger Reef Hotel | Waikiki Royal Hotel |
| Outrigger Reef Lanais | Waikiki Shore Apartments ★ |

**THE BREAKERS** ★ (hotel)   *Moderate*
250 Beachwalk, Honolulu, HI 96815 (923-3181), US: 1-800-426-0494. The Breakers and Hawaiiana Hotels could be twins - both were done by the same architect and both have excellent reputations for catering to families. The 66 studio and one bedroom units, recently remodeled, overlook a central atrium with exotic trees and a large inviting pool. Both the courtyard and clean, natural wood rooms have a distinctive old-time Hawaiian flavor. Air conditioning,

parking, TV. This is a hotel people return to year after year. It's an oasis well located near beach, bus, and Kalakaua Avenue. A very comfortable place to stay. *S BR w/kit'net $74-80, 1 BR suite w/kit'net $116, extra person $8*

**HALE PUA NUI (apt. hotel)**   *Inexpensive*
228 Beachwalk, Honolulu, HI 96815 (923-9693), US 1-800-433-3828, Canada 1-800-433-5424. A small (22 unit) apartment hotel 1-1/2 blocks from the beach. Minimum stay 3 nights. No room telephone service. Weekly and monthly rates available. Studios with kitchenettes. *S BR w/kit'net $39-56*

**HALEKULANI ★ (hotel)**   *Deluxe*
2199 Kalia Road, Honolulu, HI 96815 (923-2311), 1-800-367-2343. Agent: Leading Hotels of the World 1-800-223-6800, Canada 1-800-341-8585. This is one of the beautiful old "grande-dame" hotels of Hawaii, now charmingly renovated and modernized carefully to retain its elegant heritage.

In 1833 Robert Lewers built a two-story family home on this site, surrounded by hau trees. Fishermen storing their outrigger canoes beneath these trees were made so welcome they named the house "house befitting (heaven or) royalty." In 1917 Clifford Kimball (former manager of the Hale'iwa Hotel on O'ahu's North Shore) leased the property and maintained it as a hotel. In 1931 Kimball razed the Lewers home and built the present lobby building.

---

DID YOU KNOW...that "Charlie Chan", the famous fictional detective, was based on real-life Chang Apana, a detective with the Honolulu Police Department in the early 1900's? Chan's creator, novelist Earl Derr Biggers, is said to have created the first Charlie Chan novel while staying at the Halekulani Hotel in 1925. The novel is called *House Without a Key*, the name of one of Hale-kulani's restaurants, and takes place on the site of the present hotel.

---

In addition to casual dining or cocktails in the House Without a Key, cocktails in the Lewers Lounge or afternoon tea service in the Living Room or Veranda, guests can dine in the oceanside Orchids Dining Room or in the award winning French restaurant La Mer.

Today the Halekulani is synonomous with deluxe accommodations, with the same style of elegance and graciousness that the hotel first brought to Waikiki visitors in the early 1900s. Reflective of Halekulani's quality is its five-diamond (highest possible) rating by the American Automobile Association (AAA) for two consecutive years, and its dual membership (only hotel in Waikiki so honored) in both the Preferred Hotels Worldwide and the Leading Hotels of the World, two associations of independently owned and managed luxury hotels in 17 countries. More than 90% of the 456 spacious guest rooms face the ocean directly outside the five interconnecting buildings (ranging from 2 to 16 stories) surrounding secluded, tranquil courtyards and gardens.

Send for a brochure. For those who value an oasis of luxury on the beach, discover the Halekulani. *S BR g.v. $190, c.v. $220, o.v. $265, o.f. $295 Diamond Head o.f. $325, Suites $425 - 2400*

### THE HAWAIIANA HOTEL ★ *Moderate*
260 Beachwalk, Honolulu, HI 96815 (923-3811), 1-800-367-5122. The real spirit of aloha is alive at The Hawaiiana - people are important here. The hotel is built in a hollow rectangle, creating a lush tropical garden courtyard inside. Coconut leaf umbrellas shade guests near two swimming pools. The traditional-style low Hawaiian buildings offer a welcome change from high-rise hotels. Newly-redecorated air conditioned rooms all have complete kitchens, TV, and complimentary electronic safe. The little things here mean a lot - a freshly picked, sweet pineapple on arrival, Kona coffee and fruit juice by the pool in the morning, a daily newspaper at your door, beach mats and towels, and parking is available. This oasis is well located near beach, bus, and Kalakaua Ave. shops. Families are especially welcome here - a real vacation treat! Special rates for stay of 2 wks. or longer. *S BR sup. $75/70, dlx. $85/80, 1 BR (max 4) $125/105*

### IMPERIAL HAWAII RESORT *Moderate-Expensive*
205 Lewers Street, Honolulu, HI 96815 (923-1827), US 1-800-367-8047 ext. 225, Canada 1-800-423-8733 ext.225. Located less than one block from Waikiki Beach, this condominium offers convenience and the flexibility to dine in or out. Studio, one and two bedroom units, some with kitchenettes and others with full kitchen facilities. Restaurant and 24-hour coffee shop located off the lobby. Daily maid service, adjacent grocery and sundry store, travel and activity desk, air conditioning, and direct-dial telephones in every suite. As close to beachfront as you can get for off-the-beach prices.
*S BR (max 2) $75, 1 BR (max 4) $92-135, 2 BR (max 5) w/full kit. $160*

### KAI ALOHA APARTMENT HOTEL *Inexpensive*
235 Saratoga Road, Honolulu, HI 96815 (923-6723). The tiny (18 unit) Kai Aloha offers lanai-studios and one bedroom suites with tradewind-cooled bedroom and living-dining room. All have modern kitchenettes with two burners, refrigerator, and disposal. One bedroom units have full kitchens. All units have daily maid service, air conditioning, lanais, telephone, and use of ironing and laundry facilities. Kai Aloha is well located, close to beach, bus, and Kalakaua Avenue. *S BR w/kit' net $44-47, 1 BR w/kit. $52-55, extra person $9*

### MALIHINI HOTEL ★ (apt. hotel) *Inexpensive*
217 Saratoga Road, Honolulu, HI 96815 (923-9644 or 923-3095). This small, highly rated, two-story hotel is a friendly reminder of what Waikiki used to be. Centrally located near the beach and Kalakaua Ave., the Malihini is close to the bus route and the post office. The 30 units have 10 studios with twin- or king-size bed, fan (no air conditioning) and kitchenette. The 10 lanai studios feature king or twin beds, large airy rooms with cross tradewinds, lanai or garden patio, shower and kitchenette. The 10 1 BR apts. have a king-size and twin bed (in bedroom), hall with full bath, big sitting room with kitchen, and lanai. Children are welcome; this is a great family place. Laundry facilities and common BBQ area. The brochure describes the Malihini as a "small, plain hotel with no extra frills." *Studio w/kit' net $40, Lanai Studio w/kit' net $50, 1 BR w/kit. $70*

**NIIHAU APARTMENT HOTEL**   *Inexpensive*
247 Beachwalk, Honolulu, HI 96815 (922-1607). Located between the Outrigger
Village Hotel and the Waikiki Royal Apartment Hotel on Beachwalk. Only 2-
1/2 blocks from Gray's Beach near the Halekulani, this 22-unit apartment hotel
has air conditioning, full kitchens, and once a week maid service. Three parking
stalls available. *1 BR (max 2) $42.71, 2 BR (max 4) $59.13*

**OUTRIGGER CORAL SEAS** ★ **(hotel)**   *Inexpensive*
250 Lewers Street, Honolulu, HI 96815 (923-3881), US 1-800-367-5170,
Canada 1-800-826-6786. Well located 2-1/2 blocks from great beach, 1/2 block
from the Royal Hawaiian Shopping Center and Kalakaua Avenue. Restaurants
and night spots surround this hotel. The 109 studios are basic, and well priced.
Add $10 for a kitchenette. Pool, air conditioning and TV, parking, shops. The
Outrigger Coral Seas is well-recommended as a classic Waikiki budget hotel.
*S BR wo/kit' net std.$55/45, mod. $60/50, dlx. $70/60*
*S BR w/kit' net std.  $65/60, mod. $70/65, dlx. $80/70*

**OUTRIGGER EDGEWATER**   *Moderate*
2168 Kalia Road, Honolulu, HI 96815 (922-6424), US 1-800-367-5170, Canada
1-800-826-6786. This small, 184 unit, landmark budget hotel is now connected
to the Outrigger Waikiki Tower Hotel, 200 Lewers Street, to form a single
complex, although each retains separate bookings. The two hotels share a pool
and several restaurants, including the popular Trattoria (Italian). The combination is a large, spacious facility. Amenities include air conditioning, parking,
TV, cocktail lounges, and in-hotel shops. Great location a block from the beach.
Also near Fort DeRussy military recreation area (much of which is open to the
public, including Fort DeRussy beach).
*S BR (max 2) std. $55/45, mod. $60/50, dlx. $70/60*
*S BR (max 2) w/kit' net $75/65, Suite (max 4) w/kit' net $135/110*

**OUTRIGGER REEF HOTEL**   *Expensive-Deluxe*
2169 Kalia Rd., Honolulu, HI 96815 (923-3111), US 1-800-367-5170, Canada
1-800-826-6786. One of the early Outrigger Hotels, the Reef has just undergone
major renovation, especially the lobby and pool areas. Open-air dining at the
Chief's Hut near the newly-created lobby "reefscape" with rocks and waterfalls
is very pleasant. They also serve cocktails and pupus - try the teriyaki chicken or
meat sticks; they're wonderful. Past stores and shops on the beachfront you'll
find the famous Shore Bird Broiler where you can cook your own meal. The
underwater bar and shops one level down have just been redone and are worth a
visit. Rooms also are being redone with the 7th floor for non-smoking guests.
Ask for the type of view and room you prefer; with 883 rooms they should be
able to accommodate you. This hotel is known for being a "bargain" beachfront
property. *Rooftop garden suites $350/300*
*S BR std. $90/80, mod. $110/100, dlx. o.v. $130/120, D. Hd. o.v. or o.f. $160/150*
*Kitchenettes available in all categories - add $5.00.*
*1 BR (max 4) mod. $160/150, dlx. o.v. $200/190, o.f. $225/215*

**OUTRIGGER REEF LANAIS (hotel)**   *Inexpensive-Moderate*
225 Saratoga Rd., Honolulu, HI 96815 (923-3881), 1-800-367-5170, Canada 1-
800-826-6786. Companion to the Outrigger Coral Seas Hotel fronting Lewers

Street. Air conditioning, TV, parking, restaurant/lounge. One guide suggests the best rooms are on upper floors facing Ewa. A budget accommodation with a good location near Waikiki beach (1-1/2 blocks) and Kalakaua Ave. (1/2 block). *S BR std. $55/45, mod. $60/50, dlx. $70/60, PH $90, 1 BR mod. $95, dlx. $105*

**OUTRIGGER REEF TOWERS (hotel)** *Moderate*
227 Lewers Street, Honolulu, HI 96815 (924-8844), US 1-800-367-5170, Canada 1-800-826-6786. Great (and busy) location near restaurants and night spots, the older Outrigger Reef Towers provides a basic travel bargain. Home to the top-notch Al Harrington Show, the hotel has a pool with deck and snack kiosk, 461 rooms ranging from studios to one bedroom suites. This is a dense area so views are primarily of nearby sights. Small lanais. Bathrooms have shower stall; most rooms have refrigerator and coffee maker. Kitchenettes are available. Lobby is busy, with activity desk, shops, and snack bar. Good parking facility in the hotel. The fact that many airline crews stay here reflects the hotel's convenience and affordability.
*S BR std. $70/60, mod. $80/65, dlx. $90/70, add $15/10 for kitchenette*
*S BR suite w/kit' net $95-100/80-85, 1 BR suite w/kit' net 95-105/75-85*

**OUTRIGGER ROYAL ISLANDER (hotel)** *Inexpensive-Moderate*
2164 Kalia Road, Honolulu, HI 96815 (922-1961), 1-800-367-5170, Canada 1-800-826-6786. This small hotel is well located within a block of Waikiki Beach. The 98 units include studios and one bedrooms which can accommodate up to 4 persons. Moderate and Deluxe studios are available with kitchenettes for $5 additional. All units air conditioned. TV. Restaurant and parking.
*S BR (max 2) $55-90/45-60, 1 BR (max 3) $95-105*

**OUTRIGGER WAIKIKI HOTEL** ★ *Moderate-Expensive*
2335 Kalakaua Ave., Honolulu, HI 96815 (923-0711), 1-800-367-5170, Canada 1-800-826-6786. This is the flagship hotel in the 20-property Outrigger family of hotels and condominiums on O'ahu. Set on the beach between the Royal Hawaiian Hotel and the Moana Surfrider Hotel, the Outrigger Waikiki has 530 recently refurbished rooms, large pool, and Kuhio Club on the 16th floor with keyed elevator, workout room, and concierge. A variety of beachfront activity is available, too.

Three nights every week there's a luau and entertainment hosted by Hawaii-Five-O's Doug Mossman. Open bar, sit-down Hawaiian dinner featuring kalua (roast) pig, teriyaki (marinated) chicken, pineapple and corn on the cob. Afterwards enjoy the Polynesian show. (Children's prices available.) The hotel's main and lower lobbies hold shops and restaurants, including Chuck's Steakhouse, Perry's Smorgy Restaurant (all you can eat family buffet), Wendy's Hamburgers, and Monterey Bay Canners seafood restaurant. Cocktails are available at 6 locations in the hotel including Davy Jones Locker bar under the hotel pool (open 8 a.m. to midnight). Entertainment is available at 6 hotel spots, including the Outrigger Main Showroom, featuring Hawaii's top star attractions such as the popular Society of Seven and The Krush. Dancing at the Blue Dolphin Room 8:30 p.m. to midnight.

Oceanfront rooms here are a bargain; a family of four can stay in a Pacific Lanai or Waikiki Lanai (kids stay free in parents' room with existing beds) room for less than $50 per person! * *Outrigger membership travel club*
*S BR std. $110/95, mod. o.v. $130/115, sup. o.v. $140/125*
*Pacific Lanais o.f. $165/155, Waikiki Lanais o.f. $175/165*
*S BR Kuhio Club * o.v. $145/130, Kuhio Club * o.f. $180-200/170-190*
*Suites: Jr. o.v. $185/175, 1 BR o.f. $250-285/240-275, 2 BR o.f. $415/395*

## OUTRIGGER VILLAGE HOTEL    *Moderate*
240 Lewers St., Honolulu, HI 96815 (923-3881), US 1-800-367-5170, Canada 1-800-826-6786. One of Waikiki's more recent hotels, the Outrigger Village is large enough (439 units) to offer a wide range of accommodations. Kitchenette units available with small refrigerator and hotplates. Air conditioning and TV, pool, shops, restaurants and cocktail lounges, parking.
*S BR std. $70/60, mod. $80/65, dlx. $90/70, add $5 for unit w/kit' net*
*1 BR Suites (max 4) w/kit' net $90-140/$75-110*

## OUTRIGGER WAIKIKI TOWER (hotel)    *Moderate*
200 Lewers Street, Honolulu, HI 96815 (922-6424), US 1-800-367-5170, Canada 1-800-826-8786. This hotel and the next-door Outrigger Edgewater might as well be one hotel; they share a pool, restaurants, and lobby space. The Tower itself has 440 bright rooms; most have lanais and corner rooms have kitchenettes. In the hotel is the attractive Waikiki Broiler Restaurant for casual inside-outside dining. The lobby is especially attractive and open. Just a block from the beach, this Outrigger double hotel offers some attractive bargains.
*S BR std. $70/60, mod. $80/65, dlx. $90/70, add $5 for unit w/kit' net*
*Jr. suites (max 3) $90-100/75-/85*

## PLEASANT HOLIDAY ISLE (hotel)    *Inexpensive*
270 Lewers Street, Honolulu, HI 96815 (923-0777). A great location for those who enjoy being where the action is - corner of Kalakaua Avenue and Lewers Street. Very near restaurants, Royal Hawaiian Shopping Center, and only 3 blocks from great beach. Each of the 264 rooms has air conditioning and color TV, refrigerator, and lanai. Nice-sized pool and deck near lobby. A Pleasant Hawaiian Holidays hotel. *S BR std. $42, sup. $46, dlx $51, corner dlx. $56*

BANYAN TREES                                      J. BAYOT

**SHERATON MOANA SURFRIDER** ★ (hotel)   *Expensive-Deluxe*
2365 Kalakaua Ave., Honolulu, HI 96815 (922-3111). Sheraton Res: 1-800-325-3535. Sheraton Hotels in Hawaii: 1-800-634-4747. This legendary inn, built in 1901, is the oldest major hotel in Waikiki, and the newest, too! How can that be? Because for the past several years the historic Moana has been closed for a complete $50 million renovation program. Now completed, the result is certainly spectacular. They've kept the best of the old, and added the best of the new. Three separate structures comprise the hotel, the 1901 historic main Moana Hotel building, the 1952 Ocean Lanai Wing on the diamondhead side of the Moana, and the 1969 Surfrider building on the Moana's Ewa (downtown) side. Until the 1989 renovation, all three buildings were booked separately; now they are structurally connected and function as one single grand hotel. Inside and out, the "new" Moana Surfrider Hotel will look much as she did on opening day, 12 March 1901. In the original hotel, the second floor was furnished in oak, the third in mahogany, and the fourth in maple. That feature has been replaced. In the renovated Moana, the fifth floor (added in 1918 along with the 6th floor) will be furnished with native Hawaiian koa wood, and the sixth floor will be done in cherry. The hotel's general manager states, "In style as well as appearance we will transport guests back to the turn of the century where it all began." And the Moana Surfrider Hotel staff will be expert at making you feel comfortable and an honored guest.

The Moana, Royal Hawaiian, the Kahala Hilton and the Halekulani are often close competitors as visitors' all-time favorite O'ahu hotel. The Moana, meaning "ocean, or open sea", became a household word in 1935 when the famous radio program "Hawaii Calls" began regular nationwide broadcasts which lasted for more than 30 years. Originating from the Moana banyan tree courtyard, "Hawaii Calls" was largely responsible for popularizing Hawaiian music as well as the islands themselves, all across America. Famous songs such as "My Little Grass Shack" and "Sweet Leilani" were first performed for a wide audience on this radio program. The Moana banyan tree, often called Hawaii's most famous shade tree, was planted in 1885. Robert Louis Stevenson is said to have written under this tree. The banyan is now protected under Hawaii State law as "Exceptional Tree Number 41." It received a two day physical exam and "manicure" in preparation for the hotel's grand re-opening in spring 1989.

Accommodations include a pool, three beautiful restaurants and lounges, reproductions of turn-of-the-century furniture, state-of-the-art electronic bedside controls, bathrooms featuring TV and stereo speakers, valet parking, complimentary in-room TV movies, and 24-hour room service. The banyan court will feature a restored Beach Bar, and tea will be served on the veranda overlooking the ocean.

Wherever you stay on O'ahu, visit and tour the Moana Surfrider Hotel. Stroll under the venerable banyan tree in the moonlight. Perhaps you too will glimpse shimmering scenes of a bygone era, and hear soft island melodies as the eternal magic of Hawaii calls. Tentative new rates. Grand re-opening in April 1989.
*Tower Bldg.   c.v. $155, part. o.v. $195, o.f. $235, all with lanais*
*Main Bldg.   c.v. $175, part. o.v. $195, o.f. $215*

## SHERATON ROYAL HAWAIIAN HOTEL ★ *Expensive-Deluxe*

2259 Kalakaua Ave., Honolulu, HI 96815-2578 (923-7311), 1-800-325-3535. Have you heard and read about this great hotel since you were a child? I have too, and believe me, it lives up to its reputation. First of all, everything is pink. The walls, the sheets, the bath towels, the hotel stationery, and even the phone. We challenge anyone to stand anywhere inside or outside the Royal Hawaiian Hotel and look in any direction without seeing pink. It's wonderful! Not shocking pink either, but just the right shade of pink - Royal Hawaiian Pink. Did you know that when the hotel was most recently repainted in 1987 it took 550 gallons of pink paint to cover the hotel's exterior, at a cost of $320,000?

Built in 1927, on the same site occupied by Hawaiian royalty for centuries, the Royal Hawaiian was created as a luxurious resort hotel for well-to-do tourists arriving in Hawaii aboard the new Matson Navigation Co. ocean liner, the Malolo, in the "new recreation era" of the post-World War I 1920s. The hotel took 1-1/2 years to build and cost $4 million. The six-story 400 room hotel was given the Spanish Moorish palace-like appearance made so popular during the period because of the similar settings in the films of superstar Rudolph Valentino. Old Spanish missions are suggested in the structure by cupolas resembling bell towers.

The great and famous all seemed to stay at the Royal. President Franklin D. Roosevelt stayed in the Presidential Suite on July 14, 1934. Other names on the register include Bing Crosby, Mary Pickford and Douglas Fairbanks, Rockefellers, Fords, DuPonts, Clark Gable, Al Jolson, Henry J. Kaiser, the Shah of Iran, and even the child star Shirley Temple. Guests arrived with truckloads of steamer trunks, their own servants, and often their personal Rolls Royce touring car.

During World War II the "Pink Palace" as it was affectionately called served as a rest and recreation center for U.S. Navy submariners. Since then have come major renovations and several changes of ownership. But through it all the Royal has developed into a living legend. Thanks to preservationists the Royal is still here for us to enjoy. A stay at the Royal is one of the true pleasures of visiting Hawaii.

THE ROYAL HAWAIIAN HOTEL                                    JBAYOT

Attention to detail is reflected throughout the hotel. Notice, for example, the RH embossed into the sand atop the floor ashtrays in the hotel lobby! History buffs and honeymooners might prefer the main hotel building (the palace itself), while guests desiring a lanai and spectacular ocean view may opt for a room in the connecting Royal Tower (with pink balconies). Also in the Tower are 6 split-level and several penthouse suites.

Come listen to the authentic ancient and modern Hawaiian music of the Cazimero Brothers in the elegant Monarch Room (or dance to the big band sounds of Del Courtney and his Orchestra each Sun. 5-8 p.m.). Sip a moonlight mai tai at the on-the-beach Mai Tai Bar. Enjoy a sunny Sun. brunch at the open-air Surf Room. Sample authentic Hawaiian food and entertainment at the Royal Hawaiian Luau weekly on the Ocean Lawn. Come make history at the Pink Palace! *S BR std. $145, c.v. $160, o.v. $265, o.f. $280, Jr. suite $300*

**SHERATON WAIKIKI HOTEL** ★ *Moderate-Deluxe*
2255 Kalakaua Ave., Honolulu, HI 96815 (922-4422), 1-800-325-3535. Not only is this Sheraton beachfront hotel one of the largest on Oʻahu, it's one of the most versatile. Rooms rent from $90 per night in the modest 8-story, 75-room Manor Wing, to those ranging from $120 and up per night in the 31-story ocean-front Tower.

Versatility extends to Sheraton Waikiki's dining options: restaurants include the spectacular hotel-top Hanohano Room (a Sat. morning radio program is often broadcast live during breakfast); Kon Tiki Restaurant featuring an indoor Polynesian lagoon setting and more than 70 exotic drinks; Caio!, an Italian restaurant featuring pizzas and pastas; Ocean Terrace open-air restaurant featuring buffets; Kau Kau and Beach Snack Shops; and four lounges for cocktails and pupus. This hotel also has the largest ballroom in Hawaii (with a capacity of nearly 4,000 people), Honolulu suite mini ballroom (divisible into 4 meeting areas), 15 conference rooms, and 286 exhibit spaces. All rooms have recently been completely redecorated, and the huge multi-use lobby/shopping mall is always ablaze with activity and special events. This hotel is a center of activity in Waikiki, and certainly a landmark since its 1971 opening. It's the perfect place to visit and perhaps have brunch in the Hanohano Room 30 floors up.

Everywhere you'll see evidence of the $50 million renovation program completed in 1986. One of my favorite touches is the tropical wallpaper in the halls - notice the mauka (mountain) sides of each hall show upland views while the makai (ocean) sides feature beach plants! Stand still, look down a hallway, squint a little and you can almost hear the tropical birds singing in the trees above you. Parking garage, guest laundromats, valet service, 20 gift and specialty shops, two freshwater swimming pools, a travel and entertainment center, children's program in summertime, white-sand beach, secretarial and babysitting service, electronic safes, the list goes on and on.
*S BR in Sheraton Manor $90, c.v. $120, m.v. $145, part. o.v. $170, o.f. $205*
*Large luxury o.f. $260, Suites $300-up*

**WAIKIKI PARC HOTEL**  ★   *Moderate-Expensive*
2233 Helumoa Road, Honolulu, HI 96815-1938 (921-7272), 1-800-422-0450.
One of Waikiki's newest hotels (1987), the 298-room Waikiki Parc is run by the
Halekulani Corporation (see Halekulani Hotel) which developed the hotel
around the concept of affordable luxury. One hundred yards from the beach, the
hotel features valet parking, twice-daily maid service, choice of king size or two
single beds, air conditioning, remote control TV, refrigerator, room safe, two
phones, and lanai or view balcony. Pool and deck. Rooms are bright and airy.
Two excellent restaurants: the Parc Cafe featuring Continental and American
cuisine, and Kacho, an elegant Japanese restaurant with sushi bar. Family plan
available. This hotel is a sleeper; beautiful, new, and very well located. Highly
recommended. *Std. $90, c.v./m.v. $105, o.v. $145, dlx. m.v. $120, dlx. o.v. $165*

**WAIKIKI ROYAL HOTEL**   *Inexpensive*
255 Beachwalk, Honolulu, HI 96815 (926-5641). Under new ownership, this 54-
unit apartment hotel is newly renovated. One and two-bedroom units all have
full kitchens. Maid service twice a week. Located near the Royal Hawaiian
Shopping Center, Kalakaua Avenue, and 3 blocks from excellent beach.
*1 BR $70, sup. $80, 2 BR $90, sup. $100*

**WAIKIKI SHORE APARTMENTS**  ★   *Moderate-Expensive*
2161 Kalia Road, Honolulu, HI 96815 (926-4733), 1-800-367-2353. Weekly
rates also available. This is one of the few condominium apartment buildings on
Waikiki beach. All studio, 1-bedroom and 2-bedroom units have a complete
kitchen, TV and individual-line phone, washer-dryer in the unit, and private
lanai. Units are privately owned, so each unit is individually decorated and
furnished; rooms are spacious. Many units have fans instead of air conditioning.
Minimum stay 3 nights. Family plan for children under 12. Rates for studios and
1-bedroom units are double occupancy; rates for 2-bedroom units are 1-4
people. Right on the beach and close to the Fort DeRussy recreation area.
Limited paid parking in basement. Weekly rates. If you're staying for a week or
more, this is an excellent bargain, and the views are spectacular.
*1 BR 1 bath std. $120/100, dlx. $140/120, S BR std. $95/75, dlx. $110/90*
*2 BR 1 bath std. $150/130, dlx. $175/155*
*2 BR 2 bath std. $185/165, dlx. $215/195, o.f. std. $225/205, dlx. $260/240*

# MID-MAUKA
# (MOUNTAINSIDE) WAIKIKI

Now let's turn our attention toward good places to stay in mid Waikiki
(Kalaimoko to Kaiulani) on the Mauka (toward the mountains) side of
Kalaukaua Avenue (Kalakaua to Ala Wai Blvd.).

If you're going to Waikiki for a visit, and the beach is the heart of Waikiki, a
hotel on the beach is the best place to stay, right? Not necessarily. Each part of
Waikiki has advantages. Several things happen to lodgings and neighborhoods
as you move away from the beach. Prices go down, more rooms and more room
types are available and there are more rooms with kitchen facilities. Neighbor-

hoods can be quieter. Views of the city and mountains are better and less expensive than rooms with oceanview. Because costs are less, Kuhio Ave. attracts a wider variety of fun things to do than hotel and shop-lined Kalakaua Avenue. So as you enjoy our selection of lodgings Mid-Mauka Waikiki has to offer, try them on for size to see how comfortable you would be if you made your vacation headquarters here.

444 Nahua ★
Aloha Surf Hotel
Aloha Towers
Coral Reef Hotel
Fairway Villa
Hawaiian King Hotel ★
Honolulu Prince
Ilima Hotel ★
Island Colony ★
Marine Surf Hotel ★
Miramar At Waikiki ★
Outrigger East

Outrigger Malia
Outrigger Seaside Suite Hotel ★
Outrigger Surf
Outrigger Waikiki Surf ★
Outrigger Waikiki Surf East
Outrigger Waikiki Surf West
Outrigger West
Princess Kaiulani ★
Royal Kuhio
Waikiki Beachcomber ★
White Sands Waikiki Resort

## 444 NAHUA  *Inexpensive-Moderate*

444 Nahua Street, Honolulu, HI 96815. Booking Agent: Waikiki Beach Condominiums ★, Donald R. Blum, 2 Palomino Lane, Rolling Hills CA 90274, (213)541-8813. 444 Nahua is just one of a number of buildings with beautifully furnished studios, one and two bedroom condominium units in Waikiki which are booked through Don Blum. His units range from standard to plush penthouse luxury with spectacular ocean, mountain or Diamond Head views. Some units can accommodate up to six guests. Don's one and two bedroom condo units have fully equipped deluxe kitchens (studios have kitchenettes or full kitchens) with pots, pans, dishes, silverware, mixer, blender, ice crusher, coffee pot, electric can opener, refrigerator, stove/oven, garbage disposal, dishwasher and microwave oven in most units. Most units are air conditioned, with washer/dryer in the condominium. 444 Nahua is similar to the other condominium complexes represented by Waikiki Beach Condominiums, and is located in the same general area - just a short walk to International Market Place in the "Heart of Waikiki", and close to restaurants, theaters, entertainment, and The Bus.

Rooftop recreational facilities at 444 Nahua are for your use and include a swimming pool, sauna, showers, sun lounge area, BBQ stands, picnic tables, stove, refrigerator, and party facilities. Other complexes have similar facilities, often with shuffleboard, paddle tennis and jacuzzi. A free parking stall is included with most units.

I've stayed at several of these Waikiki Beach Condominium units and can vouch for their cleanliness, elegance, and convenience. Call or write Don; he'll work with you to match your needs and will place you into a condo unit that's just right for you. And the prices are among the best in Waikiki. Surely one of Waikiki's best buys. *Studios, 1 BR and 2 BR condo units $30-80/night*

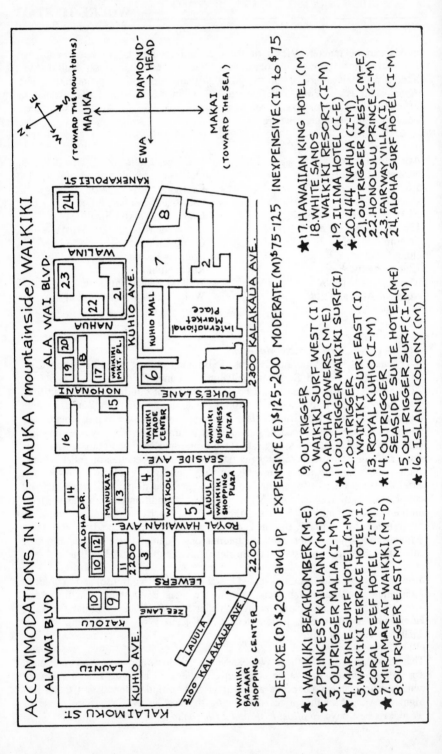

# ACCOMMODATIONS IN MID-MAUKA (mountainside) WAIKIKI

DELUXE(D)$200 and up  EXPENSIVE(E)$125-200  MODERATE(M)$75-125  INEXPENSIVE(I) to $75

★ 1. WAIKIKI BEACHCOMBER(M-E)
★ 2. PRINCESS KAIULANI(M-D)
★ 3. OUTRIGGER MALIA(I-M)
★ 4. MARINE SURF HOTEL(I-M)
5. WAIKIKI TERRACE HOTEL(I)
★ 6. CORAL REEF HOTEL(I-M)
★ 7. MIRAMAR AT WAIKIKI(M-D)
★ 8. OUTRIGGER EAST(M)

9. OUTRIGGER
   WAIKIKI SURF WEST(I)
10. ALOHA TOWERS(M-E)
★ 11. OUTRIGGER WAIKIKI SURF(I)
12. OUTRIGGER
    WAIKIKI SURF EAST(I)
13. ROYAL KUHIO(I-M)
★ 14. OUTRIGGER
    SEASIDE SUITE HOTEL(M-E)
15. OUTRIGGER SURF(I-M)
★ 16. ISLAND COLONY(M)

★ 17. HAWAIIAN KING HOTEL(M)
18. WHITE SANDS
    WAIKIKI RESORT(I-M)
★ 19. ILIMA HOTEL(I-E)
★ 20.444 NAHUA(I-M)
21. OUTRIGGER WEST(M-E)
22. HONOLULU PRINCE(I-M)
23. FAIRWAY VILLA(I)
24. ALOHA SURF HOTEL(I-M)

**ALOHA SURF HOTEL**   *Inexpensive-Moderate*
444 Kanekapolei Street, Honolulu, HI 96815 (923-0222), 1-800-423-4514.
Newly-renovated, this 200-room hotel on mid-Ala Wai Blvd. offers studios and
suites, with kitchenettes in about half the units. Some suites are furnished
Japanese style and offer an exotic alternative to American atmosphere. The
highly recommended Won Kee Chinese Restaurant is off the lobby, as are the
pool, shops, and hair salon. Views are spectacular from upper floors . Each unit
has a safe, lanai, air conditioning, and two twin beds or single queen-sized bed.
And while you're there, try the famous donuts at Merry's Coffee Shop. This is a
bargain spot off the main drag, and very comfortable.
*S BR std. $49, dlx. $64, sup. $54, suites $80-100*

**ALOHA TOWERS**   *Moderate-Expensive*
430 Lewers Street, Honolulu, HI 96815. Booking Agent: Hawaiian Apt. Leasing
Enterprises (714-497-4253), Calif 1-800-472-8449, Canada 1-800-824-8968,
Other 1-800-854-8843. Amy L. Smart or Ruth Smart, (521-0415) or (214-572-
7511). Twin 29-story towers house condominium apartments which rent through
several booking agencies or individuals. Room units in these modern, fully
appointed towers include one and two bedroom suites with kitchen facilities, air
conditioning, maid service on request, and five night minimum stay. The hotel
has parking, two pools, and shopping. Condominium units in these two imposing towers offer amazing views, security, and many amenities.
*1 BR suite w/kit' net $67-85, 2 BR suite w/kit' net $110-160*

**CORAL REEF HOTEL (ASTON)**   *Inexpensive-Moderate*
2299 Kuhio Avenue, Honolulu, HI 96815 (922-1262), US 1-800-922-7866,
Canada 1-800-423-8733 ext. 250, in Hawaii 1-800-342-1551. Located almost in
the geographical center of Waikiki. Rooftop pool and sundeck area. Two
restaurants, including a Chinese spot and Ferdinand's Coffee House, serving
American food and cocktails. The hotel's 245 rooms have lanais, air conditioning, color TV, refrigerator and coffee maker, and great views.

Brochures say one block to beach, but realistically it's more like two. If you
enjoy being where the action is, this is it. You're right next to major shopping
areas such as Kuhio Mall, International Marketplace, the Royal Hawaiian
Shopping Center, Waikiki Trade Center, and the Waikiki Market Place. Kuhio
Avenue is very busy, but this can be fun, especially if you don't plan to rent a
car - everything is close. The 1 bedroom with kitchenette might be the best buy
at the Coral Reef, which combines the best of both condo and hotel services.
*S BR std. $68/48, sup. $72/52, dlx. $82/62, Jr. suite $95/75*
*1 BR w/refrig. $109/89, w/kit' net $114/94*

**FAIRWAY VILLA**   *Inexpensive*
2345 Ala Wai Blvd., Honolulu, HI 96815 (922-9422). If you're going to be on
O'ahu for a week or more, you'll want to consider staying in a condominium.
This one on the Ala Wai Blvd. has a pool, parking, and 20 units for rent (out of
a total of 365 units in the building). Units all have kitchenettes, TV, and air
conditioning. one-bedroom units hold up to four; two-bedroom up to six.
Minimum stay is a week. Maid service on request.
*S BR (max 2) $35-45, 1 BR (max 4) $50-65, 2 BR (max 6) $65-85*

**HAWAIIAN KING HOTEL** ★ *Moderate*
417 Nohonani Street, Honolulu, HI 96815 (922-3894), From mainland: 1-800-727-1707. When we asked local people for a hotel with a true Hawaiian feeling, this (along with the Queen Kapiolani, Breakers, Hawaiiana, Waikikian, and several others noted above and below) is one they highly recommended.

The Hawaiian King is very near another such hotel, the Ilima (containing one of the best restaurants in Honolulu - Sergio's). This family apartment hotel ("suite resort" in the brochure) has very comfortable one bedroom suites each with full kitchen, and breakfast counter separating it from the living room. The hotel's 50 units are tastefully decorated and carpeted - even on the lanai. The hotel court-yard, with its swimming pool, is attractive; beach is 2-1/2 blocks away, and many of Waikiki's activities are just as close. This place is a sleeper, especially for a family of up to 4 people. All units have full kitchens. Send for a brochure!
*1 BR (2 max-4) std. $75, sup. $82, dlx. $98, sup. dlx. $12, extra persons $8*

**HONOLULU PRINCE (ASTON) (hotel)** *Inexpensive-Moderate*
415 Nahua Street, Honolulu, HI 96815 (922-1616), US 1-800-367-5124, other 1-800-663-1118, in Hawaii 1-800-342-1551. This ten-story Aston hotel has 125 rooms - studios with refrigerator, and one and two-bedrooms with full kitchens. Standard rooms are small; perhaps from the hotel's days as a college dorm. Near Kuhio Mall, Waikiki Market Place, Waikiki Trade Center, International Market Place. All units are air conditioned with color TV. Barber and beauty shop in hotel; Family Plan for children under 18. Some units have lanais - be sure to ask if you want one with your unit. The one and two bedroom units with full kitchen seem to be the best bet here; corner units are preferable.
*S BR std. $65/45, dlx. 75/55, 1 BR w/kitchen $95/75, 2 BR w/kitchen $115/95*

**ILIMA HOTEL** ★ *Inexpensive-Expensive*
445 Nohonani Street, Honolulu, HI 96815 (923-1877), 1-800-421-0767. The Ilima is a landmark Waikiki hotel built in 1968, with major lobby and room renovations completed in 1987. You should visit this hotel for two major reasons whether you stay here or not. First, it houses (near its lobby) Sergio's, the famous award-winning Italian restaurant owned, run by and named for, one of the most creative and highly respected chef-manager-owners in the islands, Sergio Battistetti.

The dramatic series of original Hawaiiana paintings in the lobby is the second reason to put the Ilima on your itinerary. This progression of four large paintings and a mural tells the story of the journey (Odyssey is the title of the series) of the human spirit as told in Hawaiian mythology. From the first painting, show-ing the primordial sun rising from Mother Earth at the hands of the God Maui, through the separation of humankind caused by ego and anger, through the intervention of Pele teaching man and woman how to transform human passions into devine love, to the final mural depicting Ku and Hina, the Hawaiian gods of active masculine and passive feminine aspects, submerged in dynamic balance in an ocean of eternal bliss - through this epic odyssey we can watch our own human journies unfolding before us. This wall gallery is splendid and well worth a visit.

This is one of very few Waikiki hotels that offers free guest parking. There's a pool and three separate sundecks, conference room, Sergio's Restaurant (with bar), sauna, exercise room, laundry, 24-hour maid service, color TV and air conditioning, free local calls, and one of the most friendly and upbeat staffs anywhere. Sound inviting? If you're looking for a solid bargain just three blocks' walk from a great beach, this is it. All 99 units are clean and attractive with modern fully-equipped kitchens. *Extra persons $8.*
S BR $39-70, 1 BR $79-111, 2 BR $92-124, 2 BR PH $145-157

**ISLAND COLONY (ASTON)** ★ **(condo hotel)** *Moderate*
445 Seaside Avenue, Honolulu, HI 96815 (923-2345), US 1-800-92-ASTON or 1-800-367-5124, Canada 1-800-423-8733 ext. 250, in Hawaii 1-800-342-1551. This is an elegant condominium hotel which offers you the convenience of condominium suites plus the full amenities of a hotel. 740 units - 434 are available to travelers. Studios with wet bar and under-the-counter refrigerators; studio suites with kitchenettes; and one bedroom suites with full kitchens. All units have lanai, color TV, safe, family plan, and daily maid service. Hotel amenities include a very nice pool and sun area on the sixth floor, restaurant near the lobby, jet spa and sauna, travel desk, spacious lobby area, parking, meeting rooms, babysitting, and cocktail lounge. Rooms are nicely furnished with soft colors and Hawaiian art. The staff is friendly and accommodating. Beach three blocks away. Easy entrance and exit using Ala Wai Blvd. adjacent to hotel. And don't miss the hanging tapa tapestries in the lobby! I especially enjoy the views here - they are stunning. Highly recommended hotel.
S BR $84/64, sup. $89/69, dlx. $94/74, 1 BR suite $119/99

**MARINE SURF HOTEL** ★ *Inexpensive-Moderate*
364 Seaside Avenue, Honolulu, HI 96815 (923-0277), 1-800-367-5176. This is definitely one of my personal favorites on O'ahu. The Marine Surf seems to have it all. It's located smack dab in the center of Waikiki, yet on a side street where you can pull in and out of the secure covered parking lot without waiting. I like the fact that you can go directly from your car to your room with a private key - no tromping through the lobby in your swimsuit.

The hotel is clean. The 120 rental studio apartments are all the same except for location - large rooms with full kitchens. There are one bedroom penthouse suites available which sleep up to six people. There's a laundry room on each floor, and a constant breeze caused by the angle of the building and the sliding glass windows at each end. The rooms are very spacious and bright, recently redone, with two extra-long double beds, color TV, kitchen, air conditioning and electronic safe ($2 per day). Even a small lanai.

Hotel amenities include an award-winning Italian restaurant - Matteo's, a travel desk with very helpful and friendly staff, covered parking ($2 a day - a bargain) with assigned spaces so you never have to hunt for one, nice private pool on the fourth floor, and a hotel staff always willing to help. I've seen them in action, and know they are among the best. The Marine Surf is one of those secrets you'd like to keep to yourself but can't. It's a great location, prices are reasonable, and it's comfortable. One of the best.
S BR (max 4) std. $64/50, dlx. $76/62, sup. $70/56, 1 BR PH (max 6) $125/100

## MIRAMAR AT WAIKIKI ★ (hotel)  *Moderate-Deluxe*

2345 Kuhio Avenue, Honolulu, HI 96815-2996 (922-2077), 1-800-367-2303, CA 1-800-622-0847. The Miramar is the hotel on Kuhio with the giant Chinese mural on its facade. Many people thus consider it a Chinese Club or private association. On the contrary, the Miramar is an excellent public hotel located in the hub of Waikiki activity. Redone recently, the Miramar is clean and attractive; its 368 rooms vary mostly in location and view. Each room is good sized, air conditioned, has a private lanai, color TV, refrigerator, in-room safe, and many have an ocean view (be sure to ask for a room with a view if it's important to you). Family plan for children under 12.

One of my favorite features of the Miramar, besides its central location, is its unusually-shaped swimming pool. The deck is also large and attractive. And you can be sure that a frosted tropical fruit drink from the poolside Warrior Bar will help you enjoy the afternoon sun. A beautiful Chinese restaurant, cafe, lounge and shops can also be found in the hotel. Low-key, friendly and efficient service from the staff is a hallmark of the Miramar. If you want to savor the flavor of the Orient in an elegant, quiet setting, consider staying at the Miramar.
*S BR std. $65/75, sup. $68/85, dlx. $80/90, suites $160 & up*

## OUTRIGGER EAST (hotel)  *Moderate*

150 Kaiulani Avenue, Honolulu, HI 96815 (922-5353), US 1-800-367-5170, Canada 1-800-826-6786. Located across the street from triangular Kaiulani Park, and less than a block from King's Village, the Outrigger East has 444 studios, some with kitchenettes, that will sleep four people. Rooms are good sized, with nice views on higher floors. Hotel has family plan, air conditioning, parking, pool, restaurant and lounges, shops, meeting room, self service laundry, and a pharmacy. Jolly Roger and Burger King restaurants downstairs, Perry's Smorgy (family all-you-can-eat buffet) across the street, convenience stores nearby. Good location, moderate prices, and clean.

If you have a large family, up to eight, the best buy might be the two-bedroom Penthouse Suite for $125 a night. There's a queen-sized bed in one bedroom, two doubles in the other, and a queen-sized sleeper in the living room. The view is out-of-this-world, and the kids can go to the pool and never miss the ocean!
*S BR std. $70/60, mod. $80/65, dlx. $90/70, w/kit' net $90/70*
*1 BR w/kit' net (max 4) $95-125/85-125, 2 BR PH w/kit. $125*

## OUTRIGGER MALIA (hotel)  *Inexpensive-Moderate*

2211 Kuhio Avenue, Honolulu, HI 96815 (923-7621), US 1-800-367-5170, Canada 1-800-826-6786. Great location on Kuhio in mid-Waikiki. Hotel has 328 units - studios and one bedroom Junior Suites. No kitchen facilities. Each room has air conditioning, TV, lanai, and family plan. There is a rooftop tennis court, swimming pool, restaurant and lounge, shops, a floor with rooms especially equipped for the handicapped traveler, and the Wailana Malia Coffee Shop, a popular local spot that never closes.
*S BR std. $70/50, mod. $75/55, dlx. $85/60, 1 BR Jr. suite $90/80*

**OUTRIGGER SEASIDE SUITE HOTEL** ★ *Moderate-Expensive*
440 Seaside Avenue, Honolulu, HI 96815 (922-2383), US 1-800-367-5170,
Canada 1-800-826-6786. This Outrigger condo hotel is located near the Ala Wai
Blvd. in mid-Waikiki. The 56 suites consist of one and two bedroom units, all
with kitchenettes, air conditioning, and TV. Rates are the same for up to four
persons. This hotel is excellent for families who do not require a swimming
pool. For long-term stays, too, this is a real bargain. Quiet location with easy
access to major streets for rental car tourists.
*1 BR std. $100/70, mod. $110/80, dlx. $120/90, 2 BR $150-175/120-125*

**OUTRIGGER SURF (hotel)** *Inexpensive-Moderate*
2280 Kuhio Ave., Honolulu, HI 96815 (922-5777), US 1-800-367-5170, Canada
1-800-826-6786. This is the home of Rudy's Italian Restaurant and Hideaway
Lounge (923-5949), where dinner and cocktails are available from 5:30 p.m.
daily. The hotel also offers a small swimming pool, parking, and 251 studio
units, all with kitchenettes. The deluxe rooms seem to be the best buy; some
have Japanese (shoji) screens separating bed and sitting area. Located across
Kuhio from the Waikiki Trade Center, and within a few blocks of Kuhio Mall,
International Market Place, Royal Hawaiian Shopping Center, and the Waikiki
Shopping Plaza. 2 blocks from King's Village, and not much farther to beach.
*S BR $70-90/50-60, Jr. suite (max 4) $90/80, studio suite (max 4) $95/85*

**OUTRIGGER WAIKIKI SURF** ★ (hotel) *Inexpensive*
2200 Kuhio Ave., Honolulu, HI 96815 (923-7671), US 1-800-367-5170, Canada
1-800-826-6786. This hotel is well located near a Kuhio Ave. bus stop at the
corner of Kuhio and Lewers. Near shopping, restaurants, and only two (long)
blocks to the beach. Hotel has a pool and deck; nice, busy lobby. The 288 units
vary from standard studios with no cooking facilities to studios and one
bedroom units with kitchenettes. All rooms are air conditioned with TV. Higher
floors are quieter and have better views. Kitchenette units are recommended.
There is parking, cocktail lounge, and a shopping area in the hotel.
*S BR std. $45/40, mod. $50/45, dlx $55/50, add $10 for unit w/kit' net*
*1 BR w/ kit' net std. $65/55, mod. $70/60, dlx. $75/65*

**OUTRIGGER WAIKIKI SURF EAST (hotel)** *Inexpensive*
422 Royal Hawaiian Ave., Honolulu, HI 96815 (923-7671), US 1-800-367-5170,
Canada 1-800-826-6786. 102 units, all with kitchenettes. All units have TV and
air conditioning. The hotel has a swimming pool, and parking available.
*S BR (max 2) std. $45/40, mod. $50/45, dlx. $55/50, suite (max 4) $65-80/60-75*

**OUTRIGGER WAIKIKI SURF WEST (hotel)** *Inexpensive*
412 Lewers Street, Honolulu, HI 96815 (923-7671), 1-800-367-5170. Located
within a block of the Outrigger Waikiki Surf and Outrigger Waikiki Surf East.
110 units. The hotel is 90% air conditioned with parking, pool, lounge, and
shops available at the hotel. *S BR w/kit' net mod. $50/45, dlx. $55/50*
*1 BR w/kit' net std. $70/65, mod. $75/70, dlx. $80/75*

**OUTRIGGER WEST (hotel)** *Moderate-Expensive*
2330 Kuhio Ave., Honolulu, HI 96815 (922-5022), US 1-800-367-5170, Canada
1-800-826-6786. Located just around the corner and across the street from the

Outrigger East, and very near such major shopping centers as Kuhio Mall, Waikiki Market Place, and King's Village. The hotel has a whopping 659 units. Since there are so many rooms here they should be able to match your needs and desires. So be sure to let them or your travel agent know where and what type of unit you prefer. There is an attractive pool and deck, poolside snack bar, parking, restaurants and cocktail lounges, shops, and meeting rooms available. *S BR std. $70/60, mod. $80/65, dlx. $90/70, add $5 for unit with kit' net*
*2 BR dlx. w/kit' net $95/75, 1 BR Suite w/kit' net $100-175*

**PRINCESS KA'IULANI (SHERATON)** ★ **(hotel)** *Moderate-Expensive*
120 Kaiulani Avenue, Honolulu, HI 96815-3296 (922-5811), 1-800-325-3535. Like her sister hotel, the Sheraton Moana Surfrider just across the street, the Princess Kaiulani Hotel (affectionately referred to by insiders as the P.K.) has just received a complete renovation, especially in the lobby area.

This hotel is one of my personal favorites. There is a feeling here of being in old Hawaii, yet there's a modern charm and sophistication about it too. The open, brass, tiled, and breezy lobby yields a huge private atrium around a large pool, deck, and informal dining area amidst tropical jungle foliage. You can almost feel the presence of the Royal Princess Kaiulani, in whose honor the hotel is named. Kaiulani grew up at Ainahau, a 10-acre estate on which the hotel stands. Kaiulani would have been queen if the monarchy had survived. She tried valiently to save the old Hawaii, and died at the young age of 23. Her courage, beauty, and charm have endeared her to all who know her story. Her legacy lives today in the quiet beauty of the hotel; you can see her portrait in the front lobby. And if you walk outside in back of the Food Pantry Market on Walina at Kuhio, you can still see one of the Ainahau Banyan Trees in whose shade Kaiulani may have listened to stories told to her by visiting author Robert Louis Stevenson in 1889. And for you history buffs, the original Ainahau house stood about where the Governor Cleghorn Apartments stand today, at 225 Kaiulani Avenue (Governor Cleghorn was Kaiulani's father, as well as Governor of O'ahu).

The Princess Kaiulani Hotel consists of three wings, the Ainahau Wing, the Princess Wing and the Kaiulani Wing (Kaiulani means the lofty one; the one near heaven). Rooms vary from the more modest Princess Wing to the interesting pool views and spectacular ocean views of the Princess Wing and the tallest Ainahau Wing. There are rooms for non-smokers, rooms for handicapped travelers, Kamaaina (local) specials, senior specials, and Family Plan for children under 18.

The hotel amenities are outstanding. Guests walk across the street to Waikiki's best beach. As Sheraton guests you can charge meals or activities at the other Sheraton hotels, such as the Moana Surfrider, the Sheraton Waikiki, or the legendary Royal Hawaiian Hotel. You can dine at a great Japanese restaurant, Momoyama, an excellent Chinese restaurant, the Lotus Moon, or snack under the tropical moon by the pool and see the exciting Polynesian Review in the hotel's own Ainahau Showroom. But most of all, you will feel a part of historic Hawaii. *S BR (max 3) economy to o.v. $85-140/$95-130*

**ROYAL KUHIO**   *Inexpensive to Expensive*
2240 Kuhio Avenue, Honolulu, HI 96815. Booking agents: Paradise Management Corp. (Reservations Hawaii) (808-538-7145), 1-800-367-5205 (20 units). Smedley Travel Services, Inc., (312-358-0273 or 312-358-1078), (15 units). Hawaiian Apartment Leasing Enterprises, (714-497-4253), Calif 1-800-472-8449, Canada 1-800-824-8968, other 1-800-854-8843.

This large condominium apartment complex has 385 units, some of which are privately owned and not available for rent. Those units which owners do rent are managed by several different booking companies. This is true in many Waikiki Condominiums. Some travelers avoid buildings with this type of multiple booking system; others prefer it and suggest that it gives them a better chance of finding a suitable opening, especially on short notice. Units vary from one bedroom apartments with kitchenette to two-bedroom and one bedroom suites with kitchenettes or kitchens. Units are air conditioned; have TV; and some require a minimum stay of several nights. The Royal Kuhio has weekly maid service, parking, a very inviting swimming pool, putting green, exercise room, paddle tennis, badminton and volleyball courts, sauna, shuffleboard, ping pong and pool tables, a card and TV room, private banquet-conference facilities, and excellent security. *Prices for units vary with each rental agent.*

**WAIKIKI BEACHCOMBER ★ (hotel)**   *Moderate-Deluxe*
2300 Kalakaua Ave., Honolulu, HI 96815 (922-4646), US 1-800-622-4646. Canada 1-800-338-6233. Recently redone, this elegant hotel is a real treat. It's large enough (500 units) that you can find the room you're looking for. The rooms are beautiful. Each has private lanai, color TV, air conditioning, refrigerator, room safe, family plan and stunning views. The hotel has fascinating shops, an inviting pool with snack bar and informal restaurant, meeting and banquet rooms, convenient parking underneath, cocktail lounges, and beautiful furnishings. The Beachcomber is an oasis in the midst of Waikiki's excitement. Close to everything, yet up the escalator and you're in a world of calm elegance. Many people walk or drive right past the entrance to the Waikiki Beachcomber thinking it's a part of Duke's Lane. Watch for the bellhops and escalator just past the Duke's Lane sign. It's a hotel worth finding!
*S BR c.v. $95/89, o.v. $115/105, dlx. o.v. $145/130, add $15 for 12/25 - 1/5*

**WHITE SANDS WAIKIKI RESORT**   *Inexpensive-Moderate*
431 Nohonani St., Honolulu, HI 96815 (923-7336). Booking Agent: (702) 731-6100. Its former name, White Sands Garden Hotel, accurately describes this lovely small oasis. Rooms are arranged around a lush tropical garden and shimmering freshwater pool. Rooms include studios and one bedroom suites, all with air conditioning, lanai, TV, telephone, kitchenettes, and a view of the courtyard and pool. Hidden and quiet, this little spot is tailor-made for rest and relaxation. One important note on the White Sands Waikiki Resort - it is now a "time-share hotel", meaning that members have first rights to bookings. So if you are interested, be sure to plan ahead to reserve space.
*S BR std. $52-69, sup. $59-75, dlx $69-85, 1 BR suite $78-105*

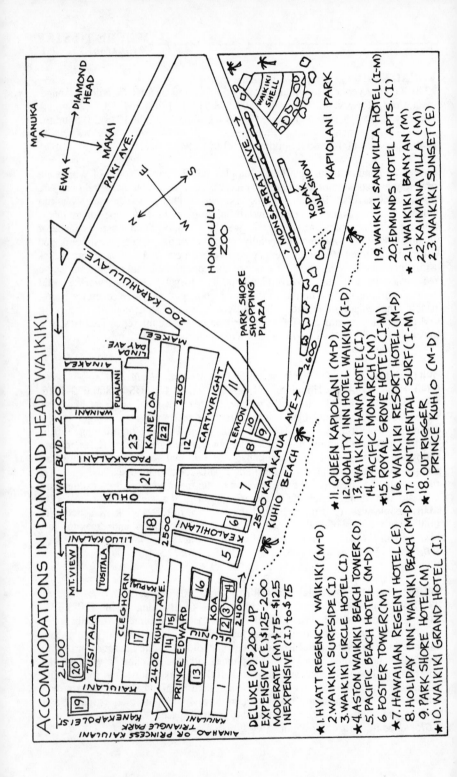

# ACCOMMODATIONS IN DIAMOND HEAD WAIKIKI

DELUXE (D) $200 UP
EXPENSIVE (E) $125-200
MODERATE (M) $75-$125
INEXPENSIVE (I.) to $75

★ 1. HYATT REGENCY WAIKIKI (M-D)
2. WAIKIKI SURFSIDE (I)
3. WAIKIKI CIRCLE HOTEL (I)
★ 4. ASTON WAIKIKI BEACH TOWER (D)
5. PACIFIC BEACH HOTEL (M-D)
6. FOSTER TOWER (M)
★ 7. HAWAIIAN REGENT HOTEL (E)
8. HOLIDAY INN-WAIKIKI BEACH (M-D)
9. PARK SHORE HOTEL (M)
★ 10. WAIKIKI GRAND HOTEL (I.)
★ 11. QUEEN KAPIOLANI (M-D)
12. QUALITY INN HOTEL WAIKIKI (I-D)
13. WAIKIKI HANA HOTEL (I)
14. PACIFIC MONARCH (M)
★ 15. ROYAL GROVE HOTEL (I-M)
16. WAIKIKI RESORT HOTEL (M-D)
17. CONTINENTAL SURF (I-M)
★ 18. OUTRIGGER
PRINCE KUHIO (M-D)
19. WAIKIKI SANDVILLA HOTEL (I-M)
20. EDMUNDS HOTEL APTS. (I)
★ 21. WAIKIKI BANYAN (M)
22. KAIMANA VILLA (M)
23. WAIKIKI SUNSET (E)

94

# DIAMONDHEAD WAIKIKI

This is the slower-paced end of Waikiki, much of which was duck pond and marsh before the 1928 completion of the Ala Wai Canal. In fact, one of the three ancient streams emptying into the ocean at Waikiki before the canal was dug flowed right through the block now occupied by the Hawaiian Regent Hotel.

Here you can still find low-rise buildings, quieter neighborhoods, and unobstructed views of beautiful Mt. Leahi, known as Diamond Head after sailors found calcite crystals there in the 19th century and mistook them for precious diamonds. People seem to feel less cramped staying in lodgings here; perhaps its the open expanses of the Zoo and Kapiolani Park nearby, perhaps the tradewinds blow just a bit more regularly here, or perhaps its the less dense ratio of buildings to land area. In any case, this Diamond Head section offers some of Waikiki's best bargain accommodations.

Continental Surf
Edmunds Hotel Apartments
Foster Tower
Hawaiian Regent ★
Holiday Inn-Waikiki Beach
Hyatt Regency Waikiki ★
Kaimana Villa
Outrigger Prince Kuhio ★
Pacific Beach Hotel
Pacific Monarch
Park Shore Hotel
Quality Inn Hotel Waikiki

Queen Kapiolani Hotel ★
Royal Grove Hotel ★
Waikiki Banyan ★
Waikiki Beach Tower ★
Waikiki Circle Hotel
Waikiki Grand Hotel ★
Waikiki Hana Hotel
Waikiki Resort Hotel
Waikiki Sand Villa Hotel
Waikiki Sunset
Waikiki Surfside Hotel

**CONTINENTAL SURF (hotel)**   *Inexpensive-Moderate*
2426 Kuhio Ave., Honolulu, HI 96815 (922-2755), 1-800-245-7873, 1-800-227-4321. Within three minutes' walk of the best Waikiki beach, the Continental Surf Apartment Hotel offers 140 studio and one bedroom suites, about half with kitchenettes. All apartments have air conditioning, TV, phone, and family plan. The hotel offers parking and strict standards of cleanliness. A good family hotel - no lanais, just minutes walk from the Honolulu Zoo, Waikiki Aquarium, and Queen Kapiolani Park. Each extra person is $10 additional.
*S BR std. $53/43, sup. $59/49, w/kit' net $66/56, 1 BR suite w/kit' net 105/85*

**EDMUNDS HOTEL APARTMENTS**   *Inexpensive*
2411 Ala Wai Blvd., Honolulu, HI 96815 (923-8381). Small and modest place, with neat, clean studios, one and two bedroom apartments, all with kitchenette. Bath and TV in each unit. No air conditioning or room phones. Extra person $4. Views of the mountains and Ala Wai Golf Course are very nice. Certainly not for everyone, but for students, singles, and adventurers out for a bargain, this is a great place. *S BR studio $28, 1 BR apt. $28, 2 BR apt. $36*

### FOSTER TOWER   *Moderate*
2500 Kalakaua Avenue, Honolulu, HI 96815 (923-6883). Booking agent: Hawaiian Apt. Leasing Enterprises, (714-497-4253), CA 1-800-472-8449, Canada 1-800-824-8968, other 1-800-854-8843. An attractive condo apartment complex located on Kalakaua next to the St. Augustine Catholic Church and Father Damion memorial (which are scheduled to be moved to make way for a new building). Foster Tower has air conditioning, TV, pool, parking, and a five-night minimum stay. *S BR w/kit' net $75, 1 BR suite w/kit' net $80/100*

### HAWAIIAN REGENT   ★   (hotel)   *Expensive*
2552 Kalakaua Ave., Honolulu, HI 96815-3699 (922-6611), 1-800-367-5370. This resort hotel is lavishly set on one entire five-acre Waikiki block directly across the street from the beach. It is among my favorite places, for many reasons. This is a fairyland of exotic sights, sounds, and scents. If you walk through the tropical jungle atrium in the Kalakaua side of the first level, past the shops, original oil paintings, past the grand staircase, and Lobby Bar to the Cafe Regent and Shirokiya Japanese Retail Store on the Kuhio Ave. side, you will fall in love with the Hawaiian Regent also. It won't surprise you to learn that the atrium (officially the Garden Courtyard) is a favorite place for weddings.

A dinner at The Third Floor Restaurant is one of Waikiki's finest dining experiences. And here's a secret - also in this hotel is one of the best places to sit outside, day or night, sip a cool drink and watch in complete privacy as the people go by on Kalakaua Avenue a few feet away. It's The Summery, and it's on the first level fronting Kalakaua. It features full breakfast, lunch and dinner service, and a late evening snack menu. The Summery's lanai terrace has cool umbrella tables and is shielded from the street by lush greenery. It's a secret garden, one of Waikiki's magical spots. After dinner you might have a liqueur in the Library and enjoy the sounds from the piano bar, before visiting the famous Point After disco (no rush, it's open 'till 4am). If you have time, visit the newly redone Kalakaua pool on the third level. Treat yourself to a drink at the Ocean Terrace Snack Bar, then stand by the railing and watch Waikiki and the beach spread out below you. A memorable scene.

Then to your room - one of 1,346 guest rooms and suites in two skyhugging towers. Your room will have a refrigerator, private lanai, twice daily maid service, an in-room safe, air conditioning, two double, queen- or king-sized beds, and a stupendous view. You can relax on your lanai while you think about your tennis match tomorrow on the hotel's championship court.
*S BR m.v. $120-140/110-130, o.v. $160/150, o.f. $185/175, corner $195/185*

### HOLIDAY INN-WAIKIKI BEACH   *Moderate-Deluxe*
2570 Kalakaua Avenue, Honolulu, HI 96815 (922-2511), 1-800-877-7666. 800 units make this hotel one of the largest Holiday Inns in the United States and its location directly across the street from a great beach and only steps from the Zoo and Aquarium make it a very popular place to stay. There are now two towers to the hotel, the 25-story Main Tower and the smaller new 72-room Mauka Tower on the mountain side. Amenities include in-room safe, air conditioning, recently refurbished rooms, lounge, pub, pool with snack bar, parking, ice machines, and an excellent travel desk.

This is also the home of one of the very best Sunday brunch spots on Oʻahu - The Captain's Table. It's served from 10 am - 2 pm, costs $15.95 per person and is a treat you'll long remember. The restaurant's motif is that of an old-time luxury liner, and the food is superb. Nearby in the Captain's Table Lounge you can have a cocktail and dance to a "ships orchestra." *Family plan available.*
*S BR std.mod.dlx. $86-117/76-107, o.v. $106-128/96-118, o.f. $150/140*
*S BR suite $165/155, 1 & 2 BR dlx. suites $475-1,050, 2 BR PH $1,000*


**HYATT REGENCY WAIKIKI ★ (hotel)** *Moderate-Deluxe*
2424 Kalakaua Avenue, Honolulu, HI 96815-3289 (922-9292). Imagine twin 40-story towers rising from opposite ends of a full city block directly across from the beach near the four ancient Hawaiian Wizard stones - which stand as sentinals in front of the towers. Imagine a towering three-level open-air atrium connecting the two towers, featuring more than 70 elegant international shops, six restaurants, six cocktail lounges, as well as a three-story cascading waterfall and pool, tropical foilage, and a custom-designed 45,000 pound sculptured chandelier suspended six floors directly overhead. Imagine yourself relaxing in your room with a view, enjoying the air conditioning, lanai, large closets, game table-desk, original art prints, private phone, in-room safe, and room service. Imagine all this, then come and experience it and more at the Hyatt Regency Waikiki. Recipient of the American Automobile Association's prestigious "Four Diamond" rating in 1988, this is one of Oʻahu's premier places to stay.

You can find excitement and entertainment around the clock here. By day, take a ride on Hyatt's 50-foot catamaran, the Manu Kai (graceful ocean bird). Or explore the special collection of shops in the Hyatt Atrium and see gifts brought to you from all over the world. Enjoy lunch at Harry's Bar, a sidewalk cafe near the Hyatt's waterfalls and mountain pool. After a swim and sun on Waikiki and after stopping by to visit and learn the legend of the Wizard Stones on the beach in front of the hotel, perhaps you'd like a trip to the Waikiki Aquarium to see the rare exhibits of live chambered nautilus and seahorses.

Then back to the Hyatt for dinner at the award-winning Bagwells 2424 Restaurant. Perhaps tonight you'll try the fresh Hawaiian Opakapaka (pink snapper) cooked with ginger, or the medallions of veal with tender morel mushrooms in heavy cream. A night at Hyatt's disco, Spats, with lights flashing and walls pounding, or a quieter interlude listening to the sounds of jazz at Trappers jazz club completes your day.

The Hyatt is a city within a city - a posh, upscale dreamscape where beautiful people stay and play. The Hyatt also reserves its top four floors for the Regency Club, offering 104 Regency Rooms with such luxuries as express check-in, iced champagne on arrival, complimentary limo service, robes, sundeck and jacuzzi atop the 40th floor, special concierge, Regency Club Lounge with continental breakfast, cocktails, newspapers and other touches. If you decide to stay elsewhere this trip, visit the Hyatt - you may someday become a guest.
*S BR c.v. $115, m.v. $140, o.v. $170, o.f. $185*
*Regency Club m.v. $195, o.v. $250, o.f. $370, suite $450*
*Suites: 1BR PH $800, 2BR PH $950, Ambassador $1,000, Presidential $1,600*

### KAIMANA VILLA (condo-hotel)   *Moderate*
2550 Kuhio Avenue, Honolulu, HI 96815 (922-3833), US & Canada 1-800-367-6060. in HI 1-800-342-8434. This condominium-hotel offers the advantages of both. Each apartment features a private lanai facing world-renowned Diamond Head, all electric, full kitchen with dishwasher, washer/dryer, color TV, in-room safe, direct dial phone, sleeper sofa in the living room, air conditioning, daily housekeeping service, and 24-hour front desk. One bedroom units have 612 square feet, full bath, and queen-sized bed in the bedroom. Two-bedroom units have 822 square feet, two full baths, queen-sized bed and two twin beds (in addition to the sleeper sofa). The hotel's location is excellent, in the older, low-rise part of Waikiki overlooking the Zoo, Aquarium, and Queen Kapiolani Park. A wonderful family place. Children under 18 stay free.
*1 BR max 4 c.v. $80/65, o.v. $90/75, 2 BR max 6 c.v. $125/110, o.v. $135/120*

### OUTRIGGER PRINCE KUHIO ★ (hotel)   *Moderate-Deluxe*
2500 Kuhio Avenue, Honolulu, HI 96815-2941 (922-0811), US 1-800-367-5170, Canada 1-800-826-6786. This newer Outrigger (1980) is well located a block from the beach in the quieter Diamond Head section of Waikiki. The 626 units vary from modest studios to deluxe studios and one and two bedroom suites; kitchenettes are available with many of the units. Each room comes with a king sized bed or two double beds, private lanai, refrigerator and wet bar, and lighted makeup mirrors in the bathroom. The lobby is huge and beautiful. On the tenth floor you'll find a pool, jacuzzi, sundeck, and snack bar. Hotel amenities include the award-winning Compadres Mexican Restaurant, Trellises Garden Restaurant featuring continental cuisine, Cupid's Lounge, services for handicapped travelers, room service and complete convention-meeting facilities. Kuhio Club on the three top floors offers exclusive rooms and suites featuring concierge, spa-exercise room, complimentary morning continental breakfast and afternoon hors d'oeuvres, guest library, plush bathrobes, and newspaper. The hotel is within easy walking distance of Waikiki's major shopping, entertainment, and recreational attractions. A favorite of tourists and locals alike.
*S BR std. $90/80, mod. $100/90, dlx. m.v. $110/100, dlx. o.v. $120/110*
*S BR Kuhio Club m.v. $130/120, o.v. $140/130*
*1 BR Jr. Suite (max 2) $195, King Suite (max 2) $300*
*2 BR Jr. Suite (max 4) $270, King Suite (max 4) $375*
*Kitchenettes available in mod. & dlx. rooms and suites, Family plans available*

DIAMOND HEAD

**PACIFIC MONARCH (condo-apts)**    *Moderate*
142 Uluniu Avenue, Honolulu, HI 96815 (923-9805), 1-800-367-6046. Uluniu (coconut grove) Street is named for the thousands of royal trees that once stood here near the King's Waikiki residence. It is said that Kamehameha I, Kamehameha V, and King Kalakaua all had a beach house near this spot. There are 216 condominium apartments - studios with kitchenette, and one bedroom suites with full kitchen. The building is beautiful, with a rooftop pool and king-size jacuzzi, parking, sauna, daily maid service, and family plan for children under 16. Weekly rates April to December. Only a block away is King's Village, a unique shopping complex re-creating the sights and sounds of 19th century Honolulu. Three short blocks from the beach, and very near The Bus.
*S BR (max 3) sup. $65/88, dlx. $75/98, 1 BR (max 4) sup. $90/113, dlx. $95/118*

**PACIFIC BEACH HOTEL**    *Moderate-Expensive*
2490 Kalakaua Ave., Honolulu, HI 96815 (922-1233), 1-800-367-6060, Canada 1-800-663-1118, inter Island 1-800-342-8434. This is the hotel with the famous three-story, 280,000 gallon Oceanarium smack dab in the middle of the 40-story Ocean Tower. You and your kids can watch as divers feed the sting ray, rock fish, barracuda, and a host of other sea creatures (even sharks); six feeding times per day at 9am, noon, and 1, 5:30, 7, and 8pm. They've created an informal restaurant facing the tank - it's called the Oceanarium. Other restaurants in the hotel include the elegant Neptune and Japanese Shogun Restaurant. In addition to the fascinating Oceanarium tank, the hotel boasts two tennis courts, pool, jacuzzi, a coffee shop, entertainment, and banquet/convention facilities among the best. Run by the HTH Corporation, which also manages the Kaimana Villa and Pagoda Hotel and Terrace. The two towers, taller Ocean Tower Mauka and lower Makai Tower, have 850 guest rooms and suites, including studios, and one and two bedroom suites. All units have air conditioning, lanais, and beautiful views of mountains, ocean, or Diamond Head. Family plan, too. Don't miss the Oceanarium. And the Neptune, one level up, is an outstanding restaurant which many tourists never hear about. Both are worth a visit.
*S BR std. $100/90, sup. $120/105, dlx. $135/120, o.f. $160/145*
*1 BR suites $240-280, 2 BR suites $300-450*

**PARK SHORE HOTEL**    *Moderate*
2586 Kalakaua Ave., Honolulu, HI 96815 (923-0411), 1-800-367-2377, Canada 1-800-663-1118. This hotel is easily remembered since the Queen Kapiolani *Park* is across one street fronting the hotel and the (sea-)*shore* is across the other. A nice spot for a hotel. Its 227 rooms, in an "L" shaped building, are all studios, with only the most expensive Pacific Lanais boasting kitchenettes. Each spacious room is air conditioned, color TV, room safe, and a view you'll never forget. Many rooms also have refrigerators. Travel desks are available in the lobby, and Guest Services can reserve a limousine to take you to the airport. A large freshwater pool and expansive sundeck await you on the second level. You can browse at a wide variety of shops and boutiques in the Park Shore Shopping Plaza, then relax at the Korean BBQ restaurant, visit the old standby McDonalds, or fill up at the Denny's with the best 24-hour view in the world! Sushi and other Japanese foods are also available.
*S BR std. $85/75, mod. o.v. $94/84, o.v. or Diamond Hd. view $106-113/96-103*
*S BR Pacific Lanai o.v. & D.H. view w/ kit' net $130/120, Extra person $12/night*

**QUALITY INN HOTEL WAIKIKI**     *Inexpensive to Deluxe*
175 Paoakalani Ave., Honolulu, HI 96815 (922-3861), 1-800-367-2317, inter island 1-800-342-1560. This hotel is much larger than it looks. Its two buildings, the Pali Tower and the Diamond Head Tower, together house 451 guest rooms and suites. In the higher Pali Tower, rooms have no kitchen facilities. Pali Tower standard and superior rooms have kitchenettes; deluxe, superior deluxe, and suites have kitchens. Both towers reserve the entire sixth floor for non-smoking units. Shops and meeting rooms are also in the hotel, as well as facilities for handicapped travelers. The hotel has two attractive pools with decks, parking, the Puna Wai Lounge with live entertainment Monday-Saturday from 6-9pm, and free pupus 4-6pm Mondays. Mala Restaurant serves breakfast (6:30-11am), lunch (11-2), and dinner (6-9pm).
*S BR std. $59/51, sup. & non-smoking $70/62, add $21 for kit' net*
*S BR with kitchen dlx. $80/72, sup.dlx. $90/82, suites $125-250*

**QUEEN KAPIOLANI HOTEL**  ★   *Moderate-Deluxe*
150 Kapahulu Ave., Honolulu, HI 96815 (922-1941), 1-800-367-5004, inter island 1-800-272-5275. This regal, 18-story, 313 room hotel is named for Queen Kapiolani (1834-1899), the wife of the last reigning King of Hawaii, King Kalakaua (1836-1891), who presented the park across the street to the people of Hawaii in 1877 and named it for his wife. The interiors of the hotel are designed to recapture the charm of the 19th Century Hawaiian Monarchy. From the full-length portrait of the Queen in the hotel lobby, to the ten-foot chandeliers, and the luxurious Peacock Dining Room on the third level featuring portraits of famous friends and relatives of the King and Queen, this is a place where you can imagine yourself in the Hawaii of old. One more thing to watch for. When Queen Kapiolani attended Queen Victoria's Jubilee in London, she wore a stunning blue velvet gown trimmed with peacock feathers (the gown is now in a glass case at the Bishop Museum). A portrait of Queen Kapiolani wearing this famous peacock gown is featured in the Peacock Dining Room.

This is also one of a mere handful of hotels where you can choose to eat all your meals in the hotel and pay a reduced price for doing so on the American Plan. At the Queen Kapiolani Hotel, the American Plan including breakfast, lunch and dinner, costs $38 a day. Modified American Plan including breakfast and dinner only, costs $28. (Be sure to add 15% gratuity and Hawaii State tax to these figures.) Dine a la carte at the Peacock Dining Room, sit and eat outside at the open-air Queen's Garden Lanai, or listen to the piano bar and enjoy complimentary pupus with your drinks at the second floor Pupu Lounge. Rooms and suites at the hotel are newly renovated, and carry out the Hawaiian Monarchy theme in their decor. All are air conditioned and most have a lanai. The hotel also has a third floor pool and sun deck. And don't miss the shops in the lobby.
*S BR std. (max 2) $85/75, sup. (max 4) $92/82, dlx. $102/92*
*S BR sup.dlx. w/kit' net (max 3) $115/105*
*1 BR w/kit' net (max 4) mt. suite $225/215, ocean suite $285/275*

**ROYAL GROVE HOTEL**  ★   *Inexpensive-Moderate*
151 Uluniu Ave., Honolulu, HI 96815 (923-7691). The Royal Grove is hard to miss - it's pink! Step inside and you'll find one of Waikiki's best bargain hotels. The older Mauka Wing and new Makai Wing together house 87 units, most with

air conditioning. And there's a pool. These modest lodgings are recommended as clean, convenient and cheap. You can splurge on the finest one bedroom unit here and still pay less than you would for the lowest category of room at many other Waikiki hotels! *S BR $28-48, w/kit' net $29-48, 1 BR w/kit' net $35-90*

## WAIKIKI BANYAN ★ (condo hotel) *Moderate*

201 Ohua Ave., Honolulu, HI 96815 (922-0555), US 1-800-367-8047 ext.125, Canada 1-800-423-8733 ext.125. Agent: Hawaiian Apt. Leasing Enterprises (714-497-4253), CA 1-800-472-8449, other US 1-800-854-8843, Canada 1-800-824-8968. 10 units - 1 BR suites (max 4) w/kit'nets $70-90 (approx.). Agent: Smedley Travel Services, Inc., (312-358-0273 or 312-358-1078). 15 units - 1 BR std. w/kit'net $90-110, 1 BR dlx. w/kitchen $110-140 (approx.).

Here is an elegant condominium hotel on the quieter Diamond Head side of Waikiki. There are two towers arranged perpendicular to each other, connected by a low-rise parking structure with recreational features such as tennis court, large pool, sun deck, barbecue area, children's play area, sauna, game room, locker room, and more. Full hotel services including laundry, 24-hour front desk, bell and maid services, valet and babysitting. These apartment-suites combine hotel convenience with condo privacy, and are only a long block from the beach, the Zoo, Kapiolani Park, Ala Wai Municipal Golf Course, and just a stroll from the Aquarium. A great family place. Family plan for kids under 12. *1 BR (max 4) std. $90/110, m.v. $100/120, part. o.v. $110/130*

## WAIKIKI BEACH TOWER (ASTON) ★ *Deluxe*

2470 Kalakaua Ave., Honolulu, HI 96815 (926-6400), 1-800-922-7866, Canada 1-800-423-8733 ext.250, in Hawaii 1-800-342-1551. If you can afford it, or want to splurge on your accommodations, this top-of-the-line Aston condominium suite resort is one to consider. Its newer (1984) bedroom apartments are luxurious with spacious living room, full kitchen, king-sized beds, gorgeous view over Kuhio beach and the ocean, expansive lanai, wet bar and cable TV, and lots of little surprises such as a collectible seashell in its own silk bag on your pillow each night. The tower has a fourth-floor pool, paddle tennis court, saunas, shuffleboard court, a concierge desk, and a four-diamond rating from the American Automobile Association (AAA). All two-bedroom, two-bath units include use of a Lincoln Town Car, with private parking space. This beautiful hotel will pamper and enchant you. *1 BR o.v. (1, max 2) $239/199, 2 BR o.v. (1, max 6) $335-380/295-340 2 BR PH (1, max 6) $455/415, 2 BR Pres. suite o.v. (1, max 6) $600*

## WAIKIKI CIRCLE HOTEL *Inexpensive*

2464 Kalakaua Ave., Honolulu, HI 96815 (923-1571). You can pick out this hotel on Kalakaua Ave. by its shape - it's 14 stories tall and cylindrical! Ocean front rooms higher up are the best bargains here, about $50 for double occupancy. No kitchen facilities. The hotel has parking, a dining room on the lobby level, lounge, and air conditioning. It's right across the street from the beach, so if your budget is limited and you want to be close to the water, this might be your spot. *S BR (1 max 3) $35-39, add' l persons $3*

## WAIKIKI GRAND HOTEL ★ *Inexpensive-Moderate*

134 Kapahulu Ave., Honolulu, HI 96815 (923-1511). Recently renovated. 113 studio rooms, all with air conditioning and color TV; kitchenettes are available. The hotel has a pool outside the lobby, and Jack-in-the-Box restaurant inside. Excellent location between Park Shore and Queen Kapiolani Hotels, and right across the street from the Zoo. *S BR std. $65, o.v. $75, dlx. w/kit' net $80*

## WAIKIKI HANA HOTEL *Inexpensive*

2424 Koa Ave., Honolulu, HI 96815 (926-8841), 1-800-367-5004, Canada 1-800-663-1118, inter island 1-800-272-5275. This recently refurbished 73-unit hotel is on the same block as King's Village. All rooms have color TV, air conditioning, full bath, and in-room safe. Some have lanais and kitchenettes. Restaurants, shops, and entertainment are all available within a few steps of the hotel. *S BR std. (max 2) $62/52, sup. (max 3) $70/60, dlx. (max 3) $78/68, sup.dlx. (max 4) w/kit' net $89/79*

## WAIKIKI RESORT HOTEL *Moderate-Deluxe*

2460 Koa Ave., Honolulu, HI 96815 (922-4911), US 1-800-367-5116. Recent renovation of the entire hotel and all 309 rooms makes the Waikiki Resort a good place to explore. Hotel offers a pool, deck, great Korean restaurant, the "Camellia", coffee shop, lounge, guest laundromat, and sundry/gift shop. Its location just two blocks Diamondhead of King's Village puts it directly across the street from the Pacific Beach Hotel (with the three-story tall aquarium tank - called the "Oceanarium") and close to major shopping and entertainment areas. Family plan is available for kids under 12, and there is no winter increase in rates. A very comfortable place where the staff is as friendly as can be.
*S BR std.- dlx. $75-85, dlx. w/kit' net $89, 1 BR suite $230, 2 BR suite $360*

## WAIKIKI SAND VILLA HOTEL *Inexpensive-Moderate*

2375 Ala Wai Blvd., Honolulu, HI 96815 (922-4744), 1-800-247-1903, in Hawaii 1-800-342-1557. This is the show headquarters for Frank DeLima, a local legend and one of Hawaii's funniest comedians. He performs regularly in the newly remodeled Noodle Shop Restaurant on the lobby level of the hotel. If you're quick you might see a celebrity or two duck into Frank's show the back way - they love to hear him poke fun at the many ethnic groups represented in the islands. His impressions keep 'em rolling in the aisles. Literally. The hotel is a 14-story, sand-colored honeycomb structure fronting the Ala Wai Blvd. and overlooking the Canal. It has a pool, a gigantic pool is planned, cocktail lounge, and parking. No kitchen facilities. Air conditioned, soundproofed rooms have lanai and wonderful views of city and mountains. Family plan for kids under 8. *S BR std. $49, sup. $60, dlx. $70, premium $85, 1 BR suite $135*

## WAIKIKI SUNSET (ASTON) *Expensive*

229 Paoakalani Ave., Honolulu, HI 96815 (922-0511), 1-800-922-7866. This Aston condominium suite resort has some of the most beautiful views of city and mountains we've seen. It's in a quiet neighborhood and has 435 units, 310 of which are available for rent. All of the one and two bedroom units have full kitchen, lanai, safe, and shower-tub. Hotel has daily maid service, pool, sauna, shuffleboard, tennis, barbecues, and sun deck. Seven night minimum during Christmas holiday. Marie's Restaurant on the 6th floor has world-class eggs

benedict. And there's a hotel mini-mart for snacks. Clean, attractive, convenient, and a bargain for its category. *1 BR sup. m.v. $134/109, dlx. o.v. $154/129 2 BR D. Head & o.v. $199/179, D. Head dlx. $215/195*

**WAIKIKI SURFSIDE HOTEL (ASTON)** *Inexpensive*
2452 Kalakaua Ave., Honolulu, HI 96815 (923-0266), 1-800-92-ASTON, in Hawaii 1-800-342-1551, Canada 1-800-423-8733 ext.250. This is Aston's budget hotel, located directly across from the beach on Kalakaua Ave. Its 80 studio rooms are basic and clean, with TV and air conditioning. Views from higher ocean-front rooms are spectacular. Restaurants, shops, and entertainment attractions nearby. *S BR std. $59/37, mod. $62/41, sup. $72/51*

# DOWNTOWN AND METROPOLITAN HONOLULU

Downtown and Metro Honolulu host a number of excellent hotels. Some of which, including The Pagoda, Ala Moana Americana, New Otani Kaimana Beach Hotel and Colony Surf Hotel, are so close to Waikiki that they are considered by many to be a part of it. And some, such as the Kahala Hilton Hotel, are among the finest O'ahu has to offer. Look closely at the lodgings in these out-of-Waikiki areas. They might have just the mix of advantages you're looking for in your vacation headquarters. Our list is not exhaustive, but it does give you a good idea of the wide variety of accommodations to be found in the Honolulu beyond Waikiki. Some advantages: less traffic, often lower rates, quieter neighborhoods, closer to major attractions and shopping areas, away from the hustle and bustle of Waikiki.

So before you decide on a Waikiki address, read and enjoy these Honolulu alternatives. You might widen your horizons!

Ala Moana Americana Hotel
Colony Surf Hotel ★
Diamond Head Beach Hotel
Haleakala
Holiday Inn-Honolulu Airport
Kahala Hilton ★
Kobayashi Hotel

Manoa Valley Inn
Nakamura Hotel
New Otani Kaimana Beach Hotel
Pacific Grand
Pagoda Hotel and Terrace ★
Plaza Hotel-Honolulu Airport

**ALA MOANA AMERICANA HOTEL** *Moderate-Deluxe*
410 Atkinson Dr., Honolulu, HI 96814 (955-4811), 1-800-367-6025. This elegant hotel has recently been renovated from top (with TV broadcasts) to bottom (the huge lobby is spectacular). It's a large hotel (1,200 units) so a variety of studios and 1 or 2-bedroom suites are available. Its location is a major plus - it even has a walkway connecting it with the famous Ala Moana Shopping Center. Hotel has pool, sundeck, wonderful Chinese restaurant, rooftop restaurant with great view, cocktail lounge, shops, meeting rooms, and parking.
*S BR $90-160, 1 BR suite $180-200, 2 BR suite $290-330, add'l person $10*

**COLONY SURF HOTEL** ★  *Expensive-Deluxe*
2895 Kalakaua Ave., Honolulu, HI 96815 (923-5751), US 1-800-252-7873, Canada 1-800-423-8733. Quiet elegance has been the trademark of the Colony Surf for three decades. There are two buildings: Colony Surf on the beach and Colony East on the mauka side. Rooms in the Colony Surf are beautiful, and huge one-bedroom suites with lovely off-white living room, full kitchen, and a breathtaking view from 25-foot long windows. Two-bedroom suites are also available here. The Colony East studios are available with generous bathroom, kitchenette, two double beds, private balcony, air conditioning and color TV. The penthouse suite is absolutely the most beautiful accommodation unit I've seen in Hawaii, and a *must* if money is no object.

The Colony Surf is also home to two restaurants, the relaxed and family-oriented Bobby McGee's Conglomeration in the Colony East, and world-famous, award-winning Michel's on the beach at the Colony Surf. Michel's was recently named the "most romantic restaurant in the world" by the CBS series "Lifestyles of the Rich and Famous." A vacation stay at the Colony Surf is an experience in comfort and savoir-faire. A first choice.

| Colony Surf: | 1 BR limited view | $130-160 |
|---|---|---|
| | 1 BR D. Head view | $175-225 |
| | 1 BR direct o.v. | $255-285 |
| | 2 BR suite | $500-600 |
| Colony East: | S BR c.v./m.v./o.v. | $100-150 |
| | Penthouse East | $1,000 |

**DIAMOND HEAD BEACH HOTEL**  *Moderate-Deluxe*
2947 Kalakaua Ave., Honolulu, HI 96815 (922-1928), 1-800-367-6046. Agent: Colony Resorts, Inc., (808-523-0411). This pink, 15-floor building houses 53 hotel-condominium units for rent, including rooms with no kitchen facilities, studios and one-bedroom units with kitchenettes. Located near Diamond Head in the Gold Coast area. Near good beach, restaurants, and Kapiolani Park. This hotel-condo inspires loyal visitors who return year after year. Parking available.
*S BR $105-130, w/kit' net $145, 1 BR $170-230*

**HALEAKALA (private villa)**  *Expensive*
Diamond Head, O'ahu. (735-9000), 1-800-522-3030. A private villa on the slopes of Diamond Head Crater, with four bedrooms, kitchen, its own swimming pool, parking, TV, maid service on request, and same rate ($825/night) for up to eight people. Minimum stay seven nights. Sounds expensive, but with a large family, group, or four couples, its moderate rate affords you luxury living during your vacation. The grounds alone are worth it!

**HOLIDAY INN-HONOLULU AIRPORT (hotel)**  *Inexpensive to Expensive*
3401 Nimitz Hwy., Honolulu, HI 96819 (836-0661), 1-800-HOLIDAY. The out-of-Waikiki location very close to the Airport is this Holiday Inn's strong suit. The 308 units feature air conditioned studios and one-bedroom suites with TV and without kitchen facilities. Guests have use of a pool, restaurant, lounge, shops, and meeting rooms. *S BR std. $68-78, sup. $86, 1 BR suite $185*

### KAHALA HILTON ★ *Deluxe*

5000 Kahala Ave., Honolulu, HI 96816-5498 (734-2211), 1-800-367-2525. The Kahala Hilton has often been described as the finest accommodation on Oʻahu. This is the place you've heard and read about - where kings, presidents, and celebrities stay and play. This imposing hotel is built above a secluded 800-foot, white-sand beach and around a private blue lagoon. The resort was built in 1969 in the fashionable residential area of Kahala on Maunalua Bay, between Diamond Head and Koko Head Craters. This is one of Oʻahu's outer-island resorts, where you can forget that Honolulu is only 20 minutes away.

Hotel amenities are nearly unlimited; the expert staff will see that you get what you desire. Some of the more exotic offerings include non-allergenic pillows, Japanese pressure-point massage (Shiatsu), 24-hour doctor-on-call, computer jacks on all phones, and a seasonal children's program. The pool is elegant; the restaurants and lounges among the best in town; and the rooms are as varied in type and style as they are spacious.

Many children have fallen in love with the hotel's three Atlantic Bottlenose dolphins, Maka, Iwa, and Nihoa, who should live to be 35 to 40 years old. Nihoa, the oldest, born in 1964, is one of the original dolphins brought here when the hotel opened. The dolphins perform the hula, play volleyball, and enjoy being fed daily at 11 am, 2 pm and 4 pm. You can also see residents such as "Spec" the female nurse shark, local reef fish, green sea turtles, and penguins being hand fed.

Are you a sportslover? Such activities as: kayaks, paddle boats and snorkel equipment; golf clubs, courses, lessons and transportation day and night; tennis courts and pro; nautilus and other fitness equipment; sport flying; and much more awaits your pleasure.

Walk into the lobby and you're likely to hear soothing romantic music coming from the grand piano by the windows. Look in the shop windows at the jewelry, antiques, and unique items from around the world. Walk by the quiet waterfall cascading across the rocks and flowing on in a winding stream to the lagoon. Sip a drink outside at the Hala Terrace and watch one of the island's best Polynesian entertainers, Danny Kaleikini, captivate you with his magic voice.

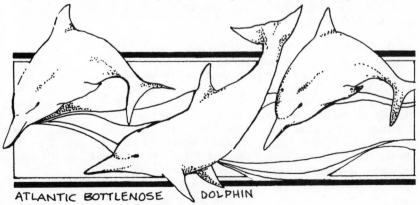

ATLANTIC BOTTLENOSE DOLPHIN

The Kahala Hilton hosts some of O'ahu's finest dining experiences. The Maile Restaurant, on the lower level, serves Continental cuisine with an a la carte and gourmet table d'hote menu from 6:30-9:30pm. At the oceanside Hala Terrace you can have a superb breakfast, lunch or dinner, and enjoy the Royal Hula Buffet from 6-10pm on Sundays. Hala Terrace is also the site of Danny Kaleikini's Polynesian show, which offers dinner or cocktails and show nightly except Sunday. Dinner show seating at 7pm; cocktail show seating at 8:45pm. One of the Hawaii's best Sunday Brunches is served in the Maile Terrace weekly from 10:30am to 1pm. Wherever you're staying on O'ahu, a Sunday drive to the Kahala HIlton for Brunch will be a high point of your vacation.

You'll love the Kahala Hilton, it's one of the very best.
*S BR m.v. $180-225, g.v. $195-225, o.v. 265-440, o.f. suites $495-1,700*

**KOBAYASHI HOTEL**   *Inexpensive*
250 N. Beretania St., Honolulu, HI 96817 (536-2377). Located in Chinatown, this budget hotel is clean and inexpensive. No frills here, but a good place for singles and students. Restaurant in the hotel serves good Japanese food at reasonable prices. *S BR $25*

**MANOA VALLEY INN**   *Moderate-Expensive*
2001 Vancouver Dr., Honolulu, HI 96822 (947-6019), 1-800-634-5115. Do you love to play the piano? There is a place in Manoa Valley high above Honolulu where you can sit on the veranda and listen, or sit in the game room and play an antique piano to fill this amazing three-story Victorian mansion with soft music. Each of the seven rooms in the mansion is named and decorated in honor of a famous person. A secluded private cottage on the grounds is also available. A continental breakfast, lush flowers in your room, and an afternoon snack of fruit and cheese are all part of this memorable accommodation. Here you can live inside a piece of Hawaiian history; an unforgettable experience. Min. age 14.
*7 guest rooms $80-110, cottage $125, suite $145*

**NAKAMURA HOTEL**   *Inexpensive*
1140 South King St., Honolulu, HI 96814 (537-1951). Some rooms here have carpeting and air conditioning. Mauka-side rooms are away from street noise. The hotel is clean and very basic. Units have private bathrooms. A good place to stay while you look around. Away from the crowds at Waikiki. No kitchen facilities. *S BR $25*

**NEW OTANI KAIMANA BEACH HOTEL**   *Moderate-Deluxe*
2863 Kalakaua Ave., Honolulu, HI 96815 (923-1555). Here's an old standby at the Diamond Head end of Waikiki Beach which has been recently renovated. The classic Hau Tree Lanai lounge has been redone and deserves a visit. The Kaimana has a variety of units (125), from a basic bedroom with no cooking facilities to studios, junior and penthouse one- and two-bedroom suites, all with kitchenettes. The hotel offers shops, the Japanese restaurant Miyako, and a wonderful beach (Sans Souci). This hotel has been a haven for many discriminating travelers in the past. Write or call for a brochure and give it a look before you choose your lodgings. *Each additional person $10*
*S BR $71-150, Jr. suite $135-170, 1 BR PH $265, 2 BR PH $305*

**PACIFIC GRAND**   *Inexpensive*
747 Amana St., Honolulu, HI 96814 (955-1531), 1-800-367-7040. Agent: Hawaiiana Resorts (808-523-7785). Condominium apartments with 75 units (out of 360) available for rent. Studios with kitchen facilities. Guests have access to restaurant and lounge, pool, daily maid service, and parking. Located a block from Holiday Mart discount food and department store. Also only several blocks from Ala Moana Shopping Center. *S BR std. $50, sup. $55, dlx. $60*

**PAGODA HOTEL AND TERRACE**   ★   *Inexpensive to Moderate*
1525 Rycroft St., Honolulu, HI 96814 (941-6611), 1-800-367-6060, inter island 1-800-342-8434. The fact that many local folks who live on the outer islands stay at the Pagoda when they come to O'ahu to shop or vacation tells you that this place is a good one. The hotel complex has two buildings - the Hotel itself, and the Terrace across the street, which is the better deal for families or groups. Hotel offers pools, sundry store, parking, shops, meeting rooms and two of the most charming restaurants in town. The Pagoda and LaSalle Restaurants are set in beautiful gardens with a cascading waterfall, and seem to float in the middle of a miniature lake filled with thousands of "good luck" koi. Entrance to these enchanted restaurants is across an old-fashioned bridge. The Pagoda Hotel is just a few blocks from the Ala Moana Center, and only five minutes from Waikiki. I found the staff here to be very cordial and willing to help. Highly recommended. *Pagoda Hotel - S BR $60-70. Pagoda Terrace - S BR $54, 1 BR $74, 2 BR $85*

**PLAZA HOTEL-HONOLULU INTERNATIONAL AIRPORT**   *Moderate*
3253 N. Nimitz Hwy., Honolulu, HI 96819 (836-3636), US 1-800-327-4570 ext. 225, Canada 1-800-423-8733 ext.225. Convenience is the key here. Parking, pool, restaurant, lounge, and meeting rooms. *S BR $79, 1 BR w/kit' net $89*

# SOUTHEAST O'AHU
# AND THE WINDWARD SIDE

There are almost no advertised hotels or condos for short term rental in the southeast region of O'ahu. However, bed and breakfast associations include a few listings in this area, especially in Aina Haina, Niu Valley, and Hawaii Kai. See the Bed and Breakfast listings. The Windward Side, especially the Kailua and Kaneohe area, is one of the major bedroom communities for Honolulu. Although there are few large hotels, there are quite a number of small rental agencies and secluded apartments and cottages for rent. If you're staying on O'ahu for a week or more, be sure to consider staying on this quieter side where you can find attractive, cheap lodgings, with discounts for extended stays.

| | |
|---|---|
| Bayview Apartment Hotel | Kailua Beachfront Vacation Homes |
| Countryside Cabins | Kailuana: Kailua Beachfront |
| Dream Home |    Vacation Homes |
| Hale Kalaheo | La Mer-Laie Vacation Villa |
| Hale Kekela Vacation Rentals ★ | Laniloa Lodge |
| Hale Pohaku | Pat's at Punaluu Condo ★ |
| Kailua Beachside Cottages | Windward Marine Resort |

## BAYVIEW APARTMENT HOTEL    *Inexpensive*
44-707 Puamoala St., Kaneohe, HI 96744 (247-3635). This 18-unit complex has color TV, kitchens, maid service, pool, lanai, and parking. Minimum 3-day stay. Overlooks Kaneohe Bay. No in-room phones. *1 BR $59/49, 2 BR $59/52*

## COUNTRYSIDE CABINS    *Inexpensive*
53-224 Kam Hwy., Hauula, HI 96717 (237-8169). If you're looking for lodgings as close to being with a local family as possible, this is it. Owned and managed by Margaret Naai, these homey unfurnished rooms and furnished studios are inexpensive and enjoyable. You'll love Margaret, her friendly dog Smokey, and the experience. Write or call Margaret for dates and current rates.
*S BR $20/nt., $140/wk., $350/mo., Unfurn. Room $12/nt., $85/wk., $200/mo.*

## DREAM HOME    *Inexpensive*
Kailua, O'ahu. (735-9000). Agent: Another property represented by Villas of Hawaii, Inc., 4218 Waialae Avenue, Suite 203, Honolulu, HI 96816. This 3-BR home near a sandy beach has kitchen, TV, parking, maid service on request, and seven-night minimum stay. *Rates are $325 a night for up to six persons.*

## HALE KALAHEO    *Inexpensive*
Kailua, O'ahu, HI. (808) 735-9000. Agent: Villas of Hawaii, Inc., 4218 Waialae Avenue, Suite 203, Honolulu, HI 96816. This three-bedroom beachfront home in Kailua has kitchen facilities, parking, TV, maid service on request, and seven night minimum stay. *3 BR w/kitchen (max 6) $225, Extra persons $25*

## HALE KEKELA VACATION RENTALS    ★    *Inexpensive*
55-113 Kamehameha Hwy., Laie, O'ahu, HI 96762 (293-9700). Hale Kekela means "place of surpassing beauty" and this place is well named. On this private estate of George and Mimi Murdock are three unusual units that only recently became available for rental - a fully-furnished and equipped three-bedroom home, sleeping 6-12, and two adjacent connecting duplex cottages, each sleeping 4-6. The one-acre private property features grassy play area, private beach, tennis court, volleyball, basketball court, horseshoes, and croquet. Located near the Polynesian Cultural Center. Resident managers Herb and Verna Calvert are Canadians who will go out of their way to make you comfortable. A private-estate residence. 3 day min. *Home $240, $1,440/wk, cottages $120/day, $720/wk*

## HALE POHAKU    *Inexpensive*
1324 Aloha Oe Drive, Kailua, O'ahu, HI 96734 (261-1936). Located in the Waimanalo area on a sandy beach, this vacation home has TV, parking, maid service on request, and minimum one-week stay. With three bedrooms and kitchen. *$135 per week (2,max 6), extra person $12*

## KAILUA BEACHSIDE COTTAGES    *Inexpensive*
204 S. Kalaheo Av., Kailua, HI 96734 (261-1653). The many hidden beach cottages and apts. on the Windward Side provide an outer-island opportunity and the 6 Kailua Beachside Cottages offer a classic example. Studios and 1-bedroom have kitchens, color TV, and laundry facilities. These are cabins in the old style - perfect for anyone who wants to taste the Hawaiian countryside within easy drive of Honolulu and Waikiki. *S BR $55, 1 BR $55, 2 BR $65-70*

**KAILUA BEACHFRONT VACATION HOMES**   *Inexpensive*
133 Kailuana Place, Kailua, HI 96734 (261-3484). Would you like to stay in a completely furnished home in a quiet Kailua neighborhood? You can, in either the one- or three-bedroom house offered here, with parking, TV, maid service on request, and five-night minimum stay. Privacy and an outer-island feeling.
*1 BR home $80-95, 3 BR home $160-190*

**KAILUANA: KAILUA BEACHFRONT VACATION HOMES**   *Inexpensive*
133 Kalulana Place, Kailua, HI 96734 (261-3484). Homes have TV, parking, maid service on request, and five-day minimum stay.
*1 BR (max 4) w/kitchen $80-95, 3 BR w/kitchen (max 6) $160-190*

**LA MER-LAIE VACATION VILLA**   *Inexpensive*
55-090 Naupaka St., Laie, HI 96762 (293-1843). Here is a large five-bedroom, six-bath home on the beach in Laie, near the Polynesian Cultural Center, Mormon Temple Hawaii, and Brigham Young University Hawaii. La Mer-Laie affords you a private and luxurious headquarters. *$200/day, $1,200/wk*

**LANILOA LODGE (hotel)**   *Inexpensive-Moderate*
55-109 Laniloa St., Laie, HI 96762 (293-9282). This 46-unit hotel is just beyond the large McDonald's restaurant at the northern end of the Polynesian Cultural Center parking lot and convenient for travelers who prefer staying overnight after a visit to the famous tourist attraction in Laie. No kitchen facilities, but the McDonald's next door is top-of-the-line, even with a waterfall! No charge for kids under 8. *S BR $49-65, suite $105-110*

**PAT'S AT PUNALUU CONDO ★**   *Inexpensive*
53-567 Kam Hwy., Hauula, HI 96717 (293-8111 or 293-9322). "Pat's at Punaluu" has been a famous restaurant on the upper Windward Side for years. It is newly remodeled and beautiful, with some of the best Kalua pig anywhere. Pat's Condominium is quickly becoming equally famous. Situated on 600 feet of sandy beach, Pat's has its own freshwater pool, saunas, gym recreation areas, convenience store, car rentals, and a tour and travel desk. Accommodations include cottages, one, two and three bedroom units, including a luxurious two-story penthouse, sleeping six. Studios and cottage units have kitchenettes; one-, two-, and three-bedroom units have full kitchens. Most units have washer/dryer and will accommodate five persons, with rollaway. In a few days or a week at this comfortable hideaway, you could see the Polynesian Cultural Center, Kahuku Sugar Mill, the world-famous North Shore beaches and other attractions, and still be back in Honolulu within an hour for dinner or a show. A very nice spot. *Cottage $42-54, 2 BR $60-75, 1 BR $50-58, 3 BR $82-100*

**WINDWARD MARINE RESORT**   *Inexpensive*
47-039 Lihikai Dr., Kaneohe, HI 96744 (239-5711), 1-800-367-8047ext.239, Canada 1-800-423-8733 ext.239. Looking for a small, rural resort on the water at Kaneohe Bay? Here, less than a hour from Waikiki, is such a retreat. Cottages with kitchens, air conditioning, TV, pool, and parking. Guests also have access to kayaks, sailboards, small sailboats, and motorboats. Discounts for extended stays. *1 BR $45-80, 2 BR $60-90, 3 BR $120*

# THE NORTH SHORE AND CENTRAL O'AHU

There are wonderful accommodations to be had on O'ahu's North Shore, but they are most often individual homes, rooms in a private residence, or hidden spots that travel by word of mouth.

Here is a selection, from the huge Turtle Bay Hilton to a gorgeous beach house. If you plan to stay on the North Shore you should watch local bulletin boards at places like Foodland on the highway past Waimea Bay, the Hale'iwa IGA, or the Surf and Sea Dive shop near the Union 76 gas station in Hale'iwa for notices of private rental properties available during your stay. Also, don't forget to check out some of the smaller places in the area, such as the Ke Iki Hale cottages in Hale'iwa. If you're with a group, look into the facilities at Mokuleia Beach Park on the way to Kaena Point. In winter, watch for small rental signs on the highway and ask at surfing beaches for other leads on places to stay. There are some real bargains to be found here, but it requires a creative search.

The Central O'ahu Valley is a bedroom community and has few hotels. Check in bed and breakfast books for private rentals available in the area.

Ke Iki Hale
Lokahi Hale
North Shore Vacation Rentals
Sunset Beach House
Turtle Bay Hilton and Country Club ★
Vacation Inns

**KE IKI HALE**   *Inexpensive-Moderate*
59-579 Ke Iki Road, Hale'iwa, O'ahu HI 96712 (638-8229). Contact Alice Tracy for more information and specific rates for this small condominium property by the beach near Foodland. On a quiet beachfront are one and two bedroom beachfront units, and some units without beachfront, about 25% less. Atmosphere is homey and comfortable. *1 BR $65-100, 2 BR $95-110*

**LOKAHI HALE**   *Inexpensive*
95-503 la Place, Mililani, O'ahu, HI 96789 (625-2117). Call for more information about this central O'ahu bed and breakfast accommodation. Parking is available. This is one of very few public lodgings in the Central O'ahu region. *1 BR (no kitchen) $36-49 (single or double)*

**NORTH SHORE VACATION RENTALS**   *Moderate-Expensive*
59-22-C Kenui Rd., Hale'iwa, O'ahu, HI 96712 (638-7289). Call Marilyne Cole for information, rates, and specific dates on these four beachfront rental homes. Both are fully furnished. All homes are adjacent, and within two miles of Turtle Bay. 3 day minimum; weekly, monthly rates. Families are invited; no pets. *2 BR 1 BA $300 deposit $625-750/wk., 3 BR 2 BA $500 deposit $950-1,050/wk.*

## SUNSET BEACH HOUSE *Inexpensive*
Northshore, O'ahu. (735-9000). Booking agent: Villas of Hawaii, Inc., 4218 Waialae Ave., Suite 203, Honolulu, HI 96816. This lovely oceanfront four-bedroom home features maid service on request, TV, parking, and sandy beach. 7-night minimum. Villas of Hawaii also handles beautiful rental homes in other parts of O'ahu. *4 BR w/kitchen (4 max,8) $275/day, ($25 each additional person)*

## TURTLE BAY HILTON
### AND COUNTRY CLUB ★ (hotel) *Expensive-Deluxe*
P.O. Box 187, 57-091 Kamehameha Hwy., Kahuku, HI 96731 (293-8811. The secret is out; you never have to leave O'ahu to have an incredible outer-island vacation. Truth is, O'ahu is three separate islands in one: 1) Waikiki, a place unlike any other; 2) Metropolitan Honolulu, America's only Island capitol and one of our most lovely cities; and 3) outer O'ahu - a hidden paradise and the last major Hawaiian island to be discovered by visitors! The Turtle Bay Hilton and Country Club is the perfect headquarters for your visit to the North Shore of this outer-O'ahu get-away.

The Turtle Bay Hilton is a complete, self-contained resort, with deluxe ocean view rooms, restaurants and lounges, gift shops, golf course, tennis courts with instruction, horseback riding, swimming pools and beaches, helicopter tours, and exciting nightlife. All on the most beautiful 800 acres you've ever seen. Would you prefer to stay in a deluxe room overlooking the ocean, or a cottage by the bay? Take your pick. Rather bathe in the tiny, sheltered Kuilima Cove where Queen Liliuokulani swam when visiting the North Shore, or take a dip in one of the two sun drenched pools on the hotel's landscaped grounds? The cove? Good choice - and a lifeguard will be on duty to assure your complete safety.

Now for dinner. The famous Cove Restaurant will prepare fresh seafood and succulent beef for you. Or yield to temptation and have the dish in the poolside Palm Terrace that has drawn people from all over the island - the melt-in-your-mouth lobster fruit salad. A legend in its own time. And of course sports. Golf tomorrow morning on a course personally laid out for you by none other than Arnold Palmer himself. Or tennis lessons with the pro - then a trail ride on horseback. Or a scuba lesson and on to the world renowned North Shore beaches. You can have it all. And you'll absolutely forget that you're only 45 minutes away from the closest other island - Waikiki!
*S BR $135-190, S BR suite $300, Cabanas/cottages $235, 1 BR suites $405-950*

## VACATION INNS *Inexpensive*
59-788 Kamehameha Hwy., Hale'iwa, O'ahu, HI 96712 (628-7838). Call the manager toll free at 1-800-367-8047 ext.438 for more information on the eight studios, six private rooms, one two-bedroom house, and private youth hostel managed by Vacation Inns. All units are located in Hale'iwa near Foodland, with laundry, telephones, and recreational equipment available. Basic lodgings, but convenient and a bargain price. Staff is friendly and helpful, too.
*Youth hostel $12/nt. (4 per room), Own rm/shared kitchen in 3 BR house $30/nt. S BR interior units $55, corner units $65*

# LEEWARD COAST

The Leeward Coast of O'ahu is the last major bastion of Old Hawaii. If you are interested in finding lodgings here, you should be willing to immerse yourself in customs and mores of the residents. People on the Leeward Coast are friendly, open, and willing to help. Some rent rooms at very low rates - you'll find listings at the Food Giant in Waianae. Stop and ask when you eat at the Makaha Drive-in or buy pottery from potter-owner Bunkie Eakutis at Pokai Pottery on Pokai Street in Waianae. People here also put a high priority on privacy, so be sure to avoid people's campsites, pickup trucks, houses, gardens, and property unless you are invited, and heed all warning signs.

Most accommodations on the Leeward Coast are condos, and require a week minimum stay. One good time of year to visit is in late February or early March during the annual Buffalo's Big Board Riding Championship, started by famous local surfer "Buffalo" Richard Keaulana. The winter surf is among the best in the world, the atmosphere is electric, and you can meet a bunch of friendly people. Stay a week, relax and enjoy the truest outer-island atmosphere and the most spectacular scenery on O'ahu. You'll fall in love with the Wainane Coast.

Makaha Beach Cabanas
Makaha Shores
Makaha Surfside ★
Makaha Valley Towers
Maili Cove
Sheraton Makaha Resort and Country Club ★

## SHERATON MAKAHA RESORT
### AND COUNTRY CLUB ★ *Moderate-Deluxe*
84-626 Makaha Valley Road, P.O. Box 896, Waianae, O'ahu, HI 96792 (695-9511), 1-800-325-3535. Every visitor to O'ahu should see the exquisite Waianae (Leeward) Coastline. Nature has had time to sculpt this older of O'ahu's two mountain ranges into fantastic shapes and textures. The scenery near Kaena Point on the north end of the coast is as breathtaking as any we've witnessed. In fact, this Leeward Coast is worlds away from Waikiki. This is real Hawaii as it used to be. Development has not yet changed the land and ocean, so you can still see Hawaiians living in harmony with the land and water.

A resort that was designed to maintain this harmony is the Sheraton Makaha. This rustic retreat might as well be on Kaua'i or Moloka'i, it's that secluded and relaxed. Golfers say the Country Club here is the finest championship golf course on the island - and perhaps in all Hawaii. You can vacation here comfortably without ever leaving the resort. For example, there are rooms in small bungalows set in lush gardens so that you have the feeling of being in a private home. Guest rooms (200) offer studios, junior suites and suites; have private lanais, refrigerators, color TV, phone, and air conditioning. You can have lunch poolside in the Pikake Cafe, enjoy dinner in the elegance of the Kaala Room serving continental cuisine, and watch the unparalleled Makaha sunset with a tropical drink at the Lobby Lounge.

The heart of this resort is sports activity. It became famous because of the 7,200 yard 18-hole championship golf course with an awe-inspiring view of mountains and coast. But there's more: an olympic-size, freshwater pool, tennis courts with instruction, escorted horseback rides, planned beach trips with a free shuttle, charter fishing and cocktail cruises. And of course bicycles, croquet, ping pong and shuffleboard all await you.

Many families come here from Honolulu to spend a luxurious weekend. It's only 30 minutes to the Airport, and yet it is a world onto itself. If you like golf, sports in general, or relaxed seclusion, come to the Sheraton Makaha.
*S BR std.$ 85, sup. $105, dlx. $125, Jr. suite $200, suite $275*

**MAKAHA VALLEY TOWERS**   *Moderate*
84-740 Kili Dr., Makaha, O'ahu, HI 96792 (695-9055). Agent: Inge's Realty, 84-1170 Farrington Hwy., Makaha, HI 96792. These condominium apartments stand alone at the base of the Waianae Mountains. Guests enter through a guarded gate after a long drive up a private road. All have kitchen facilities. Upper floors offer the best views of valley and ocean. Air conditioning, parking, TV, pool, and seven-day minimum stay. All units have kitchen facilities. Very secluded. *Studio $350/wk, 1 BR $400-500/wk, suite $500/wk.*

**MAKAHA SURFSIDE**  ★  *Inexpensive*
85-175 Farrington Hwy., Makaha, HI 96792 (969-2105). These 100 rental condo units (454 total units) offer studio and one-bedroom apartments with kitchen facilities at very reasonable rates. Guests have use of two swimming pools, sauna, and parking. Units are individually furnished and owned; most with air conditioning. Located in Makaha-Waianae area on a rocky beach. 7-day minimum stay. *S BR $29-36/day - $175-up/wk; 1 BR $39-49/day - $245-315/wk*

**MAKAHA SHORES**   *Inexpensive-Moderate*
84-265 Farrington, Hwy., Makaha, HI 96792 (696-7121). Agent: Hawaii Hatfield Realty, (808-696-8415 or 808-696-3094). 88 studios, one and two bedroom units with kitchen facilities, overlooking the ocean and surfing spots. *Studio $290-350/wk, 1 BR $400-475/wk, 2 BR $500-600/wk*

**MAKAHA BEACH CABANAS**   *Inexpensive*
84-965 Farrington Hwy., Makaha, O'ahu, HI 96792 (696-7227). Clean units with lanais viewing the water, and full kitchens, starting at $350 per week.

**MAILI COVE**   *Moderate*
87-561 Farrington Hwy., Room 110, Waianae, HI 96792 (696-4447). Pokai Bay is the premier swimming spot on the Leeward Coast. Maili Cove condominium is nearby, offering 40 one-bedroom units with kitchen facilities, pool, TV, parking, and a one-week minimum stay. *1 BR $467/week*

# OTHER TYPES AND SOURCES OF ACCOMMODATIONS

## CONDO RENTAL AGENCIES

WAIKIKI BEACH CONDOMINIUMS, Donald R. Blum, 2 Palomino Lane, Rolling Hills, CA 90274, (213) 541-8813. I've stayed at condos managed by Don and Jeanie Blum, and know them to be excellent bargains. The Blums are honest, hard working, and have the vacationer's interests at heart. Call or write them for a tailor-made accommodation you'll be very happy with.

ASTON HOTELS AND RESORTS, 2255 Kuhio Avenue, Honolulu, HI 96815 (808) 923-0745, US 1-800-922-7866, Canada 1-800-423-8733 ext.250, in Hawaii 1-800-342-1551. Aston has built a reputation in Hawaii of offering solid mid-price bargain accommodations that have elegance and charm. A good buy.

CAPITAL INVESTMENTS MARINA, Apartment Rentals and Sales, 1777 Ala Moana, Room 213, Honolulu, HI 96815

COLONY RESORTS, INC., 32 Merchant St, Honolulu, HI 96813 (808) 523-0411

HAWAIIAN APARTMENT LEASING ENTERPRISE, 1240 Cliff Drive, Laguna Beach, CA 92651 (714) 497-4253, CA 1-800-472-8449, Other US 1-800-854-8843, Canada 1-800-824-8968

HAWAIIANA RESORTS, INC., 1100 Ward Avenue, Suite 1100, Honolulu, HI 96814, (808) 523-7785, 1-800-367-7040

HILTON HOTELS IN HAWAII, 2005 Kalia Road, Honolulu, HI 96815-1999 1-800-HILTONS

IRONWOOD RESORTS, 677 Ala Moana Blvd., Suite 400, Honolulu, HI 96813 (808) 521-7854

MOKULEIA MANAGEMENT, INC., (for North Shore Rentals), 66-134 Kam Hwy., Mokuleia, HI (808) 637-3507

OUTRIGGER HOTELS HAWAII, 2335 Kalakaua Avenue, Honolulu, HI 96815-2941, 1-800-367-5170. Because they have 20 properties on O'ahu, Outrigger can offer a wide range of room types at lower prices and has developed the reputation of having O'ahu's widest selection of budget-rate accommodations.

PARADISE MANAGEMENT CORP., Suite C-207, Kukui Plaza, 50 S. Beretania Street, Honolulu, HI 96813, (808) 538-7145, 1-800-367-5205

PAT'S KAILUA BEACH RENTALS, 64 Lihiwai Road, Kailua, HI 96734
(808) 261-1653

SHERATON HOTELS, P.O. Box 8559, Honolulu, HI 96830-0559, 1-800-325-3535. You'll pay somewhat more for a Sheraton accommodation, but it's worth the difference. Sheraton (as does Aston) works hart to give their guests quality exceeding expectations.

SMEDLEY TRAVEL SERVICES, INC., 579 First Bank Dr., Suite 250, Palatine, IL 60067, (312) 358-0273, (312) 358-1078

TURTLE BAY APTS. & CONDOS, (Long and Short Term), P.O. Box 838 Kahuku, HI, (808) 293-2800

VILLAGE RESORTS, INC., 3697 Mt. Diablo Blvd., Suite 150, Lafayette, CA 94549, (Waikiki Joy Condo Hotel, 320 Lewers, 105 units)

VILLAS OF HAWAII, INC., 9218 Waialae Blvd., Suite 203, Honolulu, HI 96816

WARDAIR HAWAII, 201 Ohua Avenue, Honolulu, HI 96815, (808) 922-0555 1-800-367-8047 ext.125, Canada 1-800-423-8733 ext.125

# BED AND BREAKFASTS

BED AND BREAKFAST HAWAII, P.O. Box 449, Kapaa, HI 96746, On Oahu call 536-8421, other (808) 822-7771. This is the premier B & B outfit in Hawaii for my money. Evie Warner, Al Davis and their staff are efficient, friendly, and very interested in making the best possible matches for you with accommodations on all the Hawaiian Islands. First write for their *Bed and Breakfast Guide* ($8.95). It's worth ten times the price in information and tips. Then decide what area you want to visit, and read about the variety of places available. Put a bed and breakfast adventure at the top of your list of things to do on O'ahu.

Other Bed & Breakfast agencies include:

AKAMAI BED & BREAKFAST, (808) 263-0227

AMERICAN INTERNATIONAL BED & BREAKFAST, 1188 Bishop, Suite 2801, Honolulu, HI 96815, (808) 526-2890

BED & BREAKFAST HONOLULU, 3242 Kaohinani Drive, Honolulu, HI 96817, (808) 595-6170

BED & BREAKFAST PACIFIC HAWAII, (Maria Wilson), 19 Kai Nani Place, Kailua, HI 96734, (808) 262-6026 or 262-7865

GO NATIVE HAWAII, Box 13115, Lansing, MI 48901,

## CAMPING

Although approximately 16 City and County parks are open to visitors for camping, these are often centers for weekend and evening parties by local residents and can become very spirited. Check with the Honolulu Dept. of Parks and Recreation, Honolulu Municipal Building, 650 S. King Street, Honolulu, HI 96815, (808) 523-4525. They'll help with safety and permit information.

The State of Hawaii offers a great pamphlet on State Parks, including camping, picnicking, hiking, outdoor safety, even overnight cabins and group accommodations. Write State of Hawaii, Dept. of Land and Natural Resources, Division of State Parks, P.O. Box 621, Honolulu, HI 96809, (808) 548-7455 or 548-7456.

## HOSTELS

There are two International Youth Hostels in Honolulu: Hale Aloha Hostel, 2417 Prince Edward, Honolulu, HI (808) 926-8313 and Honolulu International Youth Hostel, 2323 A Sea View Ave., Honolulu, HI (808) 946-0591.

There is also a private hostel in Honolulu: International Network Hostel, 2051 Kalakaua Avenue, Honolulu, HI 96815 (808) 955-5457.

Each of these has its own admission requirements and regulations, so you should call or write for specifics. Studios are available at Hale Aloha Hostel for $20/night, which only admits members. The other two admit non-members for a slightly higher fee than the $9/night for a dorm room. Vacation Inns Hawaii also runs a Hostel on the North Shore (see North Shore Accommodations section).

## MISCELLANEOUS SOURCES

There are five YMCA-YWCAs on O'ahu. Write YMCA Central, 401 Atkinson Drive, Honolulu, HI 96814, (808) 941-3344 for specifics.

You can exchange your home for one in Hawaii on a short-term basis. Write Vacation Exchange Club, 12006 111th Avenue, Youngstown, AZ 85363 or Interservice Home Exchange, Box 87, Glen Echo, MD 20812.

University of Hawaii offers summer classes with inexpensive housing. They also issue listings of off-campus housing options. Write: U. of Hawaii at Manoa, Student Housing Office, 2555 Dole St., Honolulu, HI 96822, (808) 948-8177.

The two Honolulu newspapers and many local free shopping tabloids carry information on available rentals. You might also consider placing a rental ad yourself. Write *The Honolulu Advertiser* or *Honolulu Star Bulletin* at 605 Kapiolani Blvd., Honolulu, HI 96813.

# WHERE TO EAT

## *INTRODUCTION*

Now that you've arrived and are settled comfortably in your lodgings, you're probably famished, and there is no place better in the world to satisfy an appetite than right here on Oahu. It has been said in print recently that Hawaii is a "festival of foods from all over the world." And it's true. As Chinese, Koreans, Filipinos, Japanese, American Mainlanders, Europeans, Polynesians and many other people came to Hawaii over the past 200 years, they brought their dining customs with them. Herein lies another of Oahu's secrets. You can find almost any kind of dining experience on this Main Island. You could spend your entire vacation here and eat exactly as you do at home - either in the privacy of your own condo, or in a choice of restaurants. Or, you could just as easily eat every vacation meal containing only foods you've never tasted, including perhaps, chewy mini-octopus, exotic local raw fish, malasadas (sweet Portuguese sugar donuts with no hole), and even crispy salted breadfruit chips! Most of us compromise somewhere in between; so you'll have fun sampling, tasting, and letting your mouth water as you read about the bountiful variety of tastes, textures, and aromas that await you in the markets and restaurants of Oahu.

Since many more visitors are choosing to prepare some of their vacation meals in their lodgings, we have included a Dining In section which will offer you some easy and enjoyable alternatives to the traditional meal on the town.

The Dining Out section offers a choice of restaurants in each region of Oahu, as well as a variety of price ranges. Since it is not realistic to include every dining option on Oahu, (there are more than 1500 restaurants) we have done a major survey of organizations, individuals and guidebooks to identify those restaurants, caterers, markets and other eateries which are most often frequented and are most highly recommended. Using the results of this study, we have visited a wide selection of restaurants, have reviewed menus and atmosphere, and have compiled a list of establishments which we are sure you will not only enjoy reading abouat, but which will provide you with an enjoyable and satisfying dining experience. Our favorite restaurants will be accompanied by a ★, indicating that certain features caused us to favor this place over others.

Restaurants are sometimes fragile creatures which come and go quickly, and Hawaii is no exception. Many do not survive the competition. We have therefore emphasized restaurants which have prospered over time, but we have also included some of the new highly rated establishments. As the inevitable changes occur our quarterly *THE O'AHU UPDATE* will keep you informed.

# BEST BETS

### BEST MARKETS
For convenience, ABC stores are hard to beat, but prices can be expensive. Best market in Waikiki is Food Pantry, located in mid-mauka Waikiki at 2370 Kuhio. The best prices (excluding specials) and selection are at Safeway on Beretania and Times Market at 1290 S. Beretania St. You'll save money and have a ball seeing all the unusual grocery items on the shelves at these larger stores.

### BEST FARMER'S MARKET
Ala Moana Farmers Market is great on the inside. It looks like an old fashioned town with facades of old buildings suspended behind each market stall. Fish, peanuts, plate lunches, sausages and more. Best outside market is People's Open Market on Paki Playground near Diamond Head Crater. Great fresh produce and good prices.

### BEST DRUG STORE
Long's takes the cake here, hands down. Watch the Sunday paper for specials!

### BEST FAST FOOD
Zippy's, an Island cross between the plate lunch places (plate lunch is a hot box lunch containing two scoops rice, some entree such as fish, marinated beef or chicken and potato or macaroni salad, or Korean kim chee - spiced cabbage) and the fast food places you see everywhere at home. Zippy's chili and pizza are excellent. Plate lunch is a favorite too and don't miss a "Napple" from Zippy's in-house Napoleon Bakery. Best sushi is from Yanagi Sushi on Kapiolani. Try their tempura too. Burgerland is a tiny drive-in with the best teriburger in town. I went back again, and again, and everything was mouth watering.

### BEST SHAVE ICE
Oahu's most famous and most often frequented shave ice store is M. Matsumoto's in Hale'iwa. Closer to home in Honolulu is Island Snow and the Goodie Goodie Drive Inn. I like to try different flavors each time - my next cone will be vanilla and coconut syrup with ice cream in the bottom!

### BEST COFFEE SHOP
Ever since I had fried bananas with my pancakes I've loved the 24 hour Wailana Coffee House in Waikiki at 1860 Ala Moana Blvd. Parking underneath, a round lounge, and always open. A true local spot. Also one on Kuhio in the Outrigger Malia Hotel.

### BEST FAMILY RESTAURANTS
Perry's Smorgy offers all-you-can-eat buffets at good prices. The Smorgy's at 2380 Kuhio has a beautiful atrium setting. Smorgy's in the Outrigger Waikiki Hotel affords a view of the beach (and even overlooks a beach luau at night). Also a Smorgy's at the Coral Seas Hotel. You can head over to Ward Warehouse and eat at any one of a number of great, inexpensive family restaurants, including the Old Spaghetti Factory, Horatio's (seafood) and The Chowder House. Yum Yum Tree in nearby Ward Centre is also great for families.

## BEST BREAKFASTS AND BRUNCHES
Eggs 'n Things is outstanding for breakfast. Park across Kalakaua Ave. at Cilly's and have your ticket validated. Many places put on a first class Sunday brunch, but Holiday Inn has a reputation for being one of the very best, with a wide variety of choices. The Tahitian Lanai serves the world's best Eggs Benedict. Kahala Hilton's Sunday brunch is also excellent.

## BEST LUNCHEON AND SANDWICHES
Kua Aina Sandwich (66-460 Kam Highway) in Hale'iwa has the best sandwiches ever. And try their "Dawn Patrol" breakfast! For a romantic lunch, stop at the historic Crouching Lion Inn. It's often crowded so make reservations and arrive early or late. Hamburger Mary's is a hamburger gourmet's heaven.

## BEST SELECTION
At Ward Warehouse and nearby Ward Centre eat at any one of a number of great, inexpensive family restaurants, including The Old Spaghetti Factory, Horatio's, Chowder House, Yum Yum Tree and Monterrey Bay Canners.

## LOCAL FOODS
Ono Hawaiian Foods is the most popular Hawaiian restaurant with tourists; Helena's Hawaiian Food is a local favorite. Both offer the real article at very reasonable prices.

## BEST CHINESE
Best all-around is Hee Hing, on Kapahulu, only a few blocks from Waikiki.

## BEST LUAUS
We've reviewed five major luaus, and believe the best one in town is Chuck Machado's at the Outrigger Waikiki Hotel, and the best out-of-town luau is Paradise Cove, assuming you have 5-6 hours to invest.

## BEST DRINKS AND PUPUS
Hy's Steak House imported a panelled library enmasse from the east coast of North America. That and live classical guitar make it our vote for the most romantic spot for cocktails. A close second is under the Hau Tree at the New Otani Hotel. Ryan's Parkplace is a fun place for pupus and meeting people. It's classy, not-too-loud, and fun.

## BEST FINE DINING
This is a tough call; there are many fine restaurants in Honolulu (we've starred many of these in the section which follows). If we must choose, The Third Floor would be at the top of our list for its creativity and excitement. Ditto for Keo's Thai Cuisine, Castagnola's and Sergio's. For Japanese cuisine in a traditional setting close to everything our choice would be Kyo-ya. For continental cuisine with a flair at remarkable prices, don't miss L'auberge Swiss.

## BEST DESSERTS AND AFTER DINNER DRINKS
Bubbies without question has my vote for the best ice cream and homemade desserts. The romantic beachside Surf Room at the Royal Hawaiian Hotel is a best bet for after dinner drinks and conversation.

## BEST PIZZA
Sbarro's in Ala Moana Center's Makai Food Court can't be beat. Pizza Hut is a consistently good runner up.

*Here are some unique/special Hawaiian foods you'll want to try!*

Bento - Japanese cold boxed meal with variety of ingredients; usually containing an entree of sushi and vegetables.

Breadfruit chips - lighter and more crisp with less salt than potato chips

Crack seed - preserved and seasoned fruit often with split seeds; favorite snack of Island keikis (kids)

Donburi - a bowl of rice, topped with various condiments such as egg, beef and sauce, or mixed vegetables

Exotic Island drinks - Mai Tai, Chi Chi, and Blue Hawaiian are very popular

Fresh Island fish - ahi, aku, mahi mahi, onaga, opakapaka, ulua - pampano

Fresh Island fruit - pineapple, mango, papaya, guava, passion fruit

Island beer - Primo and Maui Lager are two favorites

Kalua pig - tender, juicy pork steamed in an underground imu (pit)

Kim Chee - Korean spicy cabbage with vegetable slaw, marinated with chili peppers, garlic, onion and ginger

Kona coffee - unique blend of sweet, flavorful beans from Big Island; only commercial coffee grown in the U.S.

Malasadas - sweet Portuguese hole-less donut

Plate lunch - hot boxed meal of meat, salad, and rice or potato

Poi - traditional Hawaiian starch paste of water and pounded taro root

Portuguese sausage - mild and often served as a breakfast side order or luncheon specialty

Pupus - Island style hor d'oeuvres

Saimin - Hawaiian version of Japanese ramin; noodles in spiced broth with a chicken, beef or fish base

Saki - Japanese rice wine; usually served warm and made in Honolulu as well as Japan

Sashimi - raw fish; often tuna, with sauces for dipping

Shave ice - paper cone with flavored syrup etc. over packed ice shavings

Spam - canned meat, usually served as a breakfast side dish, made popular during Hawaii's WW II meat rationing

Spring roll - Thai or Vietnamese (cha gio) delicacy; chopped meat and vegetables wrapped in thin rice paper and deep fried; often eaten with mint leaves and dip

Sukiyaki - various meat and vegetables, tofu chunks boiled in a liquid stock, often at your own table

Sushi - Japanese rice cakes with raw fish inside

Tappan yaki - meal of meat, fish and vegetables prepared and cooked by chef at special table-grill

Tempura - bite-size morsels of fish, meat and vegetables deep-fried in an egg batter

Teriyaki meat - marinated in soy sauce and spices before cooking

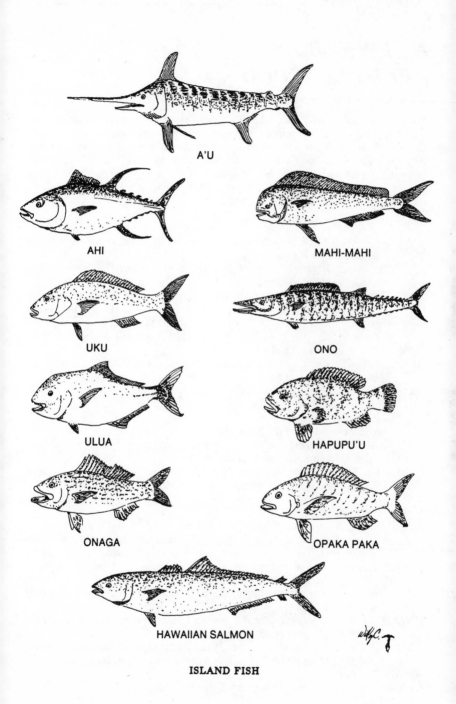

A'U

AHI

MAHI-MAHI

UKU

ONO

ULUA

HAPUPU'U

ONAGA

OPAKA PAKA

HAWAIIAN SALMON

**ISLAND FISH**

# A FEW WORDS ABOUT SEAFOOD

Whether you are dining out or buying fresh fish at the market, Hawaiian fish names can be confusing. Among the more common fish caught commercially that you'll see at the market and on restaurant menus are Ahi (yellow fin tuna), Aku (blue fin tuna), Ono (wahoo), Mahimahi (dolphin fish), and several species of marlin. Other popular table fish include Opakapaka (pink snapper) and Onaga (red snapper) which provide delicate white flaky meat. A short list of Hawaii's more popular seafood delicacies follows:

A'AMA - A small black crab that scurries over rocks at the beach. A delicacy required for a Hawaiian luau.

A'U - The broadbill swordfish averages 250 lbs. in Hawaii. The broadbill is a rare catch, hard to locate, difficult to hook, and a challenge to land.

AHI - The yellow fin tuna (Allison tuna) is caught in deep waters surrounding the Big Island. The pinkish red meat is firm yet flaky. This fish is popular for sashimi (raw, sliced thin, dipped in mustard-soy sauce) and costs $15-20 per lb. at New Year's when it is most in demand. They can weigh over 200 lbs.

ALBACORE - This smaller version of the Ahi averages 40-50 lbs. and is lighter in both texture and color.

AKU - This is the blue fin tuna, usually averaging 5-15 lbs.

EHU - Orange snapper

HAPU - Hawaiian sea bass

IKA - Hawaiian squid, used for many dishes

KAMAKAMAKA - Island catfish is a very tasty and popular dish, however, a little difficult to find at most restaurants.

LEHI - The Silver Mouth is a member of the snapper family with a stronger flavor than Onaga or Opakapaka and a texture resembling Mahimahi.

MU'U - A very mild white fish which is seldom seen on menus because it is very difficult to catch

MAHIMAHI - Also called dolphin fish but unrelated to the mammal of the same name. Ranges from 10-65 lbs. It is a seasonal fish and commands a high price when fresh. Traditionally one of Hawaii's most popular seafoods, it is often imported from other Pacific and Far East areas to meet the demand. If it's on your dinner menu, ask if it is fresh (caught in Hawaii) or frozen (imported). Excellent eating fresh and almost as good when frozen, if well prepared.

ONAGA - Red snapper, considered a bottom fish as it is caught in quite deep water. Bright pink scales, tender white meat.

ONO - This one is a member of the barracuda family but the meat is flaky, moist, and "very good", which is what Ono means in Hawaiian.

'OPAE - Shrimp

OPAKAPAKA - Pink snapper has very light, flaky, delicate meat.

OPIHI - single shell limpet, mollusk that clings to rocks on the shore. Dangerous and difficult to gather as hazardous surf can sweep pickers into the
ocean. Many have been drowned this way. But opihi are a must for an
authentic Hawaiian luau.

PAPIO - This is a baby Ulua which is caught in shallow waters and weighs 5 -
25 pounds.

HE'E - better known as octopus. This a is very popular seafood prepared
numerous ways and used in various dishes.

ULUA - Also known as Pompano, this fish has firm and flaky white meat. Often
caught along the Big Island's steep rocky coastline. Ulua can weigh up
to 100 lbs. A Papio is a young ulua usually under 25 lbs.

WANA - otherwise known as the sea urchin, many consider this a real delicacy.
Simply scoop out the contents of the wana shell and enjoy!


*Enjoy the variety of unique dining experiences O'ahu has to offer.*

One day spoil yourself - have breakfast in bed catered by room service. Then off
for a morning of relaxed shopping followed by luncheon at an elegant little cafe
hidden away in the shade. How about an afternoon snack at a local fresh fruit
stand, crack seed from a Mom and Pop store, or a cold drinking coconut or
shave ice while doing some leisurely touring outside Waikiki. For dinner, have a
luxurious, dressy evening with cocktails, leisurely dinner, and live entertainment
at one of O'ahu's finest restaurants. And then cap the evening off with a
moonlight stroll along your favorite beach.

For a less formal day how about a traditional Hawaiian plate lunch from a kau
kau (food) wagon near the white sandy beach where you've been snorkeling,
then a quiet early-bird dinner in a small ethnic restaurant in rural O'ahu, far
from the bustle of Waikiki.

Try a local food day. Enjoy an afternoon at a school carnival (Punahau School
Carnival makes the best fresh malasadas), ethnic festival (Samoans know how to
throw a party), Ho'olaulea (street party or picnic; good ones held during Aloha
Week), or celebration (1989 is Chinese Bicentennial; watch for lots of parties
and special events all year). The food at these special occasions is often the very
best of all! Then have dinner at an old-fashioned Island luau, with traditional
food and the sights, sounds and aromas of old Hawaii.

For an extravaganza of tastes a Sunday brunch at a special restaurant is a must.
For a light meal at the end of the day try a bento or specialty take-out food
enjoyed during a romantic moonlight walk or drive along a secluded stretch of
beach, in a lush tropical garden, or tableside on a private candlelit lanai overlooking Honolulu's city lights.

Enjoy your time away from the work-a-day world. Use your imagination.
Explore the multitude of dining experiences O'ahu has to offer and create
memories you'll remember long after your tropical tan has faded.

# DINING IN

Now that you've gotten settled into your lodgings, with your luggage in your room, and all your fellow travelers safely inside looking in closets, trying the TV and peeking inside the shower curtain, you can sit down, take off your shoes, and begin to think about how to spend the remainder of your day or evening. Sooner or later your thoughts (or someone else's nearby) will turn to food. Perhaps at this point someone thinks to pick up the Yellow Pages, and discover that your choices of places to eat on O'ahu are almost unlimited.

Especially if you're staying in Waikiki, you have thousands of places to try, from fast food shops to restaurants in or near your hotel or condo, to expensive restaurants that all seem to advertise the finest food at lowest prices, to luaus, dinner shows, dinner cruises, discount coupons at this spot, specials at that, Japanese, Chinese, Mexican, Italian, the list goes on. It is easy in the midst of the fatigue and confusion of travel to be frustrated and find it difficult to decide where to eat, or even how best to proceed with your dining plans.

Let us make several suggestions designed to clear the fog and make your first meals on O'ahu among the most pleasant and relaxed of your trip.

## ROOM SERVICES
First, plan your first meal to be easy and the least work for everyone. If you are energized and want to eat out, explore the dining options in or near your lodgings first. Many hotels have excellent restaurants in a variety of price ranges.

For many new arrivals, however, the easiest and quickest meal is one you can eat in your room or apartment. The easiest, but certainly not cheapest, way to accomplish this is to pick up the phone and order Room Service, assuming you are in a hotel that offers this luxury. Only you can decide on the relative merits of more expensive ordering in, compared to less expensive ordering out. Room service is an alternative you should at least consider.

A growing number of food outlets on O'ahu will deliver to your door, often for a small fee. Several such outlets, including pizza places and Wally Wok, are described in this chapter; more can be found in the Yellow Pages. Certainly less expensive than room service, and almost as convenient.

A third option involves call for take-out or going to a fast food outlet in or near your building and bringing it back to your room. If you call the front desk, or inquire at a store nearby, you can find out where you can purchase fast food in the immediate area. You'll still probably have choices of a number of kinds of ethnic food, and prices will be reasonable.

If you have a kitchen or kitchenette where you are staying, the least expensive, but most ambitious alternative is to get groceries, bring them home and prepare a meal in your own kitchen. While this is certainly the least expensive option, it does involve the most work for the grocery shopper and cook.

On our frequent trips to O'ahu, my family and I usually opt for bringing in fast food for our first meal after we arrive. It's quick, inexpensive, and we can eat while we relax in the privacy of our own living room. We've always been able to find a reliable fast food restaurant within a block of our lodgings.

## MEAL PLANNING

Before your first full day on O'ahu try to make some time to review this Chapter and discuss with your family or friends what kinds of dining experiences you want to have as a part of your O'ahu vacation (the "unique and special Hawaiian foods" on page 120 can be helpful in your discussion), and begin to make some meal plans and menus for your stay.

You have probably made some major decisions before your visit, for example, whether you'll prepare most of your meals in your vacation kitchen or not.

If you have a kitchen and plan on meal preparations, consider eating breakfasts and dinners at "home" for most of your vacation days, and expect to have lunches on the town. An alternative is to plan a late brunch in, skip lunch, and prepare an early dinner. This has the disadvantage, however, of forcing you to be in your lodgings until mid morning. We have found that a full breakfast early in the morning will encourage everyone to get an early and healthful start. You can even pack picnic lunches for the day's excursions, and plan to have everyone help with dinner preparation. You might even include visits to local markets on your day's itinerary of things to see and do.

By preparing most of your meals in your home-away-from-home, you can save enough to pay for several dining splurges at restaurants of your choice. You'll find a constellation of them in the Dining Out section which follows.

If you decide to dine out on your vacation and forget the pots and pans, you'll find that O'ahu offers excellent food at bargain prices. If you choose your places with care, you can eat three delicious, filling meals for not too much more than you could prepare the same meals at home, if you figure in the cost of time and energy of the planning, shopping, preparation and clean up involved in a home fixed meal. And by dining out you may also add a whole new dimension to your vacation, the enjoyment of visiting some of the most exotic and exciting restaurants in the world.

So whatever your priorities, you'll enjoy planning your menu, reading our restaurant reviews, and choosing which stores, markets, and dining spots you will explore while on O'ahu.

## TIPS ON COOKING IN (AND GROCERY SHOPPING)

Whenever my family and I visit O'ahu, we stay someplace with a kitchen and cook at least some of our meals (we travel with 6 - 10 people). Here are a few suggestions we have found very useful when preparing meals in a vacation kitchen on O'ahu.

Of course the most convenient places to grocery shop are the ABC Discount Stores. They're practically on every block in Waikiki, and although their prices are often higher than a super market, the convenience is sometimes worth the difference in price. And if you have to take a cab or bus to the supermarket, the savings of time, trouble, and carfare at ABC makes it a bargain.

If you're buying in any quantity, however, you'll want to visit a large grocery store for the variety, fresher produce, and lower prices. The only supermarket in Waikiki is Food Pantry, with its major outlet at 2370 Kuhio Ave. (923-9831) and another store in Eaton Square, at 444 Hobron Lane (847-3763). Food Pantry is a large grocery store with a good variety of items. When we conducted a careful survey of comparative prices at eight O'ahu grocery outlets, we found that while Food Pantry prices were significantly higher than large super markets outside Waikiki, they were lower on the average than ABC Stores or any other packaged food source in Waikiki. Visit the Food Pantry nearer you and see if it has what you need.

For a major grocery shopping trip, including stocking your vacation kitchen with staples, spices, and such necessities as toothpaste, kitchen detergent and all the odds and ends any cook needs, a trip to one of Honolulu's major supermarkets is worthwhile. If you don't have a rental car, take a taxi. Our overall favorite is Safeway, 1121 South Beretania St., (538-7315). This mega-store has it all, including excellent fresh produce, meat and fish sections, a deli in the store, and one of the best and most complete wine cellars on O'ahu. I go regularly to do my basic shopping for the week. Safeway has five stores in Honolulu, two in Kailua, and one in Aiea, Kaneohe, and Mililani (Central O'ahu). They're big, dependable, and very well stocked.

Times Super Markets also offer good discount prices and a large variety of items. There is a large Times Market near Waikiki at 1776 South King St. (955-3388) and another near Safeway at 1290 South Beretania St., (524-5711). Times has excellent produce. Three other retail grocery outlets are: Foodland at Ala Moana Center or 1460 South Beretania St. (944-9046); and 7-Eleven Food Stores, which have more than forty outlets on O'ahu; two in Waikiki, at 1901 Kalakaua Ave. and Ewa Rd. (944-8001), and 2299 Kuhio Ave. (924-7470). Another large all-purpose store is the Japanese owned Holiday Mart, near Ala Moana Center.

You'll see in the Yellow Pages under such titles as Grocers, Retail, Markets, Fruits and Vegetables, and Produce, many, many more stores and outlets for ethnic and specialty purchases. A few of these are well worth a visit. One such is Tamashiro Market, 802 North King St., Honolulu (841-8047). It's five minutes form downtown, open seven days a week, and has the largest fresh seafood selection in Hawaii, with local and imported fish.

Another exotic fresh fish outlet is the O'ahu Fish Market along King St. in Chinatown. There's an amazing variety of food items I've never seen elsewhere. While there try the People's Open Market at the Chinese Cultural Plaza (corner Beretania and Mauna Kea Streets). Its a wonderful general market with fish, meat, poultry and produce. There are at least 20 other similar Open Markets around O'ahu including one close to Waikiki at the Paki Playground near Diamond Head, from 9:45-10:45 Weds. Call 523-4808 for more information.

Across the street from the main library downtown, 478 South King St., on Wednesday morning from 9:30-10:30am is the Farmers Market, which features fruits and vegetables from O'ahu's home gardens at great prices. The Market moves from location to location, and is sometimes difficult to catch up with. Since it is regulated by the Honolulu Parks and Recreation Department, they can offer you the latest times and places. Call 527-6060.

There are many wonderful health food stores and vegetarian outlets in Honolulu, where you can find low calorie, no preservative ingredients for your home-cooked vacation meals. Look in the Yellow Pages for a full listing. Several to explore include Down to Earth, 2525 South King St. (947-7678); Vim and Vigor, Ala Moana Center; Celestial Natural Foods at the Hale'iwa Shopping Center (637-6729); and Kailua Health Foods, 124 Oneawa in Kailua (261-3530).

If you're the cook, you have a wonderful, magical opportunity to surprise your family with some Island-style dishes while on vacation in O'ahu. Sure, your family has their favorite meals that you feel obliged to fix them while on vacation just to make them fell at home. So they love hamburgers. Why not try a hamburger recipe from a Hawaiian Cookbook! Why not splurge and buy a local cookbook, bring it back to your condo or hotel kitchen, and have fun experimenting! What better place than here in Hawaii to buy and try fresh, unique Island ingredients for a recipe that could become a family favorite.

Same goes for Island drinks. Buy yourself a Hawaii Drink recipe book and try your hand at bartending. The ingredients are easier to get here (e.g. coconut syrup). You may have read elsewhere in this book that we're offering a contest - you create a new Island Tropical Drink, (can be non-alcoholic, too!) taste test it, and if successful send us the recipe (they become our property and won't be returned) and we'll publish the best in our quarterly, *THE O'AHU UPDATE*, along with the drink creator's name if you wish.

Here's a brief sample list of some of the excellent cookbooks available. Unless otherwise noted, these are available at the Shop Pacifica gift store in the Bishop Museum. Most souvenir stores, book shops and shopping centers have a good selection too. Good luck, and bon appetit!

Gray, Barbara B., Ed. *Tropical Drinks and Pupus from Hawaii*. Honolulu: Island Heritage. 1987. $5.95.

Gray, Barbara. *Take Home Aloha Recipes: Luau Recipes and other Island Favorites*. and *Take Home Aloha Recipes: Pupu Recipes and Favorite Island Drinks*. Honolulu. Food Consultants of Hawaii. 1987.

Monroe, Elvira and Margah, Irish. *Hawaii: Cooking with Aloha*. 192 pages of cookery information from salads to pupus, drinks, brunches, luaus, breads and of course desserts. $7.95. See order information at the back of this book.

*The Second Plantation Village Cookbook*. Compiled by the Friends of Waipahu Cultural Garden Park. Available from Waipahu Cultural Garden Park, 94-695 Waipahu St., PO Box 103, Waipahu, HI 96797 (677-0110).

Stone, Margaret K. *Best Tested Recipes of Hawaii*. Honolulu: Aloha Graphics and Sales. 1984. $3.95.

Tong, June. *Popo's Kitchen*. (Chinese-Hawaiian cookbook) $15. Available from Tam Co., PO Box 2904, Honolulu, HI 96802. Proceeds donated to charity. Book celebrates 200 years of Chinese culture in Hawaii. My personal favorite.

If you know someone who loves Island cooking and you want to offer than an exquisite and lasting gift, buy them the five-volume best seller *Favorite Island Cookery*, available from the Honpa Hongwanji Buddist Temple, 1727 Pali Hwy., Honolulu, HI 96813. 536-7044. The entire set is only $26.50. This will be a treasured addition to any chef's library and you'll love the results!

# DINING OUT

Paradise Guides are known for their ease in locating important information. To help you find what you're looking for easily and quickly, we have listed restaurants in two indexes; first alphabetically, and then by food type. These are followed by full descriptions of each restaurant. The same format is used for every description so they'll be easier to read and to compare.

As in our accommodations chapter, we have divided O'ahu into nine regions and have listed the restaurants in each region separately. To help you locate addresses, we have also divided Waikiki into four sections, with the restaurants located in each of the four sections listed separately. The restaurants are listed in each area by price range and then alphabetized. Price ranges are in four categories: Inexpensive (up to $15 per person); Moderate ($15 to $30); Expensive ($30 to $50); Deluxe (more than $50) for the meal. Remember to add a gratuity to this figure - the customary tip if service was prompt and pleasant is 15 - 20% of the total bill.

After the restaurant's name, the type of food emphasized and its price range are listed, followed by the address and phone number. Information on meals served is listed as Breakfast (B), Lunch (L) or Dinner (D). We do not include specific meal hours because they tend to change so often. Unless otherwise stated in the review, each restaurant listed requires reservations, accepts credit cards, has parking available, and serves cocktails, wine, and beer. We'll also comment on the restaurant decor and service, and often offer you samples from the menu. Restaurants vary their menus and prices with amazing rapidity, so if conditions vary from what we've stated, please let us know so we can update our reviews.

And as in other sections of our guide, we have starred ★ those restaurants which have some combination of atmosphere, service, cuisine, and price that make it an unusually good value and an especially enjoyable place to dine.

We hope our effort to bring you the best of O'ahu's restaurants will lead you to exciting and memorable dining experiences. Bon Appetit!

# *ALPHABETICAL INDEX*

# TYPE OF FOOD INDEX

# "BEST BET" RESTAURANTS IN RURAL O'AHU

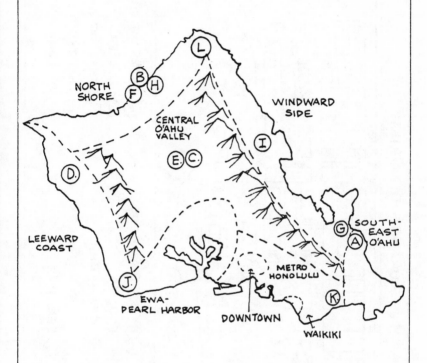

<table>
<tr><td>Ⓐ BUENO NALO</td><td>Ⓖ L'AUBERGE SWISS</td></tr>
<tr><td>Ⓑ JAMESON'S BY THE SEA</td><td>Ⓗ MATSUMOTO'S STORE</td></tr>
<tr><td>Ⓒ DOT'S IN WAHIAWA</td><td>Ⓘ PANIOLO CAFE</td></tr>
<tr><td>Ⓓ KAALA ROOM</td><td>Ⓙ PARADISE COVE LUAU</td></tr>
<tr><td>Ⓔ KEMOO FARM</td><td>Ⓚ SWISS INN</td></tr>
<tr><td>Ⓕ KUA AINA SANDWICH</td><td>Ⓛ TURTLE BAY</td></tr>
</table>

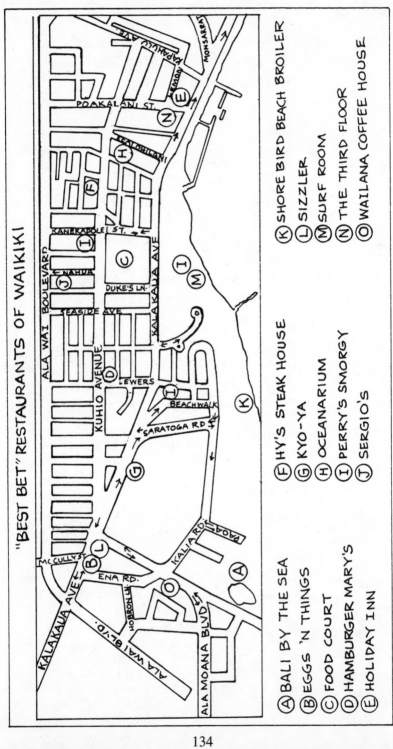

"BEST BET" RESTAURANTS OF WAIKIKI

- A BALI BY THE SEA
- B EGGS 'N THINGS
- C FOOD COURT
- D HAMBURGER MARY'S
- E HOLIDAY INN
- F HY'S STEAK HOUSE
- G KYO-YA
- H OCEANARIUM
- I PERRY'S SMORGY
- J SERGIO'S
- K SHORE BIRD BEACH BROILER
- L SIZZLER
- M SURF ROOM
- N THE THIRD FLOOR
- O WAILANA COFFEE HOUSE

# EWA WAIKIKI

**EGGS 'N THINGS** ★ *American - Inexpensive*
436 Ena Road, (949-0820). B, L; no reservations; validated parking in lot across
Kalakaua; no cocktails, wine, or beer. For breakfast at all hours (except 2-11pm)
and a filling meal, Eggs 'n Things can't be beat. Start with a cold glass of
absolutely fresh fruit juice. Then check the blackboard for Today's Specials -
they're worth considering. The omelettes are hard to resist, and if you're a
malahini (newcomer) get a side order of Spam. You can build yourself a breakfast that'll keep you happy all day. Waffles and crepes, too. And be sure,
absolutely sure, to try the coconut syrup on your stack of Macadamia Nut
Pancakes. Oooeee! No wonder there's never an empty seat.

**EL CRAB CATCHER RESTAURANT**
    **AND SEASIDE CAFE** *Seafood - Inexpensive/Moderate*
1765 Ala Moana Blvd., in the Ilikai Marina Building across from the Ilikai
Hotel, (955-4911). L, D at Cafe, Dinner only at Restaurant; no reservations at
Cafe. This is one large restaurant with two dining areas and two menus, amid
huge umbrellas, off-white table linens, fresh orchids, and a room full of lush
tropical foilage.

The open-air Seaside Cafe is a luncheon headquarters for akamai visitors and
locals, who love the Hawaiian chicken, the pasta salad with bay shrimp, or the
crab custard quiche. The more formal indoor Coral Dining Room will please
your tastebuds with such tropical drinks as the "Whaler's Coconut Cooler," non-
alcoholic "Ono Fruit Punch," or the "Panini" (fruits, bananas, OJ, and rum).
Entrees feature crab-stuffed fish, shrimp tempura, abalone (seasonal), and
Caesar salad. Then watch out. El Crab Catcher's unique naughty "Hula Pie"
(containing macadamia nuts, chocolate sauce and whipped cream) may catch
your eye. It did mine.

**FIVE SPICES RESTAURANT** ★ *N. Chinese/Vegetarian - Inexpensive*
432 Ena Rd., (955-8706), park on street or at public lot underneath Wailana
Building, corner Ena Rd. and Ala Moana Blvd. L, D; no reservations. This
small, modest restaurant continues to be very good for food of Peking,
Szechwan, and Shanghai. One specialty not to be missed is the shrimp with
lobster sauce.

But the Five-Spice claim to fame is based on their offerings of vegetarian
Chinese fare. You can order tofu (bean curd) that you'd swear was meat, gyoza
(fried dumplings), spring rolls, even vegetarian roast duck. If you're a vegetarian, this is a place you must try.

**JACK-IN-THE-BOX** *American - Inexpensive*
Six locations in Waikiki, seventeen on O'ahu; Waikiki's only drive-thru restaurant, at 1922 Kalakaua Ave., between McCully and Niu (946-3499). B, L, D;
no reservations. Two ways Jack-in-the-Box at McCully and Kalakaua is unique -
it's the only drive-thru in Waikiki, and it has the best cheesecake (99 cents a

slice), for the price, in the State! The very thing for an insomniac snack. Yum.
The Paniolo Breakfast (two eggs, Portuguese sausage, rice, passion orange juice,
coffee) is a good buy, as is the Chicken Fajita Pita. Inside seating also available. Open 24 hours.

### SIZZLER ★ *American - Inexpensive*
Eight O'ahu locations: 3131 N. Nimitz Hwy. (836-3031); 1461 Dillingham
Blvd. (847-6055); 25 Kaneohe Bay Drive, Kailua (254-3727); Koko Marina
Shopping Center (395-7433); Mililani Market Place (623-3119); Salt Lake
Shopping Center (833-1088); and 1945 Kalakaua Ave., in Waikiki (955-4069).
B, L, D, Waikiki Sizzler open 24 hours; no reservations; no credit cards. Sizzler
is a good one - famous for its huge and varied salad bar - one of the best in
town. Come early though, even the seemingly bottomless salad bar does have its
limits. Sizzler has steaks, fresh seafood, chicken, sandwiches, combination
dinners and the salad and soup bar includes seasonal fruits, cheeses, nachos,
vegetables and homemade soups. There's often a line at the Waikiki Sizzler, and
a small parking lot. So plan your visit - then enjoy a bargain meal in pleasant
surroundings.

### TONY ROMA'S *American - Inexpensive*
Three locations: 1972 Kalakaua at Pau St. (942-2121); Kahala - across from
Kahala Mall, 4230 Waialae Ave. (735-9595); Westridge Mall near Pearlridge
Kam-Drive In, 78-150 Kaonohi (487-9911). L, D; no reservations. With long
lines and a busy take out/delivery trade for years, the phrase "Tony Roma's for
Ribs" has become a Waikiki classic. If you love tender, juicy barbecued baby
back ribs loaded with sauce, get there at a not-so-crowded hour (or call 947-
7427 for delivery for all three locations), then Tony Roma's is your place.

### WAILANA COFFEE HOUSE ★ *American - Inexpensive*
Two locations: 1860 Ala Moana Blvd., in Wailana Building (955-1764); and
2211 Kuhio Ave., in Outrigger Malia Hotel (922-4769). B, L, D; no reservations. These coffee shops are among the busiest places in Waikiki - open 24
hours; good, basic food at low prices. Have you ever tasted fried bananas? You
can order them here, cooked in a buttery sauce that melts in your mouth. They
also have a circular cocktail lounge that's attractive and friendly. Park downstairs at the Wailana on Ala Moana, and get your ticket validated. Hotel parking
at the Outrigger Malia. This is an excellent place for kids - special menu, booths
and tables in the back, and highchairs available. You'll see a cross-section of
O'ahu in these two restaurants, and they'll make you feel right at home.

### BON APPETIT *French/Continental - Moderate*
1778 Ala Moana Blvd. in Discovery Bay, (942-3837). B,D. You can have a
gourmet fixed-price five-course dinner at this warm, candlelit, award-bedecked
restaurant for under $25. The menu changes every Thursday, prepared lovingly
by chef-owner Guy Banal. As you review your menu you'll see waiters pass
your table carrying such delicacies as escargot in puff pastry, caviar scallop
mousse, three-onion soup with Brie, warm leek and celery-root salad with
raspberry vinegar, and boneless breast of chicken with crab meat or shrimp! You
can order a French or California wine, by the glass if you wish, and the desserts
are varied and rich upon rich.

**CHART HOUSE**   *Seafood - Moderate*
1765 Ala Moana Blvd. (941-6669), rooftop at the Ilikai Marina Apts. Dinner only. This is one of twin open-air restaurants at the Ilikai Hotel and Apartments where you can dine overlooking the busy Ala Wai Yacht Harbor. Also a great place for drinks and pupus (5:30pm-12:30am). Their pupu menu is legendary, with escargot bourguignon, oysters on the half shell, sauteed mussels, marinated artichoke, and caramel custard for dessert. The restaurant serves dinner nightly from 5:30-10:30pm (Fri-Sat. til 11pm). A unique dish here is live lobster (Hawaiian or Maine) kept in special live tanks, prepared sashimi style (sliced, raw). Baked or steamed too, if you prefer. The abalone (tender filets dipped in egg wash, sauteed in lemon wine butter) is wonderful. There's also a menu section for "Lite Eaters." And top it all off with a sinful slice of the original mud pie (triple layer of chocolate, Kona coffee and macadamia nut ice cream with fudge and whipped cream on an oreo cookie crust).

**KOBE JAPANESE STEAK HOUSE**   *Japanese - Moderate*
1841 Ala Moana Blvd. (941-4444). Dinner only. Teppanyaki, the culinary art of preparing a Japanese meat and vegetable meal at the diner's table, is the center attraction at Kobe. If you enjoy watching as your dinner is prepared before you by a master chef, this is your place. Garden-fresh vegetables, including mushrooms, onions, green bell peppers, and bean sprouts, combine with special seasonings and exotic sauces to create a steaming hot symphony of tastes and textures. Try the teppan shrimp, or the steak and lobster combination. For dessert don't miss the special Green Tea Ice Cream. Kobe goes out of its way to cater to families with children (who'll love to watch the chef's dexterity!). Special prices for keikis under 10 years old. They'll enjoy the antiques, too; some are hundreds of years old. And you can teach your kids to say thanks in Japanese and make new friends - the word is simple - Arigato! What a great way to meet folks from another culture.

**KYO-YA RESTAURANT** ★   *Japanese - Moderate*
2057 Kalakaua Ave. (947-3911). Lunch/dinner; reservations only for parties of six or more; Japanese. A lovely piece of old-time Hawaii, this is the oldest Japanese restaurant in Waikiki. Inside and out it recaptures the style and beauty of a traditional Japanese teahouse. Your attentive waitress in kimono will serve you a complete meal, or will quietly assist you in making a la carte choices.

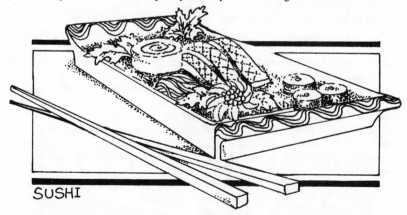

SUSHI

137

Sukiyaki is the house specialty and is highly recommended. A skilled chef will prepare beef or chicken slices, with a variety of fresh vegetables, spices, and sauces. Shabu shabu, shrimp tempura, udonsuki, sashimi, sushi, and kaiseki are also available. Complete meals served in the Japanese tea room. Lunch served 11:30am-2pm Mon-Sat.; dinner 6-9:30pm nightly. Bar is open 5-11pm. This is an easy, enjoyable introduction to Japanese dining, etiquette, and architecture. Convenient location and reasonable prices make this a best bet.

### TAHITIAN LANAI ★ *International - Moderate*
1811 Ala Moana Blvd. (946-6541) outside at the Aston Waikikian on the beach. B, L, D. Not only does the Polynesian-flavored Tahitian Lanai restaurant serve one of the most popular eggs benedict breakfasts in Hawaii, it also has one of the most romantic settings for dinner I've seen. You can reserve a traditional Hawaiian thatched hut and have your candlelit dinner for two in complete privacy. Or sit on the deck beside the pool if you prefer a more public setting for your Polynesian or American meal. And the piano bar in the adjacent Papeete Bar has a reputation far and wide for being one of Waikiki's most fun sing-along spots. Lots of pupus, frosty tropical drinks, and good company make the Tahitian Lanai a long-running favorite. While you're there stop in and see the Waikikian lobby - it's one-of-a-kind.

### THE ILIKAI YACHT CLUB *Seafood - Expensive*
1777 Ala Moana Blvd., at the Ilikai Hotel (949-3811). Dinner only. A breathtaking new open-air dining experience ovelooking the Ala Wai Yacht Club and beach below, and sister restaurant to the Chart House across the street. Try the mouth-watering carpaccio (thin slices of raw striploin of beef, garnished with pesto, dijon mustard, and sprinkled with fresh grated parmesan cheese) as an appetizer. Dinner selections: lobster thermidor (sauteed lobster and mushrooms in the shell), Alaskan king crab legs with garlic and barbon butter, or one of the combination plates, perhaps the "Yacht Club's Platter," slice of succulent prime rib served with coconut shrimp. The fresh catch of the day is always tender and mild. Open daily, 4pm-midnight. Happy hour 4-7pm, pupus served until 10:30pm. After a stroll past the schooners and yachts on the docks at the Ala Wai Yacht Harbor, a moonlit interlude and nightcap at a table overlooking the water is a perfect way to end the day.

### TOP OF THE I RESTAURANT *American - Expensive*
1777 Ala Moana Blvd., atop the Ilikai Hotel (367-8434 or 949-3811). Sunday Brunch only. During the week the restaurant serves as the home of the Comedy Club, followed by dancing and cocktails, but on Sundays it is turned into one of Waikiki's most enjoyable brunch settings. Excellent pastries, hot meat and egg entrees, and fresh fruit that will keep you coming back for more. This is a real treat, and the view from 36 stories up on the Tower Building is worth the trip.

### BALI BY THE SEA ★ *Continental - Deluxe*
2005 Kalia Rd., in Rainbow Tower at Hilton Hawaiian Village (941-BALI). Dinner only. The Bali is an award winning, open-air restaurant specializing in continental cuisine with a French flavor. Gourmet delights include sauteed Opakapaka with Watercress and Ginger, Roast Duck Lawrence, or Veal in Pepper Sauce. A fine wine list will complement your choice, and the dessert

gems must be tasted to be fully appreciated. As you enjoy your meal you can watch the ocean and beach below. An excellent restaurant in a beautiful setting.

## CHEZ MICHEL    *French/Continental - Deluxe*

444 Hobron Lane, in Eaton Square (955-7866). L, D. An award-winning hideaway in cozy Eaton Square Shopping Plaza. For lunch, sample the salads, especially the chicken salad with apples and walnuts or cold artichoke salad with a tangy vinegarette dressing. Dinner menu is even better; try the famous Michel's roast of duck in sweet fruit sauce, or medallions de veau, a veal tenderloin sauteed with a sauce of fresh mushrooms, sherry, and cream. Chez Michel's desserts are well known for variety and richness. A chilled grand marnier souffle, creme caramel, or chocolate decadence. Intimate latticed dining rooms, good service, and chocolate decadence!

## GOLDEN DRAGON RESTAURANT ★    *Chinese/Cantonese - Deluxe*

2005 Kalia Rd., in the Hilton Hawaiian Village (946-5336). Dinner only. This opulent restaurant reminds me of a room in Peking's Forbidden City - the Imperial Palace of the Chinese Emperors. You enter through a huge ornate black lacquered door, and are seated either in the teak-floored dining salon, with decor every bit as exquisite as the Emperor's Throne Room, or outside in a magic green garden overlooking the sea. There you are pampered by attentive servers attuned to your every wish even to the extent of bringing you your personal tea lady, who will gladly read your fortune in the leaves if you desire. One of nearly fifty a la carte dinner choices will be specially prepared for you, perhaps "Imperial Peking Duck," house specialty Lemon Chicken, smoked pork, lobster in Chinese black bean sauce, or the chef's special "Imperial Beggar's Chicken," so unique it requires a day's advance notice to prepare. Every portion of your dinner will be tastefully and visually exciting. Exotic desserts complement your dinner, and conclude your regal visit to the Chinese house fit for a king.

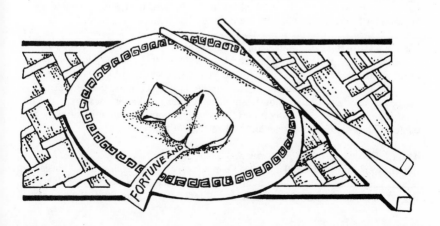

# MID-MAKAI WAIKIKI

### HOUSE WITHOUT A KEY ★ *American - Inexpensive*
Halekulani Hotel, 2199 Kalia Rd. (923-2311). B, L, D; no reservations. This wonderful lounge and restaurant offers informal dining and pupus (hors d'oeuvres). Recommendations include a delicious chilled cream of watercress soup, stir fry with beef, chicken or shrimp, Michelob on tap, and guava mousse with macadamia nuts. Live entertainment is provided nightly from 5-8:30pm, featuring such notables as Kanoe Miller (former Miss Hawaii) dancing hulas, The Islanders (Sun-Tues. and Thurs.), and the Hiram Olsen Trio (Wed., Fri., and Sat.). This is one of O'ahu's most romantic settings for cocktails or a light meal.

### IT'S GREEK TO ME *Greek - Inexpensive*
2201 Kalakaua Ave., Building A, Suite 112, in the Royal Hawaiian Shopping Center (922-2733). B, L, D; no reservations. A modern Greek cafe atmosphere. Specialties include gyros sandwich - a famous Greek combination of pita bread, sliced lamb, spices, onions, and tzatziki sauce. The Greek fries here were voted among Hawaii's best by readers of the *Honolulu Advertiser*. Kebabs, falafel (vegetables in pita bread), stuffed grape leaves, pastas, sandwiches, gourmet burgers, and complete dinners, too. And don't forget the (nightly) belly dancers!

### PERRY'S SMORGY RESTAURANTS ★ *American - Inexpensive*
Three locations - in Outrigger Waikiki Hotel, 2335 Kalakaua Ave. (923-0711), in Coral Seas Hotel, 250 Lewers (923-3881), and 2380 Kuhio Ave. at Kaneka-polei, (926-0184). B, L, D; no reservations; "All-you-can-eat buffet." Everyone talks about Smorgy Restaurants for three reasons. One, the settings are spec-tacular. The garden setting on Kuhio has a pond, waterfall, and outdoor, secluded seating. Smorgy's at the Outrigger Waikiki overlooks the beach. If you time it just right and can manage a table close to the railing, at the Outrigger Waikiki Smorgy's you can dine and watch the hotel luau entertainment at the same time. Second is the price - breakfast under $4, lunch under $6, and dinner under $8, with salad bar, beverage, dessert and tax included in that price. A true bargain. Third is the food. Such choices as hand carved round of beef, golden fried shrimp, Italian spaghetti, southern-style chicken, beef and vegetable stew. No wonder Smorgy's restaurants are favorite tourist stops on O'ahu.

### PIECES OF EIGHT *American - Inexpensive*
250 Lewers St., in the Outrigger Coral Seas Hotel (923-6646). Dinner only; no reservations. A Waikiki standby for 20 years, this steak and seafood restaurant operates its own charter fishing vessel, so the daily catch is fresh and reasonably priced. House favorites include fresh steamer clams, calamari, scallops, and the First Mate's Plate - sauteed combo of shrimp, scallops, mahimahi, calimari, and oysters. They also have a fresh and full salad/fruit bar.

### THE J. R. *American - Inexpensive*
226 Lewers St. (924-8444). B, L, D; no reservations. This small "burger 'n Island specialties" shop does a great room service business for local hotels. Breakfast is served 6am-11am; lunch and dinner from 11am-9pm. Popular items

include the complete breakfast, with bacon, sausage links or ham, two eggs, toast and jelly, and rice or potatoes; sandwiches (burgers, teriyaki chicken or beef); and teriyaki steak plus fried shrimp combo for dinner, served with macaroni or green salad, rice or French fries. If you're staying at a hotel in the Lewers, Beachwalk, Saratoga Road, or Kalia Road area, stop in at The J. R.

**SHORE BIRD BEACH BROILER** ★   *American - Inexpensive*
2169 Kalia Rd., beachfront in the Reef Hotel (922-2887). B, D; no reservations. This popular meeting place has a beachfront, cook-your-own grill where you're the chef preparing top sirloin, chicken, ribs, or fresh seafood just the way you like it. House specials: "Kal-Bi Beef Short Ribs" (Korean style), "Island Fish Filets" (when available), and famous huge "Shore Bird Burgers." Just arrived in Honolulu and anxious to meet friendly tourists and locals? This is the place, at the Shore Bird Bar and Lounge next to the Broiler. It's Waikiki's largest beachfront disco, with a laser light show, a 10-foot video screen, and nightly dancing (9pm-2am). Watch for discounts in free tourist literature. And for anyone who wants to show off, or just watch, they have a beachside bikini contest weekly, with prizes even.

**CHIEF'S HUT**   *American - Moderate*
2169 Kalia Rd., poolside with lobby cocktail lounge near the "waterscape" in the Reef Hotel (923-3111). B, L, D. Start with a cool drink and pupus in the lobby lounge (I recommend the "Mango Delight" and teriyaki meat sticks), then cross the bridge to the Chief's Hut tables poolside for a full meal. We'd suggest the "Perfect Start" lite breakfast (they even print the nutritional profile on the menu!) of fresh papaya half filled with cottage cheese and a rainbow of seasonal fruit. For lunch, a tuna melt on Hawaiian sweetbread, with either coconut snow (deep fried coconut ice cream served on a melon with custard cream) or Hawaiian sweetbread pudding with pineapple bourbon sauce. Not good to diet two meals in a row! And for dinner, prime rib au jus (from the Big Island), Hawaiian jumbo shrimp stuffed with scallops, or beef and chicken kabobs. Try hula pie for dessert. There is a wonderful casual, relaxed atmosphere here. A trio very well-known throughout Hawaii regularly entertains here and their Hawaiian music helps make the evening a very enjoyable one.

**CIAO!**   *Italian - Moderate*
2255 Kalakaua Ave., in Sheraton-Waikiki Hotel (922-4422 ext.74140). Dinner only. For those who, as I did, are having trouble with the name, it's pronounced "Chow!" - a favorite Italian greeting. Behind beautiful bevelled glass and natural wood doors, this modern restaurant located just off the Sheraton-Waikiki lobby specializes in pastas, pizzas, and other Italian favorites. You can have, for example: a mini pizza lover's pizza with thick crust; an antipasto overflowing with prosciutto, salami, pancetta, bresaola, artichoke hearts, olives, mozzarella cheese, and cherry tomatoes; or Ciao's designer pasta - you choose the pasta and the sauce. For dessert surprise yourself with Coppa Ciao (its described on the menu if you want to peek), or Zebra Pie! And of course, there's Perrier.

**HOUSE OF HONG**   *Chinese - Moderate*
260 A Lewers St. at Kalakaua (923-0202). L, D. This restaurant is an experience in Chinese art, history, and culture as well as in Cantonese cuisine. The Hong

family has collected hundreds of pieces of original art treasures and reproductions, which have been carefully placed to offer an unusual feast for the eyes, even on the ceiling! Beside Waikiki's only indoor waterfall and pool stands a camphor-wood statue representing long life. This traditional Chinese god of longevity wears an aged patina of red and gold laquer.

Five gold-on-green relief panels form a focal point in the main dining room - each representing a legend revered in the literature of ancient China. One panel shows two lovers separated because in their love they have neglected their work. They are permitted to meet only once each year, on the seventh day of the seventh moon. Pamphlets are available, as are your hosts, to describe any piece and tell you its story.

Complete dinners and a la carte selections are on the menu here. Try the abalone soup, almond duck with sweet and sour sauce, Taiwan straw mushroom beef, sliced barbecued pork (char siu), and on a very special occasion, give the House of Hong a day or two to prepare their world famous Peking duck, served with bun and hoi siu sauce. For dessert, a Chinese classic - chilled lichee fruit. To get the most from your O'ahu vacation you'll want to reach out and touch the culture and history of the Orient. You can do so at the House of Hong.

**LEWERS STREET FISH COMPANY**   *Seafood - Moderate*
247 Lewers St., in Outrigger Reef Towers Hotel (971-1000). Dinner only; dancing with piano bar until 3am. This 40's-style restaurant supplies fish from its own charter boat, and makes its own fresh pasta. Herbs and spices are grown locally on Moloka'i. House specialties include: assorted seafood with black fettucine and alfredo sauce; lobster (half-pound tail or chunks of lobster sauteed in garlic butter) served on a bed of fresh lobster pasta; and mahimahi (dolphin fish) blackened Cajun-style with black pasta and alfredo sauce. The Lewers Street fish fry (deep fried seafoods) is a kids' favorite. And their fishing boats are available for charter (call 521-2087 or 545-5411).

**SURF ROOM** ★   *International - Moderate/Expensive*
2259 Kalakaua Ave., on the beach at the Royal Hawaiian Hotel (923-7311). B, L, D. You can share languid morning breakfasts, leisurely afternoon lunches and romantic evening dinners at a table only inches from the beach at this palm decked open-air restaurant adjacent to the legendary Mai Tai Bar. My favorite time to come here is for the Royal Hawaiian Hotel's Sunday Brunch, served from 11am-2:30pm. A close second is an early dinner, at a table lit with candlelight from a tiny pink replica of the Royal's Mission Bell Tower high atop the hotel. There's no place like the Royal, and its Surf Room is one of the reasons.

**TRATTORIA**   *Italian - Moderate*
2168 Kalia Rd., in the Edgewater Hotel (923-8415). Dinner only. A standby in the Kalia Road area since 1970. Trattoria specializes in such Northern Italian food as veal saltimbocca (with mozzarella cheese and prosciutto), eggplant parmigiana, lasagne, mahimahi, and Pollo alla Romana. Begin your meal with Trattoria's excellent antipasto, and finish it with spumoni ice cream. Romantic pianist-vocalist Billy Kurch entertains nightly. Complete al a carte and table d'hote dinners nightly from 5:30-11:15pm. Wine list is extensive.

**KON TIKI**   *International/American/Cantonese - Expensive*
2255 Kalakaua Ave., upper level in the Sheraton-Waikiki Hotel (922-4646). Dinner and cocktails only. Just the walk into the Sheraton whets your appetite - it's beautiful and full of interesting art, plantings, music and lighting. Find the glass elevator and take it up to the hidden landing which leads to the restaurant's private lobby. Then enter through an arch into a re-creation of an outdoor Polynesian evening around a blue lagoon. Soft lights, tropical foliage, miniature waterfalls and Hawaiian music set the mood for Chinese and International fare. Can you resist an iced tropical drink to sip as you watch the reflections in the pool? Perhaps try an appetizer of Hawaiian barbecued baby spare ribs, marinated and finished in a smoke oven? Other recommendations include Kon Tiki specialties teriyaki steak, pineapple chicken (a Tahitian favorite, blended sweet and sour style with pineapple and green peppers), and for dessert Kon Tiki's tropical snowball! Complete meal available for $22.95. If you enjoy dining in a traditional Polynesian atmosphere, try the Kon Tiki.

**ORCHIDS**  ★  *Continental - Expensive*
2199 Kalia Rd., downstairs in the Halekulani Hotel (923-2311). B, L, D. Seaside at the unique Halekulani Hotel in an informal Hawaiian setting. For breakfast at sunrise you might order the Japanese special of grilled fish, simmered vegetables, Japanese pickles, miso soup, steamed rice, dried seaweed and Japanese tea. A wonderful way to sample a piece of Oriental culture. For an east coast (U.S.) alternative, try the lox and cream cheese on a toasted bagel. Luncheon at Orchids is a mid-day treat, with perhaps a California sandwich (dungeness crab, avocado, and tomato) or a Manoa lettuce salad. And for dinner. How about fresh broiled ahi (tuna) with julienne of cucumber, tomato, and fresh basil? And did you save room for a dessert of fresh pears poached with lilikoi (passion fruit) and served with sherbet of guava and macadamia nut ice cream? Hope so. Anyone for a jog on the beach?

**PARC CAFE**   *Continental - Expensive*
2233 Helumoa Rd., in Waikiki Parc Hotel (921-7272). B, L, D. Sunday Buffet Brunch. An upscale, new, polished restaurant done in off-whites and greenery. A buffet breakfast including hot beverage is available from 7-10am, and Sunday buffet brunch featuring eggs benedict, ginger chicken, sliced Island fruits, and assorted pastries is available from 11am-2pm. Daily luncheons feature freshly smoked salmon with avacado, Hawaiian spinach salad, and such sandwiches as roast beef on rye, or bratwurst with grilled onions. Dinners include such a la carte selections as veal with a brandy-veal glaze, prime rib of beef au jus, and grilled Pacific shrimp with a garlic butter and fresh pasta. Complete dinners are available, featuring two tender filets of beef and veal, or sauteed chicken breast with fresh pasta, appetizer, dessert and beverage.

**HANOHANO ROOM**  ★  *Continental - Deluxe*
2255 Kalakaua Ave., atop the Sheraton-Waikiki Hotel (922-5811). B, D; and Sunday Brunch. The view alone here is worth the price. Thirty stories up, after a breathtaking ride in a Willy Wonka-type glass elevator, you'll look out across the Island and its ocean from one of O'ahu's most spectacular vantage points. You can dance or just listen to the live music as you order baked crab-filled mushroom hors d'oeuvres, French onion soup, fresh catch of the day sauteed in

ginger and butter sauce, and for dessert - fresh strawberries in sabayon sauce (ice cream, Grand Marnier, wine, sugar, and egg yolk). A favorite time to come is for Saturday breakfast while a radio program is being broadcast live (a regular event), or at dusk when you can watch the city change from its day clothes to its evening finery. A spectacular Sunday brunch is served here, too. You'll feel as though you're dining on a cloud.

### LA MER ★  *French - Deluxe*
2199 Kalia Rd., in the Halekulani Hotel, on the beach (923-2311). Dinner only. Jackets required for gentlemen. This award-winning French restaurant, overlooking the ocean on the second floor of the Halekulani Hotel's historic 1930's Main Building, has won nearly universal acceptance as one of the city's finest restaurants. Decor combines teakwood panels, rich Oriental-inspired murals and tables spaciously arranged.

Diners are welcomed with a complimentary appetizer and glass of French champagne. The menu offers a la carte selections, as well as two different five-course prix fixe menus at $50 and $65. Menu selections change monthly to ensure variety. Each dish, prepared by the French chef using only the best and freshest ingredients, is decidedly French but with an Island influence. Main courses are brought to your table under silver cloches. Attention is paid to the smallest details - from your water goblet to the superb wine list and specialty desserts, prepared just minutes before being served. Your dinner at La Mer might include ravioli of snails with goat cheese and roasted garlic sauce as appetizer, then roasted breast of pheasant with savoy cabbage, foie gras and sauterne sauce. An assortment of fresh cheeses, served with walnut bread to clear the palate, then a dessert of the evening, perhaps crepes "La Mer", a trio of crepes filled with mandarin and Grand Marnier ice cream, served with almond sabayon and chocolate sauce. Finish with mignardises and truffles, and perhaps an after-dinner liqueur. A dining experience you'll remember.

### SHIP'S TAVERN  *Continental - Deluxe*
2353 Kalakaua Ave., in the Sheraton Moana Surfrider Hotel (922-3111). Dinner only. A quietly elegant restaurant overlooking the gentle curve of Waikiki Beach and Diamond Head. An attentive, considerate waiter will help you order fresh fish, steak, or chicken. A choice from the full wine list, or a frosty tropical drink will enhance your meal. Ask for a window table, and look for new touches in this recently remodeled dining salon. After dinner, take a leisurely stroll through the new Sheraton Moana Surfrider Hotel. It has been carefully restored to recapture its glamorous appearance when it opened as Waikiki's first major hotel in 1901. The century-old banyan tree is the perfect place to conclude your satisfying visit to the sparkling new Ship's Tavern.

# MID-MAUKA WAIKIKI

**CAMELLIA RESTAURANT** *Korean - Inexpensive*
2460 Koa Ave., in the Waikiki Resort Hotel (926-2039). B, L, D; no reservations. Have you tasted kim chee? It's cabbage and other vegetables marinated with chili peppers, onions, garlic and ginger. How about kal bi (thinly-sliced barbecued beef short ribs)? If you like Korean spicy food, you'll love Camellia. Ask about the bulgogi (thinly-sliced barbecued marinated steak slices, and the chop chae (stir-fried vegetables with long rice). Perhaps you'll be lucky enough to hear some Korean music and entertainment while on your visit. If not, you might inquire as to what Korean festivals or cultural events are happening during your stay on O'ahu.

**FARRELL'S ICE CREAM
PARLOUR RESTAURANTS** *American - Inexpensive*
Two locations: 2330 Kalakaua Ave., International Market Place (923-2442); and 1450 Ala Moana Blvd., Ala Moana Center (946-8686). L, D, no reservations; no cocktails, wine or beer. Typical of Farrell's chain, these two restaurants are great fun for kids, especially on birthdays. Decorated like an old-fashioned ice cream parlour, the restaurants offer sandwiches and light dinner entrees. Lots of noise, whistles, sirens, player piano music, and party atmosphere.

**FOOD COURTS** *Multi-ethnic - Inexpensive*
International Market Place, Ala Moana's Makai Market, and the Ala Moana Farmers' Market. An interesting and entertaining alternative to a dinner at a sit-down restaurant is to explore a Food Court. This is a group of small, open-air, mini-restaurants, many featuring Asian food plate-lunch style at low prices.

The largest in Hawaii (third largest in the U.S.) is the Makai Market in the center of the giant Ala Moana Center. Twenty spots to eat circle this attractive garden court, where you can sample food from across the Orient. Some of the names you'll recognize because their Food Court restaurant is an outgrowth of a well-known Honolulu establishment. In this category are Patti's Chinese Kitchen (Cantonese food), La Cocina (Mexican), and Haagen-Dazs Ice Cream. Newer enterprises include Poi Bowl, Little Cafe Siam (Thai fast-food), Jo-Ni's (Filipino), Healthy's (vegetarian), Yummy Korean B-B-Q, La Rotisserie (American/-Cajun), Panda Express (Mandarin and Szechwan), Tsuruya Noodle (Japanese buckwheat noodles), Kiawe-Q Hawaiian Barbecue (home-smoked meats and fish), Kitchen Garden (sandwiches, salads, and baked potatoes), Sbarro's (pizza; reviewed in this Chapter), Let's Make a Daiquiri (Makai Market's only frees-tanding kiosk), and The Thirst Aid Station (fresh fruit juice and ice drinks). Here you can tour Asia and sample its amazing variety of foods, all in one spot. You'll be better able to decide what fine restaurants you want to visit when you've sampled the kinds of food they offer at the Makai Market.

A similar Food Court can be found inside the celebrated International Market Place on Kalakaua Ave. in Waikiki. Rumor has it that the venerable Market Place is slated for removal in the early 1990s, so time is of the essence if you want to experience it's unique appeal. The Ala Moana Farmers Market is part Food Court and part market, but there are seats and you can make a satisfying meal of the meats, plate lunches, fresh-roasted peanuts, sweets, beverages, fresh and smoked fish and meats, specialty foods, and Hawaiian delicacies you'll find at the friendly food booths. They're located across from Ward Warehouse, at 1020 Auahi St. A full listing of stalls in the Farmers Market is on page 14 of the O'ahu White Pages.

An afternoon excursion to a Food Court is both a dining and tourist attraction, and will afford you an easy, pleasant, relaxing overview of the many exotic foods and cultures Hawaii has to offer. Most purchases will be under $5!

### HAMBURGER MARY'S
#### ORGANIC GRILL, LTD. ★ *American - Inexpensive*
2109 Kuhio Ave. (922-6722). L, D; no reservations. If you want to build a burger you'll never forget in an interesting, informal setting, Hamburger Mary's is the place. Toppings, spices, cheeses, condiments, and specials galore. In addition to hamburgers they have seafood, salads, and sweets. This section of Kuhio is a part of the O'ahu "gay" community. The area has a reputation for being clean, fun, and safe, with interesting, enjoyable places to shop and dine.

### HOFBRAU WAIKIKI, LTD. *German - Inexpensive*
2330 Kalakaua Ave., in the International Market Place (923-8982). L, D; no reservations. This basement rathskeller has delicious dark beer and rousing gemutlichkeit (comraderie) upon occasion, depending on the season and night of the week. German sausages, pretzels, and assorted dishes go well with the drinks. A fun place on a busy night; good place to party with a group.

### THE JOLLY ROGER *American - Inexpensive*
Three Waikiki locations - 2244 Kalakaua, (723-1885); 150 Kaiulani Ave. (923-2172); and 226 Lewers (924-8444). B, L, D. These restaurants, established in 1948, belong to the company which owns Sizzler, Yum Yum Tree, Monterey Bay Canners, The Spendrifter, and several other Island eateries. Try The Jolly Roger on Kalakaua Ave. with the Crow's Nest Upstairs. If you can get a table overlooking the human pageant passing by on the sidewalk, you'll have a fascinating time peoplewatching, too. Sample breakfast items: eggs benedict, pancakes, chilled juices (including guava nectar) and specialty French toast, made with Jolly Roger's orange bread.

### RUDY'S ITALIAN RESTAURANT *Italian - Inexpensive*
2280 Kuhio Ave., in the Outrigger Surf Hotel (923-5949). Dinner only. This well-advertised little Italian bistro is a good example of the many moderately-priced Italian restaurants which have sprung up in the past few years, including the Marco Polo (922-7733), Bella Italia (955-7891), Renown Milano (947-1933), Papas (949-8848), Tony Manzo's (373-5313), and Auntie Pasto's (955-7891). Most offer good food at moderate prices - with real bargains to be had if you go at an off hour and watch for specials and discounts in the free tourist pamphlets. If you enjoy Italian food, you should plan to explore one or more of these somewhat less prestigious Italian restaurants. They cater to families, and the portions are often generous.

**SERGIO'S** ★ *Italian - Inexpensive to Expensive*
445 Nohonani St., in the Ilima Hotel (926-3388). Dinner only. Imagine a deep bass voice with a heavy European accent speaking these words on the radio, with Ravel's Bolero rising to a crescendo in the background:

*"They came from all over the world. The cherimoyas from Peru, the yellow bell peppers from Holland. Rushing from New Zealand came the raspberries. Their first cousins the strawberries from California, and even the black sheep of the family, the blackberries, from Oregon. Then in their native cribs arrived the baby artichokes from Mexico, and on special assignment the black chanerelles from Vancouver Island, and right behind them from Venice appeared the famous raddicchio. Having heard of the great vegetable fever, the fish got into action. Trout swam in from the streams of the Big Island, opakapaka fought its way through the Moloka'i Channel. Oysters crawled from Florida, and jumbo prawns swam from the bayous of Louisiana. And they all met at Sergio's Restaurant. There, under the direction of Servio himself, they became part of a great gastronomic symphony. The MENU. Playing every night at Sergio's from 6pm."*

This radio spot was written and performed on Hawaiian radio by one of the most creative restauranteurs in Hawaii - Sergio himself. Fact: Tom Selleck ate at Sergio's 87 times in 1987. Fact: Sergio is the Dean of Hawaii's Italian chefs; a creative genius in the kitchen. Fact: Sergio's is probably the most highly-rated and most award-winning Italian restaurant in Hawaii. Judge for yourself. There are still excellent seats available for the symphony.

**WON KEE** *Chinese Seafood - Inexpensive*
Two locations: 444 Kanekapolei St., in the Aloha Surf Hotel (926-7606); and 100 North Beretania St., suite 106 at the Chinese Cultural Plaza (524-6877). L, D. These two excellent restaurants specialize in the blending of Cantonese-style cooking with innovative seafood dishes cooked to order. Chefs use stir-fry techniques, among others, to prepare fresh Island fish, prawns, shrimp, king crab legs, lobster, clams, and mix them with Cantonese vegetables, spices and sauces. Combinations are popular here also - steak and lobster, mixed seafood casserole, or steak and king crab legs. Specials and discounts each month - such as steak and lobster complete dinner for $8.95. The roast duck with plum sauce is a must for meat eaters. You'll also love the open-air setting and the lush tropical foilage.

**NEW ORLEANS BISTRO** *Cajun/Creole - Moderate*
2139 Kuhio Ave. (926-4444). Dinner only. One of the very few places in Hawaii serving authentic Cajun (country) and Creole (city) cooking with a chef from New Orleans. Dine inside or out daily 5-11:30pm and enjoy the jazz piano bar. Entrees include: mesquite grilled alligator tenderloin (that's right); barbecued "Shrimp Layfayette"; Cajun blackened prime ribs and steaks; corn bisque; soft shell crawfish, and fresh Island fish. But leave room for the pecan pie and coffee! It's Mardi Gras every night at the New Orleans Bistro on Kuhio.

**TOP OF WAIKIKI** *International - Expensive*
2270 Kalakaua Ave., 21st floor of the Waikiki Business Plaza (923-3877). L, D. You can pick out this building easily at night - it has a red and blue neon strip

lighting its penthouse restaurant high above busy Kalakaua Ave. There is a full luncheon and dinner menu here, but the real reason for coming is the awesome view of Waikiki and the city. If you can, come just before dusk so you can watch the lights come on and the tropical evening wash over the Island. Top of Waikiki is Waikiki's only revolving restaurant (Windows of Hawaii, also described in this chapter, is located near Ala Moana Center in Metro Honolulu and also well worth a visit). Come for lunch (11am-2pm except Sun.), cocktails, or dinner (5-10:30pm daily).

# DIAMOND HEAD WAIKIKI

**DENNY'S RESTAURANT**   *American - Inexpensive*
2586 Kalakaua Ave. (926-7200), other locations - 2345 Kuhio Ave., 205 Lewers, and Pearlridge Center. B, L, D. Offers typical Denny's food and service plus one of the nicest views of the zoo and beach in town. Full menu including entrees, sandwiches, soups, great selection of desserts and fresh salads. Be sure to try their fresh fruit pineapple boat - it's touted as the best in Waikiki!

**ROSE & CROWN PUB**  ★   *English - Inexpensive*
131 Kaiulani Ave., at King's Village (923-5833). L,D; no reservations. Now how many places serve a hearty steak and mushroom pie these days? Not many. But you can find it here, at this realistic re-creation of a British pub. What's your pleasure, mate? A round of darts? A pint of bitters? How about a pubwich, a hearty concoction specially prepared for you by the "Earl of Sandwich"? The bill of fare also has nachos, pizza, soup, salads, jumbo hot dogs (100 percent beef), wrapped if you like, Gov'nor, with a slab of cheddar. Join the voices around the nightly piano bar, then rush out at 6:10pm to witness the award-winning King's Guard drill team at the front gates of King's Village as they change the guard and put on one of the most impressive shows in Hawaii. Then back inside to make sure your seat's still warm. Arm wrestle, anyone?

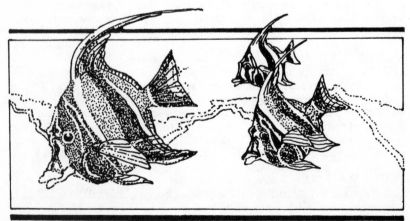

KIHIKIHI                                                    JBayot

**OCEANARIUM** ★ *American - Moderate*
2490 Kalakaua Ave., first floor of the Pacific Beach Hotel (922-1233). B,L,D. This is a must if you have kids or if you're a kid at heart! It's a unique family place where the view is half the fun. You'll be seated in front of a giant three-story wall of glass, behind which is a 26 foot tall salt water aquarium - one of the world's largest indoor tanks. As you dine you will be entertained by hundreds of sea creatures from tiny humuhumunukunukuapua'a (Hawaii's State fish) to barracuda, and even sharks. Plan to come during feeding times, which occur frequently at 9am, noon, 1pm, 6pm, 7pm, and 9pm. You can request an "Oceanarium Fact Sheet" and try to pick out which fish are which. If you have been to the Waikiki Aquarium and have a fish identification chart or booklet, bring it with you to the restaurant. And remember your flash camera, too. You'll have a ball! And, oh yes, the food. Quite good, with Porterhouse Steak, chicken parmesan, Thai Seafood Curry, and a wonderful beef stir fry, sandwiches, salads, and burgers.

**PEACOCK ROOM AND GARDEN LANAI** ★ *International - Moderate*
150 Kapahula Ave., in the Queen Kapiolani Hotel (922-1941). B, L, D. Here's what *Aloha* magazine said in a 1985 article, "Our nomination for the best all around, all-you-can-eat restaurant in town is the Queen Kapiolani Hotel. Not only do they provide a belly-busting buffet for every meal of the day, they also offer enough variety to make insatiability interesting." Served both inside (Peacock Room - an elegant, monarchy era dining salon) and outside (Garden Lanai - a cool, informal dining area on the sundeck), buffets of international cuisine from European, Asian, and Pacific countries feature a prime rib buffet, crab leg and roast beef buffet, Japanese buffet, seafood buffet, Sunday brunch buffet, and Hawaiian luncheon luau with great live entertainment (daily except Thurs. and Sun.). Japanese buffet Thurs. 11am-2pm. Breakfast buffet daily. A la carte selections are also available. This is a place where local women's groups, golfer's foresomes, and corporate teams come for an elegant lunch. You won't be disappointed. And before you eat, be sure to take a short tour of the newly remodeled hotel. It's a re-creation of the Hawaii of a century ago. Stop in the elevator lobbies for a good read of period newspapers, too. Why, you could easily make an afternoon of it!

**THE SUMMERY** *American - Moderate*
2552 Kalakaua Ave., street level in the Hawaiian Regent Hotel (922-6611). B, L, D. Open daily from 6am. A combination restaurant and coffee shop, the Summery features relaxed informal dining, with a full meal and late snack menu, weekend evening buffets and a popular Sunday Brunch. I found a secret place here that I hope you'll try. Order your drinks or meal on the outside patio, under an umbrella table amidst leafy tropical plantings and trees. You can sit hidden from view behind lush shrubbery and watch the traffic go by on Kalakaua Ave. just a few yards away. You'll enjoy this hidden garden in the middle of Waikiki. I was in the mood to try an unusual tropical drink one day on the Summery lanai, so I ordered 7-up and guava sherbet, mixed the two, and voila! A Summery Sunrise. Try one! Or better yet, create your own new tropical drink while on vacation in O'ahu! Send us a copy of the recipe and we'll publish the best along with your name, if you wish, in an issue of *THE O'AHU UPDATE*. Recipes become the property of this author and will not be returned.

### CAPTAIN'S TABLE ★ *Continental - Expensive*
2570 Kalakaua Ave., Holiday Inn-Waikiki (922-2511 or 1-800-367-8047). B, D; Sunday Brunch. If you enjoy a restaurant with a theme, and if you like Hawaiian nostalgia, you'll love the Captain's Table. The idea was to re-create the sights, sounds, and feel of boat day, in pre-jet plane Hawaii, when steamship passenger liners would dock near Aloha Tower at Honolulu Harbor, confetti would cloud the air, kids would dive for coins, and a festive atmosphere reigned. The restaurant is done to remind you of the interior of such a ship. Tuxedoed tablehelp advance the illusion, and if you squint you can see yourself dining aboard ship just prior to disembarking to supervise the transporting of your Mercedes and steamer trunks to your accommodations at the Royal Hawaiian or Moana Hotel. Say, wasn't that F. Scott Fitzgerald at the table across the way? The "Feast from the Sea for Two," is the captain's absolute favorite. And if the boat is still here on Sunday, do come aboard for Sunday Brunch at the Captain's Table. Served from 10am-2pm ($15.95 per person), it's laden with delicacies and one of the best in town. You'll be glad you made the trip.

### HY'S STEAK HOUSE ★ *American - Expensive*
2440 Kuhio, in the Waikiki Park Heights Hotel (922-5555). Dinner only. You can not only count on getting a superb steak cooked to your specifications every time you visit Hy's, but its atmosphere is right out of old Hawaii. The Canadian company which owns the restaurant bought an old Victorian house and moved parts of the interior to O'ahu to create the Victorian library motif at Hy's. You feel as though you are dining with Sherlock Holmes at his brother's exclusive British Gentlemen's Club (the Diogenes Club, yes?), with mahogany panelling, bookshelves, Oriental rugs, live classical guitar music, leather chairs, portraits framed in gold, and fresh flowers. Sizzling charcoal-broiled steaks, rack of lamb, delicate veal, Island fresh seafood, flaming desserts prepared tableside, and gracious service will complete your romantic meal. One of our favorites. The food and drink are second to none. Our favorite spot is the library, in a dark, candlelit, tapestried booth for two.

### NEPTUNE *Seafood - Expensive*
2490 Kalakaua Ave., second level in the Pacific Beach Hotel (922-1233). Dinner only, nightly 6-10pm; Sunday Brunch 10:30am-2pm. This quietly sophisticated restaurant, above the Pacific Beach Hotel's famous indoor Oceanarium (huge three-story salt water aquarium), is one of Waikiki's secrets - it's a very good restaurant overlooked by many visitors. For an appetizer try the Shrimp Dejonghe (butterflied jumbo shrimp baked in garlic butter) or Blackened Blue Ahi (seasoned and quickly seared morsels of Pacific tuna). A number of artistic dishes prepared at your table are worth considering, too, including the hot spinach salad and several steak entrees. A table d'hote (full dinner) is available including entrees of filet mignon, fresh catch of the day, or cajun seafood platter. Service and decor are impeccable; atmosphere is mellow and romantic.

### BAGWELLS 2424 *Continental - Deluxe*
2424 Kalakaua Ave., in the Hyatt Regency Waikiki (922-9292). Dinner only. If you're an adventuresome diner, at Bagwells you can order the nightly "Chef's Surprise," a six-course gala dinner with selections based on season, availability, and the chef's mood. Definitely try the Manoa lettuce, mushroom and avocado

salad to start. Then order one of the entrees you've heard about, such as the marinated Kahuku prawns on a pineapple fondue, or double breast of chicken stuffed with boursin cheese and served on a canlis of tomato and basil. As you enjoy your dinner you will appreciate the careful but subtle attention of your waiter, and will enjoy perusing the wine list, recipient of the "Top 100 Wine Lists of America" award. The director of wines will be happy to assist you with tastes from Bagwell's remarkable selection of more than 400 varieties. You'll leave Bagwells full of images: of your candlelit table; of your dessert - rainbow scoops of rich ice cream in a crisp-cookie shell, garnished with a sprig of mint; and perhaps echoes of the soft piano melodies.

### THE THIRD FLOOR ★ *Continental - Deluxe*
2522 Kalakaua Ave., third level of the Hawaiian Regent Hotel (922-6611). Dinner only; jackets suggested for men. This is among our five favorite restaurants in Honolulu (the others are Hy's Steak House, Keo's, Castagnola's, and Kyo-Ya). The openness of the main dining room, combined with the near-complete privacy afforded each table of diners by the high backed wicker princess chairs, the music of the water fountain flowing into the koi pond in the room's center, and the green live plants softly lit around the room give the illusion of dining in an open-air atrium. Since many celebrities dine here, the realization that you might be sitting near a prince or a leading lady adds an extra pinch of excitement to the atmosphere.

To describe the dinner here in detail would be like telling you the ending of a great movie. Just to mention several highlights: The fresh opakapaka (snapper) cooked in a tart butter sauce with roasted, slivered macadamia nuts and served on a heated plate was amazing; the steaming glass mug of cappuccino with blended liqueurs was the best I can remember. And the dinner's finale, well, I still wouldn't have believed they could transport a volcanic eruption from the Big Island right to my table! Pele is amazing.

Water goblets were filled just when they were low; questions were answered with aplomb; and I left the table feeling almost as pampered as a child eating Thanksgiving dinner at Grandma's. It's costly, and worth it.

# DOWNTOWN HONOLULU

**GARDEN CAFE** ★   *International - Inexpensive*
900 South Beretania St., in the Honolulu Academy of Arts (531-8865). Lunch only; reservations required, call Mon. 9am-noon, Tues-Fri. 9am-2pm. When you plan your visit to the exquisite Academy of Arts, call ahead for reservations at the Academy's Garden Cafe. Staffed by Academy volunteers, and only open from fall through spring, the Garden Cafe will provide you with a hideaway setting and a memorable luncheon soup, salad, and sandwich on a fixed menu. Dessert is extra. Ask, when you call, what the specialty will be on the day of your visit. This is one of O'ahu's hidden adventures - a morning at the Academy (its architecture alone is worth the visit) and luncheon in the Garden Cafe.

**JAKE'S DOWNTOWN RESTAURANT**   *American - Inexpensive*
1126 Bishop St., (524-4616). B, L. Rumor has it that you can see most of Honolulu's business community, half the State legislature, and on occasion even the governor breakfasting at Jake's. It's a Honolulu institution, and one not to miss when you're downtown shopping or touring. Try the waffles or pancakes, and watch for Jake's specials. This is as much a part of Honolulu's history as Wo Fat.

**MIZUTANI'S COFFEE SHOP**   *International - Inexpensive*
605 Cooke St., across the street from Seafarer's International Union hiring hall (537-9047). No reservations, cash only. I found this hidden gem by accident - I parked nearby and finally went in myself after watching a steady stream of people, in all manner of dress from swim suits to three-piece suits, hurrying inside. This tiny, local spot makes some of the best food in Honolulu, no kidding. I had a cheese steak sandwich with grilled onions that even today makes my mouth water when I think of it. Very popular also is their teriyaki beef plate lunch, shoyu chicken, and BBQ beef. Take out or eat it there, either way you're in for a true Hawaiian treat! Only seven tables; specials daily. They serve a sizzling vegetarian omelette, too.

By the way, there are so many great, hidden restaurants like this one on O'ahu that you can *always*, if you keep your eyes peeled and stop when you see a place with possibilities, find a new favorite by chance. Restaurant collecting is an art form that can become wonderfully addicting!

**WO FAT**   *Chinese/Cantonese - Inexpensive*
115 North Hotel St. (537-6260). L, D. The ads say "Hawaii's oldest restaurant" and "A downtown landmark since 1882." This old timer has become a tourist mecca - the weekly Chinese Chamber of Commerce walking tour of Chinatown even ends here for an optional lunch. Some love the food; others say it's past its prime. Either way, it's an historic spot with priceless Chinese antiques and mementos throughout. Specialties of the house include "Peking Duck" (served at the special buffet lunch Mon-Fri. 11am-1:30pm), "Hong Kong Chicken," "Honeymoon Shrimp," and "Shrimp Cashew." Waikiki Trolley Stop #14.

# METROPOLITAN HONOLULU

**BURGERLAND** ★ *International - Inexpensive*
3575 Campbell, on the corner of Monsarrat and Campbell, just three blocks east of the Zoo (732-0077). B, L, D; hours 10am-10pm seven days a week, no reservations, cash only. This local fast food place has been there forever and is so popular with locals that there's always a line (but it moves quickly). They serve a huge menu, including the best teriburger with cheese I've ever eaten. Or try their barbecued hamburgers - outstanding. I've sampled many local plate lunch drive-ins, and this is the one I keep going back to. And kids - a local custom is to skateboard into Burgerland and cool down with a slush float. I guarantee you'll like it. Unassuming, clean, friendly, and just one of the best places in town for take-out. If you choose one of a few tables under a canopy, you can watch all Honolulu walk up to the order window as you eat!

**CHOWDER HOUSE** *Seafood - Inexpensive*
1050 Ala Moana Blvd., in Ward Warehouse (521-5681). L, D; no reservations. For a mid afternoon snack or late lunch this specialty house is a quiet retreat. The Manhattan-style (tomato base) clam chowder is worth a try, with salad and fresh French bread. Lobster tail also is delicious, tender, and juicy. And I enjoyed the seafood combination platter. My favorite, though, is still New England (milk base) clam chowder - and here it's always hot, creamy, and loaded with clams. A relaxing afternoon stop.

**CHUCK'S STEAK HOUSE** *American - Inexpensive*
Six locations: 2752 Woodlawn Dr., Manoa Marketplace (988-7081); Kahala Mall (732-7861); Outrigger Hotel (923-1228); Edgewater Hotel (923-6111); Pearlridge Center (488-3055); and Mililani, at 95-221 Kipapa Drive (623-6300). Dinner only. Chuck's in Manoa (past University of Hawaii on University going mauka, then diamondhead on East Manoa Road) is the first one of the litter you should visit. It's on the balcony overlooking the Mall, with good steaks and reasonable prices. Other entrees include lobster, crab legs, and fresh catch of the day. Included are salad bar, rice, baked beans, and bread. Early bird specials. Established in 1959.

**COLUMBIA INN** *American - Inexpensive*
645 Kapiolani Blvd. (531-3747). B, L, D; no reservations. This 24-hour restaurant-coffee shop-lounge is very near the newspaper building so it has gained fame as a journalists' hangout. Drinks, pupus, TV tuned often to sports events, good food (try the tempura), and lively conversation. Here's a place you can go after a concert at the Neal Blaisdell Center nearby and still find people making a night of it.

**COMPADRES** ★ *Mexican - Inexpensive*
Two locations: 1200 Ala Moana Blvd., in Ward Centre (523-1307); and 2500 Kuhio Ave., in the Outrigger Prince Kuhio Hotel (924-4007). B, L, D, no reservations. Mexican; I appreciate Compadres' menu because they explain in English the various Mexican dishes with names in Spanish. This is a place to

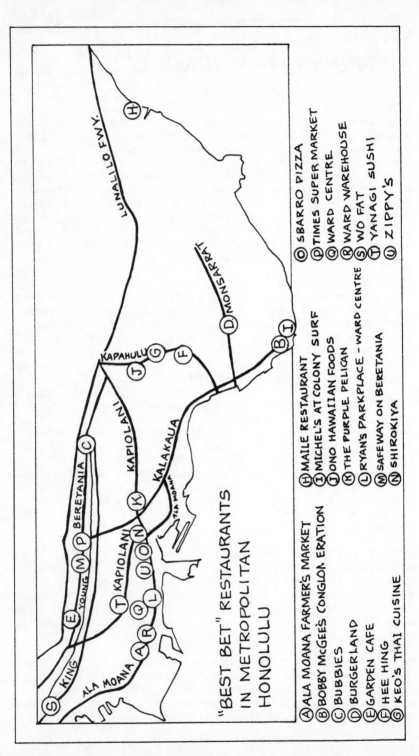

"BEST BET" RESTAURANTS
IN METROPOLITAN
HONOLULU

Ⓐ ALA MOANA FARMER'S MARKET
Ⓑ BOBBY McGEE'S CONGLOMERATION
Ⓒ BUBBIES
Ⓓ BURGERLAND
Ⓔ GARDEN CAFE
Ⓕ HEE HING
Ⓖ KEO'S THAI CUISINE

Ⓗ MAILE RESTAURANT
Ⓘ MICHEL'S AT COLONY SURF
Ⓙ ONO HAWAIIAN FOODS
Ⓚ THE PURPLE PELICAN
Ⓛ RYAN'S PARKPLACE – WARD CENTRE
Ⓜ SAFEWAY ON BERETANIA
Ⓝ SHIROKIYA

Ⓞ SBARRO PIZZA
Ⓟ TIMES SUPER MARKET
Ⓠ WARD CENTRE
Ⓡ WARD WAREHOUSE
Ⓢ WO FAT
Ⓣ YANAGI SUSHI
Ⓤ ZIPPY'S

party! Every night is Friday here, the music and talk are upbeat, the staff is energetic and hospitable, and the drinks go down very smoothly. The menu says:

*"A compadre is more than a friend, he or she is one's best amigo - someone to confide in and experience new adventures with. And Compadres is more than a Mexican restaurant and cantina. It is a place to relax and indulge the senses with good food, abundant drinks, good company, and friendly service. Ours is a place where everyone is a compadre."*

Selections: margaritas (famous here) come in four sizes - uno (big), dos (bigger), tres (giant), and pitcher. Headrests rent for $1.00. Try the guacamole or chingalinga (flour tortilla wrapped around deep-fried, sauteed chicken chunks in guacamole and sour cream), chile verde with pork, camarones al mojo de ajo (sauteed gulf shrimp in garlic butter and white wine sauce), and a grilled steak sandwich on sourdough bread with cheddar cheese and green chiles. Here's a dessert to end it all - apple chimi (fresh apple slices slow cooked with cinnamon, sugar and brandy, folded in a flour tortilla and deep fried. I'll have mine a la mode, please. I saw a Kalua-chocolate parfait go by that I'm going to order next time. That's just a taste; the menu goes on forever. Eggs, burritos, salads, weekend breakfasts with champagne, fish, enchiladas, spareribs, and combination platters. This menu even tells you in detail the proper art of drinking (hooking) tequila. I love this place! Put on your boots, cowpoke hat, and come on over. After all, it's Friday.

**CREPE FEVER**   *Continental - Inexpensive*
1200 Ala Moana Blvd., in Ward Centre (521-9023). B, L, D; no reservations. If you and your family like crepes (thin French pancakes stuffed with goodies), you'll love Crepe Fever. Its open-air, mall-side seating is easy, its counter service is fast, and its crepes are light and healthful. There are breakfast crepes stuffed with berries, lunch and dinner crepes rolled around seafood, lemon spinach vegetables, or sausage, and exotic dessert crepes with apple cinnamon, bananas and cream, and chocolate mint. Also available are homemade soups, salads, croissants, cocktails, Irish coffee, and cappuccino. Breakfast 8am-10:30am wkdys; 8am-12 noon weekends. Closes 9pm daily except Sun. 4pm.

**GARDEN COURT RESTAURANT**   *American - Inexpensive*
1450 Ala Moana Blvd., third floor in Liberty House at Ala Moana Center (945-5095). B, L, D. Since you'll want to visit Honolulu's favorite department store, Liberty House, you'll also want to know about the cool and pleasant Garden Court Restaurant on the third floor of the Ala Moana store. Perfect spot for a business breakfast, shopping break, or Sunday Brunch. Beautiful setting - elegant decor, and tasty food. If you decide to shop at other Liberty House stores on O'ahu, each one has a Gazebo Restaurant inside for a snack, lunch, or dinner. Convenient, clean, with a friendly staff.

**GRACE'S DRIVE INN**   *Island style - Inexpensive*
Three locations: 2227 South Beretania St., (946-8020); 1111 Dillingham Blvd., downtown (845-3238); and 94-866 Moloala St., Waipahu (677-9155); B, L, D; no reservations. Grace's on Beretania won *Sunset* magazine's award for "Best Plate Lunch Restaurant" several years in a row. Whatever you eat here (Grace's

on Beretania in Moiliilu is the oldest, and my favorite) don't miss the side order of macaroni salad - it's the best around. Chicken katsu is the biggest seller, and the mixed plate, with teriyaki pork, beef curry, and sweet and sour chicken, gives you a sample of several favorites. They have take-out, too. On your first visit I'd suggest sitting to the side where you can study the menu posted over the counter, and watch what local residents order. Follow their language and rhythm, and you'll be taken for a kamaaina. Grace's is a Hawaiian institution, one you should experience during your visit.

**GUILTLESS GOURMET**  *Vegetarian - Inexpensive*
1489 Kapiolani Blvd., (955-6144). B, L, D daily 11am-9pm and take-out; no reservations. This increasingly popular restaurant-bakery offers healthy, low-calorie meals and desserts. The chili is excellent, as are their fresh-baked sweets. No added fats, starches, sugars, or preservatives - just low calorie natural food with great taste and texture.

**HARD ROCK CAFE ★**  *American - Inexpensive*
1837 Kapiolani Blvd. (955-7383), just across the Ala Wai Canal from Waikiki. L, D, no reservations. You've heard of the Hard Rock Cafe: opened in London in '71, now there's one in S.F., Chicago, L.A., New Orleans, New York - and you've seen kids wearing their T-shirts. Now you can visit one of the newest (1986) Hard Rock Cafes. And you should, especially if you have kids or just love the good old '50s.

Imagine a building that looks like a small train depot with a Quonset hut roof. In the center is a square bar, with a real wooden-panelled woody (1959 Cadillac station wagon) mounted above it, complete with surfboards sticking out the back window. On the walls are 50s and 60s memorabilia from Elvis mementos, to guitars of the stars, to Jan and Dean's gold record of "Honolulu Lulu," even an aloha shirt worn by Tom Selleck! It's a museum of rock 'n roll. But that's just the start. Vintage music, just loud enough that you have to whisper in the waitress's ear. And the food. Hard Rock Cafe burgers are legendary - try #11 or #13. The other best-bet is the lime BBQ chicken or the HRC famous baby rock watermelon ribs (Texas-style ribs basted, grilled, and served with fries and a salad). Wine coolers, a mysterious HRC Hurricane (keep the glass), Clyde's iced tea (a real taste treat from Music City, USA) and thick cold shakes. And on your way out, you can kiss a statue of Mick Jagger or buy yourself a HRC T-shirt for only $10. And their motto is "Save the Planet." Not a bad thought.

**HEE HING RESTAURANT ★**  *Chinese - Inexpensive*
449 Kapahulu Ave., in Diamond Head Center (735-5544 or 734-8474). L, D. This old Honolulu favorite has a new home, so the atmosphere is even more exciting than before and the food is still excellent.

Dim sum, Hong Kong style is a house specialty you'll want to try. These are Chinese pupus, usually wrapped in a dumpling or bamboo steamer, displayed on a cart. You choose your favorites as from a dessert tray. Another specialty is Hawaiian prawns, which are grown in the North Shore aquafarm (described in the WHAT TO SEE chapter) and prepared in a variety of ways, including deep fried, steamed, sauteed, boiled, or grilled. They are out of this world - don't miss trying them. Spicy food is also available - try the Mongolian beef! If you have a group of five or more, you might consider ordering a combination of dishes such as roast spareribs, dungeness crab, sweet and sour roast duck, lemon chicken, or cold noodles. You'll have fun just looking over the extensive menu. Relax, take your time, let each course settle, and you'll walk away at the end of the evening satisfied and glad you discovered this popular Cantonese and Northern Chinese restaurant.

**INDIA HOUSE**   *East Indian - Inexpensive*
2632 South King St. (955-7552). Dinner only. Chefs tend to move from one restaurant to another, and owner-chef Ram Arora is no exception. His naan bread is still famous at The Third Floor, the place he left to open India House.

Anyone who enjoys Indian Food will love this restaurant. Samosas are crisp pastry cones stuffed with vegetables - a light and tasty appetizer. Very popular is tandoori chicken, marinated in spices, herbs, and yogurt. You can order combination dinners, such as the favorite "Maharaja Dinner", with tandoori chicken, lamb curry, and fish tikka (marinated chunks of fresh Island fish on a skewer). All kinds of curries are offered, and vegetarians will be glad to see the extensive vegetarian menu, including a delectable vegetable jalfrezi, a mixed vegetable curry. If it sounds odd to have an Indian restaurant in Honolulu, remember that Britain, with its Indian colony, had a strong influence in Hawaii for most of the 19th century. Lunch 11am-2pm Mon-Fri., dinner 5-9pm nightly.

**INN OF THE SIXTH HAPPINESS**   *Chinese - Inexpensive*
746 Kohou St. (841-0000). L, D. This one is offered to you as somewhat of an unknown quantity. I have not been here to eat, but several friends whose restaurant advice I respect have raved so much about the wonderful meals they've had here, and about how romantic the setting is that I want to ask you to be the judge. If you decide to try it, please let us know your opinion, and we'll publish your comments in an upcoming *O'AHU UPDATE*.

**KC DRIVE INN**   *American/Hawaiian - Inexpensive*
1029 Kapahulu Ave., near the H-1 Freeway (737-5581). B, L, D; no reservations. Inside dining and take-out. The most famous item in this classic restaurant (since 1934) is the KC Waffle Dog, a hot dog in a steamed waffle, available with assorted toppings. Rumor has it that when a certain famous blond country singer-actress is in town to visit her own Hawaii Kai dockside restaurant, she never fails to pull into KC in her limo and have her chauffeur order her a waffle dog or two. They are delicious - and have a unique flavor and texture. KC also serves noodles, toasted double decker sandwiches, salads, bentos (cold Japanese boxed meals, including for example: fried chicken, beef teriyaki, rice, luncheon meat, and tsukemono - pickled vegetables), complete meals, shakes, malts, and desserts. They welcome kids here and have a keiki menu for those under 13.

**KENGO'S RESTAURANT**
   **AND ROYAL BUFFET**   *Japanese/International - Inexpensive*
1517 Kapiolani Blvd. (943-1749), and Royal Buffet next door at 1529 Kapiolani Blvd. (941-2241). B, L, D; no reservations. These two dining areas offer full meal service in the restaurant, a cocktail lounge, and a superior Japanese buffet

in the building just across the parking area. The lunch and dinner buffets are very well done, with a wide variety of Japanese offerings in a beautifully decorated presentation. The staff at Kengo's is so courteous and friendly that people come back again and again. Many local folks come to Kengo's for a special occasion. Keiki menu at the restaurant includes spaghetti, steak, and teri chicken. A family place that is always good.

### LIKE LIKE (LEE-KAY)
### DRIVE INN RESTAURANT   American - Inexpensive
735 Keeaumoku St. (941-2515). B, L, D; no reservations; no cocktails, wine or beer; no credit cards. A Honolulu landmark since 1953, open 24 hours a day, this local favorite serves the best carrot cake on the Island, perhaps in the hemisphere. Also famous: saimin (Japanese noodles and spices in chicken, beef, or fish broth), plate lunch (I like the spaghetti and pot roast), sweet and sour pork ribs, Hawaiian steak (aren't the mashed potatoes addicting), and shrimp tempura. This is where the kama'ainas (native Hawaiians and old-timers) meet for coffee and a little something.

### MAPLE GARDEN   ★   *Northern Chinese/Szechuan - Inexpensive*
909 Isenberg St. (941-6641). L, D. Honolulu has many excellent Chinese restaurants, and Maple Garden is one of the best of its kind. If you enjoy spicy hot Chinese food in a no-frills, family atmosphere, this is your place. Many dishes on the menu are only mildly hot, for those, like me, who have a tender palate. If you haven't had spring rolls, try them. The braised eel is delicious, as is the sliced chicken with snow peas. Mongolian beef (hot) will clear your taste buds, just in time for one of my favorites, "Chinaman's Hat." For dessert try "Pearl Dumplings." Maple Garden is clean, inexpensive, and the food is top-notch. Call for take-out if you prefer. This place is a local favorite.

### MC CULLY CHOP SUEY   ★   *Chinese/Cantonese - Inexpensive*
2005 S. King St., corner of King and Mc Cully Streets (946-4069 or 949-9723). L, D; (no reservations). This is one of Honolulu's most popular local Chinese chop suey houses. Of course it has no sophisticated atmosphere - just good food at low, low prices. I love the Char Sui (pork marinated in spices and roasted; it has a bright red color) and the "Special Mc Cully Chop Sui." There's a different luncheon special daily that is tasty, hot, and costs almost nothing. You'll see Chinese folks, tourists, military, and lots of other locals eating here every day. It's a best bet, and they have take-out, too.

### THE OLD SPAGHETTI FACTORY   *Italian - Inexpensive*
1050 Ala Moana Blvd. (531-1513), Ward Warehouse. L, D; no reservations. This encore of the San Francisco original follows the same format - large, open area, antiques, with lots of brass and mirrors, and hearty, inexpensive food. Spaghetti, salad, bread, beer, wine, and lots of fun for families, seniors, or dates. A local favorite.

### ONO HAWAIIAN FOODS   ★   *Traditional Hawaiian - Inexpensive*
726 Kapahulu Ave. (737-2275). L, D; no reservations; park on street; cash only; no wine, beer, or cocktails. This modest, clean, busy restaurant has local flavor and real, home-cooked, quality Hawaiian food. How many places put a bench

outside so you'll be comfortable as you wait? And where else do you see three locals for every tourist? Remember that traditional Hawaiian food has tastes which may not please everyone. Lomilomi salmon is raw chunks of tender fish mixed with onion, tomato, and spices. Laulau is meat and potatoes or taro wrapped in leaves and steamed. Poi, as you know, is a bland paste made by combining taro root pulp with water. Try a fingerful with the lomilomi salmon - a perfect combination. Haupia is a white coconut custard served in squares. No one we know can eat just one! If you want to "eat local," and spend a minimum doing so, go to Ono Hawaiian Foods on Kapahulu.

**ORIGINAL PANCAKE HOUSE**   *American - Inexpensive*
Three locations: 1956 Ala Moana, in the Waikiki Marina Hotel (947-8848); 1414 Dillingham Blvd. (847-1496); and 1221 Kapiolani Blvd. (533-3005). The Waikiki location is open 6am-10pm and Sun. 6am-2pm, as are the other two locations, with dinner served 4pm-10 pm. This is a copy of the original Original Pancake House which opened in 1953 in Portland, Oregon. These restaurants use the same recipes that won world-wide acclaim for the original, which was chosen by James Beard as one of the ten best restaurants in America. You'll love this menu - with delicate French pancakes, coconut pancakes, Hawaiian pancakes (with pineapple and tropical syrup). Beside your stack of exotic pancakes you can have an omelette (I like the one with Portuguese sausage), bacon, eggs, hash, ham, or even Spam. Specialties: Dutch baby miniature German pancake, and apple pancake with fresh apples and a cinnamon glaze. Each platter is cooked to order, using only real butter, grade AA eggs, unbleached hard-wheat flour, dry-cured, hickory-smoked hams and bacon, and pure whipping cream. Natural enzymes in the batter transform food to energy and make the pancakes light and finely textured.

**RAINBOW DRIVE-IN**   *Island style - Inexpensive*
3308 Kanaina Ave., at corner of Kapahulu (737-0177). This old-timer has been recommended by *Sunset* magazine and a poll of local residents. It's just one long block from Waikiki. This busy spot now caters to a young, and well behaved, crowd who "hang out" there, so most adults order at the take-out window. Favorites at the Rainbow vary, but everyone loves the barbecued steak plate lunch. The spaghetti is great, and the beef curry is always gone before 1pm. Ditto for the daily specials - so get there early. One classic local dish you'll want to try is loco moco, hamburger on rice topped with a fried egg. If you have time, sit in your car to eat, and listen to the masters of Pidgin demonstrate this local language art form. You'll have to be invisible in order to catch it, but this is a place to hear pure Island Pidgin.

**RYAN'S PARKPLACE** ★   *American - Inexpensive*
1200 Ala Moana Blvd., in Ward Centre (523-9132). L, D. This very popular meeting place has been voted "the most popular people-watching restaurant" by readers of *Honolulu* magazine. The bar serves complimentary pupus and a large selection of beers and whiskies; the restaurant features applewood-smoked chicken, sauteed calf's liver, mesquite-grilled Island fish, and fettuccine with chicken. The atmosphere is exciting and Island-style casual with ceiling fans, lots of brass, and tropical greenery. You'll find an upbeat lunch or dinner, and perhaps a new friend or two at this chic and sophisticated spot.

### SAIGON RESTAURANT    *Vietnamese - Inexpensive*
1344 Kapiolani Blvd. (955-5040). L, D; no reservations. Rated the number one Vietnamese restaurant on O'ahu, the Saigon is famous for its use of natural ingredients and no MSG (monosodiumglutimate). The small, sparcely-decorated dining room serves appetizers such as angel wings (deep-fried stuffed chicken wings with spicy sauce), salads (the papaya salad with pork and shrimp on shredded papaya is super), soups (try the catfish soup), and beef, chicken, and shrimp entrees. The restaurant is always well-populated with military personnel, a sure sign that the food is tasty, authentic, and reasonably priced. Take-out favorites include Saigon sandwiches (ham, chicken, pork or salami on French bread), prawn casserole (sauteed prawns in mild or spicy sauce), and BBQ or lemon grass chicken plate. Flan custard or mung bean coconut milk dessert completes a meal you'll long remember.

### SEKIYA'S RESTAURANT AND DELICATESSEN    *Japanese/American - Inexpensive*
2746 Kaimuki Ave. B, L, D. Open Tues-Thurs. 8:30am-11pm, Fri-Sun. 8:30am-midnight. Closed Mondays, no reservations. A local favorite that few tourists know about. This restaurant and delicatessen serves such American dishes as sandwiches, salads, and ice cream specials, but their Japanese selections constitute the greater part of their business. This is a friendly place with a patient and courteous staff who will help you if you're just learning about Japanese food. You can sample cucumber sushi (rice and cucumber rolled in dried seaweed), donburi (steamed rice topped with cooked meat, fish or vegetables in a bowl), noodles, chicken tofu (soybean curd), or shrimp tempura (dipped in light batter and deep fried). The asparagus salad is a favorite. And their yakitori (grilled skewers of marinated chicken) and barbecued meat sticks should not be missed. Ask about their plate lunches, too.

### SEPARATE TABLES ★    *International/Island style - Inexpensive*
1028 Nuuanu Ave. (524-7787). Lunch only - 11:30am-2pm Mon-Fri. Have you searched for a cozy hidden little luncheon place where you and a friend could have a late lunch after a busy morning of shopping? Well, here it is. They have tables inside but the most fun is to sit in the cool shade under a thatched canopy and sip iced mint tea and await your generous platter of artistically displayed chicken, shrimp, or tofu in an exotic sauce on a bed of rice or pasta. Add a salad, firm sauteed vegetables, and fluffy bread, and you've got yourself a perfect Island repast. You won't want to leave when Separate Tables closes. And you can bring your own wine, since none is served. See you there!

### SHIROKIYA ★    *Japanese - Inexpensive*
1450 Ala Moana Blvd., upper floor of Shirokiya Department Store in Ala Moana Center (941-9111). This is the very best place to introduce your children, or yourself, to the culture, food, economy, language, and people of Japan.

Downstairs is a huge mixture of new electronic appliances, tapes, stereos, golf supplies (the Japanese have a love affair with golf), purses, cotton hapi coats, Japanese ceramics, hand-painted dinnerware, and a toy section you'll have to coax the kids out of. Here you can see what's new in Japan, what Japanese households are like, and what Japanese shoppers are buying.

And upstairs, the upper level has made Shirokiya famous! Most of the upper floor is devoted to Japanese foods; beautifully displayed as though you were wandering through a Japanese country market. Counter after counter are full of Japanese delicacies such as tea cakes, pickled vegetables, sushi, exotic seaweeds, and tofus. You are encouraged to take samples. Bentos (cold Japanese boxed meals) are available so you can try some foods later. Your hunger will be satisfied long before you've made the rounds, so sample carefully and be sure to ask the vendors to tell you the story behind your favorite selections.

While you're browsing with your samples, watch and listen for announcement of the Japanese arts and crafts demonstrations regularly offered in various parts of the store. Master artists and craftspersons display their talents in calligraphy, sculpting, pottery, cooking, and many other areas. Watch the daily paper for demonstration times and places. Set aside one vacation meal to have at Shirokiya. You'll enjoy a marvelous low-cost round-trip adventure to Japan and be back in time for an afternoon swim.

### SUBWAY SANDWICHES AND SALADS    *American - Inexpensive*
Ten locations on Oʻahu, including McCully Shopping Center, 1960 Kapiolani Blvd. (945-3566), and 2310 Kuhio Ave. (923-0400). 10am-2am daily. Subway franchises are clean, nicely decorated take-out or eat-in shops, featuring sandwiches such as steak and cheese, club, BLT, tuna, pastrami and spicy Italian. Build-your-own salads from a list of ingredients (they make them).

### WALLY WOK  ★    *Chinese - Inexpensive*
2320 South King St. (945-1-WOK or 943-1965), across from Old Honolulu Stadium Park. L, D; no reservations. Wally Wok is a creative new (1987) fast-food restaurant modeled after McDonald's which delivers, like Domino's Pizza, and serves Chinese health food - no MSG, low sodium, and every dish prepared when you order. This is one of the few restaurants I found myself going back to again and again. Everyone in Hawaii finds a favorite quick meal or two and a special place to go to enjoy it. For me it was a trip to Wally Wok for fried min (saimin noodles, like fried rice but long, cooked with vegetables and mini-chunks of meat), 4 won tons (fried dough packets with vegetables) with sweet and sour sauce, and a drink. I'd take this treat and drive out to the helicopter pad near the Ala Wai Yacht Harbor, park, listen to KCCN radio and watch the Waikiki skyline as I ate my Wally Wok delicacies.

You can find some gourmet fast food, then eat it in one of Oʻahu's outdoor settings that challenges any fine restaurant for atmosphere. Other fresh steaming hot and wonderful Wally Wok specialties include lemon chicken, spicy Szechwan chicken, char siu (red pork - wonderful), and pita pocket sandwich. Wally caters too, for birthdays, picnics, hotel parties, or tailgate parties before the big game. We highly recommend this new and creative restaurant.

### ZIPPY'S RESTAURANT    *American/Island Style - Inexpensive*
Sixteen locations around Oʻahu including Ala Moana Center (942-7766). B, L, D; no reservations, no cocktails, wine, or beer; some Zippy outlets have a sushi bar, and most have Napoleon's Bakery in the restaurant; all (except Ala Moana and Pearlridge) Zippy's are open 24 hours daily. Zippy's is Hawaii's answer to

McDonald's - it's the largest local fast-food chain in the Islands. Nine of the sixteen outlets offer indoor dining. Zippy's chili is the star attraction - Zippy's customers consume more than 65,000 pounds of the delicious beef and bean concoction every month! Of course Zippy's has burgers, saimin (Japanese noodles and broth), plate lunches, omelettes, salads, and beef stew. If you have cooking facilities, pick up a Zip Pac - convenient two-pound containers of chili, meat sauce, spaghetti noodles, Portuguese bean soup, beef stew, beef, chicken or hamburger curry, macaroni and potato salad, gravy, and rice. Just pop this meal-in-a-pouch into a pan and you've got yourself a Zippy meal in your condo. In one stop at Zippy's you can create an international meal of sushi appetizer, chicken curry, macaroni salad, and a famous "Napple" (apple turnover) from Napoleon's Bakery for dessert. All for under $10. What a buy.

## BOBBY MC GEE'S CONGLOMERATION ★ *American - Moderate*
2885 Kalakaua Ave., in the Colony Surf East (922-1282). Dinner only. Let's suppose one afternoon after you've just won the lottery, or you feel like you did, and you want to spend the evening with your family at some crazy, off beat place. Get dressed up in your jeans and sweater, or the clown outfit left over from last Halloween (the one you threw in your suitcase on a whim), and truck on down to Bobby McGee's. Find yourself a comfortable table in one of the dining rooms, and look around. It looks like Grandma's victorian mansion just before her first garage sale in 60 years: a conglomeration of hanging lamps, gilded picture frames, stained glass windows, Greek statues, antique bathtubs, turn-of-the-century wood burning stoves, red velvet four-poster bed canopies, overstuffed chairs, beveled mirrors, porcelain turines, candlesticks, and oil paintings. Suddenly your waiter appears - dressed as a professional magician - and announces that he is Imaka the Magnificent. You look and see that every waiter and waitress is in costume, and each table is participating in their fantasy. So you sit back, relax, and enjoy Imaka's magic show, performed just for you and your family. What a place!

And now for dinner. Don't be surprised when your salad comes to you fresh out of a clawfoot bathtub, or when you see your soup being ladled out of big pot simmering on top of a steaming wood stove. You'll love the food - the famous deep-fried zuchini or fresh potato skin appetizers, and the fresh spinach salad (served tableside - not from the tub - after a brisk shower in the kitchen). Or dig into a tender chicken cordon bleu, boneless breast stuffed with ham, swiss cheese and mushrooms, topped with sauce maltaise. Fresh catch of the day with your choice of preparations, prime rib, pork or beef ribs slow-smoked over hickory and bathed in BBQ sauce, steaks, shrimp, lobster, crab, and a sizzling tenderloin stir fry all share the menu. There's a kid's menu, and house specialty desserts (your waiter makes them appear from nowhere). Along with your healthy appetite you'd better bring your favorite joke - I suspect your waiter will ask you what it is! After dinner, you can move over into the disco portion of the restaurant. Here's where all the music has been coming from. You can dance and party every night until 2am If you come on Friday, happy hour is from 5-7:30. Dinner nightly from 5:30pm. Your clown costume was right in style; your waiter's magic show kept you on the edge of your seat; and your dinner was outstanding. You don't have to win the lottery to love an evening at Bobby McGee's Conglomeration.

## BUBBIES HOME MADE
### ICE CREAM AND DESSERTS ★ *American - Moderate*

1010 University Ave. (949-8984). Noon to midnight, Mon-Thurs.; to 1am Fri. and Sat.; to 11pm Sun.; no reservations or credit cards. The ice cream here is the best I've tasted. It is rich, creamy, flavorful, and each batch is consistently excellent. I like the lichee ice cream best, except perhaps the chocolate or macadamia nut. Then there's the papaya sherbet - I'll have one of those too. And maybe an Oreo ice cream cone to go. Bubbies' home made desserts are among the best, too. Apple pie a la mode, cinnamon twists, huge cookies just out of the oven, and "kiddie cones." Try Bubbies first, then compare with other ice cream places in town. You'll be back.

## CASTAGNOLA'S ITALIAN RESTAURANT ★ *Italian - Moderate*

2752 Woodlawn Drive, in the Manoa Marketplace (988-2969 or 988-2971). L, D. This is the classic example of a fine restaurant. First, it is small by design, so that patrons and staff both can enjoy personalized treatment of each guest. Ingredients are the freshest and finest. Only extra-virgin olive oil is used in the kitchen; only the best tomatoes and cheeses from Italy are served. They make their own sausage, and the Italian bread is baked twice daily, with unbleached flour, kosher salt, honey (no sugar) and no shortening. Fresh produce is delivered six days a week. This is also one of very few O'ahu restaurants that features authentic Portuguese dishes, including osso bucco and tripe cacciatore. Don't miss the Carpaccio (thin slices of prime sirloin, sprinkled with a spicy mustard sauce and chopped green onions) here, it's among the best in town. Get reservations for an off hour - the restaurant is cozy and lines do form regularly outside. This is a dining experience among the best Honolulu has to offer.

## FISHERMAN'S WHARF RESTAURANT ★ *Seafood - Moderate*

1009 Ala Moana Blvd., at Kewalo Basin (538-3808). L, D. This popular spot on the wharf overlooking the charter fishing boats at Kewalo Harbor is actually two dining rooms - downstairs is the Seafood Grotto; upper floor houses the Captain's Bridge. Similar menus, but different specialties. Why not opt for the upper floor view, with friendly waitresses in HMS Pinafore garb. My chilled spinach salad with shrimp and mushrooms was so superb I almost ordered another one! A wonderful, thick Boston clam chowder will start you, possibly followed by "Shrimp Tahitienne" with garlic butter, a char-broiled top sirloin, or the steam

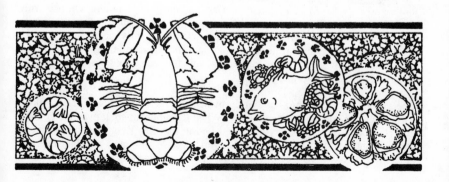

ing "Chioppino Italienne," a spicy seafood stew of clams, fish, lobster, shrimp, scallops, and crab. For dessert, try a "Queen Emma Diamond." Your visit here will remind you of going aboard an old ship for a meal. And you'll love the view from the moving-picture windows. An old standby; especially fun for families.

## GREEK ISLAND TAVERNA    *Greek - Moderate*
2570 S. Beretania St., upstairs (943-0052). L, D. This little gem is on the balcony overlooking a South Beretania mini-mall. Take a taxi or The Bus but find this place for a night of food, singing, belly dancing, music and Zorba-type fun that's hard to find these days. The food will make you think of your trip (real or imagined) to sunny Athens or the Greek Islands. Creamy gyros, bouillabaisse, kakavia, chicken and fresh kebabs, deep-fried squid, stuffed grape leaves, and kasseri cheese flambe. This is a realistic piece of Greek tastes, sounds and sights. You'll leave full of Greek hospitality.

## HAU TREE LANAI  ★   *American - Moderate*
2863 Kalakaua Ave., at the New Otani Kaimana Beach Hotel (912-1555). B, L, D. The atmosphere of this famous restaurant, under the oldest hau tree in Waikiki, is one of Oʻahu's best. I have not dined there since the recent renovation, but I'll wager the mango muffins, Portuguese sausage, and eggs benedict are still superlative. For lunch try the salads and fresh catch of the day. Dinner at sunset is wonderfully romantic - get there early for a table near the beach. There's something magic about dining in the open air of Hawaii, with the scent of flowers and the music of the Islands caressing you as you watch the tropical ocean surf. A meal at the Hau Tree Lanai is one of my favorite memories of Oʻahu.

## HORATIO'S   *Seafood - Moderate*
1050 Ala Moana Blvd. (521-5002), in Ward Warehouse. L, D. This steak and seafood grill is busy, cozy, upbeat, and exciting. Come at an off hour to assure a good table and prompt service. Any of the fresh seafood dishes here are excellent, especially shrimp, fresh Island fish, and crab. Horatio's is one of the most popular restaurants in Ward Warehouse - it's always busy because of the consistent quality of its ingredients and cooking. Also sandwiches and soups.

## KEO'S THAI CUISINE  ★   *Thai - Moderate*
625 Kapahulu Ave. (737-8240). Dinner only. You must go to Keo's. That's all there is to it. Not only is this restaurant an "in" place in Honolulu, but it is truly a memorable dining experience. What happy combination of elements makes Keo's so wonderful? First, Keo and his extended family host a party every night, are obviously having a good time, and their sincere enjoyment of life is contagious. As a guest at the restaurant you feel important, valued, and you can't help but relax and join the fun.

Keo's story is fascinating. His family owned the Pepsi franchise in Laos, along with a tobacco and shipping company. When Communists took over the country in 1975, the family lost everything, and fled to the U.S. Keo, who speaks six or seven languages, had attended the University of Washington and had recently been graduated with a degree in architecture and business. So after a year in

Tokyo, Keo came back to Hawaii, where he had vacationed as a student, and in 1977 with an investment of about $26,000, Keo and his family opened the tiny Mekong Restaurant on South Beretania. His creativity, hard work, and the loyal teamwork of his relatives have turned that investment into five Thai restaurants in Honolulu. Keo is also author of a best selling new cookbook, containing recipes from the five restaurants.

The Keo restaurant to visit first is the one on Kapahulu - Keo's Thai Cuisine. Inside you'll find an Oriental fantasy garden, with palms, orchid sprays, golden statues, huge white parasols, and soft lights. You will be seated in a secluded spot, at a table with white linen, fresh flowers, and candlelight. And dinner. On the menu each dish is labelled mild, medium, or hot, so be careful - hot can be volcanic. Don't miss the spring rolls, or the Bangkok wings (chicken stuffed with vegetables, breaded, sauteed, and served with sa-teh sauce for dipping), both appetizers. Your waiter will make sure the chef reduces the amount of spice in your entree if you request it. I'd do just that if you try the house specialty - "Evil Jungle Prince." Fresh basil, coconut milk, and red chili combined with either chicken, shrimp, or vegetables over a bed of chopped cabbage. I'm sure my patient waiter served me 10 glasses of ice water before I finished my serving, full and teary-eyed. Next visit I'm going to order the "Country-style Thai Game Hen," marinated overnight and baked to perfection. You can also have curries, fresh whole fish deep-dish fried with your choice of sauces, special Thai beverages, and desserts (such as fresh apple-bananas sauteed in fresh coconut milk). Meet Keo, enjoy a relaxed, elegant meal, and if you notice a celebrity while you're dining, don't be surprised. It might be you!

**KING TSIN**  ★  *Northern Chinese - Moderate*
1110 McCully St. (946-3273 or 947-4584), corner McCully and South King Street. L, D. This is one of the best Northern Chinese restaurants on O'ahu. The menu is extensive, ingredients are fresh and carefully prepared, cooked, and served. My abalone filets in a mild cream sauce were memorable. People in our dinner party ordered sizzling "Mongolian Beef," "Chinaman's Hat" (crepes filled with plum sauce, pork, cabbage, green onions, tender bamboo shoots, and rice, then rolled) prepared at the table, and shrimp with black bean sauce. If you have the time to call a day ahead, I heartily recommend the "Beggar's Chicken," packed with herbs and seasonings into a clay pot and slow-baked. You break open the pot at your table to reveal as succulent and tender a dish as you can imagine. This restaurant will also vary the spices in your orders if you request it. If you've never had abalone, this is the place to try it.

**MONTEREY BAY CANNERS**  *American/Seafood - Moderate*
Three locations: 1200 Ala Moana Blvd., in Ward Centre (536-6197); 2335 Kalakaua Ave., Outrigger Hotel (922-5761); and Pearlridge Center (487-0048). L, D, breakfast at Outrigger Hotel. The Waikiki location has a wonderful open-air view of the ocean, nautical decor with ceiling fans and bamboo. This is a terrific family place for late lunch or early dinner. Look for the specials, they're bargains. Among my favorites: New England clam chowder, fresh Island mahimahi dorado (make sure it's fresh, not frozen or fresh frozen), and shrimp Louis. Sandwiches, salads, burgers, soups, and rich parfaits share the menu. Try for a view table and enjoy the casual dockside flavor of this popular restaurant.

### NUUANU ONSEN TEA HOUSE    *Japanese - Moderate*
87 Laimi Rd. (538-9184). Dinner only; no cocktails, wine, or beer. Here's a riddle - how could you have dinner in Japan without leaving Hawaii? Answer: by coming up the Nuuanu Valley on the Pali Highway, turning on Laimi Road, and entering the traditional Japanese Tea House hidden there among beautiful gardens. You'll remove your shoes Japanese style, sit on traditional floor mats, and experience a Japanese dinner you would find in the finest Tokyo restaurants. Alaskan King Crab, clam soup, and picked cucumbers lead to entrees which vary regularly. If you want the most from your Oʻahu vacation, you'll want to find the mystery and beauty of Japan. This Oriental fairyland is your bridge into another world. You'll enjoy the trip. Reservations must be made 24 hours in advance; minimum party of 6; 10% deposit in advance. And its still worth it.

### PAGODA FLOATING RESTAURANT  ★  *International - Moderate*
1525 Rycroft St., at the Pagoda Hotel (941-6611). B, L, D. Before you cross the bridge to enter the two-tiered Pagoda Restaurant, take a few moments to step from stone to stone over the bubbling stream, past the ornamental Japanese plants and trees, and around the quiet pond in which regal, spotted koi swim silently. Across a bamboo bridge and past a waterfall of lava rock, you enter one of the most tranquil and secluded restaurant settings on Oʻahu.

The Pagoda has three dining areas - a round, two-story structure "floating" in the koi pond, with the Pagoda Restaurant on the lower level, and the LaSalle Restaurant on the second level directly above. There are also a few private tea houses set in the pond around the central circular restaurant, available for small groups and private family dining. The lower-level Pagoda Restaurant menu features American and Japanese complete dinners and a la carte selections, while the upper-level LaSalle Restaurant features Japanese and continental entrees with sushi bar, buffet, and early-bird specials. Try the lower level for breakfast or lunch, and the more formal upper level for dinner. Request a table overlooking the koi pond, and enjoy dining at one of Hawaii's most popular restaurants.

### THE PURPLE PELICAN  ★  *Moderate*
Second floor of McCully Shopping Center with free parking in basement, 1960 Kapiolani Blvd. (979-1000). Lunch 11-2, dinner nightly 5-10, Sun. brunch 9-2. Reservations recommended. This stylish new restaurant is a comer! Seating at private tables affords a view of the glass-enclosed kitchen, where you can watch such delicacies being prepared as teriyaki moonfish, shrimp, lobster, sliced roast beef and turkey breast. You can sample scallops, opakapaka (pink snapper), or even flavorful, chewy, delicious baby octopus. The bouillabaisse is one of the best anywhere, and the dessert table will amaze you. Buffet $13.95 for lunch, $16.95 for dinner. ($14.95 Sunday, Monday and Tuesday).

### THE PALM GRILL    *International - Moderate/Expensive*
1221 Kapiolani Blvd. (531-7256). B, L, D. One of Oʻahu's best dining bargains is Sunday Brunch at The Palm Grill. The restaurant looks like an exclusive private club, with shining brass appointments, lush palms throughout, and a courteous, pleasant staff. Sunday Brunch is served from 10:30am-2:30pm, for a remarkable $9.95 with champagnes or juices. A lavish breakfast is served Mon-Fri. from 6:30-10am, with eggs, fresh fruit, ham, and fried potatoes.

Luncheon or dinner at The Palm Grill features a flavorful wild game pate appetizer, warm goat cheese salad, seafood angel hair pasta (scallops, crab, shrimp and fish simmered in a saffron sauce with smoked salmon and white fish caviar), filet mignon and scampi provencale, and house specialty - seafood platter for two with fresh live Maine lobster, shrimp, fish, clams and oysters Rockefeller. For dessert, if you have room, sample the rose petal or lilikoi sorbet. A cup of Kona blend coffee, cappucino, or expresso completes your Palm Grill adventure. Tell your friends about one of Honolulu's legendary restaurants in-the-making.

**PHILLIP PAOLO'S ITALIAN RESTAURANT**   *Italian - Moderate*
2312 South Beretania St. (946-1163). Dinner only. Here's a novel idea - you're staying in Waikiki and you don't have a car. You see an ad for a little Italian restaurant in Honolulu and you want to go, but it's dark and you're a stranger in town. Then you see that this restaurant - Paolo's - has a limo service that will provide door-to-door service at an affordable price. (Paolo's limo service, 946-5588). This is only one of Paolo's many good ideas. The restaurant is in a bungalow, with tables inside, outside, under trees, on the porch - everywhere. Settings and service are informal but friendly - you're a dinner guest in an Italian home. The food is superb: the calamari (squid) marinara is sweet and tender; linguine with clam sauce is always in demand, and the seafood lasagna with crab and salmon has gotten rave reviews. Cheesecake and Kona coffee for dessert, then a relaxed, chauffeured ride back to your lodgings. Just in time for a walk toward the beach for a nightcap. Paolo's - remember the name.

**POTTERY STEAK & SEAFOOD RESTAURANT**   *American - Moderate*
3574 Waialae Ave. (735-5594). Dinner only. Inside this unique restaurant you'll find a potter's studio where the plates, cups, bowls and other pottery are made for use in the restaurant. Often you can watch the potters as they create the pieces. Take care here if you order an appetizer - several are so filling that they could be considered full dinners, especially the baked ham and spinach quiche. You'll also like either the fresh mushrooms in wine sauce or the jumbo shrimp. My favorite dish here is the boned Cornish game hen, stuffed with wild rice and served in its own clay pot, which is yours to keep. The steak and prawns on a bed of rice is also very tasty. Apple pie, cheesecake, or chocolate mousse somehow taste better when served on homemade crockery. And almost any plate, pot or mug you see is for sale. It's a country-style place, and one you'll really enjoy, especially if you leave with a souvenir clay pot from your dinner.

**STUART ANDERSON'S CATTLE COMPANY**   *American - Moderate*
1050 Ala Moana Blvd., in Ward Warehouse (523-9692), also 98-1262 Kaahumani St., Pearl City (487-0054). L, D. You've probably eaten at Stuart Anderson's at home. These two restaurants are typical of the chain - a pleasant meal of grilled steak on generous platters at down-home prices. However, no mainland Cattle Co. I've visited offers teriyaki sirloin steak marinated in a tangy sauce and served with fresh-grilled pineapple, lemon chicken, prepared tempura style, or filet of mahimahi. This is Anderson's Hawaiian style. And be sure to have the freshly brewed Kona-blend coffee with your rocky road pie or fresh-baked hot apple (homemade each day with fresh apples and sweet pastry crumbs, and served with sweet cream or vanilla ice cream). Chow time.

**THE WILLOWS** ★ *International - Moderate/Expensive*

901 Hausten St. (946-4808). L, D. A century and a half ago Hawaiian royalty entertained honored guests with lavish outdoor feasts in open-air thatched huts set around an ancient pond in the Moilili section of Honolulu. The spring that fills the pond was named after the Hawaiian creator-god, Kane, and is said to have healing powers. The spring flows into the pond from a hidden underground stream large enough to carry a canoe. Legends say that this subterranian stream was used as a secret passageway by warriors caught in battle, who could emerge undetected in the Manoa Valley several miles away.

This property was purchased by a local family, the Haustens, who began serving meals in the yard surrounding the pond in 1944. Gradually the tradition became a business, named after the beautiful trees that thrive near the water's edge. Today, the underground spring can still be seen (the entrance is protected by an iron grate), the pond is still fed by the healing waters of Kane (Ka-wai-a-Kane) Spring, and the age-old tradition of feasting under the willows continues, thanks to new owner and former manager of the prestigious Halekulani Hotel, Randy Lee.

The Willows is a magic tropical oasis of ancient Hawaiian grass houses hidden among jungle foilage around a central pond and waterfall. Each of these open hales (houses) offers a different dining atmosphere, reminiscent of old Hawaii. The chef, Kusuma Cooray, is a native of Sri Lanka who arrived in Hawaii after training in London and Paris. Her traditional Hawaiian curry, featuring chicken, shrimp, or vegetables, is an award winner you'll love. She makes the best chutneys in Honolulu, too.

The full lunch and dinner menu includes fresh oysters on half shell, The Willows "Prized Curry Salad," a "Paniolo Omelette" (a whopping mid-day special with ground beef, Maui onions, green peppers, and Portuguese sausage), lean strips of choice beef from the wok, sandwiches (try the "Missionaries' Mischief" - a double decker with crabmeat, bacon, and plump ripe avocado), and desserts that will attract you like a magnet (I missed the "Mile High Pie" and have regretted it ever since - don't make the same mistake).

Three features of The Willows deserve special mention. One is the Kama'aina Suite, possibly The Willows' finest feature. This room seats only 30 for one seating per evening, dinner only. The fixed price gourmet dinner ($42.50 per person) includes appetizer, entree (which changes monthly), a sorbet, a second entree, a salad, selections from a dessert cart, then coffee or tea. All who have eaten in this penthouse dining salon have given it an A+. Guests often spend three to four hours at the table. The second feature is Poi Thursday, an old-fashioned, Hawaiian luau with laulau, lomi salmon, poi, pipi daula (dried salt beef), salad and more. Third is The Willows Sunday Brunch (10am-1pm), a lavish buffet with fresh Island fruits and cheeses, hot baked breads, wilted spinach salad, cold meats, salmon steaks, stuffed egg florets, champagnes, sauteed mahimahi, chicken in puff pastry, saffron rice, apple crepes, lemon tarts, French pastries, petit fours, black forest torte, and soft Hawaiian music throughout the gardens.

## WINDOWS OF HAWAII
### REVOLVING RESTAURANT ★ *American - Moderate*
1441 Kapiolani Blvd. (941-9138), atop the Ala Moana Building at Ala Moana Center. L, D. America's first revolving restaurant (formerly called the La Ronde) serves New England cuisine with fresh fish, butcher-cut meats and fresh vegetables, homemade pastries and New England style ice creams. I'd suggest you try to come here soon after you arrive on O'ahu, perhaps for cocktails in late afternoon or for the champagne brunch served Saturday and Sunday 10am-2pm. The view from a window seat is the best inside view I've seen in Hawaii, because of the restaurant's location and the once-an-hour revolution of the restaurant. It is spectacular. Bring a city map so you can identify the streets and landmarks, and ask for the children's card showing highlights of the 360 degree view. A bird's eye view of the Island! The children's menu features a "Windowburger" for lunch and teriyaki chicken for dinner. Brunch entrees offer choice of eggs benedict, fluffy omelettes, seafood newberg, teriyaki, or beef bourguignon, plus access to the salad, fruit and other buffet selections.

## YANAGI SUSHI ★ *Japanese - Moderate*
762 Kapiolani Blvd. (537-1525). L, D. Sushi (finger-sized rolls of seasoned rice with a variety of condiments, usually wrapped in dried seaweed), is a Japanese art form. No matter what each little slice contains - cucumber, raw fish, vegetables, fried soybean curd - each slice is prepared with care to look and taste delicate. At Yanagi Sushi the master chefs prepare a mosaic of sushi for you to enjoy. The fish is very fresh, the vegetables are crisp and cold, and the rice is always tender. The tempura (mouth-sized chunks of fish or vegetables dipped in a flour and egg batter, then deep fried) is crisp and light, too. This is a small, plain restaurant that's always crowded because of the consistently excellent quality of ingredients and preparation. If you break the bonds of Waikiki and discover Yanagi Sushi just a few blocks down Kapiolani, you'll see a cross-section of all Honolulu there. And if you get full, take a bento home for a romantic midnight walk on the Waikiki beach tonight. Two meals in one, and both mouth-watering.

## SBARRO PIZZA ★ *Pizza - Moderate*

1415 Ala Moana Blvd., in the Makai Market (955-1665). 9am-9pm weekdays; 9:30am-6pm Sat.; 10am-5pm Sun. Before Sbarro, most people would have pointed out that Pizza Hut has very good pizza on Oʻahu. Pizza Hut is still very good pizza - the phone book lists 23 Pizza Hut locations from Aiea to Waikiki, and all around the island. But Sbarro has simply stolen the show - it has the best pizza on Oʻahu. Period. A Brooklyn, New York family started this fast-growing business thirty-some years ago. Everything is top quality. The dough is made fresh and hand-thrown. The toppings are liberally applied, and the sauces are made with fresh garlic, Romano cheese, imported Italian tomatoes, and the best olive oil. The whole island is beating a path to their door. And it's not expensive - whole pizzas range from $9 to $12. If you're shopping at Ala Moana (as we all do sooner or later) and you love pizza (available by the slice here, too!), remember the name Sbarro. It's a mouthfull.

## ALFRED'S AT CENTURY CENTER *International - Expensive*

1750 Kalakaua Ave. (955-5353), at Century Center. L, D. Named for its Swiss chef-owner Alfred Vollenweider, this restaurant has a varied menu with French, German, English, American mainland, and Hawaiian dishes. Veal, steaks, weinerschnitzel, fresh fish, crisp chilled salads with shrimp and apple, and European desserts such as souffle glace Grand Marnier, strawberries romanoff, black forest cake, German cheesecake, apple strudel, and caramel chantilly. A meal at Alfred's is a step into old Europe - a cultured atmosphere, soft music, and fine food.

## THE BLACK ORCHID *American - Expensive*

500 Ala Moana Blvd., 6D at Restaurant Row (521-3111). L, D. Have you heard about Restaurant Row? It's a brand new (1988) area on Ala Moana featuring upscale dining, shopping, and entertainment spots. Scheduled to open in stages, these are places you'll be hearing us talk about in *THE OʻAHU UPDATE* as they bloom: Sunset Grill, Rose City Diner, Paradise Bakery and Cafe, Marie Callender's, and many more. Studebakers and The Black Orchid are flagships of the group and were among the first to open. The Black Orchid restaurant is right out of "Magnum PI," Tom Selleck's long-running TV detective series filmed in Hawaii. Look for the Magnum PI memorabilia sprinkled throughout the restaurant. Colors, of course, black and orchids with neon colors used in some unusual ways. At the grand opening in mid-1988, part owner Tom Selleck described the Black Orchid's decor as "art deco of the 1930's combined with a contemporary look." When asked if diners would ever see him at his restaurant (there are four partners - Larry Manetti is among them), Selleck said, "This is a good excuse for me to come back to the place I love. I'll certainly eat here whenever I'm in town." Selleck also praised Hawaiian locals and visitors for adhering to the Hawaiian tradition of allowing celebrities maximum privacy in public places. Says Selleck, "No one likes to be interrupted in mid bite. People here are wonderful." One of Selleck's favorite dishes on the menu - "Black and Blue Ahi" appetizer. As for entrees, he likes them all, of course.

On the menu are some treats: baluga caviar and Maryland crab cakes might make Selleck revise his vote as best appetizer; warm spinach salad is excellent; entrees to consider include braised pheasant with pomegranate sauce and macadamia nuts; broiled papio (baby ulua - AKA pompano); and if you like it hot, don't miss the Thai scallops or red hot prawns.

And the name Black Orchid? Tom Selleck said that it came from the name of one of the early Magnum episodes - titled, what else, but "The Black Orchid."

Transporation is easy - take the Waikiki Trolley. You can spot Restaurant Row easily after dark, too - look for the bright red neon chord connecting its establishments. Look around, it's the place people are talking about.

**BYRON II STEAK HOUSE**   *Continental - Expensive*
1450 Ala Moana Blvd., at Ala Moana Center (949-8855). L, D. Decor is rich (panelled walls), staff is expert yet subtle, and the cuisine deserves all the praise it regularly receives. You can always get a good steak here. Among the most highly recommended dishes are Fettucine Alfredo, Caesar Salad, Steak Teriyaki, and Steak Diane. Byron's grasshopper pie is so famous you'll want to tell everyone back home that you ate at least one slice! Byron II is spendy, and always offers a great meal.

**NICHOLAS NICKOLAS, THE RESTAURANT**   *Continental - Expensive*
410 Atkinson Dr., 36th Floor Penthouse of the Ala Moana Americana Hotel (955-4466). Dinner only. You can spend an entire evening at Nicholas Nickolas - cocktails in the lounge at 5:30 (to 4am nightly), then dinner at the Restaurant (5:30-11:30pm), and afterward drinks and dancing when the Restaurant magically becomes a cabaret (after 11:30pm). Through it all you'll have one of the best wrap-around views of the Honolulu city lights far below you. On the menu, look for fettucini Alfredo and Korean ribs among the appetizers. Nick has a patent pending, no less, on his "Classic Salad." And try the Greek lamb chops, keawe-broiled steaks, fresh Island fish, or steak Hong Kong. For parties or large dinners, the Restaurant has a 35-seat, glass-enclosed, private dining room, "Nick's Lanai," overlooking the city. Come up for cocktails; you may find yourself staying for the evening.

**JOHN DOMINIS** ★   *Seafood - Expensive*
43 Ohui St., at Kewalo Basin (523-0955). Dinner only. Our dining survey asked local diners and tourists to name the place they would take guests for dinner in Honolulu if price were no object, and John Dominis was one of the most often-named restaurants in response. The setting above the charter boat harbor is gorgeous, with Diamond Head in the distance, and saltwater lobster ponds decorating the restaurant's interior. Come at an off-hour so you can enjoy a relaxed meal. Start with the tender, melt-in-your-mouth ahi sashimi or cherrystone clam appetizer, then order either lobster - the Dominis centerpiece - or one of the fresh Island fish that catch your eye in the restaurant's sumptuous central display. Steak, linguini and lamb fill out the menu for those few not here for the seafood. For a special occasion, enjoy cocktails and a unique dining experience at one of O'ahu's most often recommended fine dining locations.

## MAILE RESTAURANT ★ *Continental - Deluxe*

5000 Kahala Ave., lower level in the Kahala Hilton Hotel (734-2211). Dinner only; jacket required for gentlemen. "The maile leaf is to Hawaii what the laurel was to Rome: an honored symbol of victory, strength, growth, and good fortune. Once woven into leis to give glory to the alii, Hawaii's royal regents...today the garlands grace all celebrants. From the regal maile leaf the Maile Restaurant takes its name." So says the menu.

Down a staircase which curves around a volcanic rock wall of living orchids, through the dimly lit Maile Lounge, you enter the Kahala Hilton's signature restaurant, dedicated to the standard of excellence represented by its name. The beautifully-appointed dining room is windowless, allowing you to focus in on the intimate experience you are about to enjoy.

An appetizer of "Ragout of Escargot and Shrimp on Puff Pastry." "It starts with inspiration and escargot. Next, an herb and butter sauce accents an arrangement of shrimp and mushrooms on puff pastry. A sprinkling of shallots and freshly-ground pepper completes the picture." A chilled melon soup, served with shrimp. Then a fillet of Hawaiian sunfish on a saffron-butter sauce, with lobster dumplings in spinach leaves and black linguine. Or "Roast Duckling Waialae," served with a Grand Marnier orange sauce with lychees, burgundy peaches, banana and mandarin sections. To finish, a selection from the pastry cart, and Kona coffee. For those to whom it matters, a complete dinner with selection of appetizer, soup or salad, main course, dessert, and coffee or tea is $48. Come bathe in the liquid island luxury of the Maile Restaurant.

Note: One of O'ahu's finest Sunday Brunch experiences is offered weekly in both the Kahala Hilton's Hala Terrace, a multi-tiered open air dining terrace facing the ocean and lagoon (11am-2pm), and the Maile Terrace, overlooking the dolphin lagoon (10am-1pm). The menu at this dual-location brunch is extensive, and as exciting as that offered in the Maile Restaurant. Reservations required. Highly recommended.

The Plumeria Cafe and Bar, open to the public as are the Maile Room and Hala Terrace, serves light meals, pupus, and offers a full bar in a casual open-air setting. Open 11:30am to midnight.

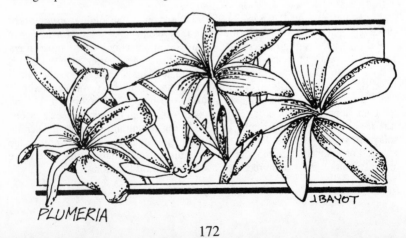

PLUMERIA

JBAYOT

**MICHEL'S AT THE COLONY SURF** ★ *French - Deluxe*
2895 Kalakaua Ave. (923-6552). B, L, D. Michel's has won many of the highest restaurant awards, including a Gold Plate from Cartier, the prestigious Travel/-Holiday Award every year since it opened in 1962, and the "Most Romantic Restaurant in the World" from CBS' Lifestyles of the Rich and Famous.

Its setting is spectacular, on the beach with wall-to-wall windows and the ocean only a few yards away. Its service is superb. Knowledgable waiters attend to your every desire with understated flair and charm. Its decor is simple and stylish, with crystal chandeliers, fine art and sculpture, and silver and china on white linen tablecloths. But it is the food which has brought Michel's its well-deserved notoriety. Breakfast features the renowned "Eggs Benedict Colony Surf," petit filet mignon and eggs, and crepes filled with fresh strawberries and orange slices. For lunch you might try the "Pate Maison Cheese Souffle," stuffed artichoke, or onaga (red snapper) broiled and served in sauce meuniere. Jackets are required for men at dinner, which offers a tantalizing "Lobster Bisque," "Carre D'Agneau Provencale" (rack of lamb for two with mint sauce), and "Plat Des Fruits de Mer" (Michel's famous seafood platter, with lobster, Alaskan king crab leg, Kahuku salt water prawns, shrimp, and opakapaka - pink snapper). Cheesecake, pies, tortes, and flambes will send you home satisfied. A good way to sample Michel's is to come to the Sunday Champagne Brunch. Open daily for breakfast and dinner; weekdays for lunch.

# SOUTHEAST OʻAHU

**BUENO NALO** ★ *Mexican - Inexpensive*
41-865A Kalanianaole Hwy., Waimanalo (259-7186). Dinner only; no reservations; no cocktails, wine, or beer; no credit cards. If you've travelled in Mexico, you've had the pleasure of walking into a cantina in an adobe building in a sleepy, hot town and finding an oasis of cool refreshing drinks, hospitable waitresses, and food that tasted so good that you soaked up the last little bit on your plate with your tortilla.

Bueno Nalo (combining "good" in Spanish with the last syllables of Waimanalo) is just such a cantina. Sitting squarely on the highway in quiet, rural Waimanalo, this simple two-room twenty table "Restaurant Mexicano" has the most realistic south-of-the-border atmosphere and some of the best-tasting Mexican food in the islands. Decor is hanging pinatas, ceiling fans, and bullfight posters. Tables are simply set and cloth covered. Yet somehow the place has a cantina magic about it - my chimichanga, a deep-fried burrito stuffed with tender grilled chicken and covered with salsa, guacamole and sour cream, filled the platter (and me) with an unforgettable combination of tastes and textures. The menu is simple: soups; tacos; tostadas; tamales; burritos; enchiladas; chimichangas; combination plates (taco, tamale, enchilada, and beans); "Special Delights" such as guacamole dip, two chile rellenos (fresh green chiles, peeled, roasted, stuffed with cheese, and fried in egg batter) or huevos rancheros (fried eggs on a corn tortilla covered with refried beans, cheese, and a ranchero sauce); and desserts (I didn't have room), including pina colada cheesecake and flan (custard). They'll box up your order to go, if you're on the road. But hopefully you can slow down, relax and take time to savor this Mexican oasis in the lovely country town of Waimanalo. Viva el Bueno Nalo!

### SHOWBIZ PIZZA PLACE    *Pizza - Inexpensive*

5200 Kalanianaole Hwy. (373-2151), in Aina Haina Shopping Center. L, D. Another pizza extravaganza that kids love, with games to play, buttons to push, and loud, loud music. The pizza is good but the real draw here is the entertainment for kids. Let us know how you, and they, liked it.

### STROMBOLI'S RISTORANTE    *Italian - Inexpensive*

7192 Kalanianaole Hwy., in Koko Marina Shopping Center, Hawaii Kai (396-6388). L, D. Koko Marina is fast becoming another Restaurant Row, with many new and interesting restaurants which we'll be exploring in *THE O'AHU UPDATES*. Examples: John Richards, La Hacienda, Domino's, Sizzler, Yummy Korean Barbeque, McDonalds, Baskin Robbins, J. Higby's Yogurt & Treat Shoppe, Zippy's and Mrs. Field's Cookies. A brilliant star in this new constellation of eateries is Stromboli's, recently chosen "Favorite New Restaurant" by readers of *Honolulu* magazine. Named for the famous Italian active volcano, Stromboli's looks out through huge windows over Kuapa Pond, Hawaii Kai, Mariner's Ridge, and the beautiful Hahiaone Valley. Your family will enjoy Stromboli's concept of eating Italian family-style - sharing a tureen of steaming soup, serving helpings of salad from a single large bowl placed on your table, breaking bread together. The menu: freshly-made pasta, traditional sauces, "Vitello Parmigiana," "Scampi Monte Carlo," pizza, prawns, lobster, and good wines. Complete dinners from $7.50. As you tour O'ahu, stop in and say hello to owner-chef Paul Sikora, general manager Robert Fierek, and assistant manager Bill Vanderbyl.

### DOCKSIDE PLANTATION    *American - Moderate*

377 Keahole St. (395-2930), in Hawaii Kai Shopping Center. Lunch is served from 11am-3pm and dinner from 5pm-11pm daily. This Dolly Parton creation reflects her upbeat charm and desire to show you "Southern hospitality" in a down-home setting. There are several dining rooms, including Dolly's Room, an open-air gazebo, the Maitre D's Room, providing mature couples a place to enjoy quiet old-fashioned meals, and a veranda-style porch over the water. Every table has a view, and the overall atmosphere is that of a Southern plantation, with a touch of Cajun, tropical atmosphere, and all with Dolly's imprint. When she is in town she greets guests and is very much in evidence at the restaurant.

### SWISS INN  ★    *Continental - Moderate*

5730 Kalanianaole Hwy. (377-5447), in Niu Valley Shopping Center. Dinner only. Here's a place you can get a gourmet meal at less than gourmet prices. Chef Martin Wyss left the Kahala Hilton in 1982 to open Swiss Inn with wife Jeanie. He has created a fine restaurant here. Decor is European; complete dinners include soup, salad, entree, and beverage. Specialties vary, but often include such delicacies as weinerschnitzel, pork sausage, veal, rainbow trout, and excellent salads. This place is fast becoming the spot to drive to from Honolulu. The Niu Valley is beautiful; only twenty minutes' from Waikiki.

# CENTRAL O'AHU

**DOT'S IN WAHIAWA** ★ *Japanese/American - Inexpensive*
130 Mango St., Wahiawa (622-4115). B, L, D; open 6:30am-9pm daily; no
reservations, no credit cards. This place is a local institution - would you believe
it opened in 1938 and has been going strong ever since? It's true. And one
glance at the menu tells you why - great food at low prices. Examples: house
specialties teriyaki beef steak or large shrimp tempura on a complete dinner for
under $8; "Special Plate" (spare ribs, teri chicken, and minute steak) $5.95;
stuffed seafood crepes (with scallops, crabmeat, shrimp, lobster, or mahimahi)
only $6.95. Full Japanese dinners, sandwiches, and a la carte entrees also on the
menu. Dot's cream and fruit pies are fresh baked daily, and the salad bar on Fri.
and Sat. evenings (5-9 pm) is worth planning your meal around. Remember
Dot's when you're in the Wahiawa area. It's one of O'ahu's best bets.

**HELEMANO PLANTATION RESTAURANT** *American - Inexpensive*
64-1510 Kam Hwy., next to the Dole Pavilion, Haleiwa (622-3929). Luncheon
only, 10:30am-2:30pm; no reservations. This is a unique place on O'ahu, set up
to offer productive employment to Hawaii's handicapped citizens. Run by
Opportunities for the Retarded, Inc., the five-acre farm grows flowers and
vegetables, trees, and other tropical plantings. After a stroll through the beauti-
fully-kept grounds, enjoy a full luncheon at the open-air restaurant. Specials
each day. Then visit the gift shop and support this one-of-a-kind plantation.

**KEMOO FARM** ★ *American - Inexpensive*
1718 Wilikina Dr., across from Schofield Barracks, Wahiawa (621-8481). L, D.
Pronounced Kay-MO-o, this farm began in 1909, and opened a country store on
this site in 1916. The farm operation was discontinued in 1934, and the present
dining room was built in 1935. The history of Kemoo Farm is closely intertwined with that of Schofield Barracks. One staff member, Margaret Itagaki,
started working at Kemoo Farm as a teenager and still comes in to arrange the
flowers after 61 years. In fact, General Westmoreland comes in to the restaurant
occasionally and requests the same type of salad that Margaret first served him
in the 1930's!

Servings are family style, with fresh trout, duck, and a variety of Hawaiian
entrees, including roast duck, scampi, and red snapper. Twice a week, on Sun.
and Wed., a buffet brunch with the legendary entertainer Charles K. L. Davis
and friends is offered in an old-fashioned dining room overlooking the Lake
Wilson reservoir (which supplies 50,000,000 gallons of water a day to irrigate
local sugar cane fields and is one of O'ahu's best fishing holes).

Please try the smooth Keoki coffee liqueur after your meal. Then look for
several items in the antique filled lobby: a sideboard from pineapple king James
Dole's home, and one of the first electric laundry irons in Hawaii. And be sure
to ask about the famous "Mauna Loa Happy Cake," baked here and sold all over
the world. On your way to North Shore, take time to have lunch (Sunday, if you
can) in this living landmark of an era gone by.

# NORTH SHORE

**CAFE HALE'IWA** ★ *American - Inexpensive*
66-460 Kam Hwy., Haleiwa (637-5516). B, L; no reservations, no credit cards. No ritzy decor, just the best breakfasts in town and lots of locals and surfers who can tell you about surf conditions and current happenings. House specials include omelettes, French toast, whole wheat banana pancakes, and quiche. Early bird specials from 6-7am. Closes at 2pm. They even serve homemade refried beans. One of North Shore's best eateries.

**KUA AINA SANDWICH** ★ *American - Inexpensive*
66-214 Kam Hwy., in Haleiwa across from the courthouse (637-6067). Open daily 11am-9pm, no reservations. Five tables in, three outside this cozy sandwich, burger, and salad haven which has been winning converts since 1975. "Best burgers on O'ahu," some writers have stated. Whatever you order here will be good, and you can get it to eat here or to go. Recommendations: the World's Best char-grilled, fresh ground beef burger, with manoa lettuce, tomato, grilled onions and, believe it or not, a splash of vermouth! The teriyaki chicken, mahimahi burger, tuna and avocado, and roast beef are mouth-watering, too. Don't miss the home made French fries. Ever had a pineapple burger? They've got that as well. Look for the hand-carved wooden sign.

**PIZZA BOB'S** *American - Inexpensive*
66-197 Kam Hwy., Haleiwa Shopping Plaza (637-5095). No credit cards. Probably the best pizza on North Shore, and a local surfer hangout. Lots of pizza combinations, the most requested being the New York, New York (pepperoni, Italian sausage, spicy beef, mushrooms, bell peppers, onions, olives, and heaps of cheddar and romano cheese). Pizza Bob's also serves huge sandwiches, such as "The Plaza" (thinly-sliced ham with tomatoes, lettuce, sprouts, cheese, and onions) or "The Brooklyn" (meatballs, melted cheese, fresh lettuce, and onions). Also available: full Italian dinners, soup of the day, salads, daily specials, vegetarian spaghetti, great beverages (wine coolers, Moosehead beer, Michelob Dark on tap, and wine by the glass or litre), and desserts. Eat in or take out, you'll want to drive back to North Shore just to have another one.

**STEAMERS** *Seafood - Inexpensive*
Haleiwa Shopping Plaza, Haleiwa (637-5071). L, D, no reservations. Possibly the most elegant dinner spot in Haleiwa, with lots of bevelled glass, natural wood, and an outdoor lanai dining area off the main dining salon and open cocktail lounge. Appetizers are extensive here, and include steamed clams, potato skins, onion rings, teriyaki top sirloin tidbits, and deep fried calamari. An excellent luncheon choice is the spinach salad, with bay shrimp, feta cheese, garlic croutons, and honey-mustard dressing. Entrees feature Linguine Nantua (fresh pasta with lobster chunks), Steamers Vegetarian Medley (fresh Island vegetables prepared in a variety of styles), Sauteed Scallops with Mushrooms and Gruyere Sauce, and Spiny Rock Lobster Tail. Sunday Brunch at Steamers, 10am-3pm, offers all you want of their special roast beef, BBQ Pork Ribs, omelettes, fresh fruits, salads, muffins, homemade jams, fresh juices, hot breads, pies, cakes, tortes, tarts, coffees, and teas. See you there.

## TURTLE BAY HILTON
## AND COUNTRY CLUB ★ *Seafood/American - Moderate to Expensive*

56-576 Kam Hwy., Kahuku (293-8811 or 1-800-HILTONS). B, L, D; reservations for dinner only. When you tour rural O'ahu, do come explore this growing luxury resort, where a United States president and the premier of Japan once held summit talks, and where two or three more luxury hotels are planned on the immense 808 acres of ocean front land owned by the hotel.

You can find breakfast, lunch, dinner, cocktails and pupus, and late night music and dancing at Turtle Bay's three restaurants and two lounges.

The signature restaurant is the Cove, open for dinner only, and featuring seafood, with a choice of two fresh catches of the day. Menu includes sashimi, veal, fresh ahi, crabmeat soup with coconut, and Cove Coffee, an after-dinner concoction of coffee, spices, and whipped cream. Entertainment nightly in this formal restaurant overlooking Turtle Bay.

Palm Terrace, overlooking the pool, serves a la carte and buffet breakfast, lunch, and dinner from 6:30am - 11pm daily. My favorite, which I'm told brings people from all over Hawaii, is the lobster fruit salad. I could live on that dish!

The outstanding Turtle Bay Sunday Brunch, one of O'ahu's best and well worth the 45-minute drive from the city, is held from 10am-2pm, complete with champagne, in the Sea Tide Room, with a spectacular view of the ocean and coastline.

The informal sandwich/salad bar is open in the Bay View Lounge daily from 11am-2:30pm. They also have live entertainment and pupus nightly. And the Green Turtle Lounge in the lower lobby offers tropical and standard cocktails; open 11am-10pm.

So any time your itinerary puts you in the North Shore area, plan to come enjoy the cuisine that Turtle Bay chefs are preparing for you this very minute. You'll fall in love with Turtle Bay!


## JAMESON'S BY THE SEA ★ *Seafood-Moderate to Expensive*

652-540 Kamehameha Hwy., Haleiwa (637-4336). Lunch, dinner and cocktails. Reservations. Jameson's seafood, fresh from Hawaiian waters daily, is matched by one of the most stunning sunset views on the Island. Less than an hour's drive from Honolulu, Jameson's will waken your tastebuds with an appetizer of smooth salmon pate or delightful Yokohama soup made with fresh spinach and cream. Famous Manoa lettuce or Maui onion salad might be followed by an entree of fresh ulua (Hawaiian jack fish) lightly breaded and sauteed to a golden brown. Or try the shrimp curry,served in a mild curry sauce with bacon and Mango Chutney. The fresh Au (swordfish) Ahi (tuna) and steaks are also first rate. Wine, imported and domestic beers, tropical drinks and fresh fruit daiquiris will complement your meal. My after dinner Keoke Coffee (a combination of freshly brewed Kona Coffee, brandy and Kahulua), completed a dinner and sunset experience I'll long remember, and highly recommend.

# WINDWARD SIDE

**AHI'S KAHUKU RESTAURANT**   *International - Inexpensive*
Main Camp Rd., next to Kahuku Sugar Mill, Kahuku (293-5650). Breakfast
Mon-Sat. 7am-10am, lunch Mon-Sat. 10:30am-3pm, dinner, Wed-Sat. 3pm-
9pm., no reservations. This historic building used to house the Plantation Tavern
at the Kahuku Sugar Mill in the late 1800's. Now it belongs to the friendly,
akamai family of Ahi and Cherlyn Logan, who manage it with the help of their
talented children and such friends as Mairicio Ramos, who began work at the
mill when he was 27 years old and only left when it closed 25 years later.

One end of the building is the newly remodeled restaurant, kitchen is in the
middle, and the other end is their Mom and Pop store, deli, and game arcade for
the keikis (kids). Atmosphere is authentic old plantation village, staff is as nice
as can be, and the food is super. For breakfast, try the two eggs, choice of meat,
juice, pancakes, and coffee. A cheeseburger deluxe, grilled ham and cheese, or
my old standby - fried saimin for lunch sounds good. For dinner, a complete
meal of soup or salad, rolls, hot vegetable, rice or mashed potato, dessert, fruit
drink, tea or coffee and entree of: spaghetti and meat sauce, chile con carne and
franks, grilled teriyaki butterfish, breaded beef cutlet with brown gravy, and
house specialty shrimp scampi fresh as fresh can be from the famous aquafarm
only minutes away. Daily specials and plate lunches, too. When you tour O'ahu
and you visit the Kahuku Mill, stop in at Ahi's Kahuku Restaurant.

**FLORENCE'S**   *Italian - Inexpensive*
20 Kainehe St., Kailua (261-1987). L, D. This small cafe has been dishing up
the spaghetti since the mid 1950's, and you can see why when you hear that a
complete meal, with soup, salad, bread, drink, and the special entree of the day
costs less than $10. And the food is wonderful. If you're in the Kailua-Kaneohe
area, and you've spent lots of money shopping, don't worry. Have dinner here.

**HUEVOS**   *International - Inexpensive*
In Kahuku Plantation Village (293-1016), just one-fourth mile toward Kahuku
from the Sugar Mill, down a dirt road on the makai side of Kam Hwy. Watch
for sign on highway or ask for directions at Kahuku Sugar Mill; B, L, daily
7am-1pm, dinner Thurs-Sat. 5:30-9pm., no reservations. Someone at the Kahuku
Sugar Mill said to me, "You've got to eat at Huevos ("eggs" in Spanish). The
platters are huge and everything's good." So I looked for it. Down one dusty dirt
road, up another. No luck. Finally I pulled out onto Kam Hwy. to ask someone
and there was a little sign on a pole. I did find it, and had a wonderful, filling
breakfast. They close by 2 pm and reopen for dinner. I had the "House Special,"
a three-egg omelette filled with mushrooms, bell peppers, onions, tomatoes,
zucchini, cheese, with rice or potatoes and your choice of toast or two buttermilk
pancakes. I saw others eating steak and eggs, a juicy-looking breakfast sandwich, pancakes, and (if I had only known) French toast. I couldn't finish my
omelette, there was so much of it. But I had fun trying! Simple, country decor,
clean, very nice folks in charge, and family-oriented. I'd go back here in a
minute.

**KAILUA OKAZUYA**    *Japanese - Inexpensive*
440 Uluniu, Kailua. This little gem of a restaurant specializes in donburi (steamed rice topped with cooked meat, fish and/or vegetables, served in a porcelain bowl). They also serve sushi and plate lunches. Clean restaurant, very friendly staff, and tasty, beautifully prepared food. Eat in or take out.

**PANIOLO CAFE
            AND COUNTRY CLUB**  ★    *Hawaiian/American - Inexpensive*
53-146 Kam Hwy. (237-8521), on the highway in Punaluu. L, D, no reservations. Put on your boots and vest, cowpokes, 'cause you're about to enter the "home of the professional party'rs!"

*"The first cowboy arrived in Hawaii in 1830, brought by King Kamehameha III from old California to teach Hawaiians how to ride the horses given to the King as a present, and how to herd the cattle which had arrived 36 years earlier. Hawaiians called these immigrant cowboys "Paniolos" from the word "Espaniol" meaning Spaniard. From these beginnings the Hawaiian-style cowboys, or Paniolos, spread to cattle ranches throughout the Islands. With great respect, the Paniolo Cafe salutes the Paniolo of old and new Hawaii."*
So says the menu.

Every night here is an old time, down home country style Hawaiian Paniolo western jamboree, with good ranch food, live, loud music you can dance to, and enough good family fun to make you want to get up and dance. They now have a broil-your-own grill with steaks, kabobs, mahimahi, ribs, beef brisket and chicken to flame broil. From the kitchen comes whopping burgers (only the best beef!), beef brisket, seafood platter, and yes, Virginia they do serve rattlesnake chili with 100 percent pure rattlesnake meat direct from Sweetwater, Texas. Don't overlook the 20-item salad bar either! Or the pupu menu. Need a drink, stranger? Let the bartender set you up with a banana margarita, a 16-ounce original "Island Mai Tai," or a "Paniolo Chi Chi" so big it comes in a mason jar! As if that's not enough, there's live Country/Western and Hawaiian Paniolo music Friday and Saturday nights from 8pm to midnight. These folks never quit. On their 3.7 acres they offer catered parties, a sprinkler volleyball court, an outside stage, and huge luau picnics. Wednesday is ladies' night, with special live entertainment and half-price drinks for gals. Every Sunday afternoon from 3-7pm held inside is the foot stompin'est jam session you've ever seen. Try to be there for this one - it's a shin kicker!

They have a tradition here at the Paniolo Cafe that you'll want to get in on. Everyone brings their business or personal card (or makes one) and staples it to a wall or ceiling. There are thousands; and owner Jeton told me that he regularly watches in amazement as busloads of tourists will rush into the cafe to search for the card of a friend and put up their own. I couldn't resist. I put mine on the doorframe directly above your head as you go from the saloon outside onto the lanai. See if you can find me! And be sure to bring a card of your own to post! You get to choose your own spot, too. Great idea. When you need to use the lua, check out (if not occupied) the most outrageous bathrooms on O'ahu. They've added a few touches that will make you look twice.
*This is a great place, pardner.*

## SOMEPLACE ELSE  *International - Inexpensive*

33 Aulike St., Kailua (263-8833). L, D; no reservations. Since it opened in mid 1986, this increasingly popular family restaurant has built a loyal clientele by offering creative dishes with quality ingredients at moderate prices to O'ahuans who were tired of having to choose either high restaurant prices or assembly-line tastes, and were looking for "someplace else" to dine out. The restaurant is clean, bright, and unassuming, with booths and chairs on a lower level; lounge a few steps up. Local owner/operators Kern Rogerson and Sal Ricca have created a fascinating and fresh menu with: salads (make mine the Tostada salad on a flour tortilla shell with refried beans, lettuce, cheese, shredded beef, black olives, diced tomatoes, Guacamole and sour cream); sandwiches (a Kalua Cheese Steak and sandwich please, with thinly-sliced beef over grilled onions and bell peppers, mozzarella cheese on a French roll; Mexican specialities such as "Pick a Dilla" (build your own fillings in a double grilled tortilla); pastas (lasagna); chicken cordon bleu, BBQ ribs, and much more. Even a "Something Else Platter" with loads of seafood and crispy deep fried vegetables with dipping sauces, enough for a small army and priced at only $18.95.

They have live entertainment to accompany your meal from 10pm-2am every Wed to Sat; a reduced price Happy Hour Mon-Fri. from 4-6:30pm; and late night Happy Hour every Mon. and Tues. night from 10pm to 2am. On Sunday there's a full-spread Sunday Brunch from 9am-2pm. So why don't you come over the hill to downtown Kailua and find Someplace Else to eat. You won't regret it!

## YUM YUM TREE  *American - Inexpensive*

Four locations: 970 North Kalaheo Ave., Kailua (254-5861); Westridge Shopping Center (487-2487); Kahala Mall (737-7938); and Ward Centre, 1200 Ala Moana Blvd., Honolulu (523-9333). B, L, D; no reservations, senior discount. This is certainly a local favorite for families and seniors. In a very informal restaurant-coffeeshop atmosphere, the Yum Yum Tree serves very good hamburgers, omelettes, quiche, steaks, salads, pasta, and specials.

But...its claim to fame is the dessert menu. Fresh, nine-inch pies, pastries, and ice cream concoctions. Many times you've looked for a place to meet a friend and have something a little sweet with your coffee, right? Come to the Yum Yum Tree. The setting in Kailua near the canal is especially beautiful. All locations are fresh, squeaky clean, and full of the most tempting aromas!

## BUZZ'S ORIGINAL STEAK HOUSE  *American - Moderate*

Three locations: 413 Kawailoa Rd., Kailua (261-4661); off University Ave. at 2535 Coyne St., Moiliili (944-9781); and 98-751 Kuahao Place, Pearl City (487-6465). Dinner only.

The first Buzz's to open in the mid 1960's and still the best is very near the beach in the Lanikai section of Kailua, fronting Kailua Beach Park. The decor will take you back to the grass shacks of old Hawaii; you'll dine on kiawe-broiled steaks, ribs, and seafood, with an excellent salad bar and garlic bread. This is a spot Kama'ainas have been coming to for decades; worth the 40-minute drive across the Pali.

**CROUCHING LION INN**   *American - Moderate*
51-666 Kamehameha Hwy., Kaaawa (237-8511). Lunch 10:30am-3:30pm, dinner 5-9pm. First, stand in the parking lot beside the Inn, look mauka, and you'll see the unmistakable profile of a reclining lion formed by the volcanic peak rising high above the beach. Then enter the massive, timbered baronial hall of the Crouching Lion, and imagine yourself a traveller in old Hawaii as you enjoy the hospitality of the house at a table in front of the huge walk-in stone fireplace. You'll love this restaurant which opened in 1957 in an historic Kaaawa residence on a bluff overlooking the beautiful white-sand beach. "Slavonic Steak" has been the house specialty here for as long as anyone can remember - and still a favorite worth ordering. Sandwiches, salads, homemade vegetable soup, grilled meats and fish round out the menu. I can't go to the Crouching Lion without sitting outside on the covered portico for a dessert of Kona coffee and the smoothest coconut cream pie anywhere. Come before or after peak hours (when the parking lot isn't packed with tour busses). Watch for an empty lot, and you'll have a leisurely meal you won't soon forget. And before you go, take one last look at the Lion.

**HAIKU GARDENS**   *American - Moderate*
46-336 Haiku Rd., Kaneohi (247-6671). L, D. What a beautiful setting for a cool meal on a warm day! Serene lily ponds, lush tropical foliage and a close-up view of the craggy Ko'olau Mts. have made this spot one of O'ahu's favorite wedding sites. You'd never suspect, standing in this tiny hidden valley, that a major city lies just over the hill. These gardens are open to the public daily from 8:30am-6pm, in good weather. Closed Christmas and New Year's Day.

The restaurant is built around one of the area's early estate homes; the roof and kitchen walls are part of the original residence. Lunch is served in and outside from 11:30am-2:30pm Tues-Sat., dinner from 5:30-8pm Tues-Sun. A very popular Sunday Brunch is available from 10:30am-2:30pm. Specialty of the house is a hot platter of "Mandarin Spareribs," prepared with an authentic Mandarin flavor and smoked in an oaken barrel, served with pineapple, banana fritter, and fried rice. For lunch the "Monte Cristo" or "Avocado Club" (in season) sandwich is just right. There's also a low-cal lunch of lean meat or fish, cottage cheese in tomato, and fresh fruit slices on lettuce. That will leave room for the house specialty dessert - "Haupia (coconut) Cake"!

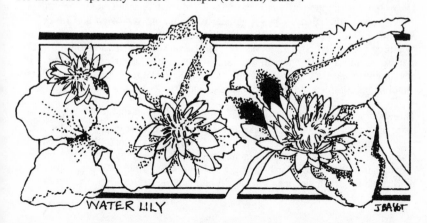

WATER LILY

Lanai tables overlook the valley (a scene right out of "Fantasy Island") and the staff will make you feel as though you're dining at your own summer estate. They have reduced-price keiki plates, too. If you're with your family, this is a perfect luncheon or dinner haven, with plenty of time and space to wander along the garden paths before you leave.

## L'AUBERGE SWISS ★ *Swiss - Moderate*
117 Hekili St., Kailua (262-4835). Dinner only, Wed. to Sun. European gasthaus (guesthouse) made its reputation with unique crepes, stuffed with such delicacies as crabmeat or mushrooms, and covered with a rich sauce. You can squint your eyes and imagine the Ko'olau Mountains are the Alps and that you are eating in snowy Switzerland. Choose from French, German, and Italian dishes which represent different parts of the Swiss culture. From Germany: weinerschnitzel, bratwurst, and potato dumplings. From Italy: chicken piccata (breast of chicken in a mushroom tomato sauce on a bed of pasta), sauteed scallops, and osso bucco (veal in a tomato-wine sauce). From France comes homemade pate, escargot bourguignonne, and the signature crepes. Other specialties: trout, and "Oysters Rockefeller." Desserts are a specialty here - a flourish of chocolate, apples, cinnamon, vanilla, and fresh fruit (try the pears in chocolate sauce, or the deep-fried apple slices in cinnamon and vanilla).

This tiny hideaway (only 40 seats) is one of O'ahu's best restaurants. So drive to the Pali, let the wind blow your hair straight, then on to Kailua to eat at L'Auberge Swiss, and get totally blown away.

## ORSON'S BOURBON HOUSE *International/Seafood - Moderate*
5 Hoolai, Hailua (262-2306). L, D. A taste of old New Orleans and Mardi Gras is alive and well at this plantation house restaurant with Southern charm and hospitality. You'll dine in a sumptuous vermillion room, amidst greenery and antiques. The menu has a wide variety of excellent selections - including "Chicken Rochambeau," sauteed fresh fish, prime rib, and a superior veal entree. Orson's is one Kailua restaurant whose patrons regularly come from all across O'ahu to enjoy the chef's unusual blend of tastes and textures.

## PAT'S AT PUNALUU *International - Moderate*
53-567 Kamehameha Hwy., Hauula (293-8502). B, L, D; (Sunday Brunch 11am-3pm). I stopped at Pat's in rural Windward Punaluu years ago on my travels around the island. I had a wonderful Kalua pig sandwich and fresh fruit. Recently (1988) they've renovated the balmy beachfront dining area - it now has gleaming natural wood, tile, brass, the most handsome driftwood furniture I've ever seen, and a huge open-air bar and lounge that's bright and friendly. Pat's has an entire tourist center here, with this "new" restaurant, an extensive lodge-motel-cabin complex, a full travel agency, and a well-stocked grocery-gift store.

There's a very private beach you can walk along after enjoying your meal, and there are colorful tee-shirts to take home to your niece or grandson. The dinner menu features such specialties as "Guava Glazed Lamb," "Kahuku Shrimp Curry," and chocolate macadamia nut pie. And ask someone in your party to order one of Pat's oven fresh tarts - a favorite since 1945! Pat's is a hideaway worth finding. It's a sleeper - one you'll be glad you discovered.

# PEARL HARBOR-EWA

**BRANDY'S BAR & GRILL**    *American - Inexpensive*
4510 Salt Lake Blvd., in Stadium Mall (486-4066). L, D; no reservations. When you're in the Aloha Stadium area for a sports event or to browse at the flea market, stop in across the street and visit the best dart-thrower's tavern on O'ahu. Men and women throwers and dart leagues. This is where the major dart tournaments are held, and where they'll be glad to teach you the game. Dart equipment is for sale, too. Food is great here - full lunches and dinners include "Brandy's Special Chicken," marinated in their secret sauce and served over crisp greens. Soups, salads (the stuffed tomato with tuna or turkey is terrific), sandwiches, burgers, fried noodles, fried rice with an egg and Portuguese sausage, even bentos (Japanese cold boxed lunches). This is a good, friendly place to relax, sip some suds, throw a dart or two, and meet the folks. And they'll sell you a T-shirt to remember your visit, if you like.

**CHUCK E. CHEESE'S PIZZA TIME THEATRE**    *Pizza - Inexpensive*
98-1258 Kaahumani, suite 101, at Times Square at Waimalu (488-8487). L, D; birthday party reservations suggested. You know Chuck E. Cheese - it's very much the same here as it is in your home town: continuous stage shows, pizza, sandwiches, broasted chicken, salad bar, make-your-own sundaes, soft drinks and beer, latest video games and kids' rides. Sound familiar? If you have kids and they have a special occasion, this is a place we're sure you want to know about. Tokens and a contained, well-monitored, and clean play area make this a favorite of the younger set. And Chuck E. Cheese himself will make a personal appearance to pose for pictures, so bring the flash.

**ELENA'S**    *Filipino - Inexpensive*
Four locations: 94-300 Farrington Hwy., Waipahu (671-3279); 70 Kukui St., Wahiawa (621-6388); 2153 North King St., Honolulu (845-0340); and Phase II, Pearlridge Center (488-2559). B, L, D, no reservations, no beer, wine or cocktails. You'll be able to find such Filipino dishes as oxtail stew, spiced pork sausage, lumpia (chopped meat and vegetables wrapped in a thin flour shell and deep fried), paella (seafood stew), sari sari (mixed vegetables and meat), and halo halo (a milk custard dessert containing fruit). Elena's is a very popular spot and a perfect place to sample quality Filipino cooking.

# LEEWARD COAST

**MAKAHA DRIVE IN**    *American - Inexpensive*
84-1150 Farrington Hwy., Makaha (696-4811). No reservations, no credit cards. This is one of the Leeward Coast's excellent local plate lunch drive-ins, where you can get a solid, flavorful meal at a rock-bottom price. Order the teriyaki chicken, pork, or mahimahi, and watch for daily specials. Another similar spot is the Nanakuli Inn, 87-2110 Farrington Hwy. (668-7878). If you're friendly, they'll go out of their way to help you find an address, beach access, or rental agency. These small, locally-owned plate lunch stops used to be all over O'ahu before the days of McDonald's; they are a part of Hawaii's past, and an experience you'll not want to miss.

**RED BARON'S PIZZA**    *Pizza - Inexpensive*
86-120 Farrington Hwy., Waianae Mall Shopping Center (969-2690). Good hot, thick pizza, salads, soft drinks and beer. Go when it's not crowded.

**RUSTY'S COAST CAFE**    *American - Inexpensive*
87-064 Farrington Hwy., in Maili Marketplace, Maili (696-6345). B, L, D. Although I've not eaten here, I've heard from folks who have that it is very nice. Breakfast served from 9am-11:30am Sat. and Sun. only, luncheon 11am-3pm, dinner from 5pm-9:30pm. I'll be able to offer you my opinion in *THE O'AHU UPDATE*. Maili is the second community you pass (after Nanakuli) driving on Farrington Hwy. toward Kaena Point on the Leeward Coast.

**FOGCUTTER**    *American - Moderate*
84-111 Orange St., Makaha (695-9404). L, D. Informal atmosphere, good steaks, ribs, and seafood make this restaurant one of Makaha's most popular.

**KAALA ROOM**    ★    *Continental - Moderate/Deluxe*
84-626 Makaha Valley Rd., Sheraton Makaha Resort and Country Club, Waianae (695-9511). Dinner only. This signature dining room is scheduled to undergo major renovation, so we'll have to wait and see how the changes affect it. Rumor is that it will be enlarged, with one of its lava-rock walls removed to permit a more open space and atmosphere. Currently the romantic Kaala Room, nearby Mount Kaala is the highest point on O'ahu, serves elegant continental dinner. When you come to the Leeward Coast to watch the surfing championships, to visit the wonderful beaches, or to enjoy the scenery and sunsets, come to Makaha Resort for a dinner in the famous Kaala Room, or a breakfast, lunch or lite dinner in the Pikake Cafe adjacent to the Olympic size swimming pool. Snacks are also available at this informal restaurant. You can have cocktails and pupus at the Lobby Lounge on the spot planned for expansion for the Kaala Room. When it occurs, look for the Lobby Lounge on the hotel's lower level.

The Sheraton Makaha Resort offers the most varied and elegant dining on the Leeward Coast. It also has the Island's finest golf course and one of Hawaii's best restored heiaus (ancient temples), Kaneakai Heiau, which you can arrange to visit by inquiring at the Sheraton Makaha Resort front desk, or by calling 695-9511. Advance reservations are required.

LOKELANI

# LUAUS

The average price for luaus ranges from $35 - $45.

**CHUCK MACHADO'S LUAU** ★ *Moderate*
Located beside the pool at the Outrigger Waikiki Hotel (921-4500). Reservations required. Held Fri., Sun., and Tues. evenings at 7pm for approximately two hours. Approximately 200-300 people served. This all-you-can-eat-and-drink luau was launched in 1963. Guests sit at long tables, and are served lomi lomi salmon, fresh Island fruits, excellent Kalua pig, chicken thighs, fresh Waimanalo corn-on-the-cob, mahimahi, coconut cake, and of course poi. The Polynesian show is well done, and hosted by Doug Mossman, who appeared on "Hawaii Five-O" and "Hawaiian Eye." This is a popular luau because it is on the beach, with no bus ride or waiting. It's small compared to other luaus, and requires only a two hour investment. Don't be surprised to see a huge audience watching and listening from hotel lanais, from the beach nearby, and from restaurants overlooking the scene. This is the best luau to take kids to, especially if you're staying in Waikiki.

**GERMAINE'S LUAU** *Expensive*
Located beachfront at Campbell Industrial Park on the Leeward Coast, 35 miles from Waikiki (40 minute drive); transportation by bus with pickup at major Waikiki hotels. Reservations required, (949-6626 or 941-3338). Seven nights a week; approx. 4 hours, serves 200-300. This all-you-can-eat-and-drink luau involves a bus ride to the site (with adult entertainment on board), a welcome lei and drink, torchlight ceremony, imu (cooking pit) ceremony, sit-down meal, and Polynesian Show Extravaganza. If you want to travel to a secluded beach, and don't want to spend six hours (as Paradise Cove requires), this is your best bet.

**PARADISE COVE LUAU** ★ *Expensive*
Located beachfront on the Campbell estate, Leeward Coast. Transportation by bus from Waikiki. Reservations required (945-3539). Seven nights a week, approx. 5-1/2 to 6 hours including bus ride. Serves 500-1,500. This largest commercial luau is the only one which offers guests the opportunity to participate in ancient Hawaiian games, to help with a hukilau (literally, huki - to pull, plus lau - ropes; to fish in a group using a seine net), to watch Hawaiian crafts demonstrated, and to watch typical Island activities such as coconut tree climbing. This is followed by perhaps the best meal of any commercial luau. The Kalua pig is well seasoned, corn is hot, the fresh pineapple spears are sweet, and the coconut cake melts in your mouth. The finale of a three-stage Polynesian review will certainly hold your attention. If you can spend up to 6 hours and want to have the fullest range of luau experiences, Paradise Cove is the best. Kids are welcome, but this is an outing better suited to adults.

**ROYAL HAWAIIAN HOTEL LUAU** *Expensive*
Located beachfront on the lawn outside the Royal Hawaiian Hotel. Reservations required (923-7311). Monday only 6-8pm. Serves 300-500. This luau starts in the open courtyard outside the Monarch Room with a fresh-flower lei greeting and complimentary drink; then moves to tables on the lawn where a full luau

buffet feast is served shortly after 6:30. Then at 7:00 the entertainment begins, on a stage between the tables and the beach. This luau is well suited for mature adults and couples. Food is good, the flower lei is beautiful, and the entertainment is loud, colorful, and exotic. The setting on the beach in the tropical moonlight is very romantic.

# DINNER CRUISES

Dinner cruises usually offer drinks, dinner, and some form of entertainment aboard a ship cruising the waters of Waikiki. Some combine dinner with an evening show in Waikiki. Average price for all dinner shows and dinner cruises is about $40 without tax. Here is a sampling:

### Aikane Catamaran Cruises
At Kawelo Basin is a fleet of four catamarans, including the newer *Aikane I*, *Aikane III* and *Aikane IV*, and the renovated *Ale Ala Kai*, once owned by Henry J. Kaiser in the 1950's. Dinner cruises have open bar with fresh ingredients, sit-down table service for dinner, audience-participation Polynesian entertainment and dancing. Free transportation to and from Waikiki. Call 538-3680.

### Ali'i Kai Catamaran
If you prefer to ride a double hulled catamaran (descendant of the ancient Polynesian voyaging canoes) this one blends ancient Polynesian design with modern technology to create the world's largest catamaran (167 feet long; carrying up to 1,000 passengers). The sunset dinner cruise aboard this floating supper club features continuous music, two open bars, a bountiful dinner feast with silverware, china and linen, a Polynesian show, dancing and transportation to and from selected Waikiki hotels. Departs 5:15pm, returns 7:30pm. A second Moonlight Dinner Cruise, 8:30pm-10:45pm, features everything included in the earlier cruise, plus a lot more partying, dancing and romance. Call 524-1800.

### Paradise Cruise
This is one of a number of cruises departing from Kewalo Basin. You board the *Pearl Kai* at 5pm, enjoy cocktails and dancing on the main deck, then return to your table for a steak dinner. Afterwards enjoy the "Paradise Cruise Review," with dance, music, and comedy on center stage. Top deck is always open for stargazing and enjoying the lights of Waikiki. Cruise ends at 7:45pm. Free round trip bus transportation from Waikiki. $36 per person plus tax. Call 536-3641.

### The Royal Prince
A smaller (165 ft.) all aluminum luxury yacht sails nightly from Pier 8 (transportation included) on a luxury dinner cruise. You'll enjoy cocktails, choice of three entrees, and first class service at your dining table. This is one of Waikiki's best dinner cruises. Call 531-1777.

### Windjammer Sunset Dinner Cruise
This is the premier 2 1/2 hour dinner cruise aboard the 284-foot, three deck, 4-masted replica of a clipper ship, the *Rella Mae*. She leaves from Pier 7 (near the *Falls of Clyde*) carries 1500 passengers, and offers drinks, dinner, and a floor

show. The ship glides toward Diamond head, then anchors off Waikiki for an unforgettable view of the shoreline. Packages are available which combine the Dinner Cruise with Flashback, re-created performances of Elvis, Marilyn Monroe, The Supremes, and Buddy Holly ($39.95 plus tax, call 922-1200). Other packages combine the Windjammer dinner cruise with the Don Ho Show ($39.95, call 924-3434) or John Rowles' (buffet at Rowles show then moonlight sail with cocktails, entertainment and dancing; call 922-1200). The best food and service on a dinner cruise is probably to be found on the special VIP Yacht Club Service aboard the *Windjammer*. For slightly more ($55 per adult; $40 for children) you'll be treated to entrees such as prime rib, scampi and chicken cordon bleu accompanied by champagne at your table with linen cloth. If you're going to take a dinner cruise, this is the top of the line.

# DINNER SHOWS

Many Waikiki headliner shows featuring top entertainers will either have two shows per night - a dinner show and a cocktail show later - or will offer one show nightly with two seatings - dinner guests are seated and eat first, then cocktail guests are seated (behind the dinner guests) just before the performance. There are advantages to choosing each package - the dinner package will get you better seats, while the cocktail package is less expensive. Dinner is some-times a buffet (as at Al Harrington) and sometimes served (as at Don Ho). Here are several recommended dinner and show performances.

### Al Harrington
Al and his fine cast of young musicians and dancers is a show you should not miss. This singer, comedian, actor, and historian is an up-and-coming super star who will introduce you to South Pacific culture, make you laugh, cry and leave the showroom with a new awareness of "aloha." This evening is more than a show; it will affect your life. Two shows nightly except Saturdays, dinner and cocktail seating available. Call 923-9861 or toll free 1-800-367-2345.

### An Evening with Danny Kaleikini
One of Hawaii's most charismatic entertainer-personalities, Danny Kaleikini has been pleasing audiences at the Kahala Hilton since the early 1970's. Kaleikini's rapport with his audience, his modesty, his beautiful voice, all combine to make you want to come back night after night. For an unforgettable evening, have dinner at the Kahala Hilton, then spend an evening with Danny Kaleikini. You won't want to leave. Two shows nightly except Sunday; dinner show at 7pm, cocktail show at 9pm.

### The Brothers Casimero
Share a memorable evening with Hawaii's most successful recording artists in the elegant Monarch Dining Room of the Royal Hawaiian Hotel. Mirrored against the music are dance interpretations of the Royal Dance Company and hulas by Leina'ala. These brothers sing a blend of ancient and modern Hawaiian music which will touch your heart and show you the romance of Hawaii's soul. Dinner seating at 6:30, Tues-Sat. Or come for cocktails and show only at 8:30. Additional cocktail show Fri. and Sat. at 10:30pm. Call 924-8211.

## Frank DeLima at the Noodle Shop

The Noodle Shop Restaurant at the Waikiki Sand Villa Hotel has recently been done over from stem to stern. Its intimate dining atmosphere will offer you a romantic dinner. Then stay for possibly the funniest man in Hawaii - he pokes fun at every ethnic group in the Islands. He's an equal opportunity mimic, and everyone knows it's all in fun. See Frank every Wed-Sun. at 9:30 and 11:30pm with an additional 12:30am show on Friday and Saturday. Call 922-4744.

## Don Ho at the Hilton Hawaiian Village Dome

"Mr. Hawaii" and friends are good, no doubt about that. The food is tasty, the show is legendary, and the Dome is unique. Dinner show nightly except Sat.; seating 6:30pm, showtime 8:30pm. Cocktail seating 8pm. Call 949-4321 ext.70105.

## Plaza Showroom

Such outstanding local entertainers as the Alii and Lullaby of Swing make this dinner show at the Waikiki Plaza Hotel one of O'ahu's best. The dinner here is superb - as top quality as the show. Cocktails are served on the open-air mezzanine before dinner. Call 955-6363.

## Polynesian Cultural Center

Spend the afternoon touring the seven authentic South Pacific Villages, then stay for the amazing evening show, "This is Polynesia." In between, get a ticket for the all-you-can-eat dinner buffet. It's lavish, in a beautiful setting, and offers a taste of many Polynesian dishes. Open Mon-Sat. from 12:30pm. Call 293-3333 or 923-1861.

## John Rowles at the Hilton Hawaiian Village

One of the most exciting and romantic entertainers in Hawaii appears at the new Tropics Surf Club Showroom at the Hilton Hawaiian Village. Mon. to Sat. You'll enjoy a lavish buffet dinner featuring roast beef, lobster, Seafood Newburg, and more. After the show, the club becomes a colorful discotheque from 9:30-2am weekdays and until 4am on weekends. Call 942-7873.

## Voyage

Live on stage, this new award-winning show on the 4th floor of the Waikiki Shopping Plaza will hold your attention with hula, Tahitian dances, brilliant cinematography and quadraphonic sound. You'll be surrounded with sights and sounds of the ancient voyage from Islands in the South Pacific to Hawaii, with special effects by the creators of Universal Studio Tour's "King Kong" and "Conan." Cocktail and dinner packages; call 922-6600 (fine dining before or after the show); dining times available from 5:15-10:15.

## Dinner and "Waikiki Calls" at Marco Polo

"Waikiki Calls" is the musical spectacle which traces the history of the Hawaiian Islands. Because the shows at 6:15 and 7:45, Mon. to Sat. at the Waikiki Shopping Center are free, lines can be long and people are often turned away. So take advantage of the offer from the Marco Polo Restaurant. Enjoy a dinner at this cozy Italian restaurant and they'll assure you of reserved VIP seats at the show. Waikiki Shopping Plaza, 4th floor. Call 922-7733.

# WAIKIKI NIGHTLIFE

Waikiki is beach, sun, and great shopping by day, but, oh, those summer nights! Three hundred sixty five of them every year. When the sun goes down, it isn't only the lights that come on at night. Waikiki becomes the heartbeat of Hawaii.

After dinner, visitors and kama'ainas alike go out in search of the perfect evening. The evening starts early with Happy Hour cocktails, then moves on to dinner, dancing, music, after dinner drinks, and entertainment to suit every taste.

We're pleased to introduce you to some of Waikiki's most popular night spots. Watch Wayne Harada's Weekend column in the Thursday paper, and thumb through the free tourist literature and the Yellow Pages for even more places to pass the night away. Have fun!

## HAPPY HOUR

Buzz's Steak & Lobster, 225 Saratoga Rd., noon-5pm daily. 923-6762
El Crab Catcher, 1765 Ala Moana Blvd, 4-6pm daily. 955-4911
Great Wok of China, Royal Hawaiian Shopping Ctr., 4-6:30pm daily. 922-5373
Hots, 2350 Kuhio Ave., 8pm-midnight daily. 922-2281
Jazz Cellar, 205 Lewers St., 2-4am nightly. 923-9952
Plaza Lounge, Waikiki Shopping Plaza, 11am-8:30pm daily. 922-6885
Rose and Crown Pub, King's Village, 11am-6:30pm daily. 923-5833
Wailana Lounge, 2211 Kuhio Ave., 10:30am-6pm. 922-4769
Wailana Lounge, Ala Moana Blvd., 10am-6pm. 955-1764

## NIGHT CLUBS

Rumors, Ala Moana Hotel, 410 Atkinson Drive. 955-4811
Annabelle's at the Top of the Ilikai Hotel, 1777 Ala Moana.
Cilly's, (video and disco music, young crowd, very popular), 1909 Ala Wai, lower level. 942-2952.
Studebaker's at Restaurant Row. 1950's rock 'n roll to juke box sounds. Staff leads the fun. Large dance floor. Open nightly till 2am. 531-8444
Honolulu Comedy Club, Ilikai Hotel. Hot stand-up comics Tues.-Sat. 922-5998
Open-air nightclub poolside at the Sheraton Princess Kai'ulani Hotel. Nightly 5:30-9pm. Features Leslie Fernandez production of Tahitian dancing to hulas and Hawaiian melodies. 922-5811
Jazz Cellar, 205 Lewers. Live rock'n roll music till 4am with specials every night. 923-9952
The Library, Hawaiian Regent Hotel. Sophisticated, romantic, cozy. 922-6611
Monarch Room, Sun. 5-8pm. Del Courtney's Band plays 30's and 40's big band dance music, for younger and older, a good time. 923-7311
Waikiki Sheraton Hotel Lounge, especially if Brother Nolan is performing Reggae, Stevie Wonder and original compositions. Hot. 922-4422

Rascals, Kuhio Mall, 2301 Kuhio Ave. Three bars on two levels - dancing down, cocktails and conversation up. Live music by Nohelani Cypriano Sun.-Fri. Dancing till 4am. 922-5566

Scruples, 2310 Kuhio Ave., in the Waikiki Marketplace. Hot and sophisticated celebrity playground. D.J.'s spin records nightly from 8pm. 923-9530

Masquerade, corner Kalakaua and McCully, near Cilly's. Hawaii's biggest dance club, with five levels. The Island's only computerized video wall, and state-of-the-art special effects. Open 7pm-4am nightly. (949-6337)

Wave Waikiki, with the wave mural outside, 1877 Kalakaua Ave. One of Waikiki's hottest spots. Live rock 'n roll nightly. 941-0424

Spats, in the Hyatt Regency Hotel. An Italian restaurant turned disco at 9pm. Upscale, lively and loud. 922-9292

## COCKTAILS, AFTER DINNER DRINKS

## AND CONVERSATION

The Chart House, 1765 Ala Moana Blvd., overlooking the Ala Wai Yacht Harbor. 947-2490

Hanohano Room, Sheraton Waikiki Hotel. Beautiful view of the city. 922-4422

Harry's Underwater Bar, Reef Hotel, 2169 Kalia Rd. 922-8886

House without a Key, 21909 Kalia Rd., Halekulani Hotel. Elegant and quiet, with live entertainment. 923.2311

Moose McGillycuddy's Pub and Cafe, 310 Lewers. A place you'll never forget! 923-0751

Rose and Crown Pub, King's Village. 923-5833

The Point After, Hawaiian Regent Hotel. 922-6611

Tahitian Lanai's famous Papeete Bar, at the Waikikian on the Beach. 1811 Ala Moana Blvd. 946-6541

Trader Vic's, International Marketplace. 923-1581

Surf Room, Royal Hawaiian Hotel, beachside, 2259 Kalakaua Ave. 923-7311

KONA COFFEE

JBAYOT

# WHAT TO SEE

## *INTRODUCTION*

Good Morning! Rise and shine, up and at 'em, let's get cracking. After all, it's a beautiful day, you're in the most famous and desirable vacation spot in all the world, and you want to make the most of every minute. Right? Right. As your personal guide, chauffeur, Master of Ceremonies, weatherman, timekeeper, and valet, it's my pleasure to tell you that you are doing great so far, and that today you're in for some fantastic surprises. Why are you doing so well? Because you have planned carefully so that your accommodations are just what you wanted, you are eating well, and are trying some new foods that you never knew existed (and wish you could get back home), and you are being akamai about keys and wallets and suntan lotion with PABA.

And why are you in store for such a memorable day? Because you're going to explore O'ahu! We suggest that you take a few minutes, over an island breakfast, to open up your faithful travel friend, *O'AHU: A Paradise Guide*, and look over this chapter on WHAT TO SEE. The island is divided into nine major areas with an in-depth description of places of special interest to be explored in each region. A detailed map accompanies each region locating many of the sights discussed in the text. As with accommodations and restaurants, we have identified with a ★ those attractions and activities which we consider to be of greatest interest and value to you, a "Best Bet," that should be seen first if your time and energy are limited. After a leisurely look at the variety of offerings, and using our tips and suggestions, select a group of sights and activities to form your itinerary for the day. Have fun, and don't worry if you haven't made it to all these sights by the time to go home - there's always next trip!

It would be an excellent idea to visit a book or souvenir store near you and purchase a large O'ahu map to use in conjunction with this chapter. And if you plan to do extensive touring, a current copy of *Bryan's Sectional Maps of O'ahu*, available at most book stores, is an essential companion. Bryan's shows easy-to-read maps of every street and highway on O'ahu, along with cross-referenced lists of cities, towns, police and fire stations, schools, playgrounds, parks, military installations, hospitals and clinics, shopping centers, points of interest, libraries and trails. We also urge you to call places on your itinerary before you visit them. Although our information is as current as possible, it's still advisable to confirm times and admission prices. You can inquire at the same time about luncheon facilities, parking, special show times, handicapped access, children's accommodations or about any other items of special interest to you and your group.

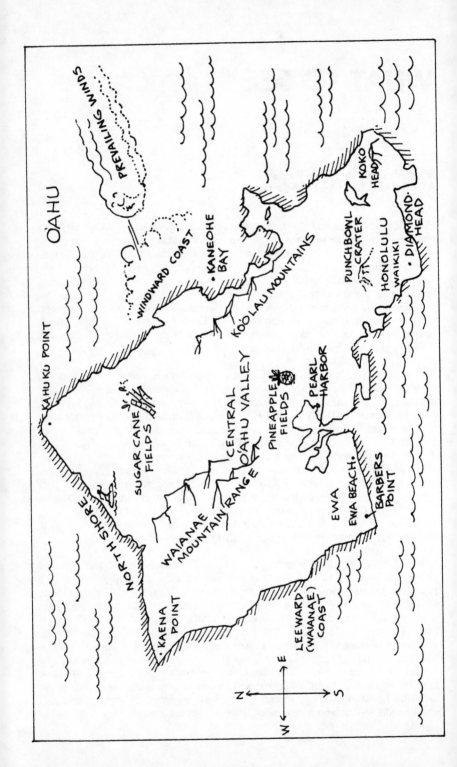

Before we begin, here's a word about making friends. You're likely to be driving more slowly than local traffic, especially when you are trying to read a tiny map or decipher Hawaiian street names. So if you find yourself going 20 in a 35 mile per hour zone, pull over and let the traffic pass. You'll make friends by doing so, and you'll confirm for the drivers behind you that visitors are thoughtful and courteous. And now, lets explore O'ahu.

# EXPLORING WAIKIKI

For our pre-tour briefing on Waikiki, let's meet at a window table in the Top of Waikiki's Revolving Restaurant (2270 Kalakaua Ave.). As we sit and look at Waikiki spread out far below us, it is hard to believe that less than 70 years ago this area was swamp, with duck farms, ponds and taro patches covering Waikiki's mauka half. In 1928 the Ala Wai (fresh water channel) Canal was completed. The purpose of this drainage canal was to catch the run off of the three major streams which emptied into the ocean at Waikiki (spurting water) and to change the swampy lowland into the vacation mecca we see around us today.

One good source to carry with you as you explore Waikiki is *Waikiki: Nine Walks Through Time* by Veneeta Ascon, available in most gift or bookstores for less than $2. It can be read for information, or used as a walking tour guide. Emphasis of the nine tours ranges from ancient history through the monarchy to modern neighborhoods and lifestyles. Its fascinating maps show you where to look for interesting sights, tell you where street names come from, and describe in detail where royal residences, early hotels, and other interesting buildings were located. It is a book you should have with you as you tour Waikiki.

Another indispensable help is a fold-out tourist map of Waikiki. Stop in at Woolworth's (only a block or so from the Top of Waikiki Restaurant) and choose one you like. With these three documents, the map, *Nine Walks Through Time*, and *O'AHU: A Paradise Guide*, you're ready to begin.

One note about transportation. If you have a rental car, it's fun to drive toward Diamond Head on Kalakaua Ave. and watch all the hotels, shops and people pass by. Then turn mauka on Kapahulu, take a left onto Kuhio and drive back toward Ewa along Kuhio, setting landmark streets, buildings, and fun centers in your mind as you drive. Driving along Kalakaua and Kuhio is a Waikiki tradition, especially on Fri. and Sat. nights. You'll see some of the most interesting people in the world along these two streets, perhaps even someone you know. A popular saying in Waikiki is that if you sit on a bench near the Banyan Tree on Kalakaua Ave., across from the Hyatt Regency, you'll eventually see someone you know walk by. Whether this is true or not, people watching is a favorite pastime on the world's most famous beach playground.

After you've driven Waikiki, the best way to really get to know it (if you have time) is to take a walking tour. Use the Exploring Waikiki map in this book as your major reference, since it is marked with most of the points of interest which you'll visit on your walking tour.

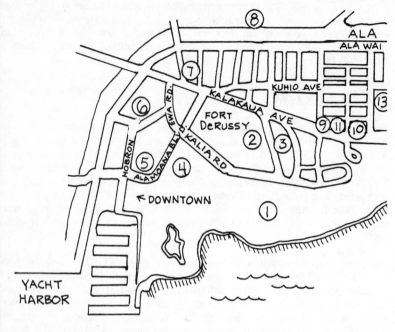

# WAIKIKI

1. U.S. ARMY MUSEUM
2. POST OFFICE
3. URASENKE FOUNDATION OF HAWAII (THE WAY OF TEA)
4. KAISER GEODESIC DOME
5. BANK
6. SMALL POST OFFICE IN EATON SQUARE
7. JACK-IN-THE BOX (ONLY DRIVE-THRU WINDOW IN WAIKIKI!)
8. CANOE HOUSE
9. BANK
10. TOP OF WAIKIKI REVOLVING RESTAURANT
11. WOOLWORTH'S
12. ALA WAI MUNICIPAL GOLF COURSE

WAI CANAL BLVD

LEAHI AVE
PAKI AVE
KAIULANI AVE
KALAKAUA AVE
KAPAHULU AVE
MONSARRAT AVE
THE FENCE

HONOLULU ZOO

WAIKIKI BEACH

KAPIOLANI PARK

MOUNTAIN (MAUKA)

EWA ← → KOKO HEAD

OCEAN (MAKAI)

TO DIAMOND HEAD

⑬ WAIKIKI TRADE CENTER

⑭ INTERNATIONAL MARKET PLACE

⑮ PRINCESS KAIULANI'S BANYAN TREE

⑯ KING'S ALLEY

⑰ KAHUNA (WIZARD) STONES

⑱ FATHER DAMIEN MEMORIAL

⑲ ST. AUGUSTINE CHURCH

⑳ LIBRARY FOR THE BLIND

㉑ QUEEN KAPIOLANI GARDENS

㉒ KODAK HULA SHOW

㉓ WAIKIKI SHELL

㉔ AQUARIUM

㉕ TENNIS COURTS

㉖ NATATORIUM

## ALA WAI YACHT HARBOR

This hidden area of Waikiki is a feast for the eyes. Beautiful sailboats, motorboats, yachts, exotic boats designed for round-the-world cruising, interesting people who are almost always willing to tell you about their craft, even a kaukau (food) wagon with one of Waikiki's best plate lunch bargains.

The docks are open to the public day and night, but be sure to respect the private property and belongings and keep in mind that since many people live on their boats, this is a residential neighborhood as well as a boat moorage.

While you're there, walk Ewa across the parking lot and explore the helicopter pad (it's fenced) and rock jetty area. This is a perfect place to enjoy a bento at dusk, or to watch the annual canoe races from Moloka'i to O'ahu - they end right here in front of the Hilton Hawaiian Village at the catamaran dock.

This is local Hawaii, right in the middle of Waikiki. If you get thirsty during your walk, try the Ilikai Hotel's Yacht Club for tropical drinks overlooking the boats. And you're only steps away from a tropical dinner at the Waikikian on the Beach, just diamondhead of the Ilikai Hotel.

---

DID YOU KNOW...that roadside signposts picturing Hawaiian Royalty (Alii) point to major island attractions and sights? They are red, white and yellow portraits of a robed Hawaiian King-Warrior, and were placed by the Hawaii Visitors Bureau. Watch for them!

---

## KAISER'S ALUMINUM DOME

Nestled near the entrance to the Hilton Hawaiian Village at the Ewa end of Waikiki is the world's first Geodesic Dome, built in 1957 by industrialist Henry J. Kaiser, to the specifications of dome inventor R. Buckminster Fuller. Amazingly, workers erected the 575 triangular-shaped panels by attaching 25,000 bolts in just under 36 hours, at a cost of $80,000. The 1200 seat dome was designed to provide a low-cost large audience space in which no interior posts obstruct the view.

Opening night, Sunday, February 17, 1957 featured legendary Hawaiian singer Alfred Apaka and the Honolulu Symphony Orchestra. The list of entertainers who have since appeared at the Dome reads like a Hollywood's Who's Who, including: Count Basie, Glen Miller's Orchestra, Joey Heatherton, Jim Nabors, and current star Don Ho.

Don Ho's show is one of Waikiki's best, and the dome is a landmark worth peaking into, even if you can't come for the show. Dinner shows are offered Sun-Fri. with seating at 6:30pm, show at 8:30pm. Cocktail show package Sun-Fri. with seating at 8:00pm for the 8:30 show. The dinner is excellent; includes fresh fruit, steak with mahimahi and bay shrimp, Japanese vegetables, Macadamia Nut Dessert and one standard or Tropical drink. Cocktail show package includes one standard or tropical drink, the show, gratuity and tax.

## EATON SQUARE MALL AND POST OFFICE

Hidden at 444 Hobron Lane near Ewa Road in Ewa Waikiki is a small, elegant shopping mall with such stores as Bushido (Japanese) Antiques, Chez Michel French Restaurant, King's Bakery and Coffee Shop (one of Honolulu's best bakeries), Pioneer Federal Savings Bank, Nell Gwynne Shoppe, and a branch of the U.S. Post Office. This tiny post office is located in the far recesses of the square behind a beautiful small fountain and pool. When the main post office at 330 Saratoga (in the Fort DeRussy area) has a long line, this little branch is usually cool and available. There is also a small post office in the Hilton Hawaiian Village and the Royal Hawaiian Shopping Center (Building B, 2nd Floor, Open 9am-4:30pm M-F).

Eaton Square is worth exploring - especially for the Japanese art and antique galleries, and several specialty food stores. When you're in the area, walk Ewa one short block and watch the fishermen and outrigger canoe teams on the Ala Wai Canal. There's shade, and places to sit to watch the water. It's a quiet, shady spot to catch your breath after shopping.

## BANK LOCATIONS

Banks aren't often considered points of interest, but an open bank is surely a sight I want to see when I'm running low on cash. Hawaii has many large full-service financial institutions. Here are the locations of three with branch offices in Waikiki. Look for them when you're in these areas so you'll know where to head in a pinch. Bank of Hawaii is the largest full-service financial organization in Hawaii. Waikiki Branch offices: Discovery Bay, across Ala Moana Blvd. from the Ilikai, 1778 Ala Moana - Space LL11 (942-6670); and 2220 Kalakaua Ave. (942-6222). First Hawaiian Bank (943-4670), established in 1858, offers complete banking and trust services. A bank machine is located in Waikiki at 2181 Kalakaua Ave. First Interstate Bank of Hawaii, with more locations in more cities and states than any other Hawaiian bank, has a Waikiki Branch at 2270 Kalakaua Ave. (923-2011).

## CANOE CLUBHOUSE

Just across the Ala Wai Canal, almost directly across from Niu Street near McCully is an old one-story building which houses the various outrigger canoe clubs. They practice on the Ala Wai Canal, and you can see them preparing their craft, discussing strategy, and entering the water at this Club House. This team sport is poetry in motion when executed by a well-trained crew. If you enjoy boating, canoeing, and the water, this Club House is a place to visit. Since it is private property, be sure to inquire where and when you are welcome to watch. Outrigger canoeing is an ancient Hawaiian tradition; the water was the highway for centuries. Hawaiians are rightfully proud of their canoeing tradition and expertise. A view of the sleek craft cutting through the water at dusk is one you'll long remember.

## WAIKIKI HOTELS

Although many visitors don't realize it, the famous hotels of Waikiki are among the most interesting places to explore on the entire Island. If you have an afternoon, read through our hotel descriptions in the accommodations section, choose three, four or five you'd like to see, and visit them. If your time is too limited to spending an afternoon, then arrange to have lunch, cocktails or dinner, or see a show at one of these major hotels, and take time to walk through them while you're there.

Some hotel adventures not to miss are: riding the exterior glass elevator at the Ilikai Hotel; walking down the torchlit jungle path at night at the Waikikian on the Beach; the lobby and Surf Room of the Royal Hawaiian Hotel; Sheraton Moana Surfrider's Banyan Court; the new lobby reefscape with flowing water at the Outrigger Reef Hotel; the Oceanarium at the Pacific Beach Hotel; the underwater bar at the Outrigger Waikiki Hotel; Halekulani's pool with the underwater orchid mosaic; Kahala Hilton's blue lagoon with dolphins; the monarchy-era motif at the Queen Kapiolani Hotel; and the central atrium at the Hyatt Regency Hotel. These are just a few of the lavish, one-of-a-kind settings you'll discover in O'ahu's fabulous hotels!

## THE BEACHES OF WAIKIKI ★
Most tourists, before they come, think of Waikiki as *one* beach. When they arrive they are amazed to find out that the famous "Waikiki Beach" is actually five interconnecting beaches with varying surf and swimming conditions.

In front of the Hilton Hawaiian Village is *Duke Kahanamoku Beach*, named for legendary Hawaiian Surfer (he introduced board surfing to Australia), swimmer (he won Olympic gold medals in swimming), charter member of the swimming Hall of Fame, and Honorary Sheriff of Honolulu. This stretch of beach is man-made, having been dredged in 1956 by Henry J. Kaiser. Sandy ocean bottom and safe swimming and surfing all year.

*Fort DeRussy Beach* in front of the Hale Koa Military Hotel is the widest single stretch of beach in Waikiki, with safe and calm inshore waters, but a rough coral bottom surrounding pockets of sand. Purchased by the U.S. Government in 1909 and named for a famous army engineer, Fort DeRussy is an "R & R" (rest and relaxation) site for armed forces personnel. By State law, all beaches in Hawaii are public, so everyone is welcome to enjoy the beach here, one of the nicest in Waikiki. The rest of the Fort's facilities are open only to military personnel, their dependents and guests.

*Gray's Beach*, fronting the Halekulani Hotel, is named for Gray's-by-the-Sea Lodging House operated here in 1912. A sandy channel here by the same name runs westward through the reef, the rest has a rocky bottom. The best swimming is in the channel and is safe all year. Surfing (wave) breaks along these beaches are named "Paradise" and "Number Threes." Surfing spots are located on either side of Gray's Channel.

*Royal-Moana Beach*, in front of the Royal Hawaiian Hotel and Sheraton Moana Surfrider Hotel, is the most sacred and historically important stretch of beach in Waikiki. It was here that for centuries the kings and queens of Hawaii had homes. King Kamehameha I lived on this spot from 1795 - 1809. A royal kou tree grove surrounded the royal residence, which was kapu (off limits) to commoners. The ocean bottom is sandy and almost coral free, with one small offshore channel.

The *Waikiki Beach Center* building stands on the site of a series of taverns, first built in 1884. This is why the surf break nearby is still referred to as "Tavern's." The City and County of Honolulu purchased the site and now maintains the Beach Center and its beach for bathers and surfers. Swimming is excellent here.

---

DID YOU KNOW...that the largest salt-water pool in the United States is on O'ahu? The Natatorium, on the Waikiki Beach next to the New Otani Beach Hotel near the Aquarium, was built in 1927 to honor soldiers who fought in World War I. Now closed, this olympic size pool measuring 40 x 100 meters once held 6,000 cheering spectators at its gala swimming and diving events.

---

*Kuhio Beach Park*, the last beach area in Waikiki proper, was donated to the people by Prince Jonah Kuhio Kalanianaole, heir to the throne and member of the U.S. Congress from Hawaii for 20 years. His beachside home was located just mauka from this site.

This entire diamondhead end of Waikiki once had a huge dike to support Kalakaua Ave. and was known as "Stonewall." A low retaining wall, which remains today, was built to keep sand from eroding. Known as "slippery wall," it is hazardous due to its slick surface. This area looks safe for kids, but is dangerous because one morning the water can be very shallow and hazardous for diving, and the same afternoon the surf can make the same area deep, with strong currents that can catch small children. If you do swim or dive in this area, use extreme caution.

The best beaches to use along Waikiki Beach are Kahanamoku, Fort DeRussy, Grays, Royal-Moana, and the Waikiki Beach Center beach.

## URASENKE TEA HOUSE ★
A public demonstration of Chado, the Way of Tea, is offered every Wed. and Fri., (except holidays) from 10:00 to noon at the Urasenke Foundation of Hawaii, 245 Saratoga Rd., Honolulu, HI 96815 (923-3059 or 923-1057). Call for more information and reservations.

What is Chado?

*"Chado, the Way of Tea, is based on the simple act of boiling water, making tea, offering it to others, and drinking it ourselves. Served with respectful heart and received with gratitude a bowl of tea satisfies both physical and spiritual thirst. The frenzied world and our myriad dilemmas leave our bodies and minds exhausted. It is then that we seek out a place where we can have a moment's peace and tranquility. In the discipline of Chado such a place can be found. The four principles of harmony, respect, purity, and tranquility, codified almost four hundred years ago, are timeless guides to the practice of Chado. Incorporating them into daily life helps one to find that unassailable place of tranquility that is within each of us."*

These are the words of Sositu Sen, Urasenke Grand Tea Master since 1964, and fifteen in an unbroken line of tea masters dating back to the 16th century A.D.

This traditional Way of Tea which so permeates Japanese society today began in Southern Asia when tea was used as medicine. Brought to China before Christ, then to Japan in the 7th or 8th century A.D., the drinking of tea was confined to the court aristocracy and Buddhist ceremonies until the 12th century. Since the underlying philosophy of Tea has evolved from Zen Buddhism, the saying "To study the way of tea is to study Zen" refers to the rigorous spiritual discipline and meditation which leads to deep spiritual insight.

Today the Urasenke Foundation has donated tea houses and gardens, tea utensils, and reference materials to cities and institutions worldwide. Branch offices and qualified tea instructors such as the ones on O'ahu teach the increasing number of individuals who desire to experience and learn about the practice of Tea. Your visit to the Urasenke Foundation, and participation in a demonstration, will allow you to experience one of the orient's most beautiful and important traditions - The Way of Tea.

## U.S. ARMY MUSEUM ★

This is really two museums in one, the Army Museum downstairs and the Army Corps of Engineers Museum upstairs. Both are among the most interesting things to see on Oʻahu - don't miss them. Open 10:00am-4:30pm daily, except Monday (438-2819). The museum is housed in a pre-World War I artillery bunker which held two 14" disappearing guns and two - 6" guns, built in 1911, as part of the defense of Oʻahu and Pearl Harbor. As you walk down the cool, dark underground bunker (which, by the way, was scheduled for demolition a few years ago, but resisted all efforts to destroy it, so they decided to make it into a museum!) you first pass the gift shop, well managed by friendly Darlene Martin, then proceed down the main tunnel. On each side you'll see rooms and work areas where the shells and powder were stored, prepared, and sent up top to be fired.

The museum staff has done an outstanding job of creating the sights, sounds, and total environment scenes from ancient Hawaiian armies (there's a fascinating display of old Hawaiian implements of war), American Revolution, Spanish American War, Boxer Rebellion, World Wars I and II, Korea, Vietnam, and (upstairs) the four modern roles of the Corps of Engineers: harbor development, shoreline protection, flood control, and resource management.

The Vietnam exhibit is so realistic that some people have to leave. You enter through an R & R "barefoot bar," a re-creation of the Waikiki bars soldiers visited on leave, and then left to make the 16-hour return flight on an army troop transport back to the jungles of Vietnam. You cannot help but feel the emotions our soldiers experienced as they re-entered the bizarre existence of combat, confusion, and sudden death. This exhibit is a fitting tribute to every American who fought in the terrible Vietnam War. A special exhibit now honors the Go-for-broke soldiers of Hawaii's famed 100th Battalion, the 442nd Infantry, and the other Hawaiian units that fought so valiantly during World War II. All Americans should know the story of their heroism, and it is well told here.

Bring your children, and help them understand the sacrifices Americans have made and continue to make in order to protect our way of life. Guided tours are available by appointment. NOTE: If you're looking for a place to buy military patches, insignia, books, memorabilia, and a wide assortment of military wear, visit the Military Shop of Hawaii, 1921 Kalakaua Ave. (942-3414). Open Mon-Sat., 9am-6pm.

## F.W. WOOLWORTH CO. ★

Almost the entire second floor of the Waikiki Woolworth Store (2224 Kalakaua Ave. on the corner of Kalakaua and Royal Hawaii Avenues, 923-2331) is devoted to souvenirs - it's great fun to just browse! They have carved wooden tiki statues, placemats with a map of an Hawaiian island on each one, Macadamia nuts in about a million varieties, whole coconuts for mailing home, pineapple packs, shells, grass skirts, sharks' jaws, candies, postcards by the ton, T-shirts, thongs, beach blankets, sunglasses, perfumes, artifact re-creations, Hawaiian music on cassette tapes, swimsuits, Island jewelry, and on and on and on. They always have discounts, and specials, too.

You can shop all over O'ahu and find yourself coming back here. They're open 8am-11pm daily. The Woolworth's in-store restaurant is open from 7am-10pm. Satisfaction on all items guaranteed - replacement or money refunded on request. There's also a parking lot just behind the store on Lauula Street, with direct access from the lot into Woolworth's. Check the variety and prices in this store before you buy elsewhere - you may decide to buy the bulk of your souvenirs right here!

### INTERNATIONAL MARKETPLACE AND DUKE'S LANE
Located in the center of Waikiki at 2330 Kalakaua Ave., this landmark is scheduled to be demolished within the next few years to make room for another high rise building. Although one plan would re-create the Marketplace in miniature within the building's lobby, the phenomenon as it has been known by generations of vacationers is doomed. So now's the time to see this village of shops and stalls clustered around an ancient spreading Banyan Tree, complete with a treehouse which was the original broadcast booth of KCCN Hawaiian Radio. You can get a temporary tatoo, or buy a pearl-bearing oyster shell. Try a squeezed-on-the-spot orange juice, or visit the International Food Court to sample foods from many countries. There's a place upstairs where you can get your picture taken riding a huge wave - so bring your camera. There are also vendors who will bargain with you - if you love to haggle over prices. You'll find hours of entertainment here.

Duke's Lane is an alley running between Kalakaua and Kuhio Avenues near the International Marketplace. It is known for having good prices, especially on coral and jade-like jewelry. You'll see exotic jewelry in wood, opal, and mother-of-pearl. It's worth a visit, if only to compare prices with those you just saw in the Marketplace.

### WAIKIKI TRADE CENTER AND SHOPPING PLAZA
These two shopping centers are within a block of each other. The Waikiki Shopping Plaza is on the corner of Kalakaua and Seaside Avenues. The Trade Center is just a block mauka. You'll find many shops to visit at both locations, plus restaurants, apparel stores, an art gallery, and (at the shopping plaza) a million dollar water fountain. A free hula show, Waikiki Calls, is presented nightly except Sun. at the Plaza, 6:30 and 9:00pm. If you make a half-day walking tour, you can easily visit these two centers, Woolworth's, the International Market Place, Dukes Lane, and King's Alley. After that you'll be ready for a swim and a Mai Tai (or two)!

### WIZARD STONES OF WAIKIKI
On the beach at Kuhio Beach Park, near the Waikiki Beach Center and the Police Sub-station are four large pieces of rock embedded in the sand. A bronze plaque tells us that the stones are a tribute to four kahuna (soothsayers) - Kapaemahu, Kahaloa, Kapuni, and Kinohi, who came to O'ahu in the sixteenth century A.D. Old stories say that the four mysterious visitors first toured the Hawaiian Islands, then returned and settled at a place called Ulukou, very near the location of the Sheraton Moana Surfrider Hotel. They came unannounced, some say from Tahiti, and during their stay became widely known for healing

by laying on of hands and other acts of great wisdom. Before they departed, they asked the people to help them erect a monument to their cures and their visit. The people chose four large rocks, brought them from the Kaimuki section of Honolulu, and placed them on the beach near where the four wizards had lived. One by one the four named a stone for him/herself (some believe there were two women and two men; others contend all four were asexual), and invested the rock with his/her personal mana (spirit; power). During ceremonies, celebrations, and prayers held in their honor through the following month, the wizards disappeared, never to return.

The stones have since been moved, buried, chipped, forgotten and recovered any number of times. Then in 1980 after being deeply imbedded in the sand since 1963, the "Wizard Stones" were moved 50 feet diamondhead to their present location under a banyan tree. To many people these stones have far more than historical significance. Do they possess healing powers? Can a person sense the mana of departed soothsayers in the rock? One thing is for certain; these stones are of great value to the people who love Hawaii, and they deserve respect and careful treatment from all who visit them.

## PRINCESS KAI'ULANI'S BANYAN TREE

Kai'ulani (1876 - 1899) was heir to the Hawaiian throne. She lived the life of a fairy Princess as a child, in a lovely home surrounded by a garden of colored flowers. Tame peacocks were her pets, eating out of her hand. She lived in a tropical paradise, with a mother and father who doted on her, and a kingdom full of people who loved her. And then the first of a series of tragedies struck, which eventually took her life when she was only 23 years old. When she was 12, her mother died. At fourteen, she was sent to school in England. Then on Monday, January 30, 1893, when she was seventeen and still at school, Kai'ulani received three telegrams. "Queen deposed. Monarchy abrogated. Break news to Princess." The gallant young girl went almost immediately to Washington D.C. to meet with U.S. President Grover Cleveland. Then in July of 1898, when she was 22, the United States annexed Hawaii. The throne was lost forever. A year later Kai'ulani was dead. Some said her heart shattered the day the Hawaiian flag was taken down for the last time. Others said she had a secret love whom she was forbidden to marry. In any case, the last hope of the monarchy died with her.

As both an only child and a princess, Kai'ulani had many acquaintances, but few real friends. One friend she loved and spent long hours with as a motherless girl of 13 was a famous storyteller, born in Scotland (as was her father), who was in Hawaii with his family for his health. His name was Robert Louis Stevenson, author of *Treasure Island, Kidnapped, Dr. Jekyll and Mr. Hyde*, and *A Child's Garden of Verses*. Stevenson and Kai'ulani would sit for whole afternoons under a spreading banyan tree on the Cleghorn Estate, or sometimes in a small grass shack in the garden. He would tell her stories of adventure and romance, and he introduced her to the tales of Scotland and England. Perhaps Kai'ulani and her new friend fed the peacocks together and talked of what life would be like for her at an English boarding school. He wrote her a long going-away poem, and departed for Tahiti, where he died several years later.

There is little left of the Cleghorn property; you can imagine the two story Victorian home standing where the Govern Cleghorn Apartments are today (on the corner of Cleghorn and Kai'ulani Streets in Waikiki). But there is one thing left from the estate - one Banyan tree still exists. It stands in the parking lot behind Food Pantry (2370 Kuhio Ave). You can stand under the old Banyan and imagine you're there for afternoon tea, listening to Robert Louis Stevenson tell you and Kai'ulani magic tales of Scottish kings and battles.

## ALA WAI MUNICIPAL GOLF COURSE
Look out your condo windows, or take a walk along the Ala Wai Canal and look across the water at the Ala Wai Golf Course. It's a marvel. Extensive renovations are underway and won't be completed for several years. What a piece of real estate this is - in the heart of Honolulu. It's interesting to just watch the activity, but if you want to play this 18 hole, par 71 public course, you'll want to call as soon as you arrive; starting times are hard as a rock to get. Facilities include a locker room, pro shop, clubhouse, carts, equipment rental, snack bar and restaurant. Call 732-7741.

---

DID YOU KNOW...the Ala Wai Canal was originally called the "Waikiki Drain Canal"? Proposed in 1905 and finished in 1928, it was designed to empty into the Pacific Ocean at both ends, but the Diamond Head end was never completed. Reason - no funds.

---

## FATHER DAMIEN MUSEUM AND ST. AUGUSTINE CHURCH
These two buildings are scheduled for demolition within a year or two, and will be relocated elsewhere in the area, so be sure to call before you visit (Damien Museum, 130 Ohua Ave., Waikiki, 923-2690)

Father Damien (Joseph de Veuster), a Catholic Priest born in Belgium, came to Hawaii and went to the leper colony at Kalaupapa on Moloka'i in 1873. For 16 years, until his death in 1889 of leprosy contracted at the colony, Damien eased the horrible conditions, bathed the sufferer's wounds, built shelters almost singlehandedly, begged for clothing from local communities and finally built a church, St. Philomena, for the patients. Father Damien is now being considered for Sainthood by the Catholic Church; 1989 is the 100th anniversary of his passing. The Damien Museum contains a number of Father Damien's personal possessions, and tells the story of his courageous stewardship at Kalaupapa.

Medicines now control the disease and although patients at the settlement were allowed to leave, most have stayed to live out their lives. Plans to make the area into a National Park are underway, but residents will be able to maintain their homes at the settlement. Damien was followed by Mother Marianne Kopp, a Franciscan nun from New York who spent 30 years in service at the settlement.

## KING'S VILLAGE (FORMERLY KING'S ALLEY)
This unusual shopping mall, just mauka of the Hyatt Regency Hotel, reminds one of New Orleans Square or Main Street USA at Disneyland. This half-block

village brings to life a section of Honolulu as it might have looked during the late 1880's. The shops and restaurants in King's Village fit the theme. An old English Pub is to your right, and upstairs you'll find a shop selling handsome hand-carved wooden sculptures of whales, birds and people. Many of Honolulu's best stores are represented here, including Andrade & Co. (apparel), Watumull's Department Store, and Crazy Shirts.

This is King Kalakaua's Hawaii, with the King's Guard patrolling the area wearing the Royal blue, gold, and white uniforms of the palace militia. Buildings, courtyards, cobblestone streets, all are carefully crafted to create the charm, colors, and feel of Old Honolulu. At 6:15pm sharp, the Royal Guard performs one of Waikiki's best shows as they lower the flag by numbers, then march to an inner courtyard to demonstrate a most impressive close order drill.

Located at 131 Kaiulani Ave., King's Village is open daily from 9am-11pm. Look for the giant board near the entrance posting the entertainment schedule for the week. You'll enjoy combining sightseeing with shopping at this re-creation of Hawaii's proud Monarchy era.

NOTE: In 1987 The King's Guard added another dimension to their King's Village performance. They have formed King's Guard Production, a performing group of men and women who offer shows featuring scenes from old Polynesia, the Monarchy period with classical costumes and dances, and modern themes from the 1940's, Broadway plays, and Hollywood movies. Call 922-8157 or write 131 Kaiulani Ave., Honolulu, HI 96815.

### HONOLULU ZOO ★
This fourth largest visitor attraction on Oʻahu (the first three are the Arizona Memorial, Punchbowl and the Polynesian Cultural Center) not only has one of the most creative gift shops in town (Zootique), it has things you can't see anywhere else in the world. The Zoo grounds, covering 43 acres roughly the shape of a slice of pizza, were part of the Kapiolani Park, donated in 1877 by King Kalakaua. Almost a million visitors tour the Zoo each year.

COMMON 'AMAKIHI

Have you ever seen a baby Nene (Hawaii's State bird)? This zoo is world-famous for propagating the endangered nenes for release into the wild. Do you like brilliantly colored Birds of Paradise (the bird, not the flower). Honolulu Zoo has one of the world's best collections. And wait till you see the tortoises! In 1972 the Zoo won a national award for being the first zoo to breed the Galapagos Tortoise in captivity. Look for the Madagascar Angulated Tortoise; it's the rarest tortoise in the world (only five known specimens outside Madagascar).

While you're there, be sure to see the Honolulu Federal Savings Bank's Bird Show presented Wed. to Sun. at 10am, noon and 2:30pm at the Zoo stage on the interior front lawn. A kids' favorite, the petting zoo is open from 9am-2pm daily, except Mon. (the animals' day off). Also daily at 11am (conditions permitting) you can see an elephant close up at the "Elephant Encounter" next to the "Petting Zoo." Sometimes a second presentation is held at 1:30pm. Watch the signs nearby.

For the next year or so the Zoo will be undergoing a three-phase expansion. Phase I will open the Children's and Petting Zoo, the Education Pavilion, and the Discovery Center. Phase II will see the completion of a 12-acre African Savanna exhibit, and Phase III will involve completion of an Island Bird area. Within a few years the Honolulu Zoo will be almost brand new, and waiting for a visit from you!

And on your way out, walk along the art gallery at the fence on the zoo's Diamondhead side. Open Wed. and weekends from 10am-4pm. Wonderful paintings, pen and ink drawings, watercolors, koa frames, batik, embroidery, and lots of friendly people to talk with. The Zoo has an active Friends of the Zoo society which supports and assists with Zoo functions.

Oh boy, its Zoo day!


## WAIKIKI TROLLEY

There is only one best way to get an overview of Honolulu and Waikiki with a minimum investment of time and energy: take a tour. And one of the best ways to do that is on the Waikiki Trolley.

Today's trolley is a re-creation of the Honolulu streetcar that ran from Honolulu to Waikiki at the turn of the century, except it needs no tracks. Its bright red and gold exterior is easy to spot; it's quickly becoming a moving landmark as it clangs along its route. The trolley runs from about 8:45am until 5:45pm from the Royal Hawaiian Shopping Center, to the Hilton Hawaiian Village, then toward downtown, Bishop Street, the Harbor, Hilo Hatties, Dole Pineapple Square, Chinatown, Ward Centre, and back to Waikiki. During a 90 minute tour, the driver-guide will point out and tell you about many points of interest along the way, as well as places to eat, shop, and explore. You can buy an all-day pass with unlimited stops, or a one way ticket. We suggest the all-day pass so you can take the grand tour first thing in the morning, then return to places you want to tour on foot in the afternoon.

These trolleys are also available for charter, so if you have a birthday party, a group meeting, or a family reunion, you might arrange your own private trolley tour. Call E Noa Tours (941-6608) for more information.

## LIBRARY FOR THE BLIND & PHYSICALLY HANDICAPPED

Just mauka across the Ala Wai Canal, on the access road to the Municipal Golf Course, is a modest one-story building at 402 Kapahulu Ave. Inside is a library with a difference. This is the library serving people afflicted with mental handicaps, deafness or hearing impairment, serious emotional disturbance, learning disabilities and speech impairments. Appropriations of federal and state funds enable the library to provide special materials for those who need them, including: books and magazines in Braille, large print, cassettes and records; music on records and cassettes; film loops; multimedia kits, educational games; direct reading services, community education program of lectures and seminars on blindness and other handicaps; talking books; and transcribing equipment. I went in for a brochure and ended up visiting with patrons and exploring the library. The staff welcomes your visit also. Call 732-7767. Open Mon-Fri. 8am-4:30pm; Sat. 9am-5pm. Closed Sun.

## ROYAL HAWAIIAN SHOPPING CENTER (RHSC) ★

The RHSC is made up of three connected three-story buildings which occupy what was once the front yard of the Royal Hawaiian Hotel at 2259 Kalakaua Ave. Many people, including this writer, have heaved a sad sigh at the loss of a wonderfully landscaped lawn and entrance to the legendary hotel. And yet there is a good reason for its existence. The RHSC is part of the estate given by Princess Bernice Pauahi Bishop (Bishop Museum was built by her husband as a memorial to her) for the education of Hawaiian children at the Kamehameha Schools, which today occupies a 600 acre hilltop campus in the Kamehameha Heights section of Honolulu, just mauka of the Bishop Museum. Princess Bishop was the great granddaughter and last descendent of King Kamehameha I, who united the Hawaiian Islands. The RHSC contributes significantly to the Bishop Estate, and thus supports the education of more than 47,000 students of Hawaiian ancestry. By visiting this shopping mall, you are participating in the important efforts of the Bishop Estate and Kamehameha Schools on behalf of these children, who will be Hawaii's leaders of tomorrow.

WAIKIKI TROLLEY

The Royal Hawaiian Shopping Center probably has more special events than any other shopping mall in Hawaii. Just a few of the daily free events include: Hula lessons, Hawaiian language instruction, ukulele classes, Hawaiian quilting demonstrations, pineapple cutting seminars, Polynesian Cultural Center mini show, lei making, and more. There's a free monthly calendar of events distributed throughout the RHSC. One interesting feature is the TV information person, who appears on the screen at the touch of a button and answers your questions - live!

There are more than 125 specialty shops and restaurants in the RHSC. A few favorites are: The Perfumery, where you can make your own perfume; Lefties, etc., where you can purchase a left-handed clock; Peking Marketplace and the China Friendship store; and The Little Hawaiian Craft Shop. You can have your picture taken riding a surfboard in summer, and enter a Christmas Carol contest in November. You must sit, relax, and have a cool drink in the Princess Garden Court on the Street Level near the Fountain. You'll find your own favorites here, but be careful - it's easy to spend a whole day.

Pick up a copy of the free Royal Hawaiian Shopping Center Magazine (available at most visitor information stands) and decide what shops and restaurants you want to visit most. Watch for special events, and have a great time!

# *EXPLORING DOWNTOWN HONOLULU*

There are more points of interest in Downtown and Metropolitan Honolulu than any other part of O'ahu, including Waikiki. So rather than follow the standard guidebook procedure of offering you long lists of sights which would only add to the confusing maze of choices, we offer you an insider's view of these attractions, prioritized and organized to make sure you see the most important points of interest in the time you have to sightsee.

To assist you in deciding what places to visit and which tours to take, we've included only the 15 most worthwhile sights, with the very best experiences given prominence by being described first. If you can only visit one attraction, consider going to the first or second place discussed in each of these two sections on Exploring Downtown and Metropolitan Honolulu. And when you choose a tour, pick one which includes as many of the sights described below as possible. These are the places that make Honolulu unique and ones that should be a part of your O'ahu experience.

### STATUE OF KING KAMEHAMEHA THE GREAT ★
Located outside the Aliiolani Hale (State Judiciary Building) on South King Street across from the Iolani Palace. As you stand in front of this bronze and gold statue of Hawaii's greatest warrior and leader, be aware that you are gazing on the likeness of Hawaii's George Washington. In fact, the two men had much in common - both were founding fathers of a nation, both were their new country's greatest military leader and first executive. Both were large, powerful, quiet men, and both lived during the late 18th century. Both accomplished unbelievable military and political tasks, and both are held in great esteem and

affection by their country. If you ever travel to Washington D.C., you'll see a statue of Kamehameha in Statuary Hall in the U.S. Capitol, not too far from one of George Washington. There's quite a story connected with the Honolulu statue. The original was cast in Florence, Italy, in 1880, but was lost at sea when the boat carrying it to Honolulu burned and sank near the Falkland Islands off South America. A second casting was made and installed here just in time for the Royal Coronation of King Kalakaua in 1883. Sometime later the original was recovered and now stands in front of the Kapaau Courthouse in Kohala on the Big Island where Kamehameha I was born and raised. Each year on June 10, dozens of 15-foot leis are draped across both statues in preparation for the festivities on June 11 - King Kamehameha Day, a State holiday.

## IOLANI PALACE AND GROUNDS ★

Iolani (Hawk of Heaven) Palace is a place you will never forget. It is the only royal palace in the United States, and has been the seat of government in Hawaii from its completion in 1882 until the State Capitol was built in 1969 - a period of 87 years. It was built by King Kalakaua as his official residence in 1882. Upon his death in 1891 it housed his sister-successor, the Queen Lili'uokalani until the overthrow of the Hawaiian Monarchy in 1893. During the Republic and Territory eras from 1893 until 1959, the Government was administrated from the Palace, and from the time when Hawaii became a State in 1959 until the present State Capitol was completed in 1969, the Palace served as the executive building. During the past decade Iolani Palace has undergone extensive renovations, until today it looks much the same as it did during the elaborate parties and balls of Kalakaua's reign.

Two main floors of the Palace are divided into quadrants. Upstairs are the private apartments of the King, on the Ewa side, and the Queen and her guests on the Diamond Head side. Queen Lili'uokalani was imprisoned in the front guest room for nine months following the unsuccessful counterrevolution in 1895. Downstairs, the Ewa side contains an informal sitting-audience room known as the Blue Room, and the formal Dining Room, with three massive sideboards specially made in Boston. On the Diamondhead side of the main floor is the huge Throne Room. Decorated in royal crimson and gold, this was the scene of royal audiences, receptions, and balls during the Monarchy. Tragically, the trial of Queen Lili'uokalani for "treasonable acts" against the Republic was also held in this room in 1895.

IOLANI PALACE

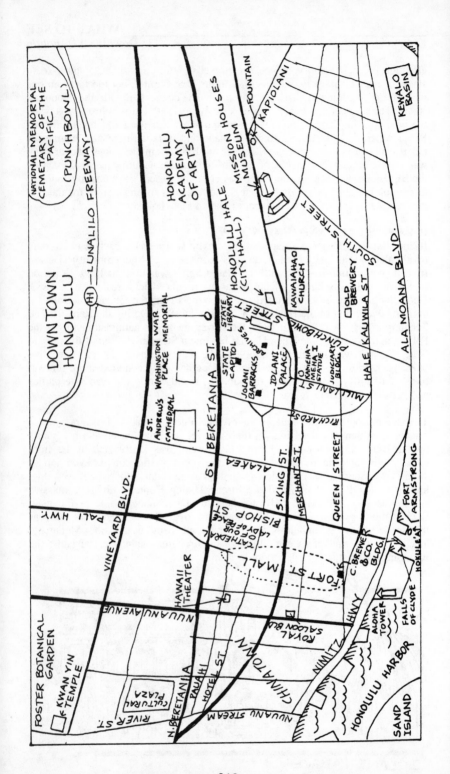

On the Palace grounds stand four monuments you should visit. The *Iolani Barracks*, in the shape of an old castle, housed the King's Household Guard. It was moved from its original location near the present State Capitol to permit new construction in the late 1960's. It now houses the Palace Gift shop and tour ticket office. The *Coronation Pavilion*, in which Kalakaua and his Queen, Kapiolani, sat during the 1883 Coronation ceremony, now hosts band concerts every Friday noon by the Royal Hawaiian Band. On the mauka Diamond Head side of the grounds is an impressive building housing the *Hawaii State Archives*. A grass mound makai from the Archives marks the location of the *Royal Mausoleum* before the present Royal burial plot was completed in 1865. In that year the royal coffins were carried in a solemn torchlight procession from here to the Nuuanu Valley to their new resting place.

If you visit only one place in Hawaii, go to the Iolani Palace. Tour the interior, and walk the grounds. You'll get a glimpse into the glory and tragedy of Hawaii's past.

## MISSION HOUSES MUSEUM ★

Would you like to walk into the first western-style frame house built in Hawaii by Congregationalist missionaries in 1821? Would you enjoy watching as characters from Old Hawaii tell Island ghost stories around a small campfire? Would you like to watch as a page is printed in the Hawaiian language on an 18th century Ramage press in a missionary print shop? You can do all this and more at the Mission Houses Museum, 553 South King St. (531-0481). The museum is made up of three historic houses, on their original site and grounds, built between 1821 and 1841 by Protestant missionaries from New England, and used as the central station for their mission to bring Christianity to Hawaii. Today these houses are restored and used as the setting for Saturday living history presentations of life as it was at the Mission in the 1820's and 30's.

As many as four families occupied the 1821 Frame House, which was shipped in pieces around the Horn and assembled on the site it now occupies. Gradually sixteen other mission stations were founded throughout the Hawaiian Islands, but this one remained the headquarters. Here was the vital printing press, which issued thousands of pages of The Bible, textbooks, copies of laws, and hymnals in the Hawaiian language. Here also, was Chamberlain House, a large two-story storehouse built in 1831 to hold the Mission's supplies ordered by Levi Chamberlain, the business agent for the entire Sandwich Island Mission. This house was built with coral rocks from the coral flats near shore, and with lumber salvaged from wrecked ships. As the mission population grew, a third house was built in 1841, as a bedroom wing attached to the main Frame House. This building has now been restored and serves as the Print House.

The Mission's unique living history program allows you to witness everyday Mission life as it was: Ships' captains being entertained in the communal parlor, dinner of fresh fish, taro, bananas, and New England pies being cooked in hanging pots and ovens in the kitchen, water being drawn from wells near the house and filtered through coral dripstones to remove impurities (you can still see the dripstones), families gathering for prayer and quiet activities (translating the Bible into Hawaiian for men; sewing and journal writing for women) in their bedrooms at night. Every Saturday, and special days such as Christmas and the Fourth of July, costumed volunteers and museum staff present skits, tours and scenes like these from Mission activities. It's like walking into a time machine and suddenly being there, as it was, when these three houses stood alone on the dusty plain that connected the village of Honolulu with the coconut groves and swamps of Waikiki. One of Honolulu's most enjoyable places. Open daily for guided tours from 9am-4pm except major holidays. Adults $3.50; youths ages 6-15, $1. Under 6 free.

The Museum also offers the best walking tour of Historic Honolulu, an alternative to the Waikiki Trolley tour we recommended in the Exploring Waikiki section above. The two hour tour begins at 9:30am, Mon-Fri. at the Mission Houses Museum, and includes admission to the Museum. Adults $7, children 6-15 $2, under 6 free. Reservations required; call 531-0481.

## THREE FAMOUS CHRISTIAN CHURCHES ★

Three major Christian Churches reflect the faiths that were brought to Hawaii in the 1800's. First, Protestantism arrived with Congregational Missionaries in 1820, who completed the coral block *Kawaiahao Church* in 1842 on the site of four previous churches of thatch and timbers. Second, Catholic Priests arrived and built *Our Lady of Peace Cathedral*, started in 1840 and completed in 1843, after local harassment of Catholics had eased. The Anglican Church, *St. Andrew's Cathedral*, was begun in the 1860's during a period of close relations between the Hawaiian and British monarchies. Many of the stones and decorations in the Cathedral were imported from England.

Each of these churches represents an important era in Hawaiian history. By far the most historically important of the three, Kawaiahao was the official church of the monarchy for most of its years. It was here that many Hawaiian kings and queens were christened, married, and given last rites. Here also is buried the only Hawaiian king (other than Kamehameha I, whose remains were secretly hidden to prevent desecration) not buried in the Royal Mausoleum. King William Lunalilo asked to be buried close to his subjects. You can see his Gothic Mausoleum built in 1879 in the front church garden. Around the crypt is a piece of the high stone wall which once enclosed the church property.

Also notice the Adobe School House behind the church cemetery. Built in 1835 as a school and meeting house, this is the only adobe building left in Honolulu.

Hawaii's first Catholic missionaries were expelled in 1831, but returned in 1839 when King Kamehameha II, under the influence of a French gunboat, issued an edict granting religious toleration. Originally, the Cathedral was a simple coral block rectangle with steeple. Balconies were added in 1871, and front columns in 1929. The church has been recently renovated by its large congregation.

King Kamehameha IV and Queen Emma brought the Episcopal Church to Hawaii. Emma had been raised by an English father, and the royal couple favored Britain. The Cathedral was begun in 1867, but not completed until 1902. It was named for the Saint on whose feast day Kamehameha IV died in 1863. The front was extended in 1958 in order to create a wall of stained glass.

## HONOLULU FOUNTAIN

As you tour Honolulu you're sure to pass the new City Fountain in the triangle where three major streets meet - Kapiolani Blvd., South Street, and South King Street, adjacent to the building housing the Star Bulletin and Honolulu Advertiser newspapers. This controversial sculpture was completed in mid-1988 by local artist Chuck Watson, who was commissioned by the City. People seem to either love it or hate it. The theme is a good one for a city - a tumbling waterfall cascades over lava rock, past Island greenery, into a pool below. Its Hawaiian name is Ka-Mea-Kui Upena which means "The person who stitches the nets."

Next time you drive, walk, or ride past this intersection (the best view is while driving diamondhead on South King Street), take a look and let us know your vote: awesome, or awful. It's just a block from the Mission Houses Museum to the fountain, so why not take a short walk after your visit to the Museum? Every time I pass the fountain on a warm Honolulu afternoon I have the greatest urge to jump in! Guess that means I love it.

---

DO YOU KNOW...the origins of some Honolulu Street names? *Lunalilo Freeway*, is named for Lunalilo, sixth king of Hawaii who ruled only a year (1873-74) and left his estate to establishe Lunalilo Home for the aged. *Kapiolani Boulevard*, is named after Queen Kapiolani, wife of Kalakaua. *Fort Street*, now Fort Street Mall, is named for the fort built by Kamehameha I in 1816 and torn down 30 years later. *Bishop Street*, is named for Charles R. Bishop, financier and creator of The Bishop Museum as a memorial to his wife Princess Bernice Pauahi Bishop. *Beretania Street* is the Hawaiian version of "Britain."

---

## HAWAII MARITIME CENTER ★

Located at Pier 7 of the Honolulu Harbor. From the arrival of the first Polynesian voyagers, Honolulu harbor has been the scene of ever increasing maritime activity, such as the whaling industry, which made Honolulu the largest whaling port in the world by 1852.

In the 1880's elaborate harbor boat houses such as the Myrtle Boat Club were built for luaus, card playing, and outrigger canoe storage. King Kalakaua had a private boat house near Pier 7 where he lavishly entertained such VIPs as sugar magnate Klaus Spreckels and author Robert Louis Stevenson.

Four-masted sailing ships made regular stops in Honolulu Harbor to unload goods or take on passengers. The famous steam passenger liners of the early 1900's followed, in the era when weekly boat day meant confetti, dockside bands, hula girls, and youngsters diving into the harbor waters for coins thrown by passengers aboard the huge ocean liners. The tallest building and best known landmark to arriving passengers was the 10-story *Aloha Tower*, built in 1926 and known to every passenger who came down a ship's gangplank in her shadow.

Now, for the first time all these eras are being celebrated in one new Hawaii Maritime Center. **King Kalakaua's Boat House** has been re-created and serves as the centerpiece of the museum complex. The Boat House will have two levels connected by glass elevators. A theater on the lower level will feature rotating exhibits and live stage presentations. A widow's walk 80 feet up will afford visitors a spectacular panorama of the harbor. Exhibits will show visitors many traditional fishing techniques, display whaling items, tell tales of Hawaiian shipwrecks and rescues, encourage children to handle parts of a ship in a special hands-on area, and suspend double-hulled canoes from the ceiling.

Outside the Kalakaua Boat House on Pier 7, you'll be able to see the types of plants that were carried here by ancient canoe voyagers, and visit two of the most historic and fascinating vessels in Hawaii, the *Hokule'a* and the *Falls of Clyde*. The *Hokule'a* is a 60 foot reproduction of the ancient Polynesian Voyaging Canoes which are thought to have brought the first humans to Hawaii 1500 years ago. This amazing craft has become famous by making the same voyage, using ancient navigational techniques. You can see this craft moored at the end of Pier 7. The *Falls of Clyde* is the only original four masted full rigged sailing vessel still afloat, the sole surviving sailing oil tanker, and one of the few riveted wought iron ships in existence. It was saved from salvage by donations from the Hawaiian people, and today is a part of the Marine Center. You can board her, see the under-deck quarters of the captain and crew, and hear stories of her voyages and adventures.

The legendary Aloha Tower is also a part of the Center, with an expanded role as the plans unfold during the next several years. Among the plans for the Tower are a maritime library, photo archives, special exhibits (perhaps of boat day), and a maritime art gallery.

If you love the sea, ships, and stories of adventure they have to tell, put the Hawaii Maritime Center toward the top of your itinerary. This is what Hawaii is all about. Hawaii Maritime Center (523-5511) is open 9am-5pm daily. Admission $6 adults, $3 juniors (ages 6-17), kids under 6 free. *Falls of Clyde* open 9:30am-4pm. Adults $3, children 6-12 $1, under 6 free.

## CHINATOWN ★

The Chinese Bicentennial celebration during all of 1989 suggests the tremendous importance of the Chinese culture in Hawaiian history. Although there are documented arrivals of Chinese in Hawaii aboard three ships from the Orient in 1788, the first Chinese immigrants to arrive in large numbers came as contract workers from China's Kwang Tung Province to work the Hawaiian sugarcane in 1852. These workers banded together, forming the Chinese Associations and Societies which provided each individual an extended family. By 1882, Chinese made up nearly 49% of the total plantation working force, and nearly outnumbered Caucasian men in the islands.

Chinese workers were enterprising and hard working. They preferred to work for themselves, and valued education. Within ten years of the arrival of the first Chinese immigrant group, 60% of the wholesale and retail businesses in Hawaii were owned by Chinese. By 1880 they owned 85% of the Hawaiian restaurant licenses. This trend was worrisome enough to the Hawaiian legislature that in 1892 it passed an act restricting Chinese immigration. As Chinese operated more and more stores (with living quarters above them), and built buildings to house them close together in order to be near friends, relatives and Chinese society associates, a crowded, wooden-building section of Honolulu called Chinatown grew larger and larger.

In 1886 calamity struck; 7,000 Chinese homes in eight blocks of Chinatown were destroyed by fire. The Chinese rebuilt. Then on December 12, 1899, a Chinese bookkeeper named Yu Chong died of bubonic plaque. Panic swept Honolulu and Chinatown again burned, this time at the hands of the Fire Dept. All went fine until a wind came up which led to the destruction of every block from Beretania to the docks. Ultimately the fire burned for 17 days, destroyed 38 acres and the homes of 4,000 people. Chinatown was never the same again. By 1900 only 40% of the Chinese population lived in here; by 1960 it was only 5%. Today, most prosperous Chinese live in the hills overlooking the city. But Chinatown continues to be a busy and vibrant business area.

Walk or drive through Chinatown, visit the lei stands (my favorite is Sweetheart's at 65N North Beretania) and the many exotic specialty shops that sell everything from Oriental herbs to fresh pig's heads. Two excellent walking tours are offered. The ***Chinese Chamber of Commerce*** (533-3181) offers one every Tuesday at 9:30am leaving from the Chamber offices at 42 N. King St., call for reservations. Another sponsored by the ***Hawaii Heritage Center*** (521-2749), Mon-Fri. starts at 9:30am. Or take a walking tour of your own. Pick up a copy of Francis Carter's easy-to-read little book, *Chinatown*. It has a self-guided walking tour in it; pick and choose what you want most to see.

A word about Hotel Street. This is Honolulu's official red-light district, very seedy and run down. It is a remnant of the rough waterfront bars and hotels that thrived here during the whaling days of 1800's. Hotel Street in this section is closed to traffic and well-patrolled by police. It's interesting to drive by, but a dangerous and tough area to go looking for entertainment.

GINGER

## THREE MAIN GOVERNMENT BUILDINGS

Many tourists bypass these three buildings simply because they are unaware of their beauty and importance to Hawaii's past. Let's visit each one briefly and hopefully you'll be stimulated to explore them further.

*Honolulu Hale* (City Hall) is the handsome white Spanish-style building just across South King Street from Kawaiahao Church (Hale means house). This is the official home of the Honolulu Mayor, City Council, and major city staff agencies. The building has a tiled, open-roof atrium modelled after a palace in Florence, 1500 pound bronze front doors, and some of the most amazing chandeliers you've ever seen in the central courtyard. Open Monday to Friday, 7:45am-4:30pm, 530 South King Street.

*Aliiolani Hale* (House of the most high royalty) was built in 1874. This impressive building looks like a palace because it was designed to be one, then modified when the need for government offices was deemed greater than that for a royal residence. The building housed the courts and Parliament during the daytime, and King Kalakaua used it at night for royal balls and receptions. It housed the Courts after 1893, when the executive and legislative functions were housed at Iolani Palace. Back wings were added in the 1940's. As you look at the entrance and staircase, imagine King Kalakaua receiving members of the city's high society while the royal orchestra played dance music for his guests.

*The State Capitol Building*, which is scheduled to be closed for renovations between 1990 and 1992, is a classic example of symbolic architecture in which every major aspect of the structure represents an important concept. If you stand inside the open central courtyard, you can see that the 60 foot pillars which surround and support the upper levels represent Hawaiian palm trees. The moat surrounding the building reminds one of the ocean surrounding the islands, and the cone-shaped legislative chambers resembling volcanoes rise from the sea-like reflecting pools. The open roof suggests both the sunlit climate of Hawaii and the openness and Aloha of her people. The Capitol's furnishings, too, reflect the beauty and uniqueness of the State. Koa wood from the Islands is used for interior trim and panelling. Sand from Moloka'i paves the courtyard. And an 8-foot bronze statue of Queen Lili'uokalani, last monarch of Hawaii, stands at the entrance. She, Kamehameha the Great, and Father Damien are the only historical figures honored with public statues. You are invited to attend regular sessions of the Hawaii State Legislature, which meets here each January through May. The opening ceremonies of each Legislative Session include hulas, flowers, and feasting. This is a major annual event which you can watch on TV if you can't be there in person.

## WASHINGTON PLACE

You can't go inside since it is not open to the public, but you can do as countless tour buses do and pull over, stop, and look at this beautiful home and grounds through the fence. Built in the 1840's by a ship's captain named John Dominis (who was lost at sea shortly thereafter), the house became home to Queen Lili'uokalani who married the captain's son, John Owen Dominis. Following her deposition from the throne in 1893, the Queen returned to Washington Place and lived there in retirement until her death in 1917. Since

1921, the Governor of Hawaii has occupied the house, which was named for General George Washington. Washington Place is the oldest continuously occupied home in Honolulu.

## HONOLULU ACADEMY OF ARTS ★

Before you go in (which is a must) look at the high peaked roof, designed to follow the roofline profile of a grass house. This is "Hawaiian" architecture, and as you enter you feel as though you were entering a Roman villa or a Chinese home. Thirty exhibition galleries surround five garden courtyards. Sit for a few moments under the entry portico and familiarize yourself with the floor plan. Then resist the urge to start off on your own, and instead join a tour group about to depart. The descriptions and overviews offered by your talented docent will help you decide which galleries and pieces you want to re-visit on your own.

Watch for several special collections; the Picasso, Van Gogh and other western masters; the oriental scrolls, paintings, tapestries and sculptures from Korea, China and Japan; and the wonderful delicate statue of Kuan Yin, Chinese goddess of Mercy. Walk through the air-conditioned contemporary art wing, and the sculpture garden.

You can have lunch, Tues. to Fri., 11:30am and 1pm seatings, from September to May in the *Garden Cafe* (531-8865 for reservations), which is run by volunteers who serve one of Honolulu's most intimate meals. Then visit the *Academy Shop* for treasures you can take home. The Hawaiian gallery is small, since most pieces are in the British Museum, but the feather and ivory fishhook leis, and the carved wooden calabashes are worth seeing. The Academy (538-3693) is open, Tues., Wed., Fri. and Sat. 10am-4:3pm; Thurs. 11am-8pm, Sunday 1pm-5pm. Closed Monday. Admission is free. Guided tours Tues-Sat. 11am.

---

DID YOU KNOW...members of the Hawaii affiliate of the American Institute of Architects voted the Academy of Arts the "best building" in Hawaii? The C. Brewer building was runner up.

---

## FORT STREET MALL

What is now a seven block pedestrian shopping mall started as the city street that took you to the fort at Honolulu Harbor. Built in 1816 by Kamehameha the Great to protect the harbor from invasion by foreign vessels, Honolulu Fort became a jail for rowdy whalers until it was torn down in 1857 to make space for more waterfront warehouses. For a century afterward Fort Street served as a major Honolulu thoroughfare in the heart of the city's mercantile district. In 1969 the City closed Fort Street to vehicular traffic, added landscaping and created a successful shopping plaza, which today hosts many street parties and special events. Fort Street Mall is also the site of one of Honolulu's hottest bread and sandwich shops, *Ba-Le Sandwich*, at 1154 Fort St. Mall (521-4117). While you're exploring the Mall, stop into the Ba-Le for a Vietnamese sandwich on fresh French bread that has the most unique taste in Hawaii. People come from all over O'ahu to buy them.

### THREE HISTORIC DOWNTOWN BUILDINGS

You could easily, and happily, spend a full day exploring Honolulu's historic buildings. But since our time for such luxuries is limited, we've chosen three you will want to stop by and see.

*The Old Brewery*, a four-story red building just makai of Kawaiahao Church, at 553 Queen Street, was built in 1900 as the original home of Primo (and later Royal) beer. Materials to build and equip the steel (enclosed in gray stone and brick) structure were shipped from the mainland by chartered schooner, making it one of the most modern breweries of its day. It produced beer until 1960.

*The C. Brewer & Company Building*, at 827 Fort Street, is one of my favorite buildings on O'ahu. It reminds me of an old Island home. In reality it was built as recently as 1930. Reinforced concrete and fitted stone are finished with textured stucco and plaster. Its interior is as elegant as its exterior, with two-story rotunda and floors of Island sandstone. The building, on the same site as an earlier store operated by the 165 year-old trading firm, is surrounded by a beautiful walled garden.

*Royal Saloon*, 14 Merchant St., is the only building left from Honolulu's rough and rowdy 19th century waterfront. Built in 1890 on the site of an earlier bar (the old Royal Hotel Saloon), the Royal Saloon saw many a shotglass raised by whalers and merchant sailors in old Honolulu. Rumor has it that during renovations a secret door was uncovered which was probably used to shanghai unconscious sailors after their drinks had been liberally spiked by the management or by a crimp (an unscrupulous talent scout for ship captains). This building is one of the last authentic pieces of Honolulu's days as a rip-roaring port town.

### THE HISTORIC HAWAII THEATER

The people of Hawaii are currently supporting a community-wide effort to restore the Hawaii Theater in Downtown Honolulu, and make it into a Performing Arts Center. As the campaign unfolds, the theater is being kept open for all sorts of performances - ballet, dixieland jazz, vaudeville, organ recitals, silent movies, fashion shows, concerts, and more.

Why bother to restore an old theater? Built throughout America and Europe in the 1920's and 30's, ornate movie "palaces" provided places where people of modest means could enjoy popular entertainment in a grand setting. As the first movie palace built in the Islands, and the only remaining theater with a stage in downtown Honolulu, the Hawaii (which opened in 1922) has the potential to become a much-needed cultural and entertainment facility for local residents and visitors alike. Phase I of the renovations is already well underway, involving repairs to roof, stage and seats, and projection booth. Phase II will see lobbies and facade renovated. Phase III will expand such facilities as rehearsal rooms, storage areas, reception rooms, and will add new restrooms.

The Hawaii Theater is now open and you're invited to attend one of the many gala events held here during your visit to O'ahu. Call development advisor Larry Ogle at 533-6400 for more information, or watch the Honolulu newspapers for dates and times of upcoming events. We'll see you at the Hawaii Theater!

## FOSTER BOTANICAL GARDENS

In 1855 a young German doctor named William Hillebrand started a botanical garden at his Nuuanu Street estate. He experimented by introducing into his garden various species of plants, birds, and animals that were new to Hawaii. The estate was sold to Captain and Mary Foster, who expanded the garden. When she died in 1930, Mrs. Foster provided for the conversion of her home into the present public display of Hawaiian flora.

On this fertile 20-acre site nearly 4,000 species of tropical plants and flowers are represented, including a special collection of palms, a bromeliad garden with hundreds of species of pineapple, and many varieties of wild orchids. Tours are offered Mon. to Wed. at 1:30pm. We recommend these guided walks since the narration brings to life the many species and varieties that might otherwise escape your notice. Reservations are recommended. Call 533-3406. 180 North Vineyard St. Admission charge.

## KUAN YIN TEMPLE

Have you ever visited a Chinese temple? This one is the oldest and most often visited of such shrines in Honolulu. Located near Foster Gardens, at 170 North Vineyard (531-1939) the Temple is dedicated to Kuan Yin, Chinese goddess of mercy.

It was originally constructed in the 1880's but has been rebuilt a number of times since then. The center alter holds a large gilded statue of Kuan Yin sitting on a lotus blossom. On the alter to the right is Wei Tor, guardian of faith. On the left is Kuan Tai, protector of truth and justice. The lotus represents purity, the pearl provides light, and the broom whisks away evil. Joss sticks are used by temple priests and priestesses to foretell the future. Incense and food are offered as symbols of respect and reverence to the Gods. Visitors can show respect for the temple and its worshippers by not taking flash pictures, and by not interrupting worshippers. Open daily 9am-4pm. No admission charge.

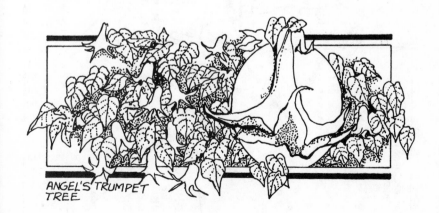

ANGEL'S TRUMPET TREE

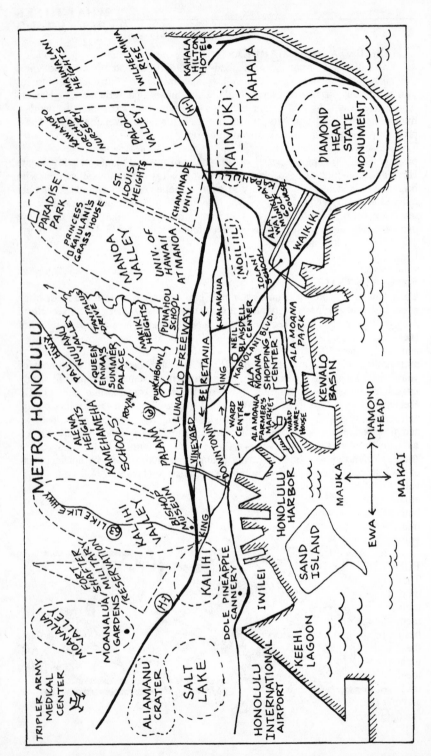

220

# EXPLORING METRO HONOLULU

Visitors usually look around Waikiki for things to see, visit downtown Honolulu on a tour, and all too often run out of time and energy before they visit many of the points of interest spread out across the city. Perhaps that's part of the problem - metropolitan Honolulu encompasses a huge amount of territory, from Tripler Army Medical Center near Moanalua Valley all the way across Waikiki, past Diamond Head Crater to the Kahala area and Waialae Country Club. Metro Honolulu also includes all the neighborhoods (between those north and south boundaries) which lie between the mountains and the sea. Did you know that much of Honolulu can be found in the series of alternating valleys and ridges that begin in the Ko'olau Mountains and gradually widen out to become the low plain that lies like a blanket between the ridges and the beach?

If you look carefully at a map of Honolulu you'll see five of these major valleys. (starting from the Ewa side - **Moanalua Valley**, **Kalihi Valley**, **Nuuanu Valley** (which flattens out to become Downtown), **Manoa Valley** (containing the University of Hawaii) and **Palolo Valley**. In between these are five ridges or rises, including from the Ewa side - the **Fort Shaffer Military Reservation**, **Alewa Heights** (where Kamehameha Schools are located), **Makiki Heights** (with famous Tantalus Drive), **St. Louis Heights** (home to Chaminade University), and the ridge comprising **Wilhelmina Rise and Maunalani Heights**. Take a moment to locate these features on a city map - if you are familiar with them you'll be much better able to picture in your mind the locations of the points of interest we'll be discussing below. A rough rule of thumb is that the Lunalilo Freeway (H1) running north and south through the city, separates the ridge-and-valley uplands of Honolulu from the city's flatlands below (downtown, Waikiki and the connecting plains).

Although many visitors see almost exclusively the sights in the lowland sections of Honolulu, there are many important points of interest in the upland ridge-and-valley areas of the city. So we offer you descriptions of some of the best attractions in all quadrants of Metropolitan Honolulu, Ewa and Diamondhead, both mauka and makai, in the hope that you will discover many of the hidden treasures the city has waiting for you to enjoy. Have fun, and let us know when you locate a treasure we have yet to find, won't you?

## PUNCHBOWL CRATER AND THE ROYAL MAUSOLEUM ★
These two sites, although different in scope, have important elements in common. Both are sacred ground, holding the remains of men and women who gave their lives in service to their nation in times of war or other crisis. And both are memorials to these people, to their acts of heroism, and to those who served beside them but whose names are not recorded on these stones. The fact that these cemeteries are among the most often visited sites in Hawaii reflects the great value we all place on both the men and women who rest here, and on the ideal of sacrifice which they so nobly represent. When you visit these shrines, take a fresh flower with you to leave as a tribute to each person interred here, as a symbol that we remember and appreciate their struggle to protect their nation's freedom and way of life.

***Punchbowl Crater (National Memorial Cemetery of the Pacific)*** is probably, except for the Arizona Memorial, the most solemn and difficult place to visit in all Hawaii. This extinct volcanic cone was known to ancient Hawaiians as "Puowaina," hill of sacrifice. At one time alii (royalty) were secretly buried here, at another time kapu-breakers were sacrificed on these slopes. In the early 1800's, the crater was a major stronghold for warriors defending O'ahu against attack by the Army of Kamehameha the Great.

Today Punchbowl Crater (named for its shape) is the hallowed resting place of American Armed Forces in the Pacific during World War II, the Korean War, and the Vietnam War, including those soldiers from all three who were missing in action or lost at sea.

At the far end of the cemetery stands the Honolulu Memorial, comprising a nonsectarian chapel; two map galleries with narrations describing such World War II Pacific battles as Coral Sea, Midway, Tarawa, Kwajalein, and Iwo Jima; a monumental stairway flanked by ten courts of the missing with inscribed names from World War II, Korea, and Vietnam; and an engraved Dedicatory Stone. On the front of the chapel tower is a 30-foot female figure holding a laurel wreath. Inscribed under the figure are the words spoken by Mrs. Abraham Lincoln to Mrs. Bixby, mother of five sons killed during the Civil War: "The solemn pride that must be yours to have laid so costly a sacrifice upon the altar of freedom."

The National Memorial of the Pacific (546-3190) is located at 2177 Puowaina Drive, Honolulu, HI 96813. Summer hours (March 2 - Sept. 29) 8am-6:30pm; winter (Sept. 30 - March 1) 8am-5:30pm.

---

DID YOU KNOW...that money was hidden inside Punchbowl Crater during World War II? The crater was honeycombed with storage tunnels dug into its inner makai-side walls in which was stored U.S. currency. As you can imagine, the crater was very heavily guarded, and kapu (off limits) throughout the war.

---

***The Royal Mausoleum*** is one of the most sacred places in Hawaii. Within its gates rest the mortal remains of every modern Hawaiian king and queen, with the exception of two. King William Lunalilio has a crypt on the grounds of the Kawaiahao Church in Honolulu. King Kamehameha the Great had one of his most trusted chiefs hide his bones so that they would never be disturbed. To this day, no one knows the location of the great king's final resting place.

After a memorable tour of the Mausoleum guided by the Kama'aina curator, Lydia Namahana Maioho, and her talented son William, I asked about the legend that the chief who hid the bones of Kamehameha I was killed immediately thereafter to prevent him from disclosing the secret he possessed, for in those days, Hawaiians believed that if an enemy possessed your bones they could control your immortal soul. To my amazement, Lydia told me that she and

William are direct descendants of the chief entrusted by Kamehameha with his remains, and that the legend of the chief's subsequent murder is untrue. She has allowed us to publish, for the first time, the true story of those events in 1819. Here are her own words.

*"This is to share with you about the hiding of the Bones of King Kamehameha the Great. Two Chiefs - Hoolulu and Hoapili, who were brothers, were chosen by the King to hide his bones secretly - till this day no one knows where. Many have said that Hoolulu was killed. This could not have happened because when any event took place - and a child is born during that event - he or she is given a name in honor of the event. This happened to Hoolulu - after the hiding of the King's bones, Hoolulu returned to his wife who had given birth to a son. Hoolulu named his son Kai heekai (meaning the receding waters). Today we tend to think that the bones of King Kamehameha I were hidden in an undersea cave. Hoolulu may have been killed later. As a descendent of this chief (Hoolulu), I can say that this is the true and correct story of this historical event. Lydia Namahana Maioho."*

So not only did Hoolulu return alive to his wife and new child (as reflected in his son having been named for an event only he knew about), but also his son's name offers us a clue to the secret location of Kamehameha's bones.

The remains of many ancient and modern chiefs and monarchs had been interred in various places in Hawaii such as the Royal Crypt at Iolani Palace, and the Heiau at the City of Refuge on the Big Island. When the Royal Mausoleum was completed in 1910, these remains were moved, as tradition dictated, in a torchlight procession at night, up into the Nuuanu Valley to their final resting place in the Royal Mausoleum. A pilgrimage to the Royal Mausoleum is not for the casual tourist; search out this place only if you love the history, culture and people of Hawaii, and if you want to spend a quiet hour in meditation and tribute to these remarkable leaders of a remarkable kingdom.

## BISHOP MUSEUM ★

Here's a riddle for you to try on someone who can't see the heading of this paragraph. "Where can you see all of the following items in one place: King Kamehameha the Great's royal feathered cape; the stars above Hawaii in the year 500 A.D.; a real grass house from Old Hawaii; King Kalakaua's Crown; a life-size sperm whale swimming through a sea of air; petroglyphs (ancient Hawaiian rock carvings) that you can make prints of with paper and crayon; wooden bowls with human teeth imbedded in the outside; and preserved pieces of the biggest shark ever caught - Megamouth." You'll see these things and more at Hawaii's Bishop Museum in Kalihi, a district of Honolulu two miles west of downtown.

If you're a resident of Hawaii or on active duty in the military, you can get in free and go to a theme party besides if you go to Family Sunday, first Sunday of every month. On the lawn they set up a big tent, with food booths, crafts to make, and entertainment for every member of the family.

The Museum was started in 1889 as a home for the treasures of the Kamehameha family. Princess Bernice Pauahi Bishop was the last direct descendant of Hawaii's first king, and in her will she left all the heirlooms from her large family to her husband. He created this museum as a tribute to her and as a storehouse of this Hawaiiana. The Museum has gradually expanded its collection, and its research, until today it is considered the best museum of its kind in the world. Because the collection is so vast, you'd be ahead to take a guided tour, then re-visit the halls you like most. And don't forget the Planetarium, a favorite of kids young and old. Next door is the Shop Pacifica, where you can buy a stuffed dinosaur, the most handsome Hawaiian greeting and Christmas cards I've found, and books and reproduction of artifacts. The Bishop Museum is a place you can come back to again and again, and see new things on every visit. You'll be glad you came. Museum hours: 9am-5pm, Mon-Sat. and the first Sunday of every month; $4.95 adults, $2.50 kids 6-17. Planetarium hours: 9am-4pm, Mon-Thurs.; 9am-8pm, Fri., Sat., & Sun; $2.50 adults, $1.25 kids 6-17 years. Call 847-3511.

SPECIAL NOTE: 1989 is the Centennial Anniversary of the founding of the Bishop Museum. Watch the local newspapers, radio and TV for special events to be held at the museum all year. Better yet, join the Bishop Museum and they'll send you a monthly newsletter, Ka 'Elele, with all the information you'll need!

## WAIKIKI AQUARIUM ★

Newly remodeled and air-conditioned, this popular visitor attraction has one of the world's most unusual collections. Have you ever watched a live Chambered Nautilus swim and breathe? I hadn't and for me it was like watching a ten million year old fossil come to life. I was surprised that its flesh coloring matches its shell! In 1976 the Waikiki Aquarium was the first to display a live chambered nautilus, and in 1985 it became the first aquarium to breed them in captivity. Another big surprise to me was that certain young fish (convict tang) are transparent! You can look through their skin and see their innards at work, like a clock with a clear plastic case. It's fascinating - and you can see it on the videotape about reef fish at the shark exhibit.

Don't miss the display showing the Megamouth shark, a new genus, species and family of shark discovered 26 miles Northeast of Kahuku in November 1976. The one and only specimen of this gargantuan creature was quick frozen and is now preserved in the fish collection of the British Museum, which I'm told displays it on special occasions. (Check with the Bishop Museum for details). You'll also see one of Hawaii's few native sea animals, the Monk seal, in the newly expanded outdoor Seal Pool. An endangered species with fewer than 1,500 surviving today, the Monk seals are in residence at the Aquarium by special permit. Look for the giant clams in Tank 38, and the hazardous marine life in Tank 9. And be sure to walk through the Hawaiian exhibit.

Before you go to Hanauma Bay to snorkel, come to the Aquarium and visit Gallery 2, which re-creates Hawaii's coral reefs, tidepools and deep-water reefs. Your snorkeling, scuba or snuba (see the WHAT TO DO chapter) excursions will be more fun when you can identify the reef life.

Before you leave the Aquarium be sure you've seen the little fish with the big name, Hawaii's State fish in Tank 13, the Humuhumunukunukuapua'a. There are knowledgeable and friendly volunteers outside at the Edge of the Reef Exhibit to answer your questions, and the well-stocked gift shop with consolation items for those unfortunates who couldn't be here in person. For the young at heart the museum holds short classes on a variety of topics - including limu cuisine (cooking with seaweed), night reef walks, fish printing, and tidal art.

You can see why the Waikiki Aquarium (within easy walking distance of Waikiki) is one of O'ahus most visited attractions. Located at 2777 Kalakaua Ave,, Honolulu, HI 96815 (923-9741). Open daily 9am-5pm. Closed major holidays. Adults $2.50 donation, kids 15 and under free.

## DIAMOND HEAD CRATER ★
Leahi, as it was known to Hawaiians, is a 760-foot tall volcanic cone created by an explosion in recent geologic history, less than half a million years ago and long after the rest of O'ahu was formed. Ancient Hawaiians considered it a sacred spot, using it not only for a navigational landmark but also a heiau (temple). King Kamehameha I worshipped and offered human sacrifices at this heiau on Leahi's western slope.

In the early nineteenth century a group of sailors found what they thought were diamonds in the crater, so Kamehameha put a kapu (taboo) on the area until his advisor John Young discovered the "diamonds" were only worthless calcite crystals. The name "Diamond Head" became popular during the incident and has been the common name for Leahi (which means either brow of the A'hi fish - referring to the shape of the crater's rim, or wreath of fire - referring to the ceremonial bonfires lit around the crater's rim to help spot deep water fishing grounds at night) ever since.

The walk to the top is 7/10 mile long and open daily from 6am-6pm. A road off Diamond Head Road, between Makapuu Road and 18th Avenue (across from Kapiolani Community College) takes you by car through a tunnel to the floor of the crater. From there the trail leads through trees and tunnels to the 760 foot summit. You will need a flashlight (since you will walk through several tunnels), a pair of binoculars if you have them, and something to drink. Your

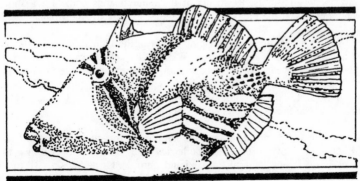

HUMUHUMU NUKUNUKU APUAA

children will enjoy the walk, especially the deserted pillboxes, gun emplacements, and tunnels built as a part of the Pacific defense network before World War II.

You might also stop in at the New Otani Kaimana Beach Hotel, 2863 Kalakaua Ave. (923-1555) or the Diamond Head Beach Hotel, 2947 Kalakaua Ave. (922-1928) for more information about Diamond Head Crater and area. They have been helping visitors for years and are very friendly.

The oceanside area makai of Diamond Head Crater from Kapiolani Park to Black Point is called the Gold Coast, and is some of Hawaii's most exclusive and expensive real estate. These fashionable cliffside villas, protected by gates and high walls, have been home to such celebrities as Doris Duke, the Kennedys, and Dorothy Lamour. Not far behind are the beautiful homes along Kahala Avenue between Black Point Road and Kealaolu Avenue. This continuation of Diamond Head Road is the closest street to the beach in the exclusive Kahala residential area, and is fun to drive through on your way to a picnic lunch at Waialae Beach Park or Sunday Brunch at the Kahala Hilton Hotel just past the Park.

This is the area where Presidents Nixon, Ford and Reagan have vacationed, and where some of O'ahu's most beautiful homes are located. After your Sunday drive through Kahala, stop at the Kahala Mall on Kealaolu and Waialae Avenues near the H-1 Freeway. There you'll find more than 50 shops, department stores, restaurants, and professional offices to explore, including Long's Drugs, the House of Almonds, Bank of Hawaii, Waldenbooks, A Yum Yum Tree, Vim and Vigor Foods, and Young Laundry and Dry Cleaning.

The Diamond Head area is one you'll enjoy exploring. Wth your walk to Diamond Head summit, a short driving tour and a trip to Kahala Mall, give yourself a half-day.

### ALA MOANA CENTER ★

"It's the best place to shop in Hawaii!" That's what I was told by a little Hawaiian grandma on the Bus. And she's right. Stewardesses arrive in cabs to buy gifts between flights. Residents of the outer Islands come for a shopping weekend and stay at the Pagoda Hotel so they can walk to Ala Moana.

Billed as the "largest open-air shopping center in the United States," Ala Moana is just across the Ala Wai Canal from Waikiki. Its 180 stores and restaurants on two levels are arrayed between Liberty House Department Store at one end and Sears at the other, with Shirokiya Japanese Department Store, J.C. Penneys, Long's Drugs, Foodland, and Woolworth's sprinkled among small specialty shops in between the two giants at either end.

This is a shopper's paradise, where you can browse through the likes of Crabtree and Evelyn, Purveyors of Fine Toiletries and Comestibles (things to eat produced in the countryside of England and Europe). Or perhaps a visit to Island Shells, Hawaii's largest seashell specialty shop selling chambered nautilus, spirally volutes, and whelks (you'll have to look those up!) Who can resist wandering into Chocolates for Breakfast, or peeking into Tahiti Imports. You can literally find anything here - from Andrade (fashions) to Zippy's (fast food).

Hungry after all that exciting shopping? You're in luck, because Ala Moana Center is home to O'ahu's largest family of restaurants. Start at the Makai Market Food Court, with more than 20 gourmet fast food restaurants. Patty's Chinese Kitchen and Sbarro's are among my favorites. If you're in the mood for a leisurely meal after you shop, try Byron II or the Fishmonger's Wife. And a trip to Shirokiya's upper level to sample Japanese food items is a treat, and a great place to take a breather, any time of day.

Entertainment on the Ala Maoan Center's "centerstage" brings artists and performers from all across Hawaii. This is where the free *Young People's Hula Show* (an Island tradition since 1969) performs every Sunday at 9:30am.

Ala Moana Center is open Mon-Fri 9:30-9pm, Sat. 9:30-5:30pm, and Sunday 10am-5pm. You can get there on the #8 bus from Waikiki (without the portable "Ward Avenue" sign), or any bus marked "Honolulu." Returning to Waikiki take the #8 or #20 Waikiki Beach and Hotels or #58 Hawaii Kai/Sea Life Park. Buses #8 and #20 board at Ala Moana Blvd; #58 boards at the suburban stop.


## SANS SOUCI BEACH ★
Located between the Natatorium and the Colony Surf Hotel, Sans Souci is one of O'ahu's best beaches. The name Sans Souci comes from Frederick the Great's Palace in Potsdam, and is the French phrase for "without a care." A series of family resorts and hotels have been built on this beach since 1884. A century of guests have enjoyed the shallow, clear water, the sandy bottom, and the excellent snorkeling and swimming the beach provides. The only danger at Sans Souci comes from youths jumping off the Natatorium wall into the coral-bottom ocean surrounding it. Stay away from the dangerous closed Natatorium and you'll find Sans Souci beach safe and enjoyable for your entire family.

## NEAL S. BLAISDELL CENTER
Known as the NBC, and sometimes called by its former name, the Honolulu International Center, this is Honolulu's biggest concert hall, exhibition center, and sports arena, located at 777 Ward Ave., Honolulu, HI 96814, 521-2911. Neal S. Blaisdell, Honolulu's Mayor from 1955 - 1969, was born in the city and served as a teacher, employee of Bishop Trust Co. and Hawaiian Pineapple Co., and as a member of the Territorial House and Senate.

Here's where the circus performs, where you can hear (sort of) rock groups, and watch basketball, boxing, and sumo wrestling (you should go to a sumo match, or watch one on local TV). The NBC is also home to the Honolulu Symphony Orchestra. Watch the local papers, because in June there is a wonderful hula competition, and various ballet troupes perform throughout the year. Also watch for the Parents' Fair, sponsored by the Boys and Girls Club of Honolulu (call 949-4773 for dates). As you drive by look at its electronic signboard on the corner of Kapiolani Blvd. and Ward Ave. which has notices of upcoming events.

## WARD WAREHOUSE AND WARD CENTRE

These two shopping-dining centers are located across the street from each other in long warehouse-type buildings, mauka from Kewalo Basin (Fisherman's Wharf on some maps) and Ala Moana Beach Park. They are unique because of their architecture and because their location puts them slightly off the beaten track. The pace is slower here, the mix of people more balanced between visitors and residents, and the atmosphere is very relaxed and informal.

*Ward Warehouse* is the less assuming of the two. The nautical theme of an old Hawaiian wharf-front warehouse is carried throughout the more than 50 shops and 9 restaurants on three floors. Shops run the gamut from Aloha Health Foods to the Liquor Connection. Just the names of many shops are intriguing - Candyman, Child's Play, Cookie Kitchen, Fine Things, In Bloom, Kris Kringle's Den, Neon Leon, Pomegranates in the Sun, Town & Country Surf Shop and Forever Summer. Three restaurants I particularly enjoy are located here: The Old Spaghetti Factory (I grew up in the one in San Francisco), Horatio's (especially for lunch) and Orsons (great view).

This is the perfect place to come after a morning tour of Historic Downtown Honolulu, after you've gotten your mate off on a charter fishing trip out of Kewalo Basin, or after attending the 10:30 Sunday worship service at Kawaiahao Church. Warehouse shops are open Mon-Fri. 10am-9pm; Sat. till 5pm; Sun. 11am-4pm. Restaurants are open for breakfast, lunch and dinner. Enjoy free Hawaiian entertainment every Fri., noon-1pm at the Food Express area. Free parking. Take Waikiki Trolley or Bus #8 from Waikiki. Ward Warehouse is two blocks Ewa from Ala Moana Center, at 1050 Ala Moana Blvd. (531-6411).

*Ward Centre*, just one block Diamond Head of the Ward Warehouse, is aimed at a slightly more upbeat clientele, with fewer, more expensive shops than the Ward Warehouse. Specialty shops include Imperial Collections, Haimoff and Haimoff Creations in Gold, Polo/Ralph Loren, Regency Shoes, and Willowdale Galleries. This is certainly a good place to come for restaurants too. Keo has a Thai restaurant here (see Dining Out Section), Compadre's Mexican Bar and Grill is great when you're in a party mood, and Monterey Bay Canners is a family standby. Ryan's Parkplace is a good place to meet people (plus having super pupus), and the Yum Yum Tree is always full of shoppers. Also for something different, especially before a concert or show when you want something light, Crepe Fever fills the bill. Open 10am-9pm, Mon-Fri.; 10am-5pm, Sat.; and 11am-4pm, Sun. Located at 1200 Ala Moana Blvd. Take the Trolley or the #8 Bus from Waikiki.

The nice thing about The Ward Warehouse and Ward Centre is that they're so close to each other you can explore them together and have a delicious, relaxing meal in the process.

## DOLE CANNERY SQUARE ★

Wouldn't it be fun to show the folks back home a snapshot of you and Kenny Rogers standing arm-in-arm in a field of ripe pineapples? Even more, wouldn't you like to know where the pineapples you've enjoyed for so many years come from? And aren't all these questions making you thirsty? Wouldn't you appreciate an ice cold cup of something to drink, say, for example, fresh pineapple juice? You can find all of these things at Dole Cannery Square, in the Iwili section of Honolulu. Though the Dole Cannery has been giving tours for five decades, Dole Cannery Square is one of O'ahu's newest major attractions.

DID YOU KNOW...that James Dole came to Hawaii almost penniless in 1899, fresh out of college? He found investors, raised $20,000, and started his pineapple production company on a 12-acre homestead farm very near the Central O'ahu site of today's Dole Pineapple Pavilion near Wahiawa. 20 years later Dole was able to buy almost the entire Island of Lanai for 1.1 million dollars.

Phase I, now open, saw the creation of a street level visitor reception area under a giant three-story skylight. Here you begin your tour by reading about Dole's modest beginnings, viewing a scale model of the cannery, and having the opportunity to get your photo taken next to a lifesize cardboard mock-up of Dole spokesman and popular entertainer Kenny Rogers. Then you enter a multi-media 60-seat theater to view a ten minute slide-tape presentation telling the fascinating story of the history of the pineapple industry in Hawaii. After the slide show you tour the cannery on foot, climbing a ramp to an upper level where you walk above the machines and watch televised video tape explanations of each step in the canning process. The Ginaca Machines, which were first built in 1913 and made the modern pineapple industry possible, are especially interesting to watch as they peel and core 98 pineapples per minute on the floor below your walkway.

After the tour, which concludes with delicious ice cold fresh pineapple juice, you enter Phase II of the new Square. On the upper level they've built a re-creation of an old Hawaiian Pineapple Plantation Village, with stores and shops on either side of the Main Street. As you stroll through the village you are met by the sights and sounds of turn-of-the century O'ahu. There are more than 17,000 square feet of shops with the "Made in Hawaii" theme to explore. Then

explore. Then down an escalator to Dole's brand new 25,000 square foot visitors' atrium with gourmet food shops, a food court (serving fresh salads, sandwiches and desserts), cafe seating, Dole's dessert pavilion (where your tour ticket is redeemable for a complimentary Dole Whip (only 20 calories per ounce), a gift shop and a fresh pineapple shipping center.

Phase III, with construction well underway across the street, will see the completion of a nine-story Visitor Orientation Center with retail areas, restaurants, meeting rooms, parking area, and a bus terminal.

Speaking of buses, Dole Cannery Square has its own! The "Pineapple Transit" is a fleet of 25 passenger mini buses that stop every five minutes at 13 major Waikiki hotels, as well as major shopping areas and tourist attractions in the Downtown area, and provides non-stop service to Cannery Square, all for only 50 cents per destination for each rider. You can also get here on the Waikiki Trolley, or by taking the #19 (Airport-Hickham) Bus. If you have a rental car, just travel Ewa on Ala Moana Blvd. (Highway 92) until it becomes Nimitz Highway, then start looking for the famous pineapple water tower. There's free parking right under the pineapple. Hours: Open daily 9am-5pm at 650 Iwilei Rd., with 10-minute multi-media presentations running continuously. Adults $5.00, children 12 and under free, Kamaainas $2.50.

## THE BEACHES OF METROPOLITAN HONOLULU
Amazing as it seems, one of the ten best beaches on O'ahu is located in Metro Honolulu. It is *Ala Moana Beach Park*, the most popular beach park among Honolulu residents. The park runs from makai of Ala Moana Center all the way down to Kewalo Basin. On weekends the park and beach are crowded with local residents playing baseball, throwing frisbees, flying model airplanes, and playing in the water. But on weekdays, the beach is often nearly deserted.

Daily lifeguard service is provided by the City and County. One word of caution, this is not one of the best beaches for young children. A deep channel was dredged parallel to the beach years ago to connect the Ala Wai Canal with Kewalo Basin for small boat traffic. Now unused, the channel is still 20 - 30 feet deep offshore. The slope from the beach is gradual, but at low tide children can wade out near it. Also, tradewinds can blow inflatable rings and rafts into deeper water, which children may chase without being aware of the dropoff. So while this beach is excellent for adults, water conditions are safe and calm all year and there are no strong currents, it is not recommended for kids.

On the Diamond Head end of Ala Moana Beach Park is *Magic Island*, known officially since 1972 as *'Aina Moana* (land from the ocean). This man-made peninsula was filled in to accommodate a resort hotel that was never built. The beach part of the project, however, was completed, and provides a safe and calm place to swim or wade. Seawalls placed to keep the sand from eroding form a small lagoon. Swimming inside the lagoon is safe, but anyone climbing the rocks or breakwater risks danger from waves breaking over them. Anyone using 'Aina Moana should be warned to swim only inside the lagoon; children should be carefully supervised. With proper precautions these two areas offer great beach and good swimming all year.

## QUEEN EMMA'S SUMMER PALACE

This modest summer home deserves your attention because it is such a good example of the getaway homes enjoyed by well-to-do families of early Honolulu. The Nuuanu (cool heights) Valley was Honolulu's first suburb. High up the slopes of the Koolau Mountains amidst lush tropical vegetation and frequent mauka showers, one could escape the heat, sun and blowing dust of the Honolulu summer.

Emma was the granddaughter of John Young, the sailor who became advisor to Kamehameha I and later Governor of the Big Island. She inherited the summer house from her uncle John Young II, who had it shipped in pieces from Boston. When she married King Kamehameha IV (Alexander Liholiho) two years into his reign (1856), the royal couple spent many days here relaxing away from the cares of the crown.

As you enter the 2-bedroom house you will see mementos of the short life of their son and heir to the Hawaiian throne, Prince Albert, who died at the age of four in 1862. His christening robe, the canoe-shaped cradle made in Germany for him, his clothing, and even locks of his hair are on display. Every room of the home is full of royal memorabilia, including a magnificent tiger claw necklace given to Emma by an East Indian Maharajah. Feather kahilis which marked the presence of royalty are displayed throughout the home, along with portraits of many members of royal family. King Kamehameha IV and Queen Emma favored British society, and the furnishings in this house reflect this preference. Look at the ornate British clock, the piano built in London, and gifts sent to the family by Britain's Queen Victoria (Albert's Godmother).

The home is well cared for by the Daughters of Hawaii. Located at 2913 Pali Highway (#61), Honolulu (595-3167). Open daily 9am-4pm. Adults $2, children under 15, 50 cents.

## NUUANU PALI ★

About a mile up the Pali Highway from Emma's Summer Palace on the right is the turnoff to the ***Nuuanu Pali Drive***. Drive through a beautiful native forest on your way up Nuuanu Valley to the famous Pali (cliff) Lookout. Just after Nuuanu Pali Drive rejoins the Pali Highway, watch on your left for the ***Upside Down Waterfalls***. One of many legends about the Nuuanu Valley tells that the water from these falls, which never reaches the ground but is blown into a veil of tear-like mist as it drops, represents the tears of a maiden who eternally weeps for her fallen warrior lover.

Continue up the Pali Highway until, just after Nuuanu Reservoir #4 on your right, you take the turn off to the right marked ***Pali Lookout***, and find the lookout parking lot. Here is one of O'ahu's most famous viewpoints. The wind blows all year here, so hard that it sends airborne any hats, hairdos, scarves, and skirts one might be wearing. You can almost lean windward at a 45 degree angle and not fall over, except as soon as you do there will be a lull in the blast and you'll find yourself on your knees.

As you stand at the viewpoint and admire the panoramic view of windward O'ahu laid out before you, you should know of two popular stories about the Pali, and should realize that most likely neither is true. In April 1795, after the young warrior chieftain Kamehameha and his armies had won control of the Big Island, Maui, and Moloka'i, they landed at Waikiki beach and prepared to battle for control of O'ahu. The battle, according to legend, was joined and fought in Nuuanu Valley with the armies defending O'ahu pushing further and further up the slopes and ultimately hundreds or thousands were pushed (or jumped) over the Pali cliff to their deaths 1000 feet below. Historians today tell us that whereas a few stragglers might have gone over the Pali, the major battles for control of O'ahu were fought in Honolulu and on the lower stretches of Nuuanu Valley, not at the Pali. It makes a good story, though, doesn't it.

The second Pali myth says that Nuuanu Valley has always been as it now is, lush and green, covered by flowering native trees and jungle vegetation. In fact, a famous photograph taken at the turn of the century shows a Nuuanu Valley devoid of all trees, shrubs, or plants and covered instead only by scrub ground cover less than a foot tall. Whether natives burned the valley to facilitate hunting, or whether plantings were not introduced until after 1900, the fact remains that Nuuanu Valley until recently was a barren, windswept canyon.

The legends and stories connected with Nuuanu Pali, combined with its spectacular view and wind, and the fact that the present tunnel and highway were not completed until well after World War II, make this one of O'ahu's most enjoyable tour sites. So bundle up, take your camera, and wear shorts!

## UNIVERSITY OF HAWAII AND EAST-WEST CENTER
Drive or take a bus (#4 Nuuanu) up University Avenue to the University of Hawaii at Manoa (UHM) campus. Get a campus map and pamphlets from the Office of University Relations in Hawaii Hall, Room 2, or from one of the guard stations on campus. UHM has an enrollment of 45,000 students in its nine-campus system on four Islands, and a faculty of nearly 7,000.

As you drive or walk through the luxurious campus, you'll be able to locate the **UHM Student Center** on your map. Stop in and ask for information on campus happenings, housing, summer programs (with 50% discount on airfare if you're coming from the mainland), and even restaurants, discos, and cultural events around town. While you're there visit the **UHM Bookstore**, open Mon-Fri. 8:15am-4:15pm, and Sat. 8:15-11:45am. And the **University Art Gallery** on the third floor has excellent rotating exhibits.

Now on to our primary destination, the **East-West Center (EWC)**. Established in 1960 by the U.S. Congress, the EWC is a non-profit educational institution, associated with but separate from the University, designed to bring together people from the United States, Asia, and the Pacific to study and seek solutions to problems of social, economic, and cultural change. Funding comes from Congress and nearly 25 Asian and Pacific governments as well as private foundations and public agencies. EWC scholarships annually support more than 300 students from 40 countries who live and study at the EWC and UHM. The Center's three residence halls house 600 students.

The East-West Center's 21 acre landscaped campus is located on East-West Road on the Diamondhead side of the UHM campus. Our first stop is *John Burns Hall* near the corner of East-West Rd. and Dole St. In the lobby you can pick up a self-guiding map and illustrated brochures about the EWC. If you can, you should take the guided tour of the Center, which will give you a look at its functions, inside and out. Call 944-7111 for reservations.

Next let's visit the *Thai Pavilion*, a gift from the King of Thailand, adjacent to Thomas Jefferson Hall. This ornate building is made of solid teak. Behind Jefferson Hall is a hidden treasure discovered by very few tourists. A complete Japanese garden and teahouse named *"Jakuan"* (House of Tranquility) which offers shade, quiet and a solitary park in which to walk and meditate. This is one of O'ahu's most lovely spots on a warm afternoon. The murals and other art inside the teahouse are handsome.

As you leave, drive mauka on East-West Rd. stop at the *Center for Korean Studies*. Stop and examine this fine building, modelled after Kyongbok Palace in Seoul. Inside the artwork is elaborate and colorful as the exterior.

The best way to conclude your tour of UHM and the East-West Center is to meet and talk with some of the students and staff. They are anxious to meet visitors, to share their interests, and to find out about yours. A good way to do this is to attend one of the frequent lectures, seminars or other sessions hosted by the Center. You may meet a person from another part of the world whose lifestyle will enhance your own, and make a new friend. In the long run that's what the East-West Center is all about.

---

DID YOU KNOW...that Honolulu has a brand new Contemporary Art Museum? Open since late 1988, the new museum is housed in an historic old estate in the Makiki Heights section of Honolulu at 2411 Makiki Heights Dr. It features Hawaiian and other art created during the past 40 - 50 years. One gallery is 20 feet high, another is small and intimate. In all the Museum has 12,000 square feet of exhibition space. Hours: 10am-4pm, Mon-Sat., noon-4 pm on Sun. Free admission Thurs. (808) 526-1322.

---

### TANTALUS/ROUND TOP DRIVE ★

Ask local residents where they would take first-time visitors to O'ahu to show them the city, and nine times out of ten a drive around Tantalus and Round Top will be high on the list. Few cities are blessed with winding country roads high above the town, complete with a lookout affording a spectacular view of the entire cityscape far below. Luckily for Honolulu, Tantalus-Round Top is just that. The beginning can be a little tricky to find, but is easy with a map and these directions. Go mauka on Piikoi, the street at the Ewa side of Ala Moana Center. When Piikoi forks, take the right fork, Mott-Smith Drive, and follow it until it becomes Makiki. Turn right off Makiki onto Tantalus Drive and you're on your way.

As you drive leisurely over the 2,013 foot high cinder cone you'll pass beautiful estates, parks, hiking trails and every kind of tropical vegetation you can imagine. Bring your camera and your botany ID book, because this is a modern Garden of Eden! Pull over and let those in a hurry go by, and enjoy the picture postcard views around every corner. Near the summit, just before Kalaiopua Place, there's a hiking trail to the rim of the crater. If you can find a place to park off the road it's a good hike and wonderful view.

From here the road becomes Round Top Drive, winding past a Boy Scout Camp and down to *Puu Ualakaa State Wayside*. This park closes at dusk, but offers the very best view of Honolulu, Waikiki and the entire southern shoreline from Koko Head to the Waianae Mountain Range. One of the two or three most photographed spots on O'ahu (along with Nuuanu Pali, Kamehameha's Statue, and Waikiki-Diamond Head.)

Contact the Sierra Club (1212 University Ave., Honolulu, HI 96826, 946-8494) for a $3 packet on Hawaii's trails, or request the *O'ahu Recreational Map* from the Division of Forestry, 1151 Punchbowl Street, Honolulu, HI 96813 (548-2861), containing detailed descriptions of Tantalus-Round Top trails.

## PARADISE PARK AND KA'IULANI'S LITTLE GRASS SHACK
Deep in the cool Manoa Valley, mauka from the U. of Hawaii at Manoa, is an attraction especially for the kids. *Paradise Park* has five features that make it worth visiting: the setting - gardens, streams, ponds and waterfalls; the birds - macaws, parrots, flamingos; the famous "Dancing Waters" show with colored lights and 30-foot tall jet streams; the buffet luncheon restaurant and snack bar; and best of all, the puppets and costumed creatures who entertain the kids.

The tropical birds perform in a 340-seat amphitheater, and kids can have their picture taken holding a feathered companion. The Dancing Waters show comes on at 11:25am, 2:15pm and 4:30pm. Free shuttle service two times daily from seven major Waikiki hotels, or take the #8 Ala Moana Center Bus (without Ward Ave. sign) and transfer to bus #5 at Kona St. Paradise Park is located at 3737 Manoa Rd. (988-6686). Open daily 10am-5pm. Adults $7.50, juniors (13-17) $6.50, keikis (4-12) $3.75. Call 988-2141 to arrange for free transportation.

PARROTS

If you're real plant lovers try to plan your visit to Paradise Park on the first Friday, third Wednesday, or third Saturday of the month. These are the only three days monthly when *University of Hawaii's Lyon Arboretum* (just up the road apiece from Paradise Park) is open. You'll need a reservation (988-3177), but the free guided tours are well worth it. The Friday and Wednesday tours begin at 1 pm. Saturday tour starts at 10am. They'll show you 124 acres full of coffee plants, spices, vanilla, cinnamon, ginger, palms, heliconia, taro (200 plus species, Hawaii's largest collection), and more. A botanist's heaven. 3860 Manoa Rd., Honolulu, HI 96822.

Back down O'ahu Avenue a mile and a half or so is the reconstructed *Grass Shack* which Robert Louis Stevenson was supposed to have stayed or written in during his 1889 stay on O'ahu. This shack stood on the Ainahau property where the 13 year old princess lived and was entertained by the famous author's stories and poems. Years later when the estate was broken up, a group purchased the shack to save it, and moved it into the Manoa Valley to the now closed Waioli Tea Room, owned and operated by the Salvation Army. The shack has since been re-thatched and a porch has been added, but it is supposed to contain the original rustic furnishings used by Stevenson. It is located at 3016 O'ahu Ave. I recommend stopping there as you explore the enchanted Manoa Valley.

## HONOLULU SAKE BREWERY

Here are two experiences for you adventuresome souls who want a challenge few tourists would undertake. Above Honolulu in the Pauoa Valley (between Nuuanu Valley and Tantalus at 2150 Booth Road) is a group of old buildings. This unlikely setting is the first Sake Brewery in the United States. Founded in 1908 and only one of a handful of such breweries outside the Orient, this brewery follows the time-honored tradition of making rice wine (sake) by hand. It also produces soy sauce. You might want to call before you go (537-9068). I have not been to the factory yet, but it is at the top of my list. This is one of those adventures that could prove to be most memorable. I'll report in *THE OAHU UPDATE* what I discover about sake brewing in Hawaii. Please write me with the results of your visit to this unique site.

## KAWAMOTO ORCHID NURSERY

A second expedition will take you into the Palolo Valley between St. Louis Heights and Maunalani Heights. Here at 2630 Waiomao Rd., you will (hopefully) find the Kawamoto Orchid Nursery. If you want to take the easy way out, you can call them at 732-5808 for directions.

This place is amazing; 3 1/2 acres of orchids! All varieties, sizes and shapes, and color schemes. They'll take you around and show you how an orchid nursery operates, so for anyone who loves flowers this is a trip worth taking. Most orchids in Hawaii are grown on the Big Island, so this orchid nursery is another outer island point of interest right here on O'ahu. The folks are friendly, patient, and very knowledgeable. Open 7am-3:30pm. Mon. to Sat.; Sundays by appointment. They have a catalog, too.

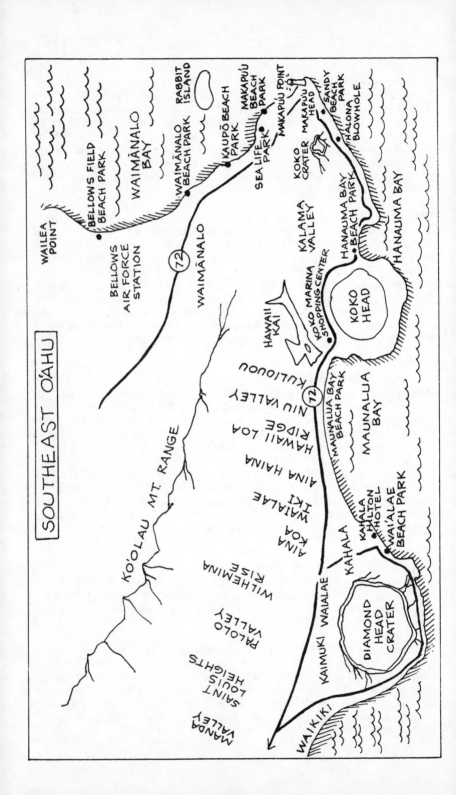

SOUTHEAST OʻAHU

# EXPLORING SOUTHEAST OʻAHU

What a beautiful day for a drive! We'll start early (6:30am) to miss the morning traffic, and be able to see the beautiful morning sun on the south Oʻahu coast. Get onto Kalanianaole Hwy (72) heading east toward Koko Crater and Hanauma Bay. As you drive past the beautiful valleys and ridges on your left, see if you can spot any caves high up in the cliffs. Ancient Hawaiians lived in each of these valleys, and stories are told about the numerous caves that were discovered recently during clearing for subdivisions power lines, and other development. One cave reportedly contained a canoe, calabashes, and household artifacts.

Be sure to have our map of Southeast Oʻahu handy so you'll be able to spot these points of interest as they appear. And don't be afraid to stop. Being from the mainland, I was so used to long distances that it took me weeks of sight-seeing to realize that Oʻahu is a compact island, where nothing is very far from anything else. So you can relax, pull over, get out, look at the incredible scenery, and take comfort in the fact that the entire southeast coast covers less than a 15 mile distance. Lots to see, but in a relatively small space.

On your left you'll see *Aina Haina Shopping Center*, home of Showbiz Pizza Place, Giftland, Kathy-Ray Casuals, The Poodle Salon, and a number of restaurants. Nearby, on the makai side of the highway is *Calvary by the Sea Lutheran Church*, 5339 Kalainaole Highway, where the Honolulu Chamber Music group plays wonderful concerts regularly each month. Call the church (377-5477 or 732-7677) for more information.

If you enjoy geology, you'll want to remember that we're following a line of volcanic tuft cones formed recently (100,000 - 3,000,000 years ago) by ex-plosions caused by steam from lava meeting subterranean sea water. You can see this line on your map connecting Diamond Head Crater, Koko Head, Koko Crater, Makapuʻu Head, and Rabbit Island. These craters all broke through the older underlying lava flows which had formed this end of the Island during the active period of the Koolau volcanic craters.

Passing the green velvet slopes of the Niu (coconut) Valley, we approach the *Maunalua* (Two mountains) *Bay* popular for small boat water activity and jet skiing. See if you can spot any jet skiers or scuba excursions out on the bay. Watch on your right for *Maunalua Bay Beach Park*, with the only public small boat ramp between Honolulu and Kailua. This beach is not a good one for swimming, since its bottom is coral-mud, and the small boat channel on its eastern side makes for dangerous currents and depths.

This entire area, now known as *Hawaii Kai* was developed in the 1950's by industrialist-builder Henry J. Kaiser who leased land containing Hawaii's largest ancient fish pond (Kuapa Pond, originally covering 523 acres), brought in his pink bulldozers, and created a planned residential community which today includes marinas, shopping centers, parks, schools, and recreational areas. Within the past several years a large number of shops and excellent restaurants have opened in the area, including Koko Marina Shopping Center, and the Hawaii Kai Shopping Center. Several of these are reviewed in the WHERE TO

EAT chapter, and you'll see more appearing in *THE O'AHU UPDATE*. Hawaii Kai is fast becoming one of O'ahus most fashionable places to have dinner. A good vantage point from which to view this growing area is from ***Koko Crater Viewpoint*** on Kalanianaole Highway east of Hawaii Kai just before the turnoff to Hanauma Bay. From this high spot you can see the entire Hawaii Kai community laid out far below.

Turn makai off the Highway onto Hanauma Bay Road, and drive through the multi-sectioned parking lot. If you're a hiker, you'll enjoy the ***trail from Hanauma to the Blowhole*** which leaves from the east end of this parking lot. There's also a ***Koko Crater Trail*** which takes off from the Hawaii Job Corps property at the end of the Koko Head Park Road across the Highway from the Hanauma Bay entrance. ***Hanauma Bay*** ★ is one of the best places to snorkel and swim on O'ahu, and has therefore become one of the Island's premier tourist attractions. No doubt you'll read and hear about this State Underwater Park on local TV, in the tourist literature, and in person from tour desk and tour company folks. And you should come back here. It's a perfect place to observe reef fish and corals, swimming is good when its not too crowded, and you can get information from the interpretive kiosk in the beach park pavilion.

There are several tips you should follow to make your visit to Hanauma Bay most successful. First, go on a weekday tour so that you don't have to drive or carry your valuables. Second, go in the early morning, arrive if you can before 7am - swim until 9 or 10 and then leave. By 10am the park is packed and it becomes a zoo. Third, rent your snorkeling or scuba equipment before you go, or as a part of the tour package. Best bet if you can is to bring your own gear or get fitted for equipment prior to the day of your trip. Fourth, take with you a towel, sun lotions, sunglasses, very little cash, your equipment, your beach wear, your camera (you can rent an underwater camera for not too much), and, if you like, a waterproof card or booklet to identify the underwater creatures. Go with a friend, or group if possible, or find a buddy to take turns watching your things. It's also fun to take a box of frozen peas; the fish will eat them out of your hand, and peas won't fall apart in the water as bread will. Meet the lifeguard and ask what you should and shouldn't do given the day's conditions, then relax, enjoy, and you'll have a morning you won't forget.

On down the highway about 1 1/2 miles you'll come to some of the Island's most spectacular seaside scenery. On your left is **Koko Crater**, highest tuft cone on O'ahu at 1,208 feet. You can see that the tradewinds were blowing from the northeast on the ancient day when it exploded because the southwest rim of the crater (just as on Diamond Head) is by far the taller and more substantial.

Stop at the **Halona Blow Hole** ★ viewpoint where a natural vertical volcanic tunnel sends geysers spouting high in the air. Notice **Halona Cove** on the right side of the parking lot as you face the Blow Hole. This beach is right out of a movie - secluded, tiny, and hard to reach. It is certainly not recommended for kids, since the cove can be turbulent with large surf and dangerous currents. But for adults who want a romantic spot to get away for an afternoon dip (stay close to shore; currents can suck a swimmer into the Blow Hole to almost certain disaster). This is a unique place. This was the location of Burt Lancaster and Deborah Kerr's love scene in the surf in the movie "From Here to Eternity."

Back toward Hanauma Bay from the Blow Hole a few hundred feet, on the other side of Halona Cove, is **Halona Point**. This has been both one of the favorite locations for O'ahu's shoreline fishermen, and one of the most dangerous fishing spots on O'ahu. You can see the **Statue of O-Jizosan**, Japanese guardian god of anyone near dangerous waters or cliffs, at the small pull-off area high on the cliff. These statues are usually placed where people have been killed, and should be viewed as a solemn reminder of the power and fury of the ocean here, especially from Koko Head to Kaupo Bay just past Sea Life Park.

Another mile southeast of the Blow Hole is **Sandy Beach Park**. Lifeguards here and at Makapu'u make more rescues per year than do guards at all other beaches on O'ahu. The beach drops off quickly so large waves break directly onto the beach - this shorebreak makes Sandy Beach O'ahu's best body surfing beach for experts and the worst for injuries. More bodysurfing injuries have been sustained on this beach than on all other O'ahu beaches execpt Makapu'u. So unless you're a veteran, watch the local youngsters bodysurf here and try the sport at Waikiki. One thing you should try here is the food at the **Kaukau wagons** often stationed across the highway from Sandy Beach. Food here hits the spot while you're checking out the scene in the water and on the beach. And be sure to ask the lifeguards about water conditions before you enter the water.

After you leave Sandy Beach you'll see the Kalama Valley and Queens Gate residential areas on the mauka side, and you'll pass the famous **Hawaii Kai Championship Golf Course**. There is one Championship course, 18 holes, par 72; and one Executive par 3 course designed by Robert Trent Jones, 18 holes par 55. Facilities for both courses include clubhouse, proshop, rental equipment, driving range, PGA pro. Both courses are private but open to the public but reservations are required (395-2358). Now we'll wind up and around through wind sculpted terrain past the lighthouse at Makapu'u Point and stop at the Lookout just beyond it, overlooking Makapu'u Beach Park.

**Makapu'u Point** rises to 700 feet from the water and marks the eastern-most tip of O'ahu. Legend says that when Pele, Goddess of Fire, left O'ahu forever she stepped off the Island at Makapu'u Point. The famous **lighthouse** has been flashing its 2.8 mile beacon (the largest in any American lighthouse) over the dark Pacific since 1906. The 150,000 candle power beacon and radio beacon, which can be heard 200 miles at sea, are operated by three U.S. Coast Guardsmen who live at the lighthouse with their families. From the *Makapu'u Lookout*, on a clear day, you can see Moloka'i 26 miles across the 2,000 foot deep Kaiwi Channel. Below you is *Makapu'u Beach Park*, O'ahu's most famous bodysurfing location. In the summer the surf is usually calm, but winter brings big surf and dangerous conditions for all but the experts. And experts come here from all over the Islands to show their bodysurfing skill.

From the Lookout you can see one of my favorite landmarks, *Manana* (stretched out) *Island* offshore (the largest of four volcanic tuft cone islets), commonly called Rabbit Island. Pet rabbits were kept there in the 1800's, but the name comes from the Island's profile, that of a rabbit's head facing Makapuu Point, with its ears back. Once your eye sees the rabbit in the profile, you'll always see the same likeness every time you look at the Island, as if mother nature had purposefully sculpted it.

---

DO YOU KNOW...why Winchester repeating rifles were once buried in the sand on Manana (Rabbit) Island off the southeast O'ahu Coast? The arms were to be used in 1895 in a counterrevolution to put Queen Liliuokalani back on the throne of Hawaii. The plot was discovered, and the secret cache of guns and ammunition was never used.

---

Coming down off the hill turn in at the *Sea Life Park* ★ entrance and find a place to park. This is one of the five best paid visitor attractions on O'ahu. The problem here is not enough time. The best way to see the Park is to come on a Thursday, Friday or Sunday when it's open from 9:30am-10pm. That way you can see each of the four shows and six major exhibits, take the Behind-the-scenes Tour (to see the one and only Wholphin in captivity), enjoy a leisurely open-air dinner at the Gallery Restaurant, do a bit of shopping at the shopping arcade, and clap to the "Salute to the Hawaiian Islands" review at 8:30pm starring radio personality Kimo Kahoano, and Auntie Myrtle K. Hilo!

If you can't spend a day, let us suggest what to see first. You must visit the 300,000 gallon salt water *Hawaiian Reef Tank* near the entrance, and take time to stop, stand and watch at each level as you look through the glass into this three story underwater world of a Hawaiian coral reef. Different creatures inhabit the various depths of the reef; you'll see more than 2,000 specimens as you descend the spiral ramp down to a level nearly three fathoms (18 feet) below the surface, and listen to the fascinating taped story of this ocean community. Graphics posted along the way will help you identify your favorite specimens. See hammerhead sharks, sting ray, tiger cowrie, and the popular human divers who enter the tank several times a day to feed the creatures and bring some of the most unusual ones close to the windows for you to see.

Second priority on your Sea Life Park agenda should be a visit to the *Ocean Science Theater*, where you'll see: dolphins who play catch, jump, and ride a surfboard; sea lions who can talk their trainers into almost anything; and a pack of pesky penguins that steal the show - and the food!! This is an educational as well as an entertaining show.

Next, be sure to take a *Behind-the Scenes Tour*, given several times each day and limited to 16 lucky people on each tour. This is when (unless you see her in a show) you'll get to see Kekaimalu (the peaceful sea), the hybrid cross between false killer whale and an Atlantic bottlenose dolphin - affectionately called a wholphin. Now she's in training, and someday she'll become a working member of the Sea Life Park troupe.

One exhibit you can't leave without seeing is the *Pacific Whaling Museum* which first opened to the public in 1979. Harpoons, whale oil, baleen, knives, a giant skeleton of a 38-foot sperm whale, scrimshaw, giant shark teeth, and many other whaling artifacts are displayed along with the glorious and horrible story of whaling. A gift shop attached to the Museum offers scrimshaw kits, jewelry, nautical gifts and marine artifacts connected with Hawaii's whaling era during the early and mid 1800's.

Must you leave? You have just started to explore the Park, and the show at the Whaler's Cove is coming up, where you'll hear legends of old Hawaii, and see a 500 pound dolphin soar 25 feet to the yardarm of a 5/8 scale model of a square masted sailing ship. You haven't fed the seals yet at the Sea Lion Feeding Pool, or seen the Shark Gallery. So why not spend the day! No matter how long you can stay, keep your eyes open for some of the superstars of the park: Fat Fred the penguin; Kamoana the baseball-playing dolphin (he has performed at the Ocean Science Theater for 15 years); Makapuu, the 1700 pound female false killer whale, and Kihei, the outrigger canoe riding dog. You'll spot them as they perform in various parts of the Park. If you've been to Sea Life Park, you can imagine how romantic and exciting it looks all lit up for the evening performances. You'll just have to stay and see for yourself!

As you reluctantly leave the Park, look up toward the *Ko'olau Mountains* which rise 2,000 feet from sea level only a few thousand feet back from the surf behind Sea Life Park. This is a favorite take-off spot for hang gliders, who ride the thermals high above the coast. One local hang glider, Jim Will, may still hold the record with his amazing 34 1/2 hour ride. The gliders are very friendly and if not committed to another flight before dusk, will be glad to talk to you about the sport. Contact the Hawaiian Hang Gliding Assoc. (395-6490) or Tradewinds Hang Gliding (396-8557). For glider ride info try Glider Rides (623-6711), Soar Hawaii (637-3147) or Honolulu Soaring Club (677-3404).

*Kaupo Beach Park* is located between Sea Life Park and *Makai Pier* which houses Park boats and sealife acquisition equipment. It is best known for its board surfing, since the small offshore surf in the cove is ideal for beginners. Swimming is safe, but discouraged by patches of onshore coral.

Driving past Makai Pier you enter the Waimanalo area. One of the estates you'll pass on the makai side of the highway near Waimanalo Beach Park was the setting for Magnum's house in the TV series "Magnum PI."

Stop at **Waimanalo Beach Park**, the site in the late 1800's of the Waimanalo Landing, a dock used by interisland steamers and cargo ships visiting the several sugar plantations and plantation villages in this area. While the beach lacks a full-time lifeguard, it is sandy and calm most of the year. The Beach Park has cooking facilities, a comfort station, and ball fields. This is a nice spot for lunch or an afternoon picnic on the beach.

Back on Highway 72, heading northwest, you pass the the home of one of Hawaii's premier musical families, the Pahinuis. The late and great entertainer Gabby Pahinui left a legacy which is being carried on by Mrs. Pahinui, sons Bla, Martin and Cyril, and their families. Waimanalo is their home, and if you love Hawaiian music you might be able to feel their spirit as you pass through their well-loved home town.

---

DID YOU KNOW..that Waimanalo is paniolo country as well as farm country? Several large ranches operate in the area; a few offer riding and Hawaiian hoe-downs. One of Waimanalo's biggest events is the annual Thanksgiving Rodeo at the New Town and Country Stables (41-1800 Kalanianaole Hwy. (808) 259-9941). Riders also compete at the Waimanalo Polo Club (41-1062 Kalanianaole Hwy. (808) 259-8904) on Sat. at 3pm, March thru August.

---

On your right, just before passing through the town of Waimanalo, is the Main Gate to **Bellows Air Force Base**, where you'll find the best swimming beach in this area and one of O'ahu's ten best beaches, **Bellows Field Beach Park ★**. Follow Tinker Rd. for 2 miles to the beach area, between Puha Stream on the south and Waimanalo Stream on the north. Although it is only open to the public on weekends (noon Fri-midnight Sun.) and national holidays, this is a beautiful sandy beach with calm water and lifeguards. Keep children away from the two streams, which can develop strong currents as they empty into the ocean. Watch for Portuguese man-o-war washing up on shore here when tradwinds blow. These transparent jellyfish have a painful sting and should be avoided on all beaches. For safety, sand, and good swimming conditions, Bellows Beach Park (523-4525) can't be beat. Camping permits are issued to the public by the City and County of Honolulu for 50 campsites and 4 trailer sites.

Back out the Bellows Main Gate turn right and drive slowly through the proud and historic town of Waimanalo. Waimanalo has always had the feeling of real Hawaii about it, shunning tourist developments and clinging to traditional Hawaiian values. After the sugar plantation closed in the 1940's, Waimanalo increased production of bananas, papayas, anthuriums and other local fruits and vegetables, such as famous Waimanalo sweet corn. Proceed up Hwy 72 toward the Kailua Jct. On the right is the Enchanted Lake residential area (originally one of Kailua's largest fish ponds) and on the left, Olomana Peak, the 1,643-ft mountain said to be the first piece of the Ko'olau side of O'ahu to break the surface of the ocean eons ago. This ends our initial exploration of S.E. O'ahu. You can either continue on up the windward coast on Hwys 72 and 83, or turn left at Hwy 61 in Kailua and drive back thru the Pali Tunnel to Honolulu.

# EXPLORING CENTRAL OʻAHU

For our tour of the Central Oʻahu Valley we'll travel north, beginning at the junction of the H-1 (Lunalilo) Freeway, the H-2 Freeway, and the Kamehameha Highway (#99) between Pearl City and Waipahu, just south of Seaview, since most visitors follow this path as they travel from Waikiki to Oʻahu's North Shore. If you are traveling south from North Shore, follow this section in reverse order of entries.

Since we have plenty of time on our tour, let's drive north through the Central Oʻahu Valley on old HIghway 99 (Kamehameha Highway) so that we can stop and see points of interest on the way. If you're in a rush, or on your way back to the city, then take the H-2 Freeway which parallels Highway 99 from Wahiawa to the Pearl City junction.

As we drive through the center of this plateau between the older Waianae Mountain Range on the west and the younger Koʻolau Mountains to the east, it is important to remember that we're crawling across an ancient lava flow which spewed out of the Koʻolaus. As it flowed out it built a bridge across the ocean channel that separated Koʻolau Island from Waianae Island, and eventually lapped against the walls of the Waianae Mountains to form the sloping Schofield Plateau (near the present site of Schofield Barracks). From sea level at the coral plain of Ewa near Pearl Harbor, this Leilehua Plateau gradually rises to 900 feet above the sea at the Del Monte Pineapple Test Garden just north of Wahiawa. Then close to the North Shore the high central valley slopes steeply toward the sea, cut by three major rivers (Anahulu, Helemano, and Poamoho) which form in the Koʻolaus and empty into Waialua Bay.

Central Oʻahu offers a majestic countryside which many visitors rush through on their way to the North Shore. If you travel on Hawaiian time, relaxed and curious about the surprises that surround us, you'll find this green valley in the sky one of Oʻahu's most precious gifts.

As we drive north on Hwy 99 from our starting junction, you'll see on your right the residential areas of Seaview, Waipiolani, Crestview, and Waipio. This scene will be repeated up the valley, since Central Oʻahu is known as a series of bedroom communities for Honolulu, especially the sections between Seaview and Wahiawa. This is suburban Oʻahu, just as the Kailua-Kaneohe area, but with a greater feeling of middle America. If you want to see the area close up, turn right in Waipio on Waipio Uka, follow the loop past the Waipio Shopping Center, through the community, then left on Ka Uka Blvd. and a right turn back onto Kam Hwy.

After bridging deep Kipapa Gulch, Highway 99 brings us through the heart of **Mililani Town**, Oʻahu's planned suburban community built in the 1960's and carved out of 3,000 acres of pineapple fields. Featured are: single family homes, garden townhouses, and low-profile apartments; two public parks; four recreational areas; a shopping center; Mililani Town Center; a full public school system; even Mililani Montessori Center. On the left edge of Mililani Town

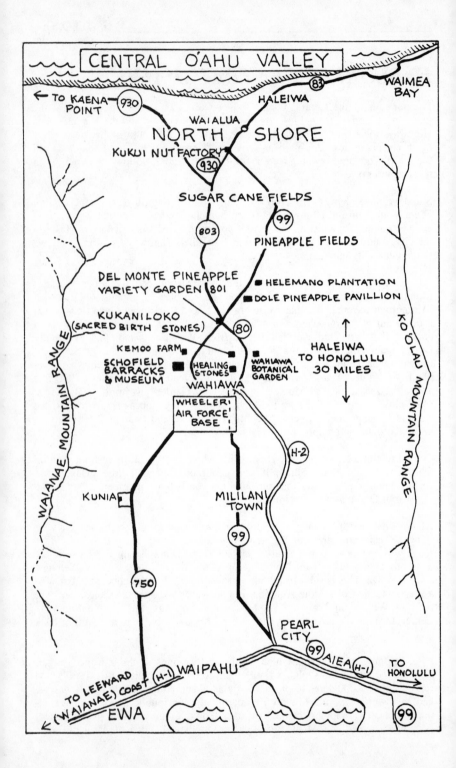

going north on Kam Highway is the **Mililani** (to praise or give thanks) *Golf Club*. This shady 18 hole, par 72 private course (open to the public) was created from sugar cane fields. Facilities include clubhouse, pro shop, rental equipment, carts, PGA pro, and restaurant. Located at 95-176 Kuahelani Ave. (623-2222).

Leaving Mililani Town, we'll cross the Waikakalaua Gulch and Melemanu Woods on the right. On your left will be part of *Wheeler Air Force Base*, one of three Air Force installations on O'ahu, (along with Hickham at Pearl Harbor and Bellows near Kailua on the windward side). Constructed in 1922, Wheeler has seen many historic aviation events, such as the first nonstop mainland to Hawaii flight in 1927, and the first solo flight from Wheeler to California by Amelia Earhart in 1935. The airfield was attacked by the first wave of 355 Japanese naval aircraft on December 7, 1941; 37 were killed and 146 American planes destroyed. In front of Headquarters today stands a replica of a P-40, the aircraft destroyed at Wheeler in the Japanese attack. During the Korean conflict, Wheeler AFB expanded and today the base employs 3,500 personnel and shares facilities with the army. Wheeler offers flying lessons and parachute jumping instruction to military personnel. Call 655-4804 (skydiving) or 624-9524 (flying) for more information.

---

DID YOU KNOW...that one man turned the Ewa plain from desert into farmland? In 1877 Irish sailor-turned-planter, James Campbell, purchased 40,000 acres on the arid Ewa plain. He discovered that O'ahu was a storehouse of fresh water held in a lens inside the Island's porous rock. He drilled an artesian well and the rest is history. By 1888 Campbell's wells had turned Ewa into one of O'ahu's most fertile sugarcane producing areas, and made him a multimillionaire who retired seven years later!

---

The town of *Wahiawa* (meaning landing place or roaring place) which grew as a plantation town and is now a shopping and support community for military personnel stationed at nearby Wheeler Air Force Base and Schofield Army Barracks. The town stretches between the north and south forks of the Wahiawa Reservoir, ending in Lake Wilson. This 300 acre reservoir stores and disperses water for irrigation of surrounding sugarcane fields. At the same time, the reservoir supports a variety of fresh water activities including excellent fishing (bass, sunfish, catfish and carp), boating and swimming.

The highway splits here; Highway 99 goes to the left around Lake Wilson, Highway 80 goes through Wahiawa and reconnects with 99 just north of town. We'll take Route 80, the town's main street, to California Ave., turn right and drive half a mile to the *Wahiawa Botanic Garden* at 1396 California Ave. Here you can explore 27 acres of rare trees, ferns, shrubs, many varieties of orchids, and a special garden of rare Hawaiian plants. This park specializes in plants that thrive in wet, cool, mountainous regions of O'ahu. Admission is free, open daily from 9am-4pm, with picnic spots available.

Still on California, but back across Ohai Street (Kam Highway #80) you'll find a beautiful Buddhist temple and grounds, the *Ryusenji Soto Mission*, 164

California Ave. (622-1429). On the opposite side of Kaala Elementary School, 130 California, in a small cinderblock shelter built in 1948, where you can see the legendary *Healing Stones of Wahiawa* ★. An old Hawaiian tale tells us that two sisters from Kauai used their supernatural powers (which only worked at night) to fly to Kukaniloko, the famous birthplace of kings near Wahiawa on Oʻahu. Just as they arrived the first rays of dawn touched them and turned them to stone. The two stones, one shaped like a huge shoe and the other like a surfboard ( 6 ft. by 2 ft.), became famous when they were reported to affect miraculous cures during the 1920's. As word spread, thousands of visitors came to pray, leave various offerings, and touch the "healing" stones. Years later the stones were moved to the old Wahiawa Cemetery at 108 California Street where they remain today (the rest of the cemetery has since become a housing development). Many skeptics have discounted any powers attached to the stones, although visitors continue to seek out the shrine and leave offerings.

Before leaving Wahiawa how about a spot of lunch? There's a Big Way Supermarket (corner of California and Kilani), Jack-in-the-Box (11 S. Kam Hwy.), McDonald's (144 S. Kam. Hwy.), and Burger King (30 S. Kam Hwy.). Or, if you'd prefer some plate lunch fixings at Wahiawa Oriental Market (302 California Ave.) then drop by Shan's Cake Shoppe (1036 Kilani Ave.) and pick out a cake with all natural ingredients, or one of their still-warm loaves of bread and some sweets. Then drive around the block to the Botanic Garden picnic area and enjoy a homemade Wahiawa-style feast in a secluded rural Oʻahu hideaway.

Just after leaving town on the Karsten Thot Bridge over the north fork of the Wahiawa Reservoir, you'll see Whitmore Rd.(#804) off to your right. This leads up to *Whitmore Village*, Dole's plantation community. A short tour through this residential area on Circle Mauka or Ihiihi Ave. will give you an idea of how Wahiawa (also a plantation town) might have looked in its early days.

Back down Whitmore Ave. and across Highway 80 at the light will bring you to the sacred birthing place of alii (royalty), *Kukaniloko* ★. There were only two places in all Hawaii designated as sacred birth sites for children of high chiefs - this one and another in Wailua, Kauai (see *KAUAI, A Paradise Guide*.) At the Kauai site, labor and delivery took place in a shelter near a stone which afterward provided a hiding place for the infant's umbilical cord. Here at Kukaniloko, the mother-to-be reclined on one of the massive stones, shaped to hold her comfortably. On either side of this birthing chair was a row of eighteen stones, supposedly inhabited by spirits able to absorb pain. A high chief stood sentinel in front of each stone. Labor and birth were accompanied by drums, chanting, and sacred rituals. When the royal child was born, it was taken to a nearby heiau (temple) where its umbilical cord was severed and hidden in a crevice among the birthing stones. Birth at this special place conferred upon the child an enhanced mana (spirit and power).

During this century the site of the *Wahiawa Royal Birthing Stones* fell into decay and even suffered vandalism. Recently, however, groups have worked hard to restore this ancient site to its former condition. To the Hawaiians, then and now, birth and children are held with special reverence and affection. This open-air ancestor of a maternity hospital symbolizes continuity of the all-important life force through the miracle of birth. It is fitting, therefore, that

Kukaniloko has been translated as meaning "an inland area from which great events are heralded."

***Schofield Army Barracks*** was built in 1909 as a companion installation to Fort Shafter (1907) which houses the U.S. Army's major command in the Asia-Pacific area (USARPAC). Schofield is home to the 25th Infantry Division (Light), a rapid strike force of nearly 11,000 soldiers known as the "Tropic Lightning" Division. Born of elements of the famous "Hawaiian Division" in 1941, this tough Division is comprised of three infantry brigades, an aviation brigade, division artillery, a division support command, and a complement of separate battalions. The 45th Support Group at Schofield provides support to the 25th Infantry division (Light) and non-divisional units in USARPAC's area of operation. The base has opened a ***Tropic Lightning Museum*** with military exhibits dating back to the war of 1812. Enter through the main Macomb Gate. Request permission at the Gate to drive through the installation.

Across Kam Highway (99) from Schofield's Main Gate is ***Kemoo Farm***, which overlooks Lake Wilson and the Wahiawa Reservoir. Here you can get a fresh trout dinner and hear traditional Hawaiian music (see dining section of this guide). You can look out over one of O'ahu's best fresh water fishing spots, or get your tackle out of the trunk and put a line in the water (be sure you have a local license). Kemoo (Kay-mo-o) Farm is worth a visit just to inquire in the restaurant lobby about the history of the area (do they ever have stories to tell!) or look around their Snack Bar and Country Store. They've been going strong since 1927.

After that short detour, let's resume our northern direction and make a stop at the fascinating ***Del Monte Pineapple Variety Garden*** ★ at the junction of Hwys. 99 and 80 just north of Wahiawa. Created in 1954, this triangular plot of 29 varieties of pineapple and other bromeliads, has signs that tell you about each one and the history of pineapple in Hawaii. Del Monte was started by a Wahiawa homesteader named Alfred W. Eames in 1906 as the Hawaiian Island Packing Company. He built a cannery at Wahiawa, which merged with the California Packing Company in 1917. The third pineapple packing company in Hawaii is the Maui Pineapple Company, started in 1903 by the Baldwin family. Three pioneers, Dole, Eames, and Baldwin are responsible for today's Hawaiian pineapple industry.

Let's visit the brand new 10,000 square foot ***Dole Pavilion*** next; it's just a mile north of the Del Monte variety garden on Kam Hwy. 99. The plantation-style, one-story building with wide lanai and traditional gently sloping roof offers fresh pineapple, ice cold juice, food service and a large gift shop with clothing and souvenirs featuring the Dole logo. As you know if you've visited Dole Cannery Square in Honolulu, or have found our description of it above, a young college graduate from Massachusetts named James Dole came to Hawaii in 1899 to seek his fortune through "agricultural opportunities." He came, he saw the fledgling pineapple industry, and he conquered the obstacles which prevented its success up to that time. Starting production on 12 fertile acres of farmland in Wahiawa, Dole's genius created a business that has grown to an annual production valued at more than 100 million dollars.

Across the parking area from the Dole Pavilion is ***Helemano Plantation ★***, 64-1510 Kam Highway (622-3929). This working farm is operated by Hawaii's mentally handicapped citizens with assistance from a sponsoring organization. Residents and day employees raise fruits and vegetables, operate a bakery and restaurant utilizing ingredients they have grown themselves, demonstrate crafts, offer classes in which you can learn to make traditional Hawaiian gifts, and run a small shop selling handmade objects and local craft items. Helemano Plantation gives handicapped men and women the chance to earn money and respect in a productive, well supervised environment. It's a pleasure to tour the farm, see the talents these individuals possess, and offer support to this proud and productive place. I think you'll come away feeling good and glad you came.

Once you pull out of the Halemano Plantation parking lot you're not far from Oahu's North Shore. Look around you; this is pineapple country! As you drive through field upon field of low spiky-leafed ***pineapple plants ★***, you can get lost in the beauty of the rolling hills and green expanses of fields surrounding you. Reddish soil reminds you of its volcanic origins and high mineral content. If you look to the left you can see the full expanse of the Waianae Mountain Range separating Central Oʻahu from the Leeward Coast.

Do you see a dip in the profile of the Mountains at about 8 o'clock? That is ***Kolekole Pass***, a primary route across the mountains to Waianae. On the leeward side of Kolekole Pass was the ancient volcanic shield crater that erupted to form the western side of Oʻahu.

Gradually, as you drive along enjoying the landscape around you, you'll realize that something is changing. Something outside is different, but what? Then it will hit you - the low green spikes of pineapple have somehow given way to tall, green plants that remind you of fields of corn. At the same time you feel the highway sloping downward, first at a shallow, then at a steeper and steeper angle. Of course; it's ***sugarcane ★***. Then all at once you look out, and over the crest of a rolling sugarcane hill there bursts into sight one of Oʻahu's most awesome scenes - the golden, sparking waters of the sea, laid out against the light blue horizon stretching like a seam in the distance, and fields of green cane carpeting rolled out across hills sloping gently down and down to meet the tide at a white threshold of sandy beach. Welcome to the North Shore!

FRUIT STAND

J Bayot

248

# EXPLORING THE NORTH SHORE

Tourists approach The North Shore from several directions. Some come north from Kahuku, others approach from Central O'ahu on 99 (Kamehameha Highway) or 803 (Farrington Highway). For our tour of this region of O'ahu we'll start at Kuilima Cove at Turtle Bay and work our way west past Hale'iwa and the mill town of Waialua to Mokuleia and Kaena Point. If you're coming another way just reverse the order of our stops.

*Kuilima Cove* is one of the most beautiful and safest of all North Shore beaches. It is sometimes called Kalokoiki, the little pool, because of its crescent shape and small, protected and calm lagoon. Stay in the cove, though, because a channel along Kuilima Point on the Cove's left side often has a dangerous current pulling toward the open ocean. Inside the cove, however, conditions are excellent for swimming, and Turtle Bay Resort provides a daily lifeguard.

*Turtle Bay Hilton and Country Club* ★ is just next door to Kuilima Cove, and is well worth a tour. Here, on 808 expansive acres, is the North Shore's only real hotel and resort complex, built in 1972 as the original Del Webb Kuilima Hotel. You'll enjoy walking or driving through the grounds, past two swimming pools, retail shops, golf, tennis, and horseback riding areas, helicopter port (with tours available), three restaurants, and the Bay View Lounge, hosting live entertainment every night until 12:30am. People regularly come here, stay for a week or more, and never leave the grounds during their visit.

Those who prefer this outer island atmosphere marvel that this "country resort" is less than an hour by car from Waikiki. With very little traffic, but lots of privacy and security, and a full menu of restaurants, shops and activities, Turtle Bay offers a very attractive alternative to accommodations in Waikiki. And the owners are planning to build two more luxury resorts on the 808 acres within a year or two. So when you swim at Kuilima Cove and explore Turtle Bay, look at this area as a possible headquarters for your next visit to O'ahu.

Continuing west on Kamehameha Highway (#83) you'll pass by (1 1/2 miles from Turtle Bay) another one of O'ahu's hidden treasures and never see it from the road. *Kawela Bay Beach* is only accessible to the public from the water. It's a great place to swim during the summer months when the water is clear and calm. Here is a beach tailormade for paddlers with an inflatable craft who want to explore a secluded and beautiful bay. No lifeguard, few people, just sun, surf, and solitude await you at Kawela Bay Beach.

Watch for Oopuola Street on the mauka side of Kam Highway about two miles toward Waimea Bay from Kawela Bay. This is the famous and best launching beach for windsurfers on the North Shore. Take Oopuola to the beach and enjoy watching and meeting some of the world's best sailboarders.

Get out your map because we're coming up on a stretch with some of the world's most famous beaches and surfing breaks. Within a few miles we'll pass beaches with famous names like Sunset, Bonzai, Pupukea and Waimea Bay, and

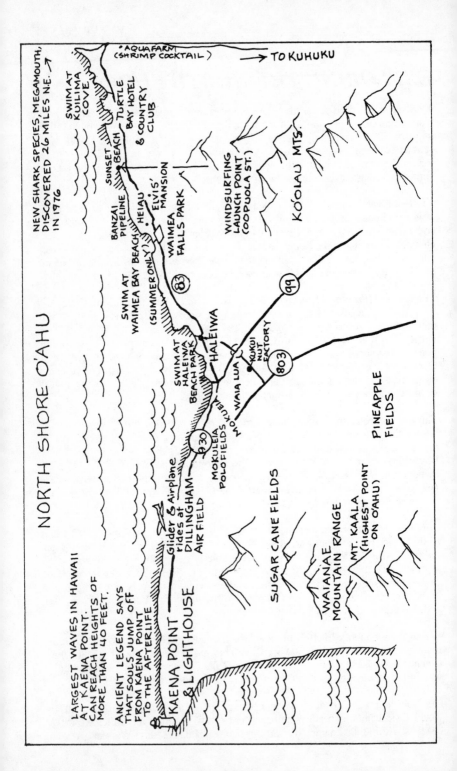

NORTH SHORE O'AHU

TO KUHUKU

AQUAFARM
(SHRIMP COCKTAIL)

NEW SHARK SPECIES, MEGAMOUTH,
DISCOVERED 26 MILES N.E.
IN 1976

SWIM AT
KUILIMA
COVE

TURTLE
BAY HOTEL
& COUNTRY
CLUB

SUNSET
BEACH

WINDSURFING
LAUNCH POINT
(OOPUOLA ST.)

KO'OLAU MTS.

BANZAI
PIPELINE

HEIAU

ELVIS'
MANSION

WAIMEA
FALLS PARK

SWIM AT
WAIMEA BAY BEACH
(SUMMER ONLY)

83

99

SWIM AT
HALEIWA
BEACH PARK

HALEIWA

KUKUI
NUT FACTORY

803

MOKU WAIA LUA

930

MOKULEIA
POLO FIELDS

PINEAPPLE
FIELDS

Glider & Airplane
rides at DILLINGHAM
AIR FIELD

SUGAR CANE FIELDS

WAIANAE
MOUNTAIN RANGE

MT. KAALA
(HIGHEST POINT
ON O'AHU)

LARGEST WAVES IN HAWAII
AT KAENA POINT.
CAN REACH HEIGHTS OF
MORE THAN 40 FEET.

ANCIENT LEGEND SAYS
THAT SOULS JUMP OFF
FROM KAENA POINT
TO THE AFTERLIFE

KAENA POINT
& LIGHTHOUSE

surf breaks to match, including Kammie Land, Gas Chambers, Pupukea, Banzai Pipeline, Back Doors, Off-The-Wall, Log Cabins, and Cloud Break. You can park at any of these beaches in the winter and see some of the best (and most dangerous) surfing in the world. Don't even think of going into the water here when the winter surf is up. You'll have enough of a challenge just finding a place to park and a square foot of sand from which to watch the action. Don't forget your camera.

Which beach is best for spectating? Stop at one like **Sunset Beach** ★ across from the Sunset Beach Elementary School and Neighborhood Park, 59-360 Kam Hwy. Park off the road and ask a lifeguard (look for the tower) where to watch, what the conditions are, and what (if any) events are going on. You can tell immediately when the surf's up, even while driving in Honolulu - it'll be all over the radio and on everyone's lips.

A little more than a mile toward Waimea Bay from Sunset Beach you'll see Pupukea Road next to Foodland on the mauka side of Kam Highway. Turn and follow it up the hill until you see the turnoff on the right to **Puu O Mahuka Heiau** ★, a Hawaii State Monument. This Heiau, which was once used for human sacrifices, is laid out in three sections separated by fitted rock walls. The lowest section is in ruins and includes several holes or pits which may be dangerous and should be avoided. If you walk down the path beside the Heiau you'll come to a lookout with a panoramic view of the coastline and ocean below. The offerings you see on the Heiau walls are stones, flowers, or food wrapped in ti leaves and left in honor of the gods and people whose stories are intertwined with this sacred place.

When you leave the Heiau parking area, turn uphill and follow Pupukea Road to another left onto Alapio Road. This will take you past a huge mansion, surrounded by a hedge, which was supposedly the O'ahu *hideaway of Elvis Presley* during his frequent visits. Also in Sunset Hills you'll pass the impressive *Nichiren Shoshu of America (NSA) Buddhist Mission* and grounds.

"Three Tables" and "Shark's Cove" are two of the most popular spots at *Pupukea Beach Park* just east of Waimea Bay. Although conditions here are very dangerous during the winter months, in the summer this stretch of water is a favorite place of snorkelers and scuba divers. Large tidal pools are fun to explore and the scenery is breathtaking. This is one of my favorite summer beach spots, but it is to be avoided during the winter.

*Waimea Bay* ★ is one of O'ahu's best known locations. For hundreds of years the Waimea Valley was home to Hawaiian kahunas (priests) and their families. After a major flood in 1894 most valley residents moved to other areas on the island. Waimea Bay is also known as the place where the first white explorers set foot on O'ahu. On February 27, 1779 the remainder of Captain Cook's squadron put into Waimea Bay for fresh water a few days after his violent death at Kealakekua Bay on the Big Island. During these times the Waimea River flowed into the ocean without obstruction, and canoes were paddled down river and on out into the bay. Today a sand bar prevents such movement, and the river's mouth has become marshy.

**Waimea Beach Park** in the summer is often calm as a lake, with excellent swimming. But in winter this surf becomes a monster; it is known to have the largest ridable surfing waves in Hawaii. People come from all around to watch the winter surfers at Waimea Bay. On the east hill overlooking the bay is the **Mission of Saints Peter and Paul** established in 1953 in buildings which had belonged to a rock crushing plant used to make the gravel which built Kamehameha Highway from Waimea to Kahuku.

Across the highway from Waimea Beach Park is the entrance to **Waimea Falls Park ★**, one of O'ahu's 10 best places to visit. This private 1800 acre park is on the site of ancient Waimea Valley, which has been the home of O'ahu's high priests since 1092 A.D. Here was the residence of Paao, the powerful high priest and ancestor of many Hawaiian kahuna families. Paao came to Hawaii from the South Pacific in the 13th century. Finding the royalty too weak, Paao imported high chiefs who became the ancestors of all great chiefs of Hawaii, including the five Kamehamehas, and three other regents during the 1800's. Paao introduced many customs to Hawaii that lasted for 600 years. Among them were heiaus, human sacrifices, feather leis and capes, and the cornerstone of the ancient Hawaiian culture - Kapu (taboo). Paao's descendants lived for centuries in Waimea Valley and advised all the high chiefs in matters of religion, war, and politics. It was not until the Christian era in Hawaii that Paao's family went underground, and Waimea Valley ceased to be the power center of the Islands. Since 1837 the Valley has had a procession of private owners, and Waimea Falls Park continues that tradition.

Luckily many of the ancient sites in the Valley have been preserved, and the major physical features of the ancient sacred area are in tact. Waimea Falls Park is dedicated to the preservation and display of Hawaii's plants, animals, and culture. When you enter the gates you are stepping back hundreds of years into the Hawaii of yesterday. The best way to visit the park is to send for a guide-book and map ($3.00 plus postage, see address below) before your visit, become familiar with the park and its many points of interest, then take the 60-minute guided tour when you arrive. Your expert guide will take you to each section of the park, and will introduce you to plants, animals and customs of Old Hawaii that the casual visitor might miss. After this overview, ride the open-air tram to the top of the valley and walk down, stopping at your own pace to explore further the exhibits and gardens which interest you most. I could spend hours watching the high divers at the Falls as they somersault from a 60 foot cliff into the natural pool below. And they had to drag me away from the performance of ancient hulas, with costumes and music as they were centuries ago.

You'll see a reconstructed home site, visit the ruins of a chief's house, try your hand at such ancient Hawaiian games as bowling, spear throwing, and konane (similar to checkers). You'll explore gardens with some of the rarest and most endangered plants in the world. Don't miss the lei garden where you can see the lei flowers in their natural state, as well as palms, gingers, sugarcane, heliconia, bananas, and taro. You can watch wild boar being fed, see Nenes (Hawaii's State Bird) with their young, identify and spot birds you never knew existed, and photograph water lilies big enough to sit on.

There's a gift shop, an education center for parents and teachers, a restaurant with live entertainment nightly until 9pm, moon walks twice a month during the full moon (many animals and plants such as the night blooming cereus are best viewed at night), wedding arrangements (this is one of O'ahu's most popular wedding locations), and annual world-famous Makahiki (harvest) Festival weekend in early October. This is a re-creation of an ancient festival which was held each year in ancient times in honor of Lono, God of Fertility and Agriculture. If you can't come, or want to see a preview, there's now a videotape available for $24.95 from Charlie's Country Store in the Park. Hours are 10am-5:30pm daily. Proud Peacock restaurant serves dinner until 9pm (638-8531). For more information contact Waimea Falls Park, 59-864 Kamehameha Highway, Hale'iwa, HI 96712 (638-8511). Park is open daily 10am-5:30pm. Admission $7.50 adults, $5.25 juniors age 7-12, $1.25 children 6 and under.

About three miles west of Waimea Bay on the mauka side of Kam Highway is the ***Meadow Gold Dairy Farm***, where small children are encouraged to meet tame animals at their petting zoo. On the Waimea Bay side of the dairy, slightly east of Pohaku Loa Way (a short road loop makai of Kam Highway) is ***Chun's Reef***, not a good place to swim but one of the North Shore's most popular board surfing beaches. The shallow coral bottom and strong currents make this a beach for veteran surfers, not beginners. There is no lifeguard, so especially in the winter this is a place to watch board surfing, not learn it. On the west side of the dairy, between Pohaku Loa Way and Papiloa Road, is ***Laniakea Beach***, similar to Chun's Reef in that swimming is dangerous (offshore currents are present even during low surf) but the winter board surfing waves are excellent. No lifeguard, and no parking area mean you'll have to find a spot off the highway if you want to watch the many surfers who enter the water here.

The old resort town of ***Hale'iwa*** ★ is our next stop. This unique town has gone through a number of stages in its 150 plus years. In the early 1800's it was a missionary outpost commemorated by the large Liliuokalani Protestant Church and cemetery, dating from the 1830's. For centuries before the missionaries came, Hawaiians had lived in villages on the banks of the Anahulu River. Missionary homes were built there too, and when the O'ahu Railway built the Hale'iwa Hotel on its banks in 1899, the area became O'ahu's most famous rural beach resort. During World War II the hotel was taken over by the military, and eventually torn down.

NIGHTBLOOMING CEREUS

253

In the 1960's Hale'iwa became a hippie and surfing haven, looking like a displaced California coastal community. Today Hale'iwa is an interesting balance of all its pasts. You can visit Liliuokalani Church, 66-090 Kam Highway, and see stone markers from the 1830's cemetery. On the back wall inside the church is the famous clock given by the Queen to the congregation. Look closely; it has seven dials and seven hands which tell the months, days of the week, weeks of the year, days of the month, phases of the moon, and hours of the day. There are no numerals - instead the hands point to the twelve letters in the Queen's name.

You can watch at Kaiaka Bay's east end as the summertime Japanese O-Bon Festival concludes when hundreds of candlelit paper lanterns set into the water beneath the full moon, each tiny boat honoring a departed ancestor.

Or you can shop in one of Hale'iwa's many one-of-a-kind stores. Buy an original painting of the waterfall at Waimea Falls Park in the Fetig Gallery, Kam Hwy., pick up the makings of dinner at Hale'iwa Super Market-IGA, 66-197-Kam Hwy. Browse in Oogenesis Boutique, 66-249 Kam Hwy., a survivor of the hippie days of the 60's and still going strong. Visit the Hale'iwa Shopping Center in the center of town. But whatever you do, don't miss getting yourself the Island's most famous shave ice at M. Matsumoto Store, 66-087 Kam Hwy., a remnant of Hale'iwa's plantation days when the store owner rode around the area taking orders for tailor-made clothes. Then Matsumoto's was a general store; now people line up outside for O'ahu's most popular shave ice.

We've rated *Hale'iwa Beach Park* ★ as the 4th best beach on O'ahu because of its wide expansive beach, its proximity (across Kam Hwy.) to Hale'iwa Regional Park, its daily lifeguard service all year round, and its large size overall (13 acres). This is one beach that you can bring young children to and feel safe. The water is calm, and the bottom is shallow and sandy. This is easily the best all-around swimming beach on The North Shore.

Just over the bridge and makai is *Hale'iwa Alii Beach Park*. This is the Waimea Bay end of Waialua Beach (66-167 Hale'iwa Rd.) In the summer it's just as good as Hale'iwa Beach Park. But in the winter, look out. Deep channels and dangerous currents make this a place only to picnic from October through April. Beautiful grounds though, for frisbee, sunning, or pole fishing. And there is a lifeguard. It's fun just to drive down past the *Hale'iwa Boat Harbor* and see what they've brought in today.

Two roads lead out of Hale'iwa, Kam Highway #83, and Hale'iwa Road which intersect with Cane Haul Road leading to the Sugar Mill town of *Waialua*. Drive through the plantation town, past houses and storefronts that haven't changed much in decades. This is every bit as much Hawaii as the glamour of Waikiki. And every bit as proud and important. Although there are no longer tours available, a drive past the *Waialua Sugar Mill* will give you a glimpse of an operating mill and the town that it supports. And if you want to visit a real Hawaiian working man's bar, try the Sugar Bar and Restaurant in the old bank building (you can still see the vault in the back) at 67-069 Kealohanui. They serve food, snacks, and the coldest beer in town (637-6989).

Follow Cane Haul Road out to Farrington Highway and turn west toward Kaena Point. In three or four miles you'll come to the ***Mokuleia Polo Farm ★***. This is the site of crowded Polo matches held every Sunday afternoon from early March through July. For almost a century this sport has been a favorite of O'ahu residents, and was played for many years in Kapiolani Park. Polo at Mokoleia is a sporting event, a social event, and an outing to the country all rolled into one. If you're on O'ahu in the spring or summer, try to include a Polo match in your itinerary.

---

DID YOU KNOW..that Britain's Prince Charles has played Polo at the Mokuleia Polo Farm? And so have the Maharajah of Jarpur, the Marquis of Waterford, Lord Patrick Beresford, and visiting teams from England, Mexico, Australia, Boston, St. Louis, South American and Japan.

---

***Dillingham Airfield and Gliderport ★*** is just down the road toward Kaena Point from the Polo Farm. Small planes and gliders based here offer rides to visitors daily from 10:30am-5:30pm. One and two passenger gliders are available, with average visibility 30 to 40 miles. Sign says on a clear day you can see forever - at least to Kauai, 80 miles away! Call 677-3404 and check in with "Mr. Bill" Starr at the airfield. By the way it was the Dillingham family that helped bring Polo to O'ahu at the turn of the century. Cost for a twenty minute ride; $36 single, $45 double.

Across Farrington Highway from Dillingham Field is ***Mokuleia Beach Park***, 68-919 Farrington Hwy. This 12-acre park is a nice spot to stop for a picnic, a stretch on the grassy play area (with play equipment for kids) or overnight camping. A comfort station, cooking podiums and 65 parking stalls are provided. Swimming is not recommended; wading inshore and shell hunting in surf may be safe (unless tides are turning) in summer, but winter surf can change quickly and currents are strong. As you pass ***Mokuleia Army Beach*** and ***Camp Harold Erdman***, you'll be interested to know why they are both closed to the public. The army has leased this stretch of beach since 1970 for exclusive recreational use of military personnel. The former site for military R & R on North Shore had been located in Hale'iwa. Camp Erdman, named after a young

GREAT FRIGATE BIRD                    JBAYOT

255

member of the Dillingham family who was killed in a fall from a polo pony in 1931, is owned and operated by the YMCA as a summer camp, conference and retreat facility. It is heavily used for YMCA activities and not available for private bookings.

Just after Camp Erdman the road ends, and we must turn around. *Kaena Point* is almost three miles west of here. Most of this dangerous headland is a Coast Guard Military Reservation, with a lighthouse situated on the point. Surf here is the highest in Hawaii averaging 30-40'in winter, and are often much higher.

As we head back toward Hale'iwa let's stop at possibly the most unique factory on O'ahu, the *Hawaiian Kukui Nut Company* ★ at 66-935 Kaukonahua Road in Waialua (637-5620 or 1-800-367-6010). Coming back east from Kaena Point on Farrington Highway, you turn left onto Kaukonahua Road and drive about 1/2 mile. The factory will be on your left just after you pass Kaamooloa Road. As you get out of your car be sure to notice the young kukui tree growing at the right front corner of this ex-movie theater. Notice the light green leaves, the nuts enclosed in a fibrous husk, and the grey bark trunk of soft wood. This tree was one of ancient Hawaii's most prized resources. From its bark and roots they made dyes for tattooing, canoe painting, and tapa cloth. The sap from green fruit was used to heal wounds and soothe toothaches. The oily nuts were used as lamps (strung on bamboo and lit, or oil in bowls was lit with a wick), food (pounded roasted nuts used in a relish eaten with lomi salmon), and were strung on leis. No wonder the Kukui is Hawaii's State Tree!

As you walk inside the factory-showroom, meet the folks and they'll invite you to watch a short videotape showing you the fascinating story of the kukui. Then you'll have a chance to see the only operation of its kind in Hawaii. You'll see the amazing process used to extract the meat from the nut, grade it, grind it, polish it, and sort it for shipment. You'll find out what happens to the oil that's extracted during the process, how a growing new industry has emerged from this spot. Owners Dana and Barbara Gray and their expert crew will make your visit one you'll find yourself telling friends and relatives about. And the kukui nut leis are cheaper here, too! P.S. Don't forget to ask about the new kukui skin care products. I've tried the shampoo, it's excellent. And the lotion with PABA could well become a favorite on the beaches of O'ahu.

Less than a mile back toward Hale'iwa on Kaukonahua Road you'll hit the Weed Circle; take it southeast onto Kamehameha Highway (#99) and you're headed toward Central O'ahu and Honolulu just beyond.

# EXPLORING THE WINDWARD SIDE

Greetings! On our tour today we'll explore one of rural O'ahu's most exciting areas - the Windward Side. It's called that because the prevailing winds blow from the northeast across this part of the island first, bringing winds, rain, and the flavor of a rain forest to this side of O'ahu.

We'll start our travels at the junction of Hwys. 61 and 72 just west of Kailua, so unless you're continuing around the island from our exploration of the Southeast Coast, you should come over the Pali on Hwy. 61 from Honolulu.

Drive through the suburban city of Kailua to **Kailua Beach Park** ★ by following Kailua Rd. (Hwy 61) until it dead ends into Kalaheo; turn right and follow Kalaheo over the canal. We've listed this as O'ahu's third best beach (behind Waikiki and Hanauma Bay) with one warning: keep children away from the Ka'elepulu Canal which flows into the ocean and bisects the park. This inviting canal has holes, channels, and currents which present hidden hazards to children and non-swimmers. The rest of this 30-acre public park has a wide sandy beach, daily lifeguard, gently sloping sandy ocean bottom, a public boat ramp at Alala Point, and a small offshore Island (Popoi'a or Flat Island)with great diving and surfing. Kailua Beach Park is also one of the best windsurfing beaches on O'ahu, with sailboards passing parallel to the beach almost every day the wind is up. Find a spot along Kailua Beach Park away from the canal and boat ramp, and you're set for a morning of sun and fun on one of O'ahu's premier beaches.

I want to show you one of O'ahu's secret beaches - a place where the akami tourists and kamaainas disappear to when they want a special treat. Follow Kawailoa Road (formerly Kalaheo Ave.) south till it becomes Aalapapa Drive. Turn left onto Lanipo Drive, and another left onto Mokulua Drive, which parallels one of O'ahu's jeweled beaches, **Lanikai Beach**. Park off Mokulua Drive between Pokole Way and Aala Drive. Find a beach access between two houses and walk down the path to one of the most beautiful, quietest, gentlest stretches of beach anywhere. Conditions are usually safe; and the bottom slopes gently, making swimming a pleasure. There's no lifeguard or facilities, so we haven't included it as a Best Beach, but for a quiet swim or nap on a weekday afternoon, Lanikai is probably my favorite beach spot on O'ahu.

Head back north to Kailua Road (Highway 61) and turn mauka toward the Pali. At the 7-11 store, turn right onto Uluoa St., then right again onto Manu Aloha. Park at the end of the street in the YMCA lot, and walk makai to the **Ulu Po Heiau**. This temple from old Hawaii measures 140 feet wide at the bottom, and 30 feet in height. It was associated with family kapunas who were responsible for building Heiau where Hawaiian kings were born. Notice especially the stone work in which no mortar or pegs are used to hold the walls together.

Get back on Kailua Rd. (Hwy 61), go mauka to junction with Hwy 83, the Kamehameha Hwy. Turn right and drive under the H-3 freeway then turn left at the first (unnamed) road. This will lead you to the **Hoomaluhia Regional Botanical Park** (235-6636). This huge plant refuge, owned and operated by the City of Kaneohe, offers hikes, overnight camping, and occasional moonlight walks among the gardens. It's relatively new, very well kept, and an oasis on a warm afternoon. If you want an unspoiled wilderness area to explore, this is it.

Makai from here, at the end of H-3 freeway, is the **Mokapu Peninsula**, once the off-limits meeting place of Kamehameha I and his chiefs - a sort of Hawaiian Camp David. It is still off limits; only the occupants have changed to the U.S. Marine Corps who use it as an Air Station.

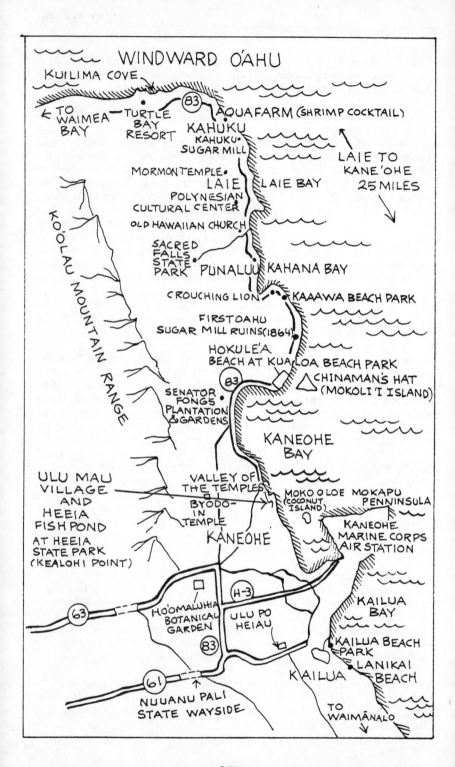

WINDWARD O'AHU

As we pass through the bedroom community of Kaneohe (meaning Bamboo man, perhaps a reference to fishermen of the area carrying bamboo tubes to keep their catch cool) be sure to turn left at Likelike Highway (63) then turn right at Kahekili Highway (83) to continue north. Within a few miles you'll see, on the mauka side, the entrance to the *Valley of the Temples Memorial Park*. Turn in, pay a few dollars and drive through this memorial cemetery with chapels and temples representing a variety of faiths, so that people of all religions can be interred in this one beautiful park.

The majestic *Byodo-In Temple* ★ stands in a small valley on the Park's mauka side. This temple of Equality, built in 1968 on the 100th anniversary of the first Japanese immigrants' arrival in Hawaii, is an exact replica of the famed 900-year old Byodo-In of Kyoto, Japan. Surrounded by quiet, manicured gardens and ponds full of koi, this red temple with blue tile roof is one of O'ahu's most tranquil settings to pause, meditate, and to renew one's feeling of balance and equality with all peoples of the world. Since Buddhism is based on the search for enlightenment about life and one's place in it, this temple is meant to be a spot which encourages such contemplation. A 3-ton brass bell is placed so you can strike it in order to create deep sounds to stimulate quiet thought. A golden statue of Buddha calls one to meditation. On the hill is a pagoda named Meditation House. And in the tiny gift shop one can buy food to feed the koi as you watch them in the quiet ponds beside the temple. Anyone, regardless of their religious beliefs, will find themselves strangely refreshed after an hour in this garden of peace and thought.

As we leave Byodo-In and continue north on Kamehameha Highway, you'll have a good view of *Kaneohe Bay* on the makai side. This is as close as Hawaii comes to having a barrier reef (the best example of which is the Great Barrier Reef in Australia). Most reefs in Hawaii are fringing reefs, which start growing on rocks along the shore and form an underwater jetty as they expand outward perpendicular to the shoreline. Barrier reefs, on the other hand, form parallel to the shoreline and form walls which create a lagoon between it and the beach. Unfortunately, the Kaneohe Bay lagoon has become polluted as a result of the development in the area, so until the problem is reversed the bay is not recommended for fishing or water activities. In fact, the glass bottom boat which used to ply the bay now takes its passengers elsewhere.

BYODO-IN TEMPLE

Do you see the small island in Kaneohe Bay between the bayfront and Mokapu Peninsula? This is **Moku O Loe** (Coconut Island). Once owned by a haole millionaire who kept a baby elephant and other animals there, this is now the site of a private resort and University of Hawaii Marine research laboratory. You have seen this Island on television, because it is "Gilligan's Island" in the opening shorts of that long running syndicated series. In fact, one water tour company offers a "three hour cruise" which includes a close up look at the famous beach (Hawaiian Overnighters 924-3434).

Paralleling Hwy. 83, clinging to Kaneohe Bay is Hwy. 830 which rejoins 83 about 2 miles above the Valley of the Temples. A mile south of this 83-830 junction is Heeia State Park, Heeia Fishpond, and Ulu Mau Village on a small peninsula just before the Heeia Kea Boat Harbor and Kaneohe Fishing Pier.

**Heeia State Park**, 46-465 Kamehameha Hwy. 830 at Kealohi Point (247-3156), offers picnicking and weekend party hall rental on a beautiful wooded peninsula overlooking the **Heeia Fishpond**, or Loko i'a (loko means pond; i'a is fish). Once 97 offshore and inland ponds existed on old O'ahu. Hawaii is the only culture to create these fish storage and fattening enclosures. Lolo i'a were engineering marvels with five foot high rock walls designed to let tidewater and young fish through, while keeping predators out. This is one of the few (only 5 on O'ahu) examples left; most have been used for building stone or filled in and sold as housing lots. Heeia Fishpond is O'ahu's largest. Also nearby was **Ulu Mau Village**, a reconstructed King's living area, remnants of which can be seen near the State Park.

Our next stop is **Senator Fong's Plantation and Gardens** ★, mauka on Pulama Rd., about a mile north of the Highway 83-830 junction. We rank this working plantation one of O'ahu's top ten paid tourist attractions, beautifully kept with a friendly staff and one of the best quality and reasonably priced gift shops on the Island. Senator Hiram Leong Fong represented Hawaii in the United States Senate from 1959 when Hawaii first became a State, until his retirement in 1976. He has many distinctions: he was the first person of Asian ancestry to serve in the U.S. Senate; he was also senior ranking minority member of the powerful Appropriations Committee and would have been its chairman had he chosen to continue in politics.

But Hawaii beckoned, and Senator Fong came home. Son Rodney had a brainchild of planting the 725 acre ex-banana plantation which Fong had purchased near his beachfront home in 1950. After years of bureaucratic red tape, the Fong family opened their botanic oasis to the public in mid 1988.

After walking through an open-air high roofed building containing a snack bar, gift shop, and dining tables, you board a tram for a 40-minute narrated tour of the valleys and ridges, each named after one of the five presidents Fong worked with during his 17 years as Republican Senator. Eisenhower Valley is home to the visitor center and parking area. Kennedy Valley holds sugarcane, ginger, ferns, giant heliconia, kikui, lauhala, and many fruit trees (watch for the famous Chinese Lychee trees). Johnson Plateau boasts more than 75 kinds of edible plants and trees while Nixon Valley holds four ethnic gardens, and Gerald Ford

Ridge contains a sculptured Northeast garden with several varieties of pine trees. You'll also see bananas, taro, and tiny dendrobium orchids (the ones hotels put on your pillow at night) being grown and harvested. You'd have to visit Maui Tropical Plantation on Maui to see anything like this - it is the only place of its kind on Oʻahu. Stay for lunch and do try the dried mango, when they have it. Next to a piece of mango fruit from a tree this is the best mango taste you'll get. Take some home along with the dried bananas. This is the place to buy those coconuts you've wanted to send home. A few dollars will buy you a big box.

Don't be surprised to see the Senator (he served in the Hawaii Territorial Legislature for 14 years before being elected to the U.S. Senate), he's often at the visitor center in the afternoon to greet you and talk about politics, plants, the Chinese bicentennial celebration he's been instrumental in coordinating, or whatever you'd like to talk with him about. I enjoyed meeting this statesman and shaking his hand.

I do much of my Hawaii gift shopping in *Fong's Plantation Gift Shop*. They import directly from China, their selection and quality are tops, and their prices are rock bottom. Look for Chinese soap and handsome wooden bowls and bracelets. The Plantation is open daily, 9am-4pm. Adults $6.50, children 5-12 $3, under 5 free. "Someone asked me when we're going to finish this," Senator Fong says, "I say maybe 500 years. It's a continuing thing. You never finish it."

As you drive on, you'll see the Waiahole Valley to mauka, famous for growing some of Oʻahu's best taro plants. On the corner of Waiahole Road and Kamehameha Highway is the old *Waiahole Poi Factory*, which made poi from Waiahole Valley taro for 67 years until it stopped production in 1971. Today the building houses a hidden gem - an artists' workshop and gallery where you can buy handcrafted Hawaiian musical instruments and other pieces of art. Notice on the outside wall the painting by Martin Charlot of an Hawaiian Adam being led out of the beautiful garden which has been his home.

Our next stop is Kualoa Regional Park and Hokuleʻa Beach (49-600 Kam. Hwy.) This has been sacred ground to Hawaiians for centuries because high chiefs (alii) resided here when they came to Oʻahu. Children of royalty were also sent here to learn and practice the ways of the alii. This area was so important that any canoes or ships that passed by were required to lower their sails. Today the Park is again famous as the ceremonial landing place of Hawaii's Polynesian voyaging canoe, *Hokuleʻa*, which was launched from a spot on this beach in 1976 to show that ancient planned voyages of exploration and settlement from Tahiti to Hawaii were possible. *Hokuleʻa's* successful voyages have proven that such voyages could have been made, and she now rests between trips in the Hawaii Maritime Center at Pier 7 in Honolulu.

Historic *Kualoa* (long way back) *Regional Park* offers visitors excellent camping, and swimming facilities at *Hokuleʻa Beach*. It's one of Oʻahu's best new parks, run by the City and County, and worth a visit. Call 237-8525 for information. One of the most popular ancient legends about the Kualoa area tells of a goddess who, while searching for a handsome local prince to kidnap for her sister Pele, was confronted by a terrifying huge Moʻo (dragon-lizard with great ferocity and power). After a long struggle the goddess dispatched the moʻo, severed its tail, and threw it into the ocean, where it turned into stone, and can still be seen today not far offshore from Kualoa Beach Park. It's known as **Chinaman's Hat** (Mokoliʻi, little dragon, in Hawaiian) because of its shape.

Just past Kualoa Beach Park on the mauka side very near the highway you'll see a rock chimney rising out of a clump of tall bushes. This is all that's left of the **Kualoa Sugar Mill**, built in 1864 by Dr. Jerrit P. Judd (an early physician and adviser to royalty) but closed and abandoned in 1871 when none of the five sugar plantations on the windward side were able to make a profit. Today these ruins are in a dangerous stage of decay, and are best avoided except for a snapshot or two from the roadside.

**Kaʻaʻawa Beach Park**, number eight on our list of Oʻahu's ten best beaches, is just across Kam Highway from Kaʻaʻawa Elementary School, about three miles north of the Kualoa Sugar Mill ruins. This is a secluded narrow 2 acre strip of white sand beach which is good for swimming and has a lifeguard daily from June through August. Although subject to occasional winter storms, the water is calm, except for the channel on the south side by the reef. If you'll swim on the northern part of the Beach Park, just across from the School, you'll find Kaʻaʻawa the perfect weekday getaway beach, and one that many locals seek out on weekends.

At the north end of Kaʻaʻawa town is the Crouching Lion Inn and profile of a lion on the mountain behind it. Stand in the upper parking lot beside the inn, look mauka through the trees, and you will see the likeness of a reclining lion silhouetted against the sky. To ancient Hawaiians, however, this was no lion. An Hawaiian legend says that when a demigod named Kauhi arrived on Oʻahu with his relative Pele, he was turned to stone for a misdeed. When he saw and fell in love with Pele's sister, Hiʻiaka, he used all his strength to tear himself loose and pursue her, but became exhausted and froze in a crouching position, which he holds to this day, frozen in his passionate attempt to escape. So as you look up at the mountain cliff, you have a choice. Which is it in profile high above, a lion, or a frozen god of ancient Hawaii?

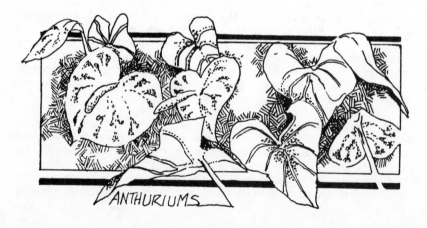
ANTHURIUMS

As you drive past the northeastern slopes of the Ko'olau Mountains from Chinaman's Hat at the upper curve of Kaneohe Bay all the way north to Kahuku, notice that the valleys stretching down to the sea have flat, not V-shaped floors. These indicate the gradual submergence of O'ahu as it moves in a northwestern direction several inches per year. Gradually O'ahu is returning to the ocean from which it came, and eventually will appear only as a small atoll or islet above the waters of the Northern Pacific Ocean.

Let's make a brief stop at **Kahana Bay Beach Park** across the bay from the Crouching Lion (Kauhi). This park and the surrounding **Kahana Valley State Park ★** are methods designed to protect and preserve this ancient valley which, retains its undeveloped way of life still practiced by valley residents after countless generations. Visitors are encouraged to explore the 5220 acres of hiking trails, picnic areas, pig hunting (permit required), swimming, and beach activities. The Huilua Fishpond, operated until the 1920's, is open for viewing on the bay's south shore. Swimming is very good at the shallow, protected beach near the Kapaeleele small boat ramp. In the "Living Park" area visitors can also witness demonstrations of traditional Hawaiian skills as they are practiced in the every day life of the Kahana Valley community. This vestige of old Hawaii offers a rare view of Hawaiian culture in its natural setting.

On up the Kam Highway you'll come to **Punalu'u**. This means "diving for coral" and refers to the coral beds here which supplied building blocks and lime for mortar. During World War II the U.S. Army trained its troops for jungle warfare on O'ahu's windward side. Punaluu Valley was "Green Valley," Kahana was "Blue Valley," and many Hawaiians still refer to them by those names. **Punalu'u Beach Park**, and the beach which extends from here all the way around Makalii Point to the Paniolo Cafe, is calm and good for swimming most of the year, except during high surf or storms. It has a sandy bottom and cooking stands, comfort station, and picnic tables at the Beach Park. No lifeguards, however. Stay close inshore and you'll enjoy this narrow beach protected by the offshore fringing reef. There is a fine stretch of beach between Papaakoko Beach on the north and Haleaha Beach on the south, near Papaakoko-Haleaha Stream. It is sandy, shallow, and good for swimming and snorkeling all year, except in high or stormy surf. There is little public access, but you can stop at **Pat's at Punaluu**, 53-567 Kam Highway (293-8111), and access the beach there, which has conditions similar to Punaluu Beach Park.

Up the road about a mile from Pat's is the entrance (mauka side) to **Sacred Falls**. Stop first at the **Garment Factory** across the highway to shop and get a map plus helpful up-to-the-minute information on conditions at the falls. While you're in the Garment Factory ask to see their famous snapshot of the falls posted on the cash register. Many visitors swear there's a ghost in the picture.

Much misinformation has been published about Sacred Falls, so let's set the record straight. First you cannot drive there; it's a 2.2 mile walk on an easy trail. Do wear tennis or walking shoes. Second, once nearly a decade ago someone was mugged on the trail; a very rare occurance, but consider going with a group as a general safety precaution anyway. Third, go in the morning and take rain gear, since occasional cloudbursts do happen. You'll pass through a narrow canyon where rocks do sometimes cascade down, so watch your head at that point. And last, remember that the water is cold and murky, so plan to swim only if you're a polar bear. Don't dive from the rocks and take along your best mosquito repellent. (They say Avon Skin So Soft does the trick.)

Nearby, across the highway, is another of O'ahu's hidden gems - the **Old Hawaiian Church**. The sign over the door says "Kamalamalama O Ke ou." Light of the World Protestant Interdenominational Church, established in 1935 and watched over since 1939 by the amazing Reverend Richard N. Gaspar (he preaches, repairs, and lives there), who will welcome you to services every Sunday at 11am. Communion service is held the first Sunday of the month at 10:30am, followed by the regular service at 11. Just meeting the Reverend Gaspar is worth the trip.

A mile further on is another church whose time has passed. **Lanakila Church** was built in 1853 by Congregational missionaries, with local coral blocks and timbers. It had 12 large windows and three panel doors, and a commanding view of the coast and ocean. By the late 1890's the village had moved south, and sadly the timbers were taken to build a smaller church in Kaluanui a mile or so south, in 1897. Since then Lanakila Church has stood in ruins, a silent monument to Hawaii's one unlimited commodity - change.

**Pounders Beach**, 55-200 Kam Highway in Laie, is one of O'ahu's most popular bodysurfing beaches. It's usually calm in the summer, and very dangerous from October through April. The pounding surf and steep shorebreak make the beach a good one to watch from the sand. Nearby is the remnant of the century old pier where ships would dock to bring supplies and pick up sugarcane and other cargo bound for Honolulu. You can still see this **Laie Landing** at the north end of Laie Beach Park and Pounders Beach.

In 1850 ten Mormon Missionaries arrived in Hawaii. By 1864 Laie became a Mormon colony. The Mormon Temple Hawaii was constructed there in 1919, and more recently the **Brigham Young University, Hawaii** opened its doors and now attracts students from throughout Polynesia. **The Mormon Temple** (55-600 Maniloa Loop) is impressive with its Taj Mahal white architecture and landscaped grounds featuring a stair-stepped reflecting pool and fountains. Guided tours are available and they have a slide show telling the history of the Church of Jesus Christ Latter-Day Saints at Laie. Call 293-9297 for more information. Centerpiece of the Laie Mormon Community for most visitors is the Polynesian Cultural Center (PCC). Opened in 1963, the Center is owned and operated by the church as a non-profit operation, with proceeds going to PCC development and to BYU Hawaii.

Here we are at the **Polynesian Cultural Center (PCC)** ★, one of O'ahu's most popular tourist attractions, located in the north windward town of Laie.

The three ticket options will give you an idea of PCC offerings. An **Explorer Passport** ($25 adult, $10 children 5-11, under 5 are free) entitles you to: admission to 7 authentic Polynesian Villages, including Samoa, Maori (New Zealand), Tahiti, the Marquesas, Fiji, old Hawaii and Tonga; access to PCC's stores and snack bar; a short "Pageant of the Long Canoes" review, performed at 1, 2, 3, and 4pm; access to the lush 42 acre PCC, with Polynesian brass band concert, island fashion show, 1850's mission house, chapel and school, games, crafts and demonstrations, continuous canoe tours, and an optional free guided tour of the historic town of Laie, the Mormon Temple grounds and BYU Hawaii Campus. This Explorer ticket encompasses the daytime activities at PCC, which begin at 12:30pm and conclude at 6 pm with a short canoe and song ceremony. The *Voyager Passport* ($37 adult, $15 child) gives you all of the above, plus an all-you-can eat buffet dinner in the Gateway Restaurant and a reserved seat for the 90 minute evening show "This is Polynesia" at the Pacific Pavilion (which seats 2800 and is usually packed). The *Ambassador Passport* ($62 adult, $40 child) gives you all of the above plus such VIP amenities as: lei greeting, personalized tour of the center, special dinner courtesies, the best seats for the Polynesian Review, and a pineapple fruit sherbet boat at intermission.

Several suggestions. Unless you spend the entire day and allocate your time to 45 minutes at each village (the Hawaii, Samoan and Tahitian villages are most interesting) you'll have to rush around the center and it will all become a blur with each village looking the same. So come early (12:30), write for an information packet and PCC map before your visit so you can become familiar with the grounds before you arrive, and especially if you have a large family, purchase the Explorer Passport, skip the buffet dinner, and eat instead at the beautiful McDonald's just across the parking lot (it even has an indoor waterfall). Divide your day (you have about 4 1/2 hours of prime daylight to tour the 7 villages, see the mini-pageant, and take a canoe or city tour), and skip the souvenirs here; you can usually get the same items in town for less. The things most worth seeing here are the 7 villages and the young BYU students who will help bring them to life for you. And if your budget or time is limited, skip the evening Polynesian show.

If you do decide to make a full day and evening of it, you can nap on the hour bus/van ride back to Honolulu. And for you explorers driving a rental car who don't want to drive at night after the show, there is a motel next to the PCC on the north side of McDonalds.

PANDANUS TREE                                                           J BAYOT

You'll get the most for your investment at the Polynesian Cultural Center if you have read about and discussed the seven Polynesian cultures represented here, before your visit. Not only will you better appreciate what you're seeing, but you'll also be better able to find out more about each culture from the BYU students who demonstrate the songs, dances, crafts and customs of their homelands, at the PCC.

Two miles north of the Polynesian Cultural Center is *Malaekahana State Recreational Area*. Enter the main gate, wind around and you'll come to a wooded beach park with swimming, picnicking, and shore activities. Overnight camping is available at the Kalanai Point section east of the parking area; lodging and fee camping at the Kahuku (northern) section, including housekeeping cabins for rent. Call 296-1736 for more information and reservations at this 110 acre State Park.

The Malaekahana area has long been the locale for the vacation beach homes of O'ahu's affluent families for many generations, and is sometimes called Cooke's Point for the family that built a large home here in the early 1900's. The beach, although without a lifeguard, has a shallow, sandy swimming area protected by *Mokuauia (Goat) Island* just offshore. As most of the small islets offshore on the windward side of O'ahu, Goat Island is a State bird refuge. However, you can wade out to the island at low tide to see the secluded lovely Mokuauia Beach, on the island's leeward shore. A summer excursion to this beach is certainly one of O'ahu's hidden treasures, and one that few visitors know about. Protect it by leaving it cleaner than you found it and by giving the birds a wide berth.

Two miles north of Goat Island you enter the mill town of *Kahuku*. This is a surprisingly self-contained community, with a community hospital and public school on the mauka side, and the *Kahuku Golf Course* to makai (9 hole, 2699 yard, par 35 course, $1.50 weekdays, $2 weekends, 293-5842).

But the town's center has long been its *Kahuku Sugar Mill* ★ and *Kahuku Mill Market Place*, at 56-700 Kam Hwy. (531-9941 or 293-2444), on the north end of town on the makai side of Kam Highway. This legendary sugar mill operated continuously from the 1880's until 1971, when high costs forced it to stop production. Five years later the mill reopened as a tourist attraction with tours through its color-coded machinery. Changes of ownership and management problems closed the venture, but recently the mill has been renovated and is now open for a self guided tour, dining and shopping. Since the O'ahu Sugar Company Mill in Wahiawa no longer offers tours, the Kahuku Mill is the only place on O'ahu where you can walk through a sugar mill and see the step-by-step process of washing, crushing, weighing, purifying, boiling, and spinning the sugar until the resulting light brown sugar crystals are collected and sent to the California and Hawaiian (C & H) Sugar refinery near San Francisco to be made into many sugar products.

You can purchase fresh sugarcane at the mill to suck and chew, just as Hawaiian kids have done for decades, stopping in the fields on their way to school and cutting pieces of cane for snacks and lunch. You can also buy a container of sweet, golden brown sugar crystals, just as they come from the milling process (now packaged from a sugar mill on Maui).

While you're at the Mill, stop and shop for unique gifts at the shops, buy a shave ice, and then explore the **Kahuku Plantation Village**, an old residential section where families of Mill workers lived for nearly a century. You can still see the old barber shop, store fronts and cafes (two of which, Huevos and Ahi's Kahuku Restaurant, are renovated and open for business (see the WHERE TO EAT chapter). This village is not a tourist attraction, but rather a lived-in section of Kahuku which looks much as it did when its inhabitants worked in the mill and the plantation that supplied it with sugarcane.

The northernmost point of interest on this windward side is the **Amorient Aquafarm ★**, located about two miles north of Kahuku on the makai side of Kamehameha Highway. At the aquafarm's little food stand on the highway you can buy the best fresh shrimp cocktail you've ever eaten. They also sell fresh prawns and fish. I only bought one shrimp cocktail on my first stop; now we buy it by the gallon. Founded in 1978, this privately owned 175 acre aquafarm devotes 100 acres to raising salt water shrimp, and 40 acres to fresh water prawns, catfish, grassfish, and silver carp. Harvesting is done at night (by draining the ponds) so that lower temperatures insure maximum freshness. Harvesting and stocking go on year-round. Tours are not allowed in order to protect the strictly controlled environmental conditions.

Nearly all the seafood raised at the aquafarm is consumed in Hawaii, although limited quantities are shipped to the mainland. Stop in at the roadside stand and judge for yourself. People from all over Hawaii stop here for a fresh-as-can-be treat. Call 293-1069 for more information.

# *EXPLORING PEARL HARBOR - EWA*

Sea level around the Hawaiian Islands is not constant. Geologists tell us that over the past million years (just yesterday in geologic time) glaciers around the world have formed and melted causing the water level surrounding Hawaii to vary as much as 500 feet. During the most recent occurrence of high water, around 80,000 - 100,000 years ago, the sea level at Oʻahu was 25 feet higher than it is today, and remained at that level for centuries. The high water created several important features which are with us today: ancient tides formed steep cliffs on the lower slopes of mountain ridges which today are far above sea level; and deep coral beds grew in the warm inland sea. On southern Oʻahu, Pearl Harbor is a remnant of that inland sea, and the land around it, from the Ewa plain on the west to the Airport, Honolulu and Diamond Head on the southeast, is all one vast coral bench which once grew on a massive reef under a shallow coastal sea that lapped high up the sides of today's mountain slopes.

So when you explore the Pearl Harbor-Ewa basin, you are driving across an ancient reef bed, which reached its greatest width of nearly five miles at Ewa, from Waipahu to Barbers Point.

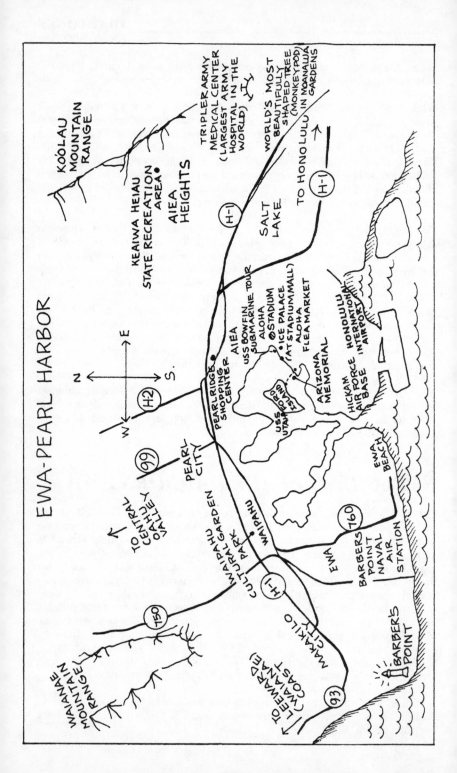

EWA-PEARL HARBOR

KOÓLAU MOUNTAIN RANGE

TRIPLER ARMY MEDICAL CENTER (LARGEST ARMY HOSPITAL IN THE WORLD)

WORLD'S MOST BEAUTIFULLY SHAPED TREE (MONKEYPOD) IN MOANALUA GARDENS

KEAIWA HEIAU STATE RECREATION AREA

AIEA HEIGHTS

H-1

TO HONOLULU

H-1

SALT LAKE

N
W — E
S

H2

PEARLRIDGE SHOPPING CENTER

AIEA

USS BOWFIN SUBMARINE TOUR

ALOHA STADIUM

ICE PALACE (AT STADIUM MALL)

ALOHA FLEA MARKET

ARIZONA MEMORIAL

HICKAM AIR FORCE BASE

HONOLULU INTERNATIONAL AIRPORT

USS UTAH / FORD ISLAND

99

PEARL CITY

TO CENTRAL OAHU VALLEY

WAIPAHU GARDEN CULTURAL PARK

WAIPAHU

H-1

PEARL CITY

EWA

EWA BEACH

760

BARBERS POINT NAVAL AIR STATION

750

WAIANAE MOUNTAIN RANGE

LEEWARD (KONA) COAST

MAKAKILO CITY

93

BARBER'S POINT

268

We'll begin our tour at the one single location which caused Oʻahu to become the principal Hawaiian Island - Pearl Harbor. For centuries before 1793, Waikiki had been the center of activity on Oʻahu. Waikiki had beautiful weather, good surf, and a sandy beach well suited to launching canoes. Then in 1793 the British trading ship "Butterworth" under the command of Captain William Brown located and entered Pearl Harbor, probably the first explorer to do so. In fact for years the area was known as "Brown's Harbor." Then as more and more foreign ships visited Hawaii, King Kamehameha I moved his court from Waikiki to the banks of the harbor in order to be nearer the anchorage chosen by most visiting ships. Before long Honolulu (meaning fair haven or protected harbor) and its port became the center of commerce and culture in Hawaii.

In 1887 King Kalakaua gave the U. S. the right to develop a coal depot at Pearl Harbor, in an agreement which included lowering the import tariff on Hawaiian sugar. After the annexation of Hawaii by the U.S. in 1898, the U.S. Navy began deepening the channel through the reef outside the harbor (completed in 1902). By 1919 when the first dry dock was completed, Pearl Harbor was fully operational, home to most of the U.S. Navy's Pacific command.

Pearl Harbor is known today for the Japanese attack on Sunday, December 7, 1941. The Arizona Memorial is one of Oʻahu's most visited places. The ***Arizona Memorial*** ★ at Pearl Harbor spans the sunken hull of the battleship *U.S.S. Arizona*. Operated along with the ***Arizona Memorial Visitors Center*** (built in 1980) on the shoreline overlooking Pearl Harbor, the Memorial was completed and dedicated in 1962. The Arizona Memorial is the final resting place for more than 1100 Navy and Marine personnel who lost their lives defending the ship during the Sunday, December 7, 1941 attack by Japanese aircraft. The attack began at 7:55am and at 8:10 the Arizona exploded, hit by a 1,760-pound armor piercing bomb. Within nine minutes she had sunk, entombing 1100 members of her crew. In all, 8 ships were sunk or beached, 13 were damaged, and 347 aircraft were destroyed or damaged; 2,403 Americans were killed, 1,178 were wounded. Other targets on Oʻahu were also hit, with hundreds of men killed at Hickham, Wheeler and Bellows Air Fields, Ewa Marine Corps Air Station, Kaneohe Naval Air Station (the first installation to be bombed during the attack), and Schofield Barracks. The unprovoked attack led directly to our nation's declaration of war, and the beginning of World War II.

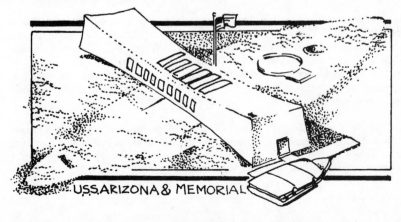

USS ARIZONA & MEMORIAL

The Memorial is operated by the National Park Service and the U.S. Navy. As you enter, the guide at the information desk will give you a brochure and ticket assigning you to a group. You move through a documentary film theater into a Navy launch and out to the floating Memorial in the harbor. Before the film you're free to tour the Museum, browse in the non-profit bookstore-gift shop, and listen to an excellent short talk by one of the Memorial's volunteers, many of whom are survivors of the 1941 attack.

---

DID YOU KNOW...that Pearl Harbor was designated a National Historic Landmark in 1965 for the significant part it has played in the defense of our country? It is the only U.S. naval base so honored.

---

Before you leave, you should also visit the *U.S.S. Bowfin*, a World War II American submarine moored on the opposite side of the Fort Island ferry landing from the Arizona Memorial, and open for tours every day except Monday. Many tourists bypass the Bowfin in a hurry to see other attractions, when this is one of the best attractions on O'ahu. Take your kids; the tour through these damp, cramped quarters is one they'll long remember.

The same day you visit the Arizona Memorial and the *U.S.S. Bowfin* is a good time to explore the numerous other points of interest in the Pearl Harbor - Ewa region of O'ahu. Just up the highway from Pearl Harbor is *Aloha Stadium* ★, football home of the University of Hawaii Rainbows, and scene of year-round sporting events including the Aloha Bowl in late December, NFL Pro Bowl, and the Hula Bowl in January. This 50,000 seat stadium made news with its air-cushion system which allows bleachers to automatically rearrange for football or baseball seating. If you're interested in attending a sporting event at Aloha Stadium, call the Box Office at 488-7731 for schedule and ticket information.

The stadium is also the Wednesday and weekend site of *The Flea Market* held in the parking area. This weekly event brings out wholesale vendors, family craftspersons, and food sellers by the hundreds. It's a great place to browse and see what open-air bargains you can find among acres of T-shirts, car stereos, and bright-patterned rolls of cloth. Expect a small admission fee.

Across the street is *Stadium Mall*, where your kids will find *The Ice Palace Iceskating Rink*. Always busy with organ music and skaters of all ages, the rink offers a cool wintry atmosphere where you can forget it's 85 degrees outside. They keep it moving on the ice with special events, couples only songs, and lessons for beginners. It's a popular place, and one where you can spend an enjoyable hour just watching. Located at 4510 Salt Lake Blvd., call 487-9921 for current times and prices.

Also at the mall is *Brandy's Grill* (486-4066), where you can learn to shoot darts and watch tournament matches. The game of darts is fascinating to watch, and can be addicting to play. And if you work up a sweat, they serve great beer, or you can visit the *Stadium Ice Cream Store* a few doors away.

Most visitors don't think of **Honolulu International Airport** as a place of interest to explore while touring the island, but it certainly is just that. You'll see the world in miniature at the airport, with more than 15 million people passing through it every year. If you like to watch people, this is the place. And there are lots of places to explore. Did you know, for instance, that the airport has its own mini-motel? It's on the upper level, near the United Airlines counter. You can take a nap, have a shower, or sleep in a small room. An eight hour sleep and shower costs less than $20.00. There is also an information booth with maps, brochures, and tips on hotels, restaurants, sights, or transportation. The airport is a place where you can have fun just looking around, window shopping at stores you once hurried past on the way to the baggage claim area, or sitting in the terminal's garden area enjoying the architecture and the peaceful feeling of not having to be anywhere on time.

There was once, when planes were boats and arrival and departure were done on the docks, a custom of offering a fresh flower lei and a hug to each arriving passenger. With air travel, that lovely ritual has shrunk until now it is almost the exclusive domain of tour companies and family gatherings. What a shame!

Adjacent to the airport is **Hickham Air Force Base**, which shares runways and taxiways with the airport. Since its construction in 1938, Hickham has grown to 2,700 acres for its 5,000 military and 2,000 civilian personnel. More than 30,000 vehicles pass through its gates daily. A major mission of the wing is to provide base and logistic support for nearly 140 associate units in Hawaii and the Pacific. The wing's 9th Airborne Command and Control Squadron flies the EC-135 J aircraft. Daily wing activities include aircraft maintenance, and the operation of Hickham, Wheeler, Bellows, and Wake Island Airfields.

---

DID YOU KNOW...that it was Prince Lot (King Kamehameha V) who revived the ancient art of hula after four decades of prohibition by the missionaries? His efforts are commemorated each July at Moanalua Gardens in the Prince Lot Hula Festival, featuring ancient and modern hula, games, crafts, demonstrations, and food.

---

Let's leave Pearl now and take the H-1 north to Moanalua Road (Highway 78) where we'll turn Diamondhead and exit at **Moanalua Gardens** ★. According to "Ripley's Believe it or Not," this is the site of "the world's most beautifully shaped tree." Whether or not the giant monkeypod (ozumbrella) tree deserves the title, it certainly does provide welcome shade on a warm Honolulu afternoon. The free guided walks here, offered on weekends, will acquaint you with the plantings in this historic valley, so sacred that Kamehameha came here to celebrate his conquest of O'ahu. Located at 1352 Pineapple Place, call 834-5334 for information and tour reservations.

Within a mile of Moanalua Gardens, sitting majestically on Moanalua Ridge high above Honolulu, is **Tripler Army Medical Center**, built in 1948 to replace a series of smaller military hospitals which had served O'ahu since the Spanish

American War in 1898. Today Tripler provides health care to one out of every four residents in Hawaii. The 550 bed facility averages 2500 outpatient visits per day and has 300 births each month. A major expansion project added three new four-story wings in 1985 and is now renovating existing Tripler facilities.

*Moanalua Golf Course* ★, located at the opening of Moanalua Valley, 1250 Ala Aolani, (839-2311), is something of a pilgrimage for those who love the game of golf, because it's the oldest golf course west of the Rocky Mountains, built around the turn of the century. It's a pretty little 9-hole course, now open to members and guests only, but worth a stop anyway since groups sometimes need a fourth.

A slight detour, and one well worth the effort, takes you past the Aiea Sugar Mill, to the end of Aiea Heights Drive where you'll find the *Keaiwa Heiau State Recreational Area*. This ancient heiau was dedicated to healing with natural medicine. Presided over by, in old times, Kahuna Lapaau (herbal physicians), this heiau was one at which lives were saved, not sacrificed as at other heiaus dedicated to the war god, Ku. Specimens of medicinal plants are on display here, as are picnic, camping and hiking areas. For anyone interested in holistic medicine or herbal medicines, this park is an excellent place to visit, accompanied by June Gutmanis' well-illustrated book on the topic.

As you come back down through Aiea, cross the H-1, travel Ewa on Moanalua Road to *Pearlridge Shopping Center* ★. This huge suburban shopping center is O'ahu's second largest after Ala Moana Center. There are 90 stores and restaurants in two clusters referred to as Phase I and II, separated by three football field lengths of parking area and landscaping. Kids will enjoy riding Hawaii's only monorail between Phases. Some shops to explore: Anna Miller's Coffee House; Bubble Gum; Crazy Shirts; Elena's Finest Filipino Foods; Famous Amos Chocolate Chip Cookies; Fernandez' Fun Factory; Fredericks of Hollywood; Honolulu Book Shops; Kay-Bee Toy and Hobby Shop; Lemonade Plus; Morrow's Nut House; See's Candies; Tape Town; Shirokiya; Tsuruya Noodle Shop, and the Zoom Surf Shop. Check the phone book for more.

Just across from the Pearlridge Shopping Center, in the Kam Drive-In theater parking lot (98-850 Moanalua Rd. 488-3835) you'll find *The Swap Meet*, open every Wednesday, Saturday and Sunday. Similar to the Flea Market at Aloha Stadium, you can negotiate for souvenirs, sarongs, silk shirts, stereos, shells, straw mats, and perhaps gold plated cockroaches. It's Honolulu's attic, and worth a look. A small admission fee is charged and parking is available.

Are you a Tom Selleck fan? Did you enjoy watching Magnum PI? If so there's a place in Pearl City you should visit. It's *Reni's*, a unique nightclub owned by Roger Mosley, co-star of the Magnum series. Open weekdays from 9pm-2am, and Fri. and Sat. until 4am, Reni's has live music, dancing and a sophisticated atmosphere. Dress code, cover charge, and valet parking. Located at 98-713 Kuhhau Place in Pearl City. Leave Pearlridge going Ewa on Kam Highway, turn right onto Kaahumanu within a mile, then left onto Kuahao. Coming from Waikiki, take the H-1 west to exit 10 and make the first three left turns.

Let's leave the residential community of Pearl City, take the Kamehameha Highway (#99), into Waipahu as 99 turns into Farrington Highway (#90). Turn right onto Waipahu Depot, pass the *O'ahu Sugar Company Mill* and turn left into the *Friends of Waipahu Cultural Garden Park and Plantation Village*.

Remember this name, because within a few years this will be one of the most spectacular and popular tourist attractions on O'ahu. The concept is unique. On the original site of the O'ahu Sugar Company plantation and worker's village, there is rising a re-creation of the turn-of-the-century Planation Village as it looked in its prime. Not only will the original buildings be rebuilt or re-created, but a full living history program (similar to that currently in operation at the Museum Houses Museum) will offer visitors a guided tour, demonstrations of period skills (such as black-smithing and charcoal making) and exhibits such as ethnobotanical gardens featuring trees, foods and medicinal plants important to the various ethnic groups living together here. And that is the key to the overall goal of the Park and Plantation Village. The Park's mission statement says:

*"Our purpose is to ensure an understanding of the accomplishments and sacrifices of the progenitors of modern Hawaii and instill a better appreciation of the origins of Hawaii's cosmopolitan society. Hawaii is a multi-ethnic State. Many of our citizens are descendants of immigrant groups who journeyed from nations around the world to live and toil on Hawaii's plantations. Contemporary Hawaii has been shaped by the results of their labor. A primary objective of the park is to depict the plantation's physical setting and lifestyle in an authentic manner which will serve as a center for preservation, programs, and study."*

> DO YOU KNOW..where the "shaka" hand greeting, so popular in Hawaii, came from? No one knows! It was popularized by surfers in the 60's, then by a local car salesman on his early TV ads. But where did it originate? A new theory from Plantation Village proposes that the custom might have originated in marble games played on plantation dirt lots, where a good kini, or shooter, had real "shocker" (shaka) power to break the pile, and where common shooting positions had the thumb and little finger extended.

Four phases have been approved and are underway. Phase I (1989-90) will present Chinese cultural influences. The 1908 Chinese Cookhouse is under restoration, a Chinese clubhouse-single men's barracks will be built, and the three dimensional interpretive scale model of Plantation Village will be completed. Phase II will stress Japanese influences in the village, and will include a tofu-ya (complete with grinding stones, tubs, and stoves), as well as the installation of the Wakamiya Inari Japanese Shrine, listed as a National Historic Site and currently in storage after being moved from Moiliili. Phase III will build Portuguese and Filipino workers' houses, with ethno-gardens and plants associated with each culture. Phase IV will re-construct the village barber shop, communal bath, wood splitter and shed, and sumo wrestling where immigrants enjoyed this sport brought with them from Japan.

Of the more than 10,000 visitors to the park in 1988, 7,500 were students who came to see the 10-minute slide presentation, tour the museum, and enjoy hands-on educational activities under the direction of the talented staff. The Museum and Park are open Mon. to Fri. 9am-3:30pm, Sat. 9am-12noon. Admission is free. Group tours available, call 677-0110. Visit now, then go back on your next visit to experience the park as the Plantation Village grows before your eyes.

Before you leave Waipahu, take an hour to explore *Arakawa's Dept. Store* ★ at 94-333 Waipahu Depot (677-3131). This wonderful, only-in-Hawaii store was started by an amazing man, Zempan Arakawa, who arrived to work in the Oʻahu Sugar Company Mill from Okinawa in 1904. Times were hard, and Zempan had a family to support. So he moonlighted as a taxi driver, as a pineapple farmer, as a self-taught tailor, and storekeeper. By 1912, people knew of his fine reputation, and his store prospered. Today it is still managed by his family, and it still has a fine reputation. No tourist shop, this. Arakawa's is a local institution; everyone eventually shops here for something. A shopping trip to Arakawa's is an adventure you can tell 'em about back home. It's an Oʻahu vacation memory you can't buy at any price. Just go, and add it to your collection of treasures.

Our next stop is the plantation mill town of *Ewa*. The Ewa Sugar Mill, built in 1891 and for decades the heart of thriving Ewa Plantation Company, is now closed. As you drive down Renton Road past handsome old houses that look empty, and parks and streets that are silent, this sleeping town sends out a muted eulogy for an industry whose time, at least here in Ewa, has come and gone. Amazingly, the town has kept its charm. People have stayed here; Ewa has become a bedroom community for someplace else. This quiet town was once prosperous, the mill highly profitable, the workers', villages or "camps" were showplaces. Take a good look; it is a way of life which is quickly disappearing.

Back to Fort Weaver Road and turn right, toward the sea, will take you down to the beachside area of *Ewa Beach* which started as a resort area for thousands of plantation workers who lived in planned housing inland. Today this small somewhat isolated community is doing very well. Drive past the Ewa Beach Shopping Center (they have a hardware store, pharmacy, and Woolworth's if you need one) and McDonald's, 91-923 Fort Weaver Rd., and on around the curve to the left as Fort Weaver Rd. parallels the beach. Just before the road turns sharply left to go around the Puuloa Rifle Range, find a place to park and walk down to *Ewa Beach Park* ★, the best public beach in the Pearl Harbor-Ewa region (don't consider swimming in Pearl Harbor, the water is dangerously polluted and beaches are muddy). This used to be one of Oʻahu's best seaweed gathering beaches; not so much any more. The park offers comfort station, picnic tables, and kids' playground equipment, but no lifeguard services. Beach is narrow, water calm inshore with a deep drop off that is dangerous for small children.

While relaxing at this beach look at your map; you'll see that you're only a stone's throw from Iroquois Point and the entrance to Pearl Harbor. So watch for some large vessels nearby. Just across the harbor entrance are Hickham Field and the Honolulu International Airport, and you are lying directly under the landing glide path (you may already be aware of that fact).

To your right and left are restricted military installations. ***Iroquois Point*** is a Navy housing area, and ***Barbers Point Naval Air Station*** is primarily an antisubmarine warfare support community. This air station, commissioned in 1942, covers 3600 acres in Ewa, and houses 3200 military personnel.

The drive back down Fort Weaver Rd. to Pohakupuna Road and on to the picnic area at the end of Papipi Road is beautiful. ***Oneula Beach Park*** is a wonderful picnic or sunbathing spot, but swimming is only fair, due to murky water and inshore coral outcroppings.

Time for a bite to eat? OK, stop at a fast food restaurant in Ewa Beach and pick up whatever you like. The perfect picnic spot is not far off. Follow Fort Weaver Road back mauka to Farrington Highway (#93), turn left and take Farrington until it curves, then take a left onto Kalaeloa Blvd. Drive makai past the ***Hawaii Raceway Park*** where, by the way, they hold auto races on some Friday and Saturday evenings (672-3267 or 682-3613 for information). Turn right onto Olai which winds around and ends at the spectacular ***Barbers Point Beach Park and Lighthouse***. The swimming is no good here, but the scenery is outstanding; there is a comfort station and picnic area. Address is 91-121 Olai Street, Campbell Industrial Park. What a setting for a picnic lunch. The view and lighthouse and breeze are all very stimulating to one's appetite!

While you're picnicking, you should know the fascinating story of how this Point got its present name. In 1795 an arrogant, tight fisted sea captain used to getting his own way stopped at Waikiki for supplies on his way to China in the trading brig Arthur, loaded with otter pelts from the Pacific Northwest. His ship ran aground at this spot, six men were drowned, and the Arthur was lost. His cargo was salvaged, however, along with ten cannons, but not before Captain Barber had left for Alaska. Upon his return several years later, Barber demanded his cargo and ten cannons from Kamehameha I. The King, also a determined negotiator, gave Barber his cargo of furs, but demanded that Barber, who needed provisions, pay for them not in the customary gold, but in gunpowder for the ten cannons. Barber, outmaneuvered, had no choice but to leave the cannons and pay the gunpowder. The sight of the wrecked Arthur became known as Barbers Point, recalled with a chuckle by anyone who knew the story of the tough old captain who was finally bested at his own game.

As we drive back to Farrington Highway, look down across the cane fields of Ewa,and up toward the ***Waianae Mountains*** where you can see the hillside homes of ***Makakilo***. It seems strange to realize that plans are now being finalized to build a "second city" in West O'ahu. This answer to Honolulu's overcrowding is planned to stretch from Pearl City to Makakilo, and cover the major part of Ewa Plain. The Ewa Coast and parts of the Leeward Coast would be developed as recreational areas for the West O'ahu City's population.

So try to explore this beautiful rich sugarcane lowland plain while its rural history is still visible. For just as glacial tides have risen and fallen across this land, a great flood of urban growth seems to be riding a wave of the future toward the Pearl Harbor-Ewa region of O'ahu.

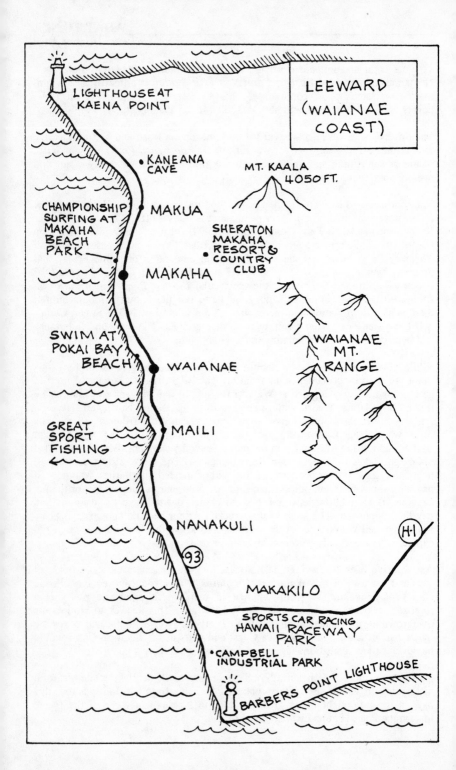

LIGHTHOUSE AT
KAENA POINT

LEEWARD
(WAIANAE
COAST)

• KANEANA
CAVE

MT. KAALA
4050 FT.

CHAMPIONSHIP
SURFING AT
MAKAHA
BEACH
PARK —

MAKUA

SHERATON
MAKAHA
RESORT &
COUNTRY
CLUB

MAKAHA

SWIM AT
POKAI BAY
BEACH

WAIANAE
MT.
RANGE

WAIANAE

GREAT
SPORT
FISHING

MAILI

NANAKULI

H-1

93

MAKAKILO

SPORTS CAR RACING
HAWAII RACEWAY
PARK

• CAMPBELL
INDUSTRIAL PARK

BARBERS POINT LIGHTHOUSE

# EXPLORING THE LEEWARD COAST

The Leeward, or Waianae, Coast is one of the last major bastions of old Hawaii to be found on the Island of Oʻahu (along with Waimanalo and a few remote communities). It is today a place of growing conflict between traditional Island ways of living and the inevitable forces of modernization, development and urbanization. U.S. Congressman Jonah Kuhio Kalanianaole successfully introduced the bill which led to the 1922 Hawaiian Homes Act, providing homestead parcels (kuleanas) for anyone with 50% or more Hawaiian ancestry. Many of the homes on the Leeward Coast were built under provisions of that law. The Hawaiians who live here have a proud heritage and a genuine aloha which make visitors feel as though they are accepted as a member of the ohana - the family group.

This is also a place where pakalolo is grown and smoked, where young people take beer to the beach on weekend evenings to have a good time and forget their troubles, and where vandalism and stealing from tourist automobiles does occasionally happen. In the past such incidents have been publicized, and have led some tour directors and guidebooks to advise visitors to avoid the Leeward Coast. We have toured this coastline from Nanakuli to Yokohama Bay and have found it to be one of Oʻahu's most enjoyable regions to explore. People have been friendly and outgoing, and we have had some of our most relaxed and memorable adventures here.

If you're looking for more Polynesian Cultural Centers and museums, the Leeward Coast will disappoint you since they don't exist here. But if you enter this Valley of the Hawaiian ready to celebrate their pride, respect their culture, and learn about their values and struggles, they will recognize you and welcome you to a treasurehouse you can find nowhere else.

On the map you can see that the Leeward Coast spans about 20 miles from Barbers Point on the south to Kaena Point. One major highway, Farrington Highway 93, parallels the beach from bottom to top, and a few small roadways run from it into the Waianae Mountain Range, which cups the oceanside valley with its crescent-shaped wall of peaks. Geologically, this is the oldest part of Oʻahu, having been formed by lava from a central vent in the Waianae Volcano (located near the present Kolekole Pass) about 10 million years ago.

We'll start our tour of the Waianae Coast where Farrington Hwy. curves north to parallel the western coastline. On your right you'll see the Hawaiian Electric Company's **Kahe Power Plant**. The beach across from it, **Hawaiian Electric Beach Park**, is private property owned by the company but opened for public use year round. Known as "Tracks" (because of the century old railroad tracks which connected Waipahu with Haleiwa and can still be seen between the beach and highway here), this is one of the best swimming and surfing areas on the south Waianae Coast. Parking is along Farrington Highway; there is a comfort station, showers, cooking pits and picnic tables; no lifeguard. In the heyday of the Waipahu Sugar Mill, this was its private recreational beach; employees would ride the train from Waipahu, and called this "Waipahu Beach."

The four major communities on the Leeward Coast (from South to North) are Nanakuli, Maili, Waianae and Makaha (Makaha and Waianae together form the largest population center on the western coast).

As you drive through *Nanakuli* slow down, pull into the *Pacific Shopping Mall* to check out their shops, then watch for *Big Daddy's Drive-In* and the *Nanakuli Trading Post*, two of the busiest places in town. *Nanakuli Super* is a good place for something cold, too. Also in Nanakuli is the *Samoa Iosua Assembly of God Church*. This handsome building has double towers and ornate facade worth inspecting. Services are held on Thursdays at 7pm and Sun. at 11am.

In *Maili* you'll find *Maili Beach Park* at 86-230 Farrington Highway. Swimming here is good; but only in summer months and only directly in front of the lifeguard stand. Daily lifeguard service is provided from June through August; there's a comfort station and picnic tables.

The town of *Waianae* is the largest on the Leeward Coast. Waianae means mullet (fish) waters, which reflects the excellent deep sea fishing to be enjoyed in the waters off the Leeward Coast. Kids won't want to leave *Fernandez' Fun Factory* in the *Waianae Mall*, on the south end of town. There are eight of these video arcades on O'ahu, the most famous one located at 2381 Kuhio Avenue in Waikiki. But this one is nicer, and certainly less crowded. It flashes, bangs, and talks to you; prizes, too! And there's a *Burger King* right across the parking lot in case your kids run out of steam. Or quarters. There's also Waianae Kau Kau (chow) Corner, 85-973 Farrington Hwy., and Waianae Coast Drive-In nearby if you prefer a more Island-style menu.

Waianae's crowning glory is definitely *Pokai Bay* ★, which you get to by turning makai from Farrington Highway onto Waianae Valley Road. *Pokai Bay Beach Park* is one of O'ahu's ten best beaches in our book, due in large part to its sheltered bay, shallow and calm swimming area, and daily lifeguard service all summer and winter weekends. Two thirds of this beach is controlled by the military and open only to their personnel. The public portion is in the area between Kaneilio Point and the first breakwater north of it. For most of the year this is the safest place to swim on the Leeward Coast, and has been since the boat harbor and jetty were constructed in 1953. If you have kids this is the only water you should let them swim in on your visit to this side of O'ahu, especially in the winter. If you're on active military duty, be sure to go to the *Waianae Kai Military Reservation Beach* here at Pokai Bay. There's a small store, a recreation center, and very good surfing conditions for beginners. Your dependents and guests are welcome to join you.

On the point forming the south side of Pokai Bay is ancient *Kuilioloa Heiau* ★, one of the few heiaus which were surrounded on three sides by water. Built around the 15th Century A.D., it was dedicated to Ililoa, the long dog (perhaps the dog who waits, since loa can mean a long time) who was patron of travellers to and from this coast. It is said that when Kamehameha the Great set sail with his peleleu (large double-hulled canoe) fleet to attack Kaua'i in the spring of 1796 (an attack which was postponed due to rough waters in the channel and never attempted again), he came here to Kuilioloa Heiau for services immediately before his departure. What a scene it must have been, with thousands of warriors, and hundreds of war canoes on the beach while the great chief and his advisors humbled themselves on the heiau's stone altar to ask favor from their gods.

Although most charter fishing boats on O'ahu leave from Kewalo Basin at Fisherman's Wharf in Honolulu, some excellent charter boats operate out of the **Waianae Yacht Harbor** just north of Pokai Bay. Enter from Farrington Highway, and enjoy the activity at this busy fishing and recreation center.

Ask anyone on the Leeward Coast where they grocery shop and you'll be surprised how many say **Tamura's Superette**, 86-032 Farrington Highway in Waianae. It's a local meeting place, where you can pick up a current copy of the *Waianae Coaster* or *Register* newspaper, which will let you in on the special local events happening on the West O'ahu Coast during your visit. Tamura's is worth going to just to see what's for sale here.

If you still have questions about the relative safety of the Leeward Coast, you might stop into the friendly and helpful **Waianae Police Station** at 85-939 Farrington Highway, 696-4221, right around the corner from Pokai Bay Beach Park. They'll be glad to provide you with information that will make your visit here even more enjoyable.

Follow the route taken by most visitors coming to the Waianae Coast. Drive north on Farrington Hwy. into Makaha, turn mauka at Cornet Village, then follow Makaha Valley Rd. to the **Sheraton Makaha Resort and Country Club** ★. Remember when we talked about O'ahu's resorts that offer you an outer-island experience less than an hour's drive from Waikiki? Well, here is one. You'll think you're on Maui when you see the Sheraton's 18-hole, par 72, championship golf course, and four day/night tennis courts surrounded by majestic Waianae Mountains and the shimmering Leeward Coastline. You could be on the Garden Isle of Kaua'i when you look out from your lanai in your two-story cottage surrounded by full tropical gardens and fragrant exotic flowers. Sitting beside the cool blue water of the Olympic size swimming pool looking across the green expanse of an ancient undeveloped valley will remind you of the Kona Coast on the Big Island.

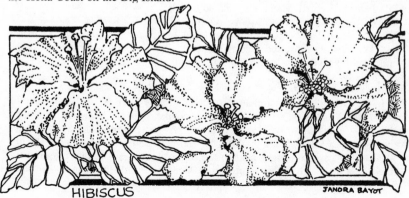

HIBISCUS                                                    JANORA BAYOT

All this, and Waikiki less than an hour's drive. But who wants to leave with a fine dining restaurant like the Kaala Room only steps away, a shuttle service to Pearlridge Shopping Center and the Airport, an activity desk that can arrange tours up in a helicopter or down into a reef. You can explore the quiet valley on horseback, explore an ancient heiau, or just lounge. You can do it all at Sheraton Makaha, or do nothing. Either way, you'll fall in love with the rustic hospitality and restful picture-postcard setting of O'ahu's outer-island Makaha Valley. So park your car, spend an hour or weekend, tour the resort, have an exotic drink by the pool, and feel the healing atmosphere of Makaha.

Stop at the desk and arrange to visit the most complete reconstruction of an ancient Hawaiian heiau anywhere in Hawaii. In many heiau today you can see ancient stone walls and platforms. But only at the City of Refuge on the Big Island and here at ***Kaneaki Heiau*** ★ in the Makaha Valley can you see the grass structures, tikis, and wicker towers which completed the temple and made it ready for ceremonial events.

Archeologists tell us that Kaneaki Heiau was built in the 14th century and used for services honoring Lono, God of Fertility and Agriculture. It is now evident that the heiau was converted for ceremonies in honor of war during the late 18th century, and became a luakini, a temple of human sacrifice. After the death of Kamehameha I in 1819, the old religion of Hawaii was abolished by the Hawaiian royalty, and heiau ceased to function as centers of worship. If you only have time to visit one heiau while on an O'ahu vacation, this is the one to see.Reservations required.

As you drive back on Makaha Valley Rd, watch for family fruit stands along the road. The fruit is tasty, fresh off backyard trees, and cheap. As good as the fruit is, the conversation you'll have with the folks doing the selling is better.

***Kepuhi Point*** between Makaha Beach Park and Kepuhi Beach is the site where the legendary Makaha International Surfing Championships were held for more than 20 years. Although most competition has moved to the North Shore, a new tradition, which began in 1978, it is worth seeing. It's Buffalo's Annual Big Board Surfing Classic, two days of competition on 12 - 16 foot, 75 pound surfboards called "tankers", plus food, entertainment, and music. It all happens in late February - early March on Makaha Beach.

Don't make the mistake of turning around at Makaha and leaving the Leeward Coast. Some of its most spectacular scenery is to be found along its northern-most stretch of highway. On the short drive to the end of the road, several places are especially worth seeing.

You must, underline must, stop and explore ***Kaneana Cave*** ★, ancient legendary home of the shark God's son. It's on the mauka side of Farrington Highway about 3 1/4 miles north of Makua Beach Park, just beyond Barking Sands (if you pass Makua Valley Road you've gone too far). Before you get out of the car to look at the cave (it's right next to the highway and requires no climbing or hiking to get to), listen to this shortened version of the old Hawaiian legend.

Once there lived in this cave a horrible creature named Nanaue, son of the Powerful Shark God Kamahaolii, who could change his appearance back and forth from shark to man at will. In the shape of a handsome young man he would lure unsuspecting travelers and neighbors into his cave, then transform into a shark and devour them near his white stone altar in the cave's watery depths. Finally he was discovered, trapped and killed by his outraged neighbors. Now you're ready to enjoy your walk into the 100 foot high mouth of the cavern (which looks like an entrance to the underworld).

Geologists tell us that Kaneana Cave, often called Makua Cave, was formed 150,000 - 200,000 years ago when the sea covered this part of the Island. It is 450 feet long inside the cavern, and far longer behind the rockslides that have sealed off its deepest parts.

Even with the bottles and cans on the ground and graffiti on the cave walls, you can still easily see how this eerie spot could cause travelers to give it a wide berth, especially at dusk. You can almost hear low guttural sounds rising from the cavern's dark interior.

*Makua Beach*, good for swimming in summer but certainly not during the winter, is just a little more than a mile north of the cave. Next time you see the classic movie "Hawaii", watch for the scenes of old Lahaina Town on Maui. In 1965 when the film was made, Makua Beach was transformed into old Lahaina, complete with false front buildings and such, for the film. Today the sets are long gone, but the pristine setting, fresh and unspoiled enough to pass for the Hawaii of 170 years ago, is still there for you to enjoy.

Another two miles north is *Yokohama Bay*, and the end of the paved highway. The area from here is part of *Kaena Point State Park*, 853 acres of remote wild coastline which offers picnicking, long hiking trail (2.7 miles one way), and early morning porpoise sightings from the point near the mouth of Kaluakauila Stream (just south of the Satellite Tracking Station Access Road).

Yokohama Bay is so named because of the hundreds of Japanese-Hawaiian fisherman who have fished here for moi (threadfish) since the 1860's. It is a nice place to sunbathe or swim in the summer, but surfing or winter swimming here can be dangerous.

Looking back as you turn your vehicle around you'll notice several white spherical pods on top of the ridge above Yokohama Bay. These are the buildings of the *Kaena Point Satellite Tracking Station*.

As you start back down the Western Coast, your view of the fluted peaks and valleys of the *Waianae Mountains* ★ will be one of the most stunning anywhere on the Island. From this point on, you're likely to have a greater understanding of the Hawaiians' love for this endangered valley, and to to be filled with an increased determination to do all you can to protect its beauty and integrity for the generations yet to come.

## LEI ILIMA

O ka ilima no kuʻu lei,
Kalia ia nei puʻu wai.
He wihi iano kuʻu kino,
ʻLei hoʻohihi a ka manao.

Iini au la i kou nani,
He hiwahiwa i kaʻu ke.
O wau kou hoa e kohu ai,
E lei ilima e iei ilima.
O ka ima.


'Tis the ilima my heart doth long for,
It is the lei so rare and lovely,
I know for me it's the only garland,
The wreath of beauty my heart adores.

Where'er I roam and where'er I wander,
I know I'll ne'er find your equal ever.
Your charms are always so fascinating,
Your praises I shall sing, lei ilima.
'Tis the ima.

(Chorus exists only in English)

O beautiful ilima,
Choice of my heart.
O sweet and charming flower,
Soft and lovely to behold.


-Song about the ilima,
the flower of Oʻahu, which is
used to make beautiful leis.
It takes some 500 ilima flowers
to make one lei.


Reprinted from Samuel H. Elbert and Noelani Mahoe, *Na Mele o Hawaiʻi Nei*.
© 1970 University of Hawaii Press.

# WHAT TO DO

The variety of recreational opportunities on O'ahu is limitless. There is something for everyone of any age, from lounging to surfing! The hardest part may be deciding which to do first. To help you decide we offer you a condensed, annotated listing of exciting things to do on land, in and under the water, and in the air. This will allow you to see almost at a glance what activities are available, and decide which ones you wish to select for your day's itinerary.

Hawaii's marvelous year round climate makes it the perfect place to enjoy outdoor activities. And there's plenty to do. On land there are tours, sports such as tennis, golf, horseback riding and garage sale-ing. On the water you can surf, ski, or paddle. Under it you can snorkel, snuba (a new activity), or take a ride in a submarine. And in the sky, you can glide on a huge kite, float under a parachute, or flightsee in a helicopter or small plane.

Lounging is of course one of Hawaii's oldest traditions. But you'll find yourself being pulled out of your beach chair like a magnet when you read about all the activities at your fingertips.

So read on and enjoy each one, even if it's from the comfort of your own lanai!

Here are some best bets to get you started:

- Double hulled canoe rides
- Surf with small or large board
- Snorkeling
- Tour of Honolulu and Hanauma Bay
- Lounging
- See a performance, go to a theater, film etc.
- Flightseeing in helicopter or small plane
- Hawaii's newest sport, SNUBA
- Walking on beach, or downtown or Chinatown
- Dancing at one of Honolulu's night spots
- A sunset or dinner cruise
- Gliding at Dillingham Field
- Hawaiian stage show
- Hiking Diamond Head Crater
- Kite flying at Kapiolani Park
- A polo match at Mokuleia or Waimanalo
- Jogging along Ala Wai Canal
- Golfing at Maunalua, the Pali Course, or Kuhuku
- Freshwater fishing in Waipahu

# WATER ACTIVITIES

## BEACHES

Beautiful beaches probably bring more people to Hawaii than any other single attraction. The image of tourists throwing their luggage in the closet, pulling on their swim suits and running into the surf is not much of an exaggeration! O'ahu is famous for its world class beaches - especially "the world's most famous beach" - Waikiki, and its other beaches which are among the best in Hawaii. Each coast of O'ahu offers beaches with good swimming, picnicking, snorkeling, and unique settings and conditions. The following 10 are probably the finest on the Island. Criteria for selection: safety, lifeguard services, sandy bottom, and good facilities.

#1    Waikiki, especially Gray's Beach
#2    Hanauma Bay
#3    Kailua Beach Park
#4    Haleiwa Beach Park
#5    Pokai Bay Beach Park
#6    Sans Souci
#7    Magic Island Lagoon (Ala Moana Beach Park)
#8    Kaaawa Beach Park
#9    Bellows Beach Park
#10   Kuilima Cove

If you'll remember to check with lifeguards before entering the water, to read and follow all rules posted at the beach, and protect yourself from sun and dangerous marine animals, your beach trips will be among your favorite vacation activities. See you on the beach!

## BEACH INDEX

We've listed more than forty of O'ahu's excellent beaches throughout the text for your beach hopping pleasure. And to help you locate each description in the book, here is a convenient Beach Index along with a brief description of the activities for which each the beach is best suited.

# BOATING

For Hawaiians, boats have historically been the major means of transportation. Hawaiians have had a love affair with the outrigger canoe for centuries, and have found the canoe a craft uniquely suited to the wave and surf conditions in the waters surrounding the islands. Recently, more and more types of boating activities have become popular. Here is a selection.

## MOTORBOATING
A number boats and yachts are available for charter:

*Hawaiian Power Boats, Inc.* (226-3300) offers hi-speed power boat rides in Maunalua Bay and Hawaii Kai.
*The Ani Ani Glass Bottom Boat* (947-9971) has tours of coral gardens and colorful marine life. Cruises depart at 10am and 11am; 1:30pm and 2:30pm. Free round trip transportation from Waikiki.
*Windward Expeditions* (263-3899) in Kailua has tours to offshore inlands and cliff caves on small boats, with personalized tours. Search for dolphins, sea turtles, Hawaiian monk seals, and whales (in season).
*North Bay Boating Club and Sailing School* (239-5711) 47-039 Lihikai Drive in Kaneohe, offers small motorboats, sailboats, kayaks and sailboards, which they'll help you learn to handle safely.

## SAILBOATING
*Honolulu Sailing Co.* features a 43-foot "Chrysalis" or new Hunter 54 available to become your private yacht for a safe and exciting sail offshore of Honolulu and Kaneohe Bay. No engine; propelled by the tradewinds. Lunches, instruction, overnight cruises available. To take the helm, call 235-8264. P.O. Box 1500 Kaneohe, HI 96744.
*Tradewind Charters* (533-0220) has private and shared half day sails, inter-island adventures, fishing, whale watching, weddings, parties, lessons, gourmet catering, champagne parties, and limo service. Credit cards accepted.
*Royal Aloha Cruises* (941-0345) has half, full day, and 3-6 day customized cruises. Free snacks and beverages or meals, and wedding packages available. Free pick-up in Waikiki.

*Aikane Catamaran Cruises* (538-3680 or 537-6355) offers swim sails, after-prom cruises, sunset and moonlight and open bar cruises, dancing and entertainmen, rock 'n roll, and pizza cruises. Senior discounts.

*All Hawaii Cruises* (926-5077) will take you aboard the Barefoot I with Captain Bob for a picnic/sailing/snorkeling adventure in Kaneohe bay, daily 10am-4pm. A four hour calm water barefoot sail with wading, glass bottom viewing and Hawaiian entertainment.

*Southern Cross Charters* (599-4757). Experience a half-day sail on an authentic reproduction of an island trading schooner. This one is at the top of my list!

## PADDLEBOATING (including outrigger canoes and kayaks)

Outrigger canoe rides are inexpensive and great fun. You'll find a number of concessions on Waikiki Beach. Beach boys (who are in reality expert watermen and lifeguards) such as Sam Mokauhi, a living legend known as "Sammy Steamboat", "Steamboat", or just "Boat" to his friends and admirers, will match you up with a canoe and conditions just right for you.

If you're serious about outrigger canoe sailing and instruction, contact the Outrigger Club, 2909 Kalakaua Ave. 923-1585 for information. Also watch the paper for notice of the numerous canoe races, and visit the Canoe Clubhouse just across the Ala Wai Canal from Ewa Waikiki. The excellent new book *Paddling Hawaii* by Audrey Sutherland contains a wealth of information about touring Hawaiian waters in small craft such as kayaks, canoes, surf skis, folding and inflatable boats. Available from The Mountaineers, 306 Second Ave. West, Seattle, WA 98119, for $12.95.

*Go Bananas*, 740 Kapahulu Ave., (737-9514) has rental equipment, kayaks, wave skis, and supplies for paddle expeditions. There are several kayak clubs on O'ahu: Hui Wa'a Kaukahi, Box 88143, Honolulu, HI 96830; Kanaka Ikaika, Box 438, Kaneohe, HI 96744; and Women's Kayak Club of Hawaii, Box 438, Kaneohe, HI 96744.

A *wave ski* is a new piece of equipment. It's shaped like a short surfboard, with an indented seat, toe straps, and bottom fins. You sit on, not in it, and propel it with a double bladed paddle. Its planing (rather than displacement) hull offers good speed on wave faces. Bob Twogood Kayaks Hawaii is reported to have the fastest surf skis in Hawaii, along with kayaks, rentals and lots of helpful information. Located between Windward Mall and the Dodge Dealer at 46-020 Alaloa Pl. Suite B6, Kaneohe (235-2352).

A *surf ski*, also a recent development, is really a kayak, not a water ski. Long (19-20 feet) and narrow (19 inches) with an indented seat and foot holes, the surf ski is designed for straight-ahead cruising and racing. Many members of six-person Outrigger Canoe racing teams use surf skis to keep in shape during the off season. Check at "Go Bananas" or with the manufacturer (there are several on O'ahu). Paddleboat dealers and manufacturers on O'ahu include: Bob Twogood Kayaks (listed above): Fiberglass shop, 91-291 Kalaeloa Bldg., B-5, Ewa Beach, HI 96707. 682-5233; and Ocean Kayak, Ltd., Mike Cripps, PO Box 438, 47-664 Kamehameha Hwy., Kaneohe, HI 96744. 239-9803.

## WATER TOURS AND EXCURSIONS

Try to make room in your vacation schedule for a water tour. Seeing Hawaii from the ocean offers a very different perspective; from this point of view you become newly aware of how beautiful and delicate these ocean mountain top islands really are. Water tours and excursions are among the most popular tourist activities while visiting O'ahu. The free travel literature on Waikiki street stands are packed with such tours, from short cruises to Pearl Harbor, to week-long inter-island tours. We have included a selection of those we consider to be the best values.

There are probably between 25 and 50 different land and water tours to Pearl Harbor. Most water tours do not permit you to board the Memorial itself. Compare carefully to decide which Pearl Harbor tour is best for you.

No private tour, land or water, can get you aboard the floating Arizona Memorial without having you enter through the Arizona Memorial Museum operated by the National Park Service and United States Navy. The Navy launch that takes you out into Pearl Harbor to the Memorial is free, as is admission to the Museum where you take a ticket and see a poignant film before boarding the Navy launch. This is a solemn tour but one that everyone should take. The volunteers at the Museum, many of whom were at Pearl Harbor on the morning of the attack, help to put the events into perspective; be sure to listen to their free presentation at the far end of the Museum courtyard while you're waiting to view the film. Children must be 45 inches tall to board the Arizona Memorial.

*Akamai Tours* (922-6485) offers a half day land and water tour which features a boat tour of Pearl Harbor and a chance to see the Museum and board the Arizona Memorial. You also visit Chinatown, Iolani Palace, and Punchbowl Crater. Pickup at Waikiki hotels at 6:45am, 9am and noon.

*Hawaiian Cruises* (944-8033) Pearl Harbor. City Tour (#10) is a full day version of the Akamai Tour, with a no-host lunch aboard your boat, the *Adventure V*. After a morning land tour to such sights as the Arizona Memorial, Iolani Palace and Punchbowl, the afternoon is spent cruising the southern coast of O'ahu through Pearl Harbor. $26.50 adults, $20.50 for kids under 12. Pickup at 6:45am, return 5-5:30pm daily. For reservations call 947-9971. *Adventure V* also makes a one hour Sunday worship cruise leaving Kewalo Basin at 7:50am. Free bus pickup.

A shorter cruise of Pearl Harbor is available on the *Pearl Kai* motor launch, sailing from Fisherman's Wharf Restaurant daily at 9:15am and 1:15pm. This narrated ocean excursion includes Waikiki, Diamond Head, and a tour into Pearl Harbor. You do not board the Memorial, however. Adults $10.50, children $5.25. (523-0195).

*The Hilton Hawaiian Village* (955-3348) *Rainbow I* catamaran takes to the seas near Waikiki on a selection of daytime and evening cruises, including a Diamond Head champagne breakfast sail and a midday "Sun and Fun" excursion.

***Aikane's Boogie Cruise*** aboard a giant catamaran offers evening sailing off-shore, two hours of dancing to live music, open bar, snacks, and people who enjoy meeting new friends. Legal drinking age in Hawaii is now 21, so ID is required. Free roundtrip transportation from Waikiki.

***Diamond Head Cruises*** (538-7733) owns Hawaii's only floating nightclub and advertises a cruise similar to Aikane's, billed as the "Rock & Roll Party Cruise" I haven't been on this one, but I'm told its a lively party. Live entertainment, open bar, cabaret seating around a large dance floor, 2 1/2 hours of packaged party with all-you-can-drink beer, wine, Mai Tais, and cocktails. Departs Fisherman's Wharf at 8:30pm sharp, boarding at 8:15, $15.99.

***American Hawaii Cruises*** (415-392-9400) has two majestic passenger liners, the *S.S. Constitution* and the *S.S. Independence*, which make regular cruises among the Hawaiian Islands. They offer 3 and 4 day cruises, an air/sea program in which your round trip flight to Hawaii is included (you can even stop off in California or Las Vegas for very little more), and a variety of cruise/hotel and family plan discounts. Both ships are U.S. registry, and the food, entertainment and staterooms are luxurious. For a brochure, contact American Hawaii Cruises, Inc., 550 Kearny St., San Francisco, CA 94108.

***Aloha Pacific Cruises*** (1-800-544-6442). The *Monterrey* also cruises inter-island. Contact them at 1350 Old Bay Shore Hwy. #400, One Bay Plaza, Burlingame, CA 94010.

# FISHING

Nowhere in the world is any more famous for its fishing than Hawaii, and some of the State's biggest and best catches are made in the waters off Oʻahu.

Start by writing to the Division of Aquatic Resources, 1151 Punchbowl St., Honolulu, HI 96815 for a free booklet and information on fishing regulations. You can get a license (necessary only for freshwater fishing, not ocean fishing) from a local sports shop, or from the Division of Conservation and Resources Enforcement. 548-5918 or 548-8766.

For fishing supplies and tall tales, try: Charlie's Fishing Supply Co., open since 1956 (they have it all) 2 blocks from Ala Moana Center at 745 Keeaumoku (949-7373); Kaya K Fishing Supply Co., carrying salt and fresh water tackle and bait, est. 1911. Senior discount. Located corner of Kekaulike and Nimitz, makai of the open fish market, downtown Honolulu, open 7 days, 901 Kekaulike, Honolulu, HI 96817 (538-1578); and Waipahu Sporting Goods, freshwater tackle, 571-California Ave., Wahiawa HI 96786 (621-6091).

## SALTWATER CHARTERS
Many Oʻahu charters fish off the protected Leeward Coast. Most depart from three locations: Kewalo Basin between Waikiki and downtown Honolulu; Pokai Bay on the Waianae Coast; and Kaneohe Bay on the Windward Side. Cost for a full day will be somewhere around $50 - $70 for a share, with six poles per

boat. Sometimes soft drinks are provided, but it's a good idea to bring some extra, and a lunch. One good idea if you have time is to go down on the wharf and talk to the charter captains. You can choose the boat you like most by finding out the captain's rules and procedures.

*The Blue Nun* (521-6441) is one of the best charters at Kewalo Basin. The captain knows his craft and is one of the few skippers to let you keep any fish you catch. Worth stopping by.

*Kono Sport Fishing* (531-0060) features a 61 foot 50 ton specially built and Coast Guard-licensed boat with an 8-person share. Docked at Kewalo Basin, they welcome beginners and furnish all equipment.

*Coreene - C Charters* (536-7472) holds the world's record for the largest Pacific blue marlin (billfish) ever caught (a 350 pound marlin is huge) - a whopping 1,805 pounds, set by the late Captain Cornelius Choy of Honolulu. His family still operates his award-winning boats after more than 20 years. Eleanor Choy is the owner, and they're good folks. Write to them at 8902 Punahou St., Honolulu, HI 96826.

*Honolulu Sailing Co.* (235-8264) in Kaneohe has a 54-foot luxury sailing yacht available for charter on fishing, diving, or snorkel trips. Other yachts 30' and up are for charter rental too. Contact them at PO Box 1500, Kaneohe, HI 96744.

*The Kamalii Kai* (696-7264), operated by Captain Jim Hilton out of Pokai Bay on the Leeward Coast, is supposed to be an excellent charter boat.


## SURF FISHING
Kamaʻainas catch fish in shallow surf by several methods, including baitcasting, throw netting, spearing, and sometimes even by hand in tidepools or fishponds. These local fishermen have their favorite spots and techniques; be careful to respect their territory and they will respond by accepting your presence. The best place to learn about local surf fishing conditions and methods is to inquire at a local sporting goods store. Follow their advice, use the tackle they recommend, and then experiment on your own.

Although conditions will vary, here are some tips to keep in mind. Light spinning tackle requires a 12-pound test line with light black wire leaders due to sharp coral and sharp teeth of reef fish. Bait can be shrimp, squid or mussels, live minnows or even banana. Buy stainless steel hooks locally, in smallest sizes for whatever range you're buying. Try artificial lures in saltwater, spools such as Kastmasters work well for castings. Plastic bait tempts reef fish and cost less.

Stop in at Charlie's Fishing Supply (745 Keeaumoku near Ala Moana Center) and ask a local fisherman to show you where and with what bait to fish for whatever surf or freshwater fish you want to catch. Often for a small fee these expert anglers will be glad to get you started so that before long you'll be pulling in fish like a local. Ask the staff at Charlie's about the going rate for this local guide service.

Many visitors see local fisherman out on the rocks and cliffs from Hanauma Bay to Makapuu Beach Park. They assume the fishing is good and safe, but when they try it they find it can be deadly. Hazards include slippery rocks, sneaker waves that can wash a person into the boiling seawater, and strong currents that can take you far out to sea or batter you against the sharp rocks. So unless you're an expert, avoid fishing from cliffs and rocky ledges.

## FRESH WATER FISHING

Be very careful where you fish in fresh water on O'ahu, because many small ponds, streams and canals contain irrigation water for the pineapple or sugarcane fields. This water is full of agriculture chemicals to protect the plants, so any fish caught in these waters could be dangerous. Stick to well posted areas where you know the fresh water is not contaminated.

One of the best freshwater fishing spots on O'ahu is the Wahiawa Reservoir near Schofield Barracks in Central O'ahu. Three hundred acres of fishable waters yield bass, catfish, carp, and sunfish. This is a huge reservoir used to irrigate the cane fields nearby.

Stop into the Wahiawa Sporting Goods Store at 571 California Ave. in Wahiawa (621-6091) and inquire as to local spots and best tackle. They'll lead you to some hot spots. If you don't connect, you can buy a delicious freshly caught trout dinner at Kemoo Farm Restaurant across from the main gate to Schofield Barracks.

Kaneohe Bay flats used to be a prime spot to wade for small saltwater fish, but unfortunately pollution has made fishing there dangerous. Until the situation is reversed, you should not consume fish from Kaneohe Bay.

Nuuanu Reservoir Number 4, in the Koolau Mountains above Honolulu, is open for fishing in May, August, and November. This 25-acre site is beautiful and a very popular fishing spot when open. Write the Division of Aquatic Resources, Dept. of Land and Natural Resources, 1151 Punchbowl St., Honolulu, HI 96813, or call 548-5897.

You may hear stories about local fishermen harvesting crab, octopus, clams and mussels, oysters, lobster, and even seaweed from local waters. All these delicacies are to be found locally, but you should not think of mounting an expedition to collect one or more of them without help from experts. If you are interested in collecting these creatures, call the State Division of Aquatic Resources (548-5897), and request information as to the legality and proper techniques of harvesting those items you are interested in. Regulations are strict, and penalties for non-compliance can be severe. Besides, knowing the law gives you peace of mind which makes your harvest taste even better. If and when you do go collecting, be sure to follow the appropriate safety precautions. Some of these animals are nocturnal or live on tidal cliffs, and you can encounter some extremely dangerous situations while collecting them. So take a friend with you, follow the State harvesting and safety guidelines, and be careful!

## JET SKIING

Most jet skiing on Oʻahu is done on Maunalua Bay near Koko Head, although some companies will take you to Keehi Lagoon (Ewa from Honolulu Harbor) or to a spot right off Waikiki Beach. If you haven't seen these machines in operation, watch for jet skiers at these places as you tour the Island. Our bet is that you'll want to try it yourself! Here are the major rental outfits.

*American Sports* (Call 395-5319) offers a jet skiing tour to Maunalua Bay with round trip transportation from Waikiki, equipment and lunch included.
*Jet Ski Hawaii* (call 9-GETWET) will take you jet skiing to Keehi Lagoon in Honolulu, featuring Kawasaki 550 Jet skis, and lessons as part of the package. Free hotel pickups. $10 off with coupon in "Spotlight Oʻahu" magazine.
*Paradise Jet Ski* (924-4941) rides let you enjoy the sport right off Waikiki beach. Ask about the earlybird special - an hour of jet skiing plus a free outrigger canoe ride. Located in front of the Outrigger Reef Hotel.
*Watersports Hawaii* (395-1647) offers jet skiing at either Manualua Bay or Keehi Lagoon. Instructors are tournament skiers.

## PARASAILING

You're sure to see these people high above the Waikiki ocean being towed by a boat while suspended under a large parachute. It's a combination of parachute jumping and waterskiing. Some have it rigged in a chair-harness so you don't even have to get wet, unless you want to, and no waterskiing experiences is required.

*Aloha Parasail* (521-2446) does it the original way, with no winches or chairs. You're securely strapped into a padded harness, life jacket, and parasail, then towed on a 300 foot line behind a powerboat. And up you go. Free Waikiki hotel pickup and return.
*Sea Breeze Parasailing* (486-9784) offers solo or tandem harness rides over Waikiki beach. Longest rides on Oʻahu, and group rates are available. $40 - $50 with coupon from free tourist magazines.
*Controlled Parasailing* (924-4941) takes you out to the boat in an outrigger canoe, where you're strapped into a comfortable chair and parasail which is then reeled out to an altitude of up to 500 feet. You'll have a bird's eye view of the Island, and not have to get wet. Call or inquire at the Ocean Sports Center on the beach in front of the Outrigger Reef Hotel in Waikiki.

## WAVE RIDING

Hawaiians have been riding the waves for centuries. The fringing reefs which protect many of Oʻahu's beaches cause waves to swell and break near shore. And a lack of such reefs at places on the North Shore allow huge winter waves to pound the beach.

The earliest form of wave riding was undoubtedly body surfing, a practice enjoyed by water-based cultures since the dawn of history. Ancient Egyptians enjoyed water sports, and Greek soldiers trained for battle by swimming. But board surfing seems to have developed in Polynesia. Petroglyphs record the sport, and ancient contests among talented wave riders (often duels between chiefs) are well documented. In the early 1900's, Hawaii's best known surfer was the legendary Duke Paoa Kahanamoku (1890 - 1968), who popularized the sport on the mainland and in Australia, and became an international hero when he saved the lives of twelve men from a capsized fishing boat in rough water off Newport Beach, California on his surfboard. The songs of the Beachboys and surfing movies in the 1950's and 60's helped to make surfing a household word.

---

DID YOU KNOW... that Duke Kahanamoku, the legendary Hawaiian athlete, developed the crawl stroke in 1910? Among this remarkable man's achievements: he introduced surfing to Australia, won Olympic gold medals in swimming, became a Hollywood film actor in 1922, served as mayor of Honolulu and was a charter member of the Swimming and Surfing Halls of Fame.

---

### BODYSURFING

Riding waves without a board is still very popular in Hawaii, especially among the younger set. Some bodysurfers use handboards (flat paddle gloves) and swim fins; others rely only on their technique (hands at sides or outstretched seem to be the two alternatives) to propel them across the break. Sandy and Makapu'u Beaches offer the best places to *watch* veteran bodysurfers; Waikiki remains the best place to learn. Open heel fins that float with fixed heel straps are the only equipment usually recommended. Quality swim fins are available at most dive shops, including: South Seas Aquatics, Ward Warehouse, 1050 Ala Moana Blvd. (538-3854); Waikiki Diving Center, 1734 Kalakaua Ave., Honolulu (955-5151); Aaron's Dive Shop, 602 Kailua Rd., Kailua (261-1211).

### SMALL BOARD SURFING

You'll see boogie boards (AKA belly boards or paipo boards) everywhere in Hawaii. These small (3 foot long) foam miniature surfboards have become kids' favorites since they're cheap (starting at $10 - $15), easy to carry, and maneuverable in the water. Many kids wear flippers when riding their boogie board for extra speed. Most surf shops sell boogie boards, including: Surf Masters Hawaii, 1860 Ala Moana, Rm. 104 in Waikiki (947-1747); and Blue Hawaii Surf, 1960 Kapiolani Blvd., Suite 108 (947-5115).

Also popular recently are skim boards (AKA sand boards) used to ride the thin cushion of water left when the water washes back from the surf after a wave. These began as belly bags or pieces of round plywood, and now commercially made boards are in vogue. Most surf shops carry them. Action Hawaii Adventures (944-6754) will teach you to boogie board in a full day adventure with snorkeling, hiking and a picnic lunch. Board and instruction provided.

## BIG BOARD SURFING

In ancient Hawaii, surfboards were of mammoth size and weight. At the turn of the century Duke Kahanamoku learned on a sixteen foot koa wood board weighing 114 pounds. Today surfboards measure between 6 and 7 feet in length and weigh only 8 to 12 pounds. Constructed of fiberglass-covered foam with a three rudder stabilizer, these modern boards are designed for maximum mobility to work the wave. Surfboarding is not difficult if you master the fundamentals; a lesson or two on Waikiki Beach usually proves to be a worthwhile investment.

As you would imagine, surf shops can be found all over the Island. Some you should visit, even if only to look around are as follows. Surf and Sea in Hale'wa, 62-595 Kam Hwy. (637-9887). Not only do they have surfboards, boogie boards, fins, sailboards, and scuba equipment, they also can tell you which surfing beaches are happening, steer you toward unadvertised lodgings, and arrange glider and small plane rides at Dillingham Field in Mokuleia. Local Motion carries surfboards, bodyboards and skateboards, beachwear, rentals, advice and will pack and ship a board home for you. Three O'ahu locations: 1714 Kapiolani Blvd. near Waikiki (955-SURF); Koko Marina in Hawaii Kai (396-SURF); and in the Windward Mall, Kaneohe (263-SURF). Open 7 days a week. If you prefer to talk with a manufacturer about a custom-made board, contact Beach Scene Hawaii, 66-119 Kam Hwy., in Hale'iwa (637-9455). They are the factory outlet for Willis Brothers Surfboards, Hawaiian design custom surfboards. Performance Hawaii (942-7932), 1459 Kapiolani Blvd., near Ala Moana Center, carries Hawaiian Tech Design surfboards by Glenn Pang.

*Surfing hotline* (945-SURF) for current O'ahu surfing conditions.

## SAILBOARDING (WINDSURFING)

Sailboarding, or windsurfing as it is popularly called, is a combination of sailing and surfboarding. You stand on a solid surfboard attached to a swivel sail which allows you to combine wind and wave power into a wild ride. Hawaii is the capital of ocean sailboarding, while Hood River on the Columbia River Gorge in Oregon is the place to go for river windsurfing. On O'ahu, Kailua Beach Park on the windward side is the home of champion and pioneer windsurfer Robbie Naish. It's also the best place to learn sailboarding techniques. To see fine windsurfing travel to the North Shore and find the most famous launching spot, located at Sunset Beach Point. Turn makai on Oopuola and enjoy.

*Naish Hawaii* is probably the most famous windsurfing shop, with 3 stores: Kailua Beach Center at 160 Kailua Rd. (261-6067); 2335 Kalakaua Ave., Waikiki (924-8600); and the main showroom, Kailua at 155-A Hamakua Drive (262-6068). *Kailua Sailboard Company Windsurfing School* (262-2555) offers lessons and rentals; 130 Kailua Rd. in Kailua Beach Center near Naish Hawaii. *Windsurfing Hawaii* (261-3539) offers lessons, sales, tours, rentals and repair at 156-C Hamakua Drive in Kailua.

Also, many local surfboard shops carry sailboards, including Hawaii Surf and Sail, 66-214 Kam Highway in Haleiwa (637-5373) and Local Motion Surfboards (see listing under Big Board Surfing).

# UNDERWATER ACTIVITIES

Hawaii's warm, clear water and fringing reefs, alive with saltwater plants and animals, have made underwater sports almost as popular as those on or above the water. Snorkeling is the easiest and most popular way to experience the under-sea world, with scuba diving a close second. Recently, two new underwater activities, snuba and submarine voyages, have appeared and are fast becominge among Oʻahu's most popular ocean adventures.

## SNORKELING
Watching underwater life has been popular since Egyptians practiced swimming, diving and sponge and pearl hunting two centuries before Christ. In the fourteenth century AD, divers in Persia began using thin clear pieces of tortoise shell to improve their underwater vision. By 1930 rubber goggles and masks with glass lenses were in use.

Today's Oʻahu snorkelers often head for Hanauma Bay (for more on Hanauma Bay, see Exploring Southeast Oʻahu). You'll need three pieces of equipment: fins, a mask and a snorkel. Find equipment that is safe, simple, and comfortable. Look for closed heel fins that fit well and float. The snorkel should be separate from the mask (not built in), without a ball arrangement at the open end. Find a mask that fits (it should stick to your face without a strap when you suck the air out), and has a double strap in back. Many people accept inferior snorkeling equipment from the grab bag offered by the snorkeling tour company, and are disappointed later because their equipment does not work correctly. The happiest snorkelers are those who find a dive shop before their snorkeling trip and rent equipment that fits their criteria. Here are some, in addition to those listed above under board surfing and sailboarding.

*Aloha Dive Shop* (395-5922), Koko Marina Shopping Center in Hawaii Kai. Complete rental service, scuba instruction, day and evening classes, and private instruction available.
*Paradise Snorkel Adventures* (923-7766) offers tours to Hanauma Bay with equipment, instruction, and transportation. Underwater cameras are also for rent, with senior discounts available. Located 270 Lewers in Waikiki.
*Hanauma Bay Watersports* (395-8947) advertises a week's snorkel rental for only $9.99. Masks, fins, prescription mask lenses,underwater cameras and film, and video instructions. Next to the Texaco Station at 6650 Hawaii Kai Drive, Suite 109 in Hawaii Kai.
*Dan's Dive Shop* (536-6181) at 660 Ala Moana Blvd., has quality snorkeling equipment and will set you up with a snorkeling tour.
*Steve's Diving Adventures* (947-8900), which also has a complete line of equipment, has full snorkeling tours with transportation, equipment, beach mats, fish food, a special guide, and underwater cameras and film available for an additional small fee.
*Seahorse Snorkeling* explores the coral gardens off Hanauma Bay on a half day tour. Transportation and gear are provided. Prescription lenses available. Film is free when you rent a 110 or 35 mm camera. Tours from 9am-1pm, 10am-2pm, 11am-3pm and noon to 4pm, $6.99 plus tax per person. Master Card and Visa.

## SCUBA DIVING

Scuba (Self Contained Underwater Breathing Apparatus) diving equipment consists of compressed air in a tank, with a regulator, hose and mouthpiece to deliver air to the diver. A mask, weight belt, fins and wet (or dry) suit are usually worn with the tank. This modern equipment using a regulator was first developed in 1943 as the Aqua Lung by Jacques-Yves Cousteau and Emile Gagnan. Since then, divers have explored the many reefs, caves, and submerged ships and planes in Hawaiian waters.

As with snorkeling, scuba divers often start at Hanauma Bay since this underwater park has a constant parade of beautifully colored and tame sealife. Other hotspots for Oʻahu scuba diving include Three Tables in summer on the North Shore, the waters around Manana (Rabbit) Island, and Black Point off Diamond Head.

You must have a current C-card showing you've had a certified SCUBA course in order to rent air on Oʻahu. You can get an introductory dive accompanied by a certified instructor for about $50. A full 3-5 day certification course will run anywhere from $150 - $300 depending on time and number of people in the course. Once you're certified, expect to pay $25 - $50 for equipment rental per day, and $40 - $70 for a single-tank boat dive.

Checking in with a reputable dive shop will save you time and money; they'll help you find the right dive package for you (there are all kinds available, from night dives and photo dives to inter-island dive tours and dive cruises). Good, full service dive centers include: Surf and Sea, 62-595 Kam Hwy. in Haleiwa (637-9887); Steve's Diving Adventures, 1860 Ala Moana Blvd. (947-8900); South Seas Aquatics, in Ward Warehouse, 1050 Ala Moana Blvd. (538-3854); Hawaiian Divers (with PAOI 5 star instruction) in Stadium Mall, 4510 Salt Lake Blvd., across from Aloha Stadium (487-8969); and Waikiki Diving Center, 1734 Kalakaua Ave., in Waikiki (955-5151).

## SNUBA

What's a cross between snorkeling and scuba diving? It's *snuba*, one of Oʻahu's newest water activities. This revolutionary shallow water dive system is an easy to learn, easy to do system with a brief (one hour) certification program. A 20-foot air line connects the inflated raft on the surface (containing a tank of compressed air) with the snuba diver below. The surface air tank and raft tow unnoticeably behind as the diver explores underwater, breathing from the attached air line. During the hour-long training course you'll spend a half hour on land, half hour in the water with only four students to each SNUBA certified instructor. SNUBA tours are currently operating in the Caribbean, Florida, California, and Hawaii. Cost of all necessary equipment is around $25 per hour. For more information contact Mick Riegel at Snuba Tours of Oʻahu, 2233 Kalakaua Ave., B205A, Suite 1271, Honolulu, HI 96815 (922-7762). Here's an exciting way that anyone, without being an athlete, can enjoy the thrill of underwater exploration.

## UNDERWATER VOYAGES

Ever since Jules Verne created Captain Nemo and his ship Nautilus, people have been fascinated with submarines. Now you can include a voyage beneath the sea in your vacation plans. Atlantis Submarines (536-2694) offers tours on a 65-foot electrically powered sub holding 46 passengers. Operating off Waikiki, the tour will last 45 minutes and cost $58 adults, $29 children 4-12 years. They explore sunken reefs and vessels up to 250 feet below the surface.

## UNDERWATER PHOTOGRAPHY

Many snorkeling tours and some dive shops offer rental of underwater 110 or 35 mm cameras and film. You can rent your own equipment at one of O'ahu's photo stores. Most will cost $10 per day for the camera with a $200 deposit, not including film. Available from: Photo Stores, with four Waikiki locations - Kuhio Photo, 2330 Kuhio Ave. (923-5505); Reef Photo, 2169 Kalia Rd. (922-1429); Outrigger Photo, 22335 Kalakaua Ave. (922-2206); and Tower Photo, 227 Lewers St. (922-8113). Action Hawaii Adventures (944-6754) will teach you the art of underwater photography on a full day tour including a hike to a waterfall, boogie boarding, and a picnic lunch. If you'd prefer just the photography, other tour packages are available.

# WATERSKIING

One does not usually think of waterskiing as being a sport found in Hawaii. But there's even an O'ahu Waterski Club which sponsors a State Championship in July and a spring open during Easter weekend, both at Keehi Lagoon. Equipment and instruction are available from Suyderhoud Water Ski Center (395-3773) in the Koko Marina Shopping Center. This company has ski instruction and skiing for 1/2 hour at $39 (1 or 2 people), and hourly rates with boat, driver, and equipment included for $75. All their waterskiing is done at the Koko Marina.

SCUBA DIVING

# LAND ACTIVITIES

## ARCHERY

Recreational archery has long been a tradition in Kapiolani Park where you can watch Japanese Zen archers on weekends. Bow hunting and archery supplies are available at Hunting Supplies of Hawaii - The Armory, 95 S. Kam Hwy., Pearl City (622-2283) or 1021 Kaheka St., Honolulu. Bows, targets, and accessories may also be purchased at King's Sporting Goods, 75 N. King (538-6764). These two shops also have information on rental equipment, target locations, and bow hunting licensing procedures.

## ATHLETIC, HEALTH AND FITNESS CENTERS

More and more travelers today want to keep up their diet and exercise programs while on vacation. Some hotels offer lap lanes in their swimming pool, workout rooms and fitness equipment. Walkers and joggers use well-worn paths such as Ala Wai Blvd. next to the Canal. O'ahu also has a wide selection of fitness centers, health spas, and indoor water exercise facilities. Here is a selection.

*Pacific Island Aquatics* (373-9348) has a year round indoor heated pool with baby classes to adult lessons.

*The O'ahu Club* (395-3300), a private membership tennis and fitness club open to the public, has a 50 meter olympic pool, fitness center, health food bar and six lighted tennis courts. 6800 Hawaii Kai Drive, Honolulu, HI 96825.

*Weight Watchers* (955-1588), 1522 Makaloa St., Suite 221, Honolulu, HI 96814. *World Gym* and pro shop specializes in co-ed weight lifting. Open 24 hours daily, 7 days a week; located in Waikiki at 1701 Ala Wai Blvd. 942-8171. Daily, weekly, monthly and yearly rates.

*International Fitness Centers* offer racquetball, Nautilus & Universal Machines and free weights. Open to men and women, 1680 Kapiolani Blvd. in Honolulu, (942-8990) and 45-608 Kam Hwy. in Kaneohe (235-5839), seven days a week.

*SPA Fitness Center* (487-5551 in Pearl City) has five locations which offer senior discount, swimming pool, sauna, whirlpool, steam room, private showers, co-ed classes, and separate workouts.

## BARGAIN HUNTING AND GARAGE "SALE-ING"

Everyone loves a bargain. Hawaii has garage sales and flea markets like everywhere else; except many of the items you'll find on sale here are unlike anything back home. Perhaps the best source is still the local newspaper, sections 718 (Garage and Lanai Sales) and 715 (Miscellaneous for Sale) are often full of interesting leads. Free local shoppers' papers such as the Pennysaver also carry notices of sales and sale items. If you enjoy a weekend drive, Honolulu suburbs often have garage sale signs posted on telephone poles and street corners.

Auctions are also a tradition on O'ahu; cash only, buyer beware, but there are some terrific bargains. Call an auction house like McLain Public Auction (538-7227) or Prinzivalli Auction (247-8444) to find dates and locations of their next auction. Also watch papers for: The Dept. of Defense Local Auctions (4455-5158) in Bldg. 4, Pearl City Junction Storage Area; Honolulu Police Department Evidence Room Auction (943-3283) or U.S. Customs Auction (546-7125).

The biggest sales of all are probably at the Aloha Stadium Flea Market (486-1529) the Kam Super Swap Meet at Pearl Ridge (488-5822) (see the WHAT TO SEE chapter), both of which certainly deserve a visit.

While you're at it why not visit one of Honolulu's numerous and legendary thrift and resale shops? Because they are well organized and have a tremendous turn over, the military thrift shops (yes they are open to the public) have excellent bargains. Try the Fort Shafter Thrift Shop (behind PX, open Tues. & Fri. 9am-1pm), Barbers Point Naval Air Station Thrift Shop, Bldg. 455 (682-5116) open Tue. & Thurs. 10am-12:30pm), and Hickam Air Force Base Thrift Shop, Bldg. 511 (449-6603), open Mon. Wed., Fri. 10am-1pm and 3rd Sat. of month 10am-1pm. In addition to the standard Goodwill, St. Vincent DePaul and Salvation Army Thrift stores (see Yellow Pages for listings), the Symphony Shop, 1023 Pensacola, Honolulu 524-7157, open Mon-Fri. 9am-noon; Punahou Thrift Shop, 1 Shade Drive, Punahou Campus, Honolulu (944-5848), open Mon. Wed., Fri. 9am-3pm; and the Liluokalani Protestant Church Thrift Shop, 66-090 Kam Hwy., Haleiwa (637-9364), open Sat. 9am-2pm, are recommended.

Orizaba (537-1826) has a permanent rack of reduced-price kimonos, all with minor imperfections and major savings, 1149 S. Beretania, Honolulu, open Mon-Fri. 9am-5pm. Variety School Thrift Shop (734-5424) has donated goods that are often new, and a special 25 cent sale on the 25th of each month, 3617 Waialae, Honolulu, open Mon. 9am-2pm, Tues-Fri. 9am-5pm, Sat. 10am-4pm. The Ultimate You (523-3888) has designer consignment fashions, furs and jewelry 50 - 90% below retail at 1112 Auahi, Honolulu, Mon-Sat. 11am-6pm.

# BICYCLING
Cycling is a fast-growing activity on O'ahu with rides almost every weekend sponsored by the Hawaii Bicycle League, Box 4403, Honolulu, HI 96813. Unless you were raised as a bicycle courier in New York City, you'll probably enjoy rural cycling more than riding in Honolulu. Roads here can be rough so a touring bike is better if you're renting. Probably the most popular beginning ride is through Kapiolani Park, past Diamond Head Crater, through the Kahala residential area toward Hawaii Kai (Kalanianaole Highway has a bike lane). The Bicycle League welcomes visitors and has a wealth of information to help you get rolling. Island Bike and Surf Rentals (949-2453) has a variety of bikes for rent including one-speed beachcruisers to 18-speed Miyata mountain bikes. Located at 2084 Kalakaua Ave., open Mon-Sat. 8am-5pm. Aloha Funway Rentals (942-9696) also rents bikes at their five locations: 1944, 1984 and 2025 Kalakaua Ave., 2976 Koapaka St., and 1778 Ala Moana Blvd.

# BIRDWATCHING
O'ahu is a bird watcher's paradise. Before you arrive, write to The Hawaii Audubon Society, Box 22832, Honolulu, HI 96822; Sierra Club, 1212 University Ave., Honolulu 96826 (946-8494), and the Dept. of Land & Natural Resources, Division of Forestry and Wildlife, 1151 Punchbowl St., Honolulu, HI 96813 (548-2861) for information and upcoming expeditions. When you arrive, visit the Honolulu Zoo, Paradise Park, Sea Life Park, and Lyon Arboretum to begin your observation of island birds and gather more information on current O'ahu birdwatching outings.

# BOWLING

Although you might associate bowling with Europe, Hawaiians have enjoyed a similar game called Ulu Maika for centuries. Players tried to roll stone disks (Maika) between two distant stakes on a grassy playing field. These stones can still be seen in museums, and kits containing carved stones and stakes can be purchased in Hawaii. You can watch Ulu Maika being played at Waimea Falls Park. Bowling is still very popular on Oʻahu, with lanes in Honolulu: Kalihi Bowl in the Kalihi Shopping Center (senior discount); Stadium Bowl-Bowl, 4618 Kilauea Ave. (949-6668); Waialae Bowl, 4618 Kilauea Ave. (734-0293); and Kapiolani Bowl, 710 Ward Ave. (536-7741).

# CAMPING

While picnicking and day camping facilities are abundant, overnight camping facilities on Oʻahu are very limited and we recommend that you postpone overnight camping until you visit one of the outer islands. Before using any campground, read the *Guide to Hawaii's State Parks*, available from the State of Hawaii, Division of State Parks, PO Box 621, Honolulu, HI 96809. It will tell you how to obtain a camping and parking permit, plus what rules you'll be required to follow in the three Oʻahu State Park camping areas.

Thirteen city and county parks are open to tent camping, and most permit RV's. Contact the City and County of Honolulu, Dept. of Parks and Recreation, 650 S. King St., Honolulu, HI 96813 (523-4525). Ask which months of the year the parks are open (dates vary) and how long in advance you must apply for a permit. Picnicking facilities are available at almost every City, County and State Park. Permits are only required for groups of 26 or more picnickers. Most picnic areas have tables or shelters, barbecue grills, drinking water, restrooms, pavilions, paved roads, and parking lots. Many beach parks also have cold showers and dressing rooms. States parks are open 7am-8pm May 1 to Sept. 30, and 7am-6:30pm from October 1 to April 30.

It is advisable to read and follow with care the safety tips in the city, county and State park literature while utilizing any of Oʻahus park areas.

For camping supplies and information try: Omar the Tent Man (836-8785), 650 A Kakoi St., Honolulu; or The Bike Shop (531-7071) 1149 S. King St.

# DANCING

Honolulu is a town for nightlife, and dancing is available at many of its glittering night spots. For the mature set, Del Courtney's Big Band plays every Sunday from 5:30-9pm in the Monarch Room of the Royal Hawaiian Hotel. Dance cruises are available (see Cruises), and some restaurants feature dancing and cocktails after the dinner hour. For sophisticated but fun dancing try Studebakers in Restaurant Row, Annabelle's at the Top off the Ilikai Hotel, and Trappers at the Hyatt Regency. The under 25 crowd is waiting in line these days to get into the Wave Waikiki (941-0424), Cilly's (942-2952), Rumours (955-4811), Rascals (922-5565), and Scruples (923-9530). Start at any one of these and you'll soon find out where else the in-crowd is currently getting together.

# GOLF

Hawaii has some of the world's most scenic golf links. You don't have to bring your clubs or shoes, since rentals are available everywhere.

Golf has become every bit as popular with tourists from the west (especially Japan) as it is with mainland visitors. Call well in advance to get the best tee times on any of O'ahu's 28 courses. Nine of the 24 are military and only open to military personnel and their guests. Four more are private and open to members only (including Waialoe Country Club, annual host of the Hawaiian Open). Of the remaining 15 courses, four are run by the City and County and eleven are private courses open to the public. Moanalua Golf Course at the foot of Moanalua Valley above Honolulu is the oldest course west of the Rocky Mountains, so if you're a true golf lover, give them a call to see if you can get on. Both the Pali and Kahuku Courses on the Windward side are good ones to try when others are booked. The Sheraton Makaka course by the hotel is one of Hawaii's best. Several companies offer golf packages including club and shoe rental plus transportation, and run from $80 - $130. Contact Alii Golf (735-0060) or Kato's Golf Tours (947-3010).

Both the Hawaii Visitors Bureau (923-1811) and the Dept. of Parks and Recreation have listings of O'ahu's golf courses. Contact: Parks & Recreation, City & County of Honolulu, 650 S. King St., Honolulu, HI 96813.

# HEALTH RESORTS

Retreats where you can pamper yourself, improve your health, and exercise your body are available on O'ahu. One such resort is the new six-acre Plantation Spa in Kaaawa. This total getaway has an exercise program complete with pool, stretch and yoga classes, low impact aerobics and weights, canoeing, volleyball and walking, massage, and gourmet lacto vegetarian cuisine. Gloria Keeling, formerly with the Waves at Wailea on Maui, will be the guest instructor here one week each quarter. A cleansing European juice and broth fast, relaxation and visualization techniques are also options. You'll be treated to Swedish health secrets and a week of TLC. Contact them at 51-550 Kam Hwy., Kaaawa, HI 96730 (237-8685).

Other resort spas include: Plaza Health Spa (671-5194), 94-939 Farrington Hwy., Suite 201; The Steam Works Baths (923-1852) for men with steam room, weight training and video rooms, at 2139 Kuhio Ave., 2nd floor; and the YWCA of O'ahu (538-7061), which offers aerobics, swimming, recreation and fitness classes, and a weight room. Located at 1040 Richards St., Honolulu.

# HIKING

Write the Hawaiian Trail and Mountain Club at Box 2238 Honolulu, HI 96804 (247-3922) and the Sierra Club, 1212 University Ave., Honolulu, HI 96826 (946-8494) for packets with information on hiking and trails on O'ahu. Craig Chisholm's book, *Hawaiian Hiking Trails* (Fernglen Press - see order information at back of this book), gives you detailed maps and trail information.

Some of O'ahu's most famous hiking areas are: Diamond Head Crater; Manoa Falls (which begins behind Paradise Park and Lyon Arboretum); Keaiwa Heiau State Recreation Area (at the end of Aiea Heights Drive above Honolulu); Manoa Cliff Trailhead at the top of Round Top Drive on Mt. Tantalus above Punchbowl Crater in Honolulu; Judd Trail starting from Reservoir Number 2 spillway on the Nuuanu Pali; Maunawili Falls Trail on the Windward side near Kailua; Koko Head Cliff Trail across from Hanauma Bay; Kahana Valley State Park (hiking permit required here) near Kaaawa; Sacred Falls near Hauula; and Kaena Point State Park at the end of Farrington Highway.

Remember to watch signs and get permission before hiking across private or military (25% of O'ahu land) property. Take water, a compass, and hike with the buddy system. Several groups conduct hiking tours, including Diamond Head Hikes (a clean air team which meets weekends at 9am in front of the Zoo), and the Lyon Arboretum Association (988-7378).

For hiking supplies try: The Bike Shop, 1149 S. King St. (531-7071); Omar the Tent Man, 650 A Kakoi St. (836-8785); The Athlete's Foot, Hawaii Kai Shopping Center (395-5050) and Pearlridge Shopping Center (486-3668); King's Sporting Goods, 75 N. King St. (538-6764; Pacific Quest, 59-603 Kawoa Place (638-8338); or Sunbird Trading Co., Tropicana Square Shopping Center on Farrington Highway in Waipahu.

## HORSEBACK RIDING

You can take a tour on horseback, go on a trail ride with real Hawaiian paniolos, or ride into Koko Crater. Here's how:

Pacific Quest-Outdoor Hawaii (638-8338) will take you on a half-day ride into the wilderness of Kaaawa Valley. Hotel pickup 12:30pm, ride ends at 5:15pm. $49.95. Keialoa Ranch (237-8202) on the windward side, and Turtle Bay Hilton (293-8693) on the North Shore offer trail rides by reservation. Koko Crater Stables at 408 Kealahou Place, Kailua, HI 96734, (395-2628) has rides into the Koko Head Crater. If you want to take lessons, contact the New Town & Country Stables at 41-1800 Kalanianaole Hwy. (259-9941) or Hilltop Ranch, with English and Western lessons, 41-430 Waikupanaha (259-8463).

To see horses in action, attend a Polo match in Waimanalo or Mokuleia on Sundays at 2 pm between mid-March and August. Gates open at 11 am, cost is $5 for adults, call the Hawaii Polo Club at 942-5210.

## HUNTING

Wild pigs and goats, pheasant, quail, partridge, and wild turkey can be hunted in fourteen hunting areas on O'ahu. You can hunt with spear, bow, or rifle. There are currently no hunting guides or tours available on O'ahu. For more information write to the Dept. of Land & Natural Resources, Division of Forestry and Wildlife Office, 1151 Punchbowl St., Honolulu, HI 96813 (548-2861). Request the Rules Regulating Game Birds and Game Mammal Hunting, and "Hunting in Hawaii." A license is necessary, and costs $7.50 for residents, $15 for non-residents, seniors free, and is good for a year starting July 1; available from the State or sporting goods stores.

## ICESKATING

Unless the lakes freeze over (unlikely!), the only place you can ice skate on O'ahu is at the Ice Palace in the Stadium Mall next to Aloha Stadium, 4510 Salt Lake Blvd. (487-9921). They have a giant covered rink, rental skates, day and evening skating, a snack bar and many special events to keep your time on the ice interesting. Admission is $5.

## LAND TOURS AND EXCURSIONS

There are thousands of land tours and excursions on O'ahu and you'll be deluged with offers and promotions from the minute you arrive. There are also hawkers on the street and in small booths selling tickets and discount coupons to practically every one of the tours available.

Although there are hundreds of land tour companies, three or four of the largest are worth sticking with unless you have reliable information recommending you to a small outfit. The big three are Polynesian Adventure Tours, E Noa Tours, and Akamai Tours. Other companies include Roberts Hawaii, Grayline Hawaii, TransHawaiian; Hawaii Adventure and Island Get-A-Ways Division of First Family Travel.

Several tips on choosing a tour and tour company will make your touring adventures more pleasant. First, look for companies with guides who have taken Hawaiiana classes from the State Dept. of Education through the community college system. Second, go in a smaller vehicle, with 6-15 people. Smaller is more personal. Third, avoid free or bonus tours on big busses, unless you don't mind large groups and cramped quarters. And last, realize you can't do it all and take selected tours of places, e.g. do a tour of Honolulu, Hanauma Bay and perhaps a specialty tour or two which you design (E Noa has such custom packages). For places like Sea Life Park, Polynesian Cultural Center, and North Shore you'll have more fun by renting a car and exploring on your own. (See the WHAT TO SEE chapter).

Be sure to explore all the options, not just the ones offered by any single tour company or activity desk. Contact individual tour companies for brochures and information on packages, discounts, and special offers. Although there are many variations, there are only five major tour itineraries offered on O'ahu:

1. A tour of Honolulu. Variations include historic downtown, Chinatown, Arizona Memorial, and Dole Cannery Square.
2. Small Circle Island Tour from Waikiki to Southeast O'ahu through Waimanalo over the Pali and back via Tantalus. Variations include Hanauma Bay and Sea Life Park Tours.
3. Grand Circle Island Tour from Waikiki past Diamond Head Crater, Koko Head, Hanauma Bay, visit to Byodo-in Temple, Halona Blowhole, Mormon Temple, visit to Waimea Falls Park, return through the Central Valley with a stop at Dole Pineapple Pavilion. Variations include Polynesian Cultural Center Tour, Circle Island Beach and Picnic Tour, and Arizona Memorial.
4. North Shore Tour, visiting Waialua, Schofield Barracks, North Shore beaches, Waimea Falls Park, and Haleiwa.

5.  Charter tours, in which you design your own tour, accompanied by a professional driver-guide. You can rent the E Noa's Waikiki Trolley ($80 per hour, up to 34 people), a mini-van ($40 - $50 an hour for up to 17 people), or even a limousine ($50 - $150 per hour, two hour minimum with lower rate).

The large tour companies also offer one day tours of Maui, Kauai, and The Big Island, all including round trip jet service, small groups, and professionally narrated sightseeing on air-conditioned mini-buses, ranging from $110 - $150.

*Island Get-Aways* (922-4400) offers two and three night tour packages to outer islands, including round trip airfare, compact car rental, and three nights accommodations for $110 - $150 per person. 222 Kalakaua Ave., Suite 211, Honolulu, HI 968156.
*Polynesian Adventure Tours* (923-8687), 2250 Kalakaua Ave., Suite 505, Honolulu, HI 96815.
*E Noa Tours* (941-6608), 1110 University Ave., Rm. 306, Honolulu, HI 96826.
*Akamai Tours* (1-800-922-6485), Waikiki Business Plaza, 2270 Kalakaua Ave., Suite 1702, Honolulu, Hi 96815.
*Trans Hawaiian Services* (735-6467), 3111 Castle St., Honolulu, HI 96815.
*Hawaiian Adventure* (947-1454 or 1-800-248-0444), 444 Hobron Lane, Vista Level, Honolulu, HI 96815.

# LOUNGING
Lounging is a time honored tradition in Hawaii, defined as: standing, moving, sitting, and lying in a relaxed or lazy way; spending time in idleness; and resting comfortably. This is an individual sport, practiced by a majority of visitors and locals alike at beaches, parks, hotels, swimming pools, and lanais throughout the islands. You need no special equipment, although lounging etiquette suggests a swim suit or shorts, a cold drink, something to read and eat, and perhaps some lovely scenery close by. Lounging is an art form which can be learned by observing connoisseurs in action, by seeking out the local fauna known as the lounge lizard (same genus as the North American couch potato), or by merely doing nothing in a comfortable location and allowing intuition to guide you. Lounging is excellent therapy for almost any ailment known to science, especially over-achievement and excessive clock-watching syndrome.

# MARTIAL ARTS
Judo, Karate, Aikido, Kendo, Tae Kwon Do, Kung Fu, and other exotic martial art instruction and equipment are available in Hawaii, where East meets West.

The largest institute of Karate in the world is in Hawaii (Japan International Karate Center, 33 S. King St., Honolulu, HI 96813, 523-5002). The International Martial Arts Center of Song Tae Kwon Do has classes available for men, women and children from 3 to 80 years old, and offers a senior discount. Kong's Siu Lum Pai Kung Fu Association teaches Shao-Lin Kung Fu, Tiger and Crane style, in day and night classes in eight locations on Oʻahu. For a free brochure contact them at 1613 Houghtailing St., Honolulu, HI 96817. 841-5228.

You can visit martial arts supply shops too. Golden Fist Self Defense Store handles all martial arts and ninja supplies and instructional videos for rent or sale, 1007 Dillingham Blvd., Rm. 201, Honolulu 845-2728. Hakabundo, Inc. has equipment and supplies for Judo, Aikido, Karate, and Kendo, 100 N. Beretania, Honolulu, 521-3805. Hawaii Martial Arts Supply Co. has books, uniforms, and equipment from China, Japan and Korea. Located across from Wo Fat Restaurant at 1041 Maunakea St., Honolulu, 536-5402.

## MOPEDDING
A moped is a cross between a bicycle and a motorcycle, and is defined as a two wheel motorized vehicle with a 50 cc or less engine and a top speed of below 30 mph. Mopeds have been a major form of transportation in Europe since World War II, where manufacturers such as Vespa, Puch, BMW, and Peugeot still build the best machines on the market.

Since mopeds have become a popular alternative to cars for the young crowd in Hawaii, accidents have skyrocketed. So if you're considering a moped for anyone in your travel group, follow these guidelines. First rent a solid, reliable machine. Second rent and use a helmet. And most importantly, realize that anyone on a two wheel vehicle with very limited speed and power is at a triple disadvantage on the highway. Avoid rush hour and weekend traffic, and give cars, trucks and busses plenty of room. Remember that roads in rural O'ahu often have shoulders in rough shape, so if you need to pull off, reduce your speed immediately. Use the buddy system whenever mopedding, exercise extreme caution and ride defensively. And since a moped can only travel up to 30 mph, be sure to pull over and offer motorists a chance to pass you in zones permitting travel speeds in excess of 30 mph.

Young vacationers on mopeds too often forget that they can be a target for motorists who can't see them or have a chip on their shoulder. So if you follow these precautions your moped excursion can be safe and enjoyable.

To rent a moped try: Inter-Island Rental with 4 Waikiki locations, 353 Royal Hawaiian Ave. (946-0013); City Bike 2469 South King St. (942-3045); and Maui Moped 2220 Kuhio Ave. (924-2401). For an alternative with more speed and power, try a motor scooter, with rentals available from: Sandy Brodie's Waipahu Cycles,94-169 Farrington Hwy., Waipahu (671-2691); South Seas Honda, 3149 N. Nimitz Hwy., Honolulu (836-1144); or Odyssey Rentals, 408 Lewers, Suite 102, Waikiki (947-8036).

## PARK HOPPING
O'ahu has beautiful parks which you and your children will love to explore. Write to these three sources for maps, brochures and recreational guides to parks and don't forget there are water parks too, such as Hanauma Bay.

Write the Hawaii Visitors Bureau (see GENERAL INFORMATION chapter for address); State of Hawaii, Dept. of Land & Natural Resources, Division of Parks, PO Box 621, Honolulu, HI 96809 (548-7455); and the Dept of Parks and Recreation, City and County of Honolulu, 650 South King St., Honolulu, HI 96813 (523-4183).

In the front of the Oʻahu phone book (white pages) under Honolulu City and County Parks and Recreation Department is a full listing of every city/county run park, playground, and recreation center on the Island. It's fun to get into your rental car, or city bus, and ride around Honolulu looking for parks and playgrounds to visit. You can also call the School District office to find out which public school playgrounds are open to visiting children and their families after school hours and on weekends (548-6911).

Some of Oʻahu's most enjoyable parks are: Queen Kapiolani Park between the Honolulu Zoo and Diamond Head Crater, Ala Moana Beach Park makai of Ala Moana Center, Thomas Square across from the Honolulu Academy of Arts, Kamanele Square on University Ave. just mauka of the University of Hawaii campus, and many of the beach parks on Oʻahu's coastline (see Beach Index). As previously discussed, you'll enjoy your park hopping most if you go during a weekday, leave before dusk, and look for posted park rules (some rules vary from park to park) and obey them. Have a great time!

# PHOTOGRAPHY - VIDEOTAPING

A visual record of your trip is a must in Hawaii. If you don't want to bother taking shots yourself or prefer to leave your expensive camera equipment at home, no problem. You can let someone else take the photos for you. Almost every souvenir shop and visitor attraction has slides, postcards, and videotapes for sale. "You're the Star" postcards (955-1693) will photograph you in the Waikiki setting of your choice, then make up postcards with you as the star. Ten postcards for $19.95. Adam Ozieblo of Video Pro Man will videotape you on a half day tour of Southeast Oʻahu, including a swim, stroll and boogie board adventure at Waimanalo Beach Park. Call 941-6786 between 5 and 8pm. You can view the tape that day, too.

If you have a camera, we suggest you buy film at the same place you plan to have it developed. And yes, you should see the results before you leave Oʻahu, both to assure the quality you desire and to avoid sending film through airport machines. Check in the local yellow pages, then choose a photo store near your accommodations or one you trust and like. Since you're buying film and processing you can expect good help with lighting, timing, or other advice. You can rent additional equipment too, including waterproof or sandproof cameras and video equipment. Here are several major photo outlets, all of which have good reputations.

In Waikiki, Fox Photo (942-8886) has five locations with cameras, equipment, one-hour developing, and video camera rentals starting at $19.95. Photo Stores has four locations in Waikiki, and features one-hour processing, camera and videotape rentals, and Hawaii's largest stock of Kodak film. Pay-n Save Stores and Long's Drug Stores have photo supplies, discount film and processing. Sears at Ala Moana Center and Pearlridge Center offers one-hour film process-ing, film and photo supplies. You can always find specials. California Photo Express (926-6500), 2139 Kalakaua Ave. sells the Fuji Quicksnap disposable 35 mm camera. It has film in it; just point, shoot, and leave it at the shop to be processed. Dollar Rent-a-Car sometimes advertises a deal in which you rent a convertible and get the use of a video camcorder free.

One famous place to calibrate your equipment and try out your technique is the free Kodak Hula Show in Kapiolani Park near the Waikiki Shell. Every Tuesday, Wednesday and Thursday at 10am you'll get shots of hula girls, flowers, and tons of photographers.

Other favorite photo spots on O'ahu include Diamond Head Crater, the Pali, Tantalus Drive and Puu Ualakaa State Park Lookout; Hanauma Bay (you'll want to rent a waterproof camera before you go); sunsets from the North Shore or the Leeward Coast, Chinatown in early morning, North Shore surfers and waves, flowers up close, and Waikiki Beach with Diamond Head Crater in the distance.

## RUNNING, JOGGING, WALKING
Honolulu is a running town, with running and jogging activities centered in the 5 mile loop around Diamond Head Crater and the 2.5 mile circuit of Queen Kapiolani Park. A popular jogging route is along the Ala Wai Canal in Waikiki. And beaches! In fact, many a tourist staggering down to the water's edge for a 7 am dip has witnessed footprints in the early morning sand.

Maybe they're practicing for the famous annual Honolulu Marathon, the 26.2 mile run attracting 10,000 runners from more than 20 countries each December. If you're interested in running, or watching the antics (some runners dress up in outrageous outfits) contact the Honolulu Marathon Association, 3435 Waialae Ave., Room 208, Honolulu, HI 96816 (734-7200). More likely all those runners on Diamond Head Loop are getting ready for one of the Honolulu Marathon Clinic's Sunday (7am) group runs. Or perhaps one of the weekly road races or fun runs held at various O'ahu spots every month. The Running Room store has a free schedule of running events and running-jogging supplies at 559 Kapahulu Ave. (737-2422). Look for The Runners Route, Ltd., another running supply store, in Ward Warehouse (523-6855), and the Windward Mall (247-5733).

## TENNIS/TABLE TENNIS
There are more than 200 tennis courts on O'ahu, including those at famous resorts such as the Ilikai Hotel, Sheraton Makaha Resort, Turtle Bay Hilton, and Kahala Hilton Hotels. There are also private tennis clubs such as the O'ahu Club (395-3300), Waialae Iki (373-1212), and the Kailua Racquet Club (264-4444) and public clubs such as the Honolulu Tennis Club (944-9696).

Most visitors play on O'ahu's 174 free public tennis courts, 106 of which are lighted and 24 have a practice backboard. A list of these courts is available free from the Honolulu Parks and Recreation Dept., 650 South King St., Honolulu, HI 96813 (523-4183). Parks with the most public courts are Keehi Lagoon (12), Ala Moana Beach Park (10), and Diamond Head Tennis Center (9) at the Diamondhead end of Kapiolani Park (which has 4 lighted courts open til 2 am).

Tennis instruction is available at the Ilikai Sports Center, Turtle Bay, Sheraton Makaha, and Kahala Hilton Hotel. For tennis supplies, try the Ilikai Sports Center, 1777 Ala Moana Blvd., Waikiki Golf and Sport Shop, 150 Kapahulu Ave. (senior discount), or Las Vegas Discount Golf and Tennis, 1020 Auahi St., Bldg. G, across from Ward Warehouse.

Table tennis has also become very popular in Hawaii with the large Chinese population. The sport began around 1900 as a parlor game and by the 1930's it had grown into a highly competitive sport throughout the world. The United States Table Tennis Association (USTTA) was formed in 1933, and governs the sport today. Did you know that table tennis is an Olympic sport? It made its debut as a medal sport during the 1988 Olympics in Seoul, Korea. A number of groups nationwide now sponsor table tennis as part of their program, including the Explorer Scout Division of the Boy Scouts of America, and the Boys and Girls Clubs of America. For information on tournaments and table tennis play on O'ahu, contact the Boys and Girls Club of Honolulu, 1704 Waiola St., Honolulu, HI 96826 (949-4743) or the U. S. Table Tennis Assoc., Olympic Ctr., 1750 E. Boulder St., Colorado Springs, CO 80909 (303-632-5551).

## THEATER/PERFORMING ARTS

Theater, films, plays, concerts, ballet, opera, and symphony; Honolulu has them all. And you can become an instant expert on weekend cultural events from one source. All you have to do is pick up the Friday edition of the Honolulu Advertiser and turn to the Living/Weekend Section B. The entire section is devoted to TGIF (The Great Index to Fun) compiled by talented Entertainment Editor Wayne Harada. I'm holding a copy in my hands. On page 1 is a potpourri of articles on radio, film, Frank DeLima (stand up comedian), dance performance and art gallery show of John Lennon's drawings. Page 3 - films showing. Page 4 - TV listings. Page 5 - Music, dance and concerts this weekend. Page 6 - happenings on neighbor islands. Page 7 - current stage productions. Page 8 - art. Page 9 - films and flings (such as church bazaars, chili cookoff and polo). Page 10 - Honolulu theater for youth, films and more films. If it has to do with music and the arts, you'll find it under TGIF. Now all you have to do is choose! To help you decide, here are a few treats you should give yourself while on O'ahu.

The Honolulu Symphony Orchestra performs its Classic Series September through April, and a summer series, Starlight Pops, in July and August. Contact them at 1441 Kapiolani Blvd., #1515, Honolulu, HI 96814 (942-2200).

Chamber Music Hawaii offers periodic concerts. For a schedule contact P.O. Box 61939, Honolulu, HI 96839-1939, enclose a self addressed, stamped envelope please. (261-4290).

Honolulu Community Theater, 520 Makapuu Ave., Honolulu, HI 96816 (734-0274); the Hawaii Performing Arts Company, 2833 East Manoa Rd., Honolulu, HI 96822 (988-6131); and the Kennedy Theater, 1770 East West Rd., Honolulu, HI 96822, produce a variety of excellent plays and musicals. The Honolulu Theater for Youth helps local youngsters perform for the public. A schedule of their performances is available from PO Box 3257, Honolulu, HI 96801.

The Hawaii State Ballet offers classical ballet training and schedules performances during the year. Write for a schedule at 1418 Kapiolani Blvd., Honolulu, HI 96814. The Hawaii Opera Theater performs three glorious operas each season, during February and March at the Neal Blaisdell Concert Hall in downtown Honolulu. Contact them at 987 Waimanu St., Honolulu, HI 96814 (521-6537).

# AIR ACTIVITIES

## HELICOPTER TOURS

You'll see ads for helicopter tours on TV, in the papers, and in the free tourist literature. They are spectacular and expensive, averaging close to $200 per hour. Tours leave from helipads at Waikiki (makai of Kahanamoku Lagoon near the Hilton Hawaiian Village), Turtle Bay Hilton, Sheraton Makaha Resort, and Kualoa Park on the Windward Side.

One company, *Hawaii Pacific Helicopters*, offers tours of: Waikiki (5-6 min., $28 per person); Diamond Head, Manoa Valley and the Kahela Coast (10-12 min., $45/person); Hanauma Bay (22-24 min., $78/person); Pearl Harbor Honolulu & Nuuanu Valley (22-24 min., $78/person); an O'ahu tour of southeast O'ahu and the Pali, a Small Circle Island Tour by air (25-30 min., $99 per person); and O'ahu Epic, which follows the coastline to Sacred Falls, Polynesian Cultural Center, North Shore Beaches, Waimea Falls Park, and returns to Honolulu via the Central O'ahu Valley (55-60 min., $187/person).

Departing from the Turtle Bay Hilton helipad, are tours of: Turtle Bay and Kahuku (5-6 min., $29/person); North Shore Tour of Elvis' mansion, beaches, heiau at Pupukea, Kaena point and whales in season (10-12 min., $47/person); Sacred Falls, Mormon Temple, Polynesian Cultural Center and Kahana Bay (25-30 min., $102/person); and a tour of O'ahu including Pearl Harbor, North Shore, Honolulu, Waikiki, Diamond Head, Koko Crater, Windward O'ahu, The Pali, and Sacred Falls (55-60 min., $192/person).

These tours are based on two passengers; but single passengers usually can be accommodated. Contact Hawaii Pacific Helicopters toll free at 1-800-367-8047, ext. 142. Other companies include: Royal Helicopters, 941-4683; Hawaii International Helicopters 839-5509; and Tropical Valley Helicopters, 833-3914.

## KITE FLYING

Queen Kapiolani Park is headquarters for serious kite flying on O'ahu. You'll see flyers from ages 3 to 100 with their kites in the sky - stunt fighters and homemade versions with newspaper and dowelling. Start your O'ahu kite adventure with a trip to a kite shop. There you'll find out if any kite contests or shows are coming up during your stay, and you'll get to see some of Hawaii's exotic kites. Talk to the owners and find out where and when you can see the best kite activity. Perhaps pick out a kite to take with you.

Then head for the park. Soon you'll be one of the flyers and you'll meet and see other kite flyers in action.

For kite supplies and information try: High as a Kite in the Royal Hawaiian Shopping Center (924-2775); High Performance Kites in Ala Moana Center near Center Stage (947-7097) - senior discount), Puck's Alley near University of Hawaii (942-8799), and Waikiki (924-7971); and Kite Fantasy, 2863 Kalakaua Ave. (922-5483).

## SKYDIVING

Here's a unique way to see the Oʻahu coastline! If you're military, the Tropic Lightning Sport Parachute Club offers instruction, rigging services and scales for personnel and their families over 16 years of age. First jump costs $90; after that, use of equipment is free to members for $10 monthly dues. The clubhouse is located on Wheeler AFB and is open on jump days, currently Wednesdays at 3 pm. Contact the USASCH Morale Support, Activities Division, Schofield Barracks, Bldg. 690 (655-4804).

For civilians, Sky Dive Hawaii Instruction will help you take the plunge from Dillingham Field on North Shore. They have FAA certified riggers and experienced instructors. Contact them at 33 South King St., Suite 504, Honolulu, HI 96813 (521-4404), or 66-485 Kilioe Place, Haleiwa, HI 96712 (637-7192).

## SMALL PLANE FLIGHTSEEING

If you prefer to enjoy the scenery from inside a plane rather than from under a parachute, try flight-seeing with or without an engine.

You've heard about the glider rides at Dillingham Field on the North Shore. This quiet air tour includes a look at the U.S. Air Force Satellite Tracking Station, a panoramic view of the North Shore coastline, aerial views of brilliant coral pools and sugar cane fields, and spontaneous entertainment offshore by leaping schools of dolphins, giant sea turtles, and occasional whales. Flights depart every twenty minutes from 10am-5:30pm every day; $35 single rider, $50 for a two passenger ride. Average visibility is 30 to 40 miles. Each ride is 15 to 20 minutes. Narration is provided by your experienced pilot-guide. Bring your camera. Contact Glider Rides (677-3404). No reservations required.

Several companies offer flightseeing in small fixed-wing prop aircraft. *Panorama Air Tours* will take you on a one-day tour of all eight Hawaiian Islands, combined with a ground tour of three major Islands: Hawaiʻi, Maui, and Kauaʻi. Flights are in an air conditioned, twin engine Piper Chieftain with panoramic view seating. Take a riverboat tour of the Wailua River to famous Fern Grotto on Kauaʻi, enjoy a no host luncheon on Maui, look at forbidden Niʻihau and Kahoʻolawe, and be back in your hotel in time for dinner. The complete air-ground tour is $185/person, plus tax. This is the oldest flightseeing operation in Hawaii, with the largest tour fleet of ten modern aircraft. Contact them at 100 Kaulela Pl., Honolulu, HI 96819 (836-2122 or 1-800-367-2671).

*Scenic Air Tours* has a variety of one-day outer island fly-drive tours in which your air and ground tour package is included in one price. For example Tour #1 takes you on a narrated air tour of five islands (Oʻahu, Kahoʻolawe, Lanaʻi, Maui and Molokaʻi) plus a continental breakfast and half day ground tour of Maui, including Wailuku, Mt. Haleakala (an extinct volcano), Maui Plantation, Lahaina Town, the Kaanapali Coast and Iao Valley State Park, all for $83 per person plus tax. Other fly-drive tours available with ground tours of Kauaʻi, Hawaiʻi (The Big Island), Maui, Molokaʻi, and an active volcano watch tour (weather permitting). Contact Scenic Air Tours, 100 Iolana Place, Honolulu, HI 96819 (836-0044). Reservations 24 hours in advance required.

## GOING HOME - DREAMS OF RETURNING

It's hard to believe that the time has gone by so fast, and the vacation you had looked forward to for so long is nearly over. But it isn't over yet, and these last few days and hours can be among your fondest vacation memories. Everyone copes with leaving Oʻahu in their own way. You may be ready to go, filled with anticipation of your arrival at home. Or you may start to feel sad and depressed as your last vacation days arrive. In either case, you can make the final days and hours of this Oʻahu vacation seem to last longer and be more filled with enjoyment if you'll follow whichever of the suggestions below are best suited to your needs and style.

Call your airline the day before you depart to confirm arrival flight and time, and to finalize arrival and transportation arrangements.

Make a written agenda for each of your last two or three vacation days during the evening before each day. This process will allow you to be sure that the sights and activities you most want to fit into these days will be included. Involve everyone in your travel group who wants to participate and make sure that everyone at least has one first choice represented on the agenda each day. Make a short list of people you've already bought presents for, and those who still need to be remembered. As you shop, buy a few extra souvenirs in case someone has been overlooked. While you're buying those last few items, you'll want to re-visit special shopping places you've fallen in love with during your vacation. As you look for bargains there, remember that holiday or birthday that is coming; a present from the islands will be a rare and cherished gift to the recipient. Consider having items boxed and sent home.

Several gifts are particularly well suited for taking home. Fresh pineapples top the list, and can be carried on the plane (in special boxes) or shipped. Fresh flower leis and exotic flowers can be sent home. The florist shops in Moiliili are excellent and among the least expensive. They'll pack the flowers you pick out and mail them, or you can save money and do your own mailing. Try: ***Flowers by Jr. Lou and T***, 2652 S. King St. (941-2022); ***Rudy's Flowers***, 2722 S. King St. (944-8844); ***Rusty's Florist***, 2700 S. King (941-2922); or in Waikiki (where you'll pay somewhat more) ***Exotics Hawaii-Waikiki***, Royal Hawaiian Shopping Center (922-2205). For fresh leis go to ***Sweetheart's*** between Smith and Maunakea St. at 65 N. Beretania (537-3011), or ***Cindy's Lei Shoppe***, 1034 Maunakea (536-6538), open Mon-Sat. 6:30am-9pm, Sun. & holidays 6:30am-7pm. You can also purchase a lei at the stands inside or outside the airport (the outside lei stands are the best buy) and they'll pack it for the trip home. Surprise those awaiting your return at the airport with a lei greeting!

Hilo Hatties Factory is not just a bargain basement of island fashions, but also features a large section of souvenirs, including the shell and seed leis which sell for well under a dollar and make wonderful gifts. While you're there, pick up a book of recipes to make exotic island drinks, and a local cookbook if you haven't already bought one. Buy some more of those 7 for a dollar post cards for the millions you've forgotten to write to. A card from the airport or even mailed from home is still a card from your Hawaiian trip.

Be sure that each piece of luggage you're carrying home, including that last minute box of pineapples, is clearly marked with your name and address, and that your children still have a label on their clothing or body identifying them, their local and home address and phone number. Count the total number of pieces you're carrying so you can keep track of them during your trip home.

If you're driving your rental car back to the airport, call a day or two in advance to confirm your return date and time. When you arrive, unload your bags first at your airline check-in (you can park there while you unload; a porter can check your bags from curbside if you desire). Allow yourself at least an hour and a half between the time you arrive and your flight time. Take your carry-on bags with you to the rental car return desk. Taxi service is available, or you may want to splurge and take a limousine to the airport. There are also affordable shuttle services. (See the GENERAL INFORMATION chapter on Getting Around)

If you get to the airport and realize you don't yet have a special present for your favorite Aunt Loucille, don't worry. There's a small city-full of specialty and gift shops between the check-in counter and your boarding gate. Not many bargain prices, but it's the last shopping mall between here and the mainland. The airport is your last chance to send a postcard home carrying an island postmark; and why not pick up the latest issue of *Honolulu* or *Hawaii* magazine to read on the plane?

You will have to have your check-in luggage and carry-on items inspected at the agricultural stations. On the airplane (remember the best views of the islands are from the left side) you can often get spectacular snapshots of Honolulu, O'ahu, and the outer islands shortly after takeoff.

Almost everyone who has visited O'ahu is filled with daydreams of a return trip. This brings us full cycle back to the first few pages of our guidebook in which you are encouraged to exercise your imagination and fantasize about the perfect Hawaiian vacation. Now that you've seen O'ahu and explored some of its mysteries, you're even better prepared to creatively visualize your return trip, and begin to make plans to turn your dreams into reality. Here are some ideas to help you with this enjoyable process:

Read *THE O'AHU UPDATE* to find new accommodations and restaurants plus special events that are happening during your next visit. You will want to plan your return to O'ahu with these events and celebrations in mind (review the Annual Events Calendar in the GENERAL INFORMATION chapter).

Consider visiting one or more of the outer islands on your next trip to O'ahu. You'll find a new world on each island when you buy and read the other books in the Paradise Guide series.

As you dream about and plan your next trip to O'ahu and Hawaii, we'll be there to assist you and do our best to make your next adventure every bit as enjoyable as this one. Bon voyage, and remember - Hawaii is a state of mind!

# RECOMMENDED READING

Acson, Veneeta. *Waikiki: Nine Walks Through Time*. Norfolk Island, Australia: Island Heritage. 1983.

Anderson, Frederick, et.al, Ed. *Mark Twain's Notebooks and Journals*, Vol. I (1855-1873) Bereley, CA: U of California Press. 1975.

Apple, Russ and Peg. *Tales of Old Hawaii*. Norfolk Island, Australia. 1977.

Ashdown, Inez McPhee, *Recollections of Kahoolawe*, Honolulu: Topgallant Publishing

Balcomb II, Kenneth C. *Whales of Hawaii*. Honolulu: The Marine Mammal Fund. 1988.

Bannick, Nancy, Agnes, Conrad and Frances Jackson, Editors. *Old Honolulu: A Guide to Oahu's Historic Buildings*. Honolulu: Historic Buildings Task Force. 1969.

Barrow, Terence. *Incredible Hawaii*. Vermont & Tokyo: 1988.

Bay, Mel. *Fun with the Ukulele*. MO: Mel Bay Publications, Inc. 1961.

Beckwith, Martha W. *The Kumulipo: A Hawaiian Creation Chant*. Honolulu: The Univ. Press of Hawaii. 1972.

Bird, Isabella L. *Six Months in the Sandwich Islands*. Seventh Printing. Vermont & Tokyo: Charles E. Tuttle Co., 1985.

Branch, Edgar M. et.al., *Mark Twain's Letters, Volume I* (1853-1866). Berkeley, CA: U of California Press. 1988.

Bryan, E.H. Jr. *Stars over Hawaii*. Hilo, HI: The Petroglyph Press. 1977.

Burningham, Robin Yoko. *Hawaiian Word Book*. Honolulu: Bess Press. 1983.

Bushnell, O.A., Ed. *The Illustrated Atlas of Hawaii*. Honolulu: Island Heritage. 7th edition. 1985.

Cahill, Emmett. *Hawaiian Stamps: An Illustrated History*. Volcano, Hawaii: Orchid Isle.

Carter, Frances. *Exploring Honolulu's Chinatown*. Honolulu: Bess Press. 1988.

Carter, Frances. *Hawaii for Free*. Conn.: Mustang Publishing Co.

Chisholm, Craig. *Hawaiian Hiking Trails*. OR: Fernglen Press. 1989.

Clark, John R.K. *Beaches of O'ahu*. Honolulu: U of Hawaii Press. 1977.

Clere, J. R. *Bryan's Sectional Maps of O'ahu*. Honolulu: EMIC Graphics. 1987.

Cohen, Stan. *The Pink Palace (The Royal Hawaiian Hotel)*. MT: Pictorial Histories Publishing Co. 1986.

Curtis, Caroline. *Life in Old Hawaii*. Honolulu: The Kamehameha Schools Press. 1970.

Day, A. Grove. *History Makers of Hawaii: A Biographical Dictionary*. Honolulu: Mutual Publishing of Honolulu. 1984.

Day, A. Grove. Ed. *A Hawaiian Reader*. Honolulu: Mutual Publishing Co., 1984.

Day, A. Grove. Ed. *Mark Twain's Letters from Hawaii*. Honolulu: U of Hawaii Press. 1983.

Finney, Ben R. *Hokule'a: The Way to Tahiti*. New York: Dodd, Mead & Co., 1979.

Goodman, Robert B. et.al. *The Hawaiians*. Sidney, Australia: Island Heritage, 1970.

Goodson, Gar. *The Many-Splendored Fish of Hawaii*. Stanford, CA: Stanford Univ. Press. 1985.

*"Guide to Hawaii's State Parks"*. Free from State of Hawaii, Div. of State Parks, PO Box 621, Honolulu, HI 96809.

Gutmanis, June. *Kahuna La'au Lapa'au*. Honolulu: Island Heritage. 1977.

Gutmanis, June. *Na Pule Kahiko (Ancient Hawaiian Prayers)*. Honolulu: Editions Limited. 1983.

*Hawaii Tourbook*. VA: American Automobile Association, 1989 (members only)

Hazama, Dorothy. *The Ancient Hawaiians*. Honolulu: Hogarth Press.

Hopkins, Jerry. *How to Make Your Own Hawaiian Musical Instruments*. Honolulu: Bess Press, 1988.

Joesting, Edward. *Hawaii: An Uncommon History*. New York: W.W. Morton & Co. 1972.

Joao, Caroline, Ed. *Ka Po'e Kahiko O Wai'anae (Oral Histories of the Old Ones of the Wai'anae Coast of Oahu)*. Honolulu: Topgallant Publishing. 1986.

Judd, Henry P. *The Hawaiian Language and Hawaiian-English Dictionary*. Honolulu: Hawaiian Service, Inc.

Kamakau, Samuel Manaiakalani. *Ruling Chiefs of Hawaii*. Honolulu: Kamehameha Schools. 1961.

Kawai'ae'a, Keiki Chang. *Let's Learn to Count in Hawaiian: Coloring and Activity Book.* Honolulu: Island Heritage. 1988.

Kyselka, Will. *An Ocean in Mind.* Honolulu: University of Hawaii Press. 1987.

Kyselka, Will and MacDonald, Gordon A. *Anatomy of An Island: A Geological History of O'ahu.* Honolulu: Bishop Museum Press. 1967.

Leach, Nicky, Ed. *Hawaiian National Parks.* CA: Sunrise Publishing. 1986.

Liliuokalani. *Hawaii's Story by Hawaii's Queen.* Tokyo: Charles E. Tuttle Co. 1979.

Lindo, Cecilia Kapua and Mower, Nancy Alpert, Eds. *Polynesian Seafaring Heritage.* Honolulu: Polynesian Voyaging Society and The Kamehameha Schools. 1980.

MacDonald, Gordon A. and Hubbard, Douglass H. *Volcanoes of the National Parks in Hawaii.* Honolulu: Tongg Publishing Co., Inc. 1982.

Malo, David. *Mo'olelo Hawaii (Hawaiian Antiquities).* Honolulu: Bishop Museum Press. 4th printing. 1980.

McBride, L.R. *Petroglyphs of Hawaii.* Hilo, HI: Petroglyph Press. 1969.

Mellen, Kathleen Dickenson. *The Magnificent Matriarch.* New York: Hastings House. 1952.

MeneHune. *Say It As It Is: Learn to Speak Hawaiian.* Honolulu: Hawaiian Isles Publishing Co. 1982.

Michener, James A. *Hawaii.* Greenwich, Conn.: Fawcett. 1973.

Mitchell, Charles and Schifflette, Colleen. *Hawaii for You and the Family.* Seattle, WA: Hancock House Publishers. 1979.

Mitchell, Donald D. Kilolani. *Resource Units in Hawaiian Culture.* Honolulu: The Kamehameha Schools Press. 1982.

Mrantz, Maxine. *Hawaii's Tragic Princess: Kaiulani, The Girl Who Never Got to Rule.* Honolulu: Aloha Graphics & Sales. 1980.

Mrantz, Maxine. *Women of Old Hawaii.* Honolulu: Aloha Graphics & Sales. 1982.

Mullins, Joseph G. *Hawaiian Journey.* Honolulu: Mutual Publishing Co. 1978.

Puku'i, Mary Kawena and Samuel H. Elbert. *Hawaiian Dictionary.* Honolulu: U of Hawaii Press. 1970.

Puku'i, Mary Kawena. *Nana I Ke Kumu (Look to the Source).* Honolulu: Hui Hanai. 1972.

Puku'i, Mary Kawena, Samuel H. Elbert and Esther T. Mookini. *Place Names of Hawaii.* Honolulu: U Hawaii Press. 1974.

Puku'i, Mary Kawena et. al., *The Pocket Hawaiian Dictionary.* Honolulu: The U Press of Hawaii. 1975.

Radlauer, Ruth and Anderson, Henry M. *Reefs.* Chicago: Children's Press. 1983.

Richardson, Jim, Ed. *The Honolulu Advertiser's Wildlife of Hawaii.* Honolulu: Honolulu Advertiser. 1986.

Ronck, Ronn. *Ronck's Hawaii Almanac.* Honolulu: U of Hawaii Press. 1984.

Roth, Steve and Paul. *My Travels in Hawaii.* Eugene, OR: Havin' Fun, Inc. 1986.

Sasaki, June. *Polynesian Crafts - Step by Step.* Hilo, HI: Petroglyph Press. 1978.

Shook, E. Victoria. *Ho'oponopono.* Honolulu: U of Hawaii Press. 1985.

Simonson, Doug (Peppo). *Pidgin To Da Max.* Honolulu: Peppovision. 1981.

Stone, Scott C.S. *Pearl Harbor: The Way It Was.* Honolulu: Island Heritage. 1977.

Sutherland, Audrey. *Paddling Hawaii.* Seattle, WA: Mountaineers. 1988.

Wisniekwski, Richard A. *The Rise and Fall of the Hawaiian Kingdom (A Pictorial History).* Honolulu: Pacific Basin Enterprises. 1979.

Zambucka, Kristin. *Princess Kaiulani, The Last Hope of Hawaii's Monarchy.* Honolulu: Mana Publishing Co. 1976.

**OTHER RESOURCES**

*The Bus Guide.* Bermuda Dunes. CA: C.P. International, Ltd.

Pahinui Records, c/o Kona-Kai Dist.Co., 2290 Alahao, Honolulu HI 96819

Pictorial Calendar: Hawaiian Service, Inc., PO Box 2835, Honolulu, HI 96803.

# INDEX

**Hawaii The Big Island**
A Paradise Guide
By John Penisten

**Maui**
A Paradise Guide
by Greg & Christie Stilson
Third Edition
Expanded & Updated

**Oahu**
A Paradise Guide
By Ken Bierly

**Kauai**
A Paradise Guide
by Don and Bea Donohugh
Second Edition
Expanded & Updated

**UPDATE NEWSLETTERS!** Each Paradise Guide features a companion newsletter. These information-filled quarterly publications highlight the most current island events. Each features late breaking tips on the newest restaurants, island activities or special, not-to-be missed events. Special feature articles are also included. *THE MAUI UPDATE, THE KAUA'I UPDATE, THE O'AHU UPDATE,* and *THE BIG ISLAND UPDATE* are available at the single issue price of $1.50 or a yearly subscription (four issues) price of $6 per year each.

# READER RESPONSE

Dear Reader:

I hope you have had a pleasant visit to O'ahu. Since this book expresses primarily my own opinions on places to stay, restaurants, and things to see and do, I would sincerely appreciate hearing of your experiences. Any updates or changes are also welcomed. Please address all correspondence to the publisher.

*FREE!* To keep you current on the most recent changes, Paradise Publications has introduced *THE O'AHU UPDATE*. A complimentary copy of this quarterly subscription newsletter is available by writing the publisher (Newsletter Dept.) and enclosing a self-addressed, stamped, #10 size envelope.

Traveling to another island? A Paradise Guide is available for each of the major Hawaiian Islands.

*MAUI, A PARADISE GUIDE* by Greg & Christie Stilson. Packed with information on over 150 condos & hotels, 200 restaurants, 50 great beaches, sights to see, travel tips, and much more. "A down-to-earth, nuts-and-bolts companion with answers to most any question." L.A. Times. 256 pages. Multi-indexed, maps, illustrations, $9.95. Third Edition - Expanded and Updated.

*KAUA'I, A PARADISE GUIDE* by Don & Bea Donohugh. Island accommodations, restaurants, secluded beaches, recreation and tours options, remote historical sites, an unusual and unique island tour, this guide covers it all. "If you need a "how to do it" book to guide your next tour to Kaua'i, here's the one." ...."this just-published guide may be the best available for the island. It has that personal touch of authors who have spent many happy hours digging up facts." Hawaii Gateway to the Pacific Magazine. 256 pages. Multi-indexed, maps, illustrations, $9.95. Second Edition - Expanded and Updated.

*O'AHU, A PARADISE GUIDE* by Ken Bierly. Let this exciting book be your personal tour guide to a Hawaii that you'll always remember. Discover why O'ahu is today's best vacation bargain, enabling the visitor to enjoy three wonderfully different vacations all on this one tropical Hawaiian isle. This guide features restaurants, accommodations, beaches, sight-seeing, and recreational and tour opportunities. 320 pages. Multi-indexed, maps, illustrations, $11.95.

*HAWAI'I: THE BIG ISLAND, A PARADISE GUIDE* by John Penisten. Outstanding for its completeness, this well-organized guide provides useful information for people of every budget and lifestyle. Each chapter features the author's personal recommendations and "best bets." Comprehensive information on more than 70 island accommodations and 150 restaurants. Sights to see, recreational activities, beaches, and helpful travel tips. 256 pages. Multiple indexes, maps, and illustrations. $9.95.

**See ordering information on following page.**

# ORDERING INFORMATION

**OTHER TITLES!**   Also available from Paradise Publications are interesting titles which may be hard to find in mainland bookstores.

*ON THE HANA COAST*, by Emphasis International Ltd. and Carl Lindquist, captures in rich color photographs and descriptive text the history of a people who arrived in double-hulled canoes to create a new life on the windward side of Maui. It is also the story of their descendents who became farmers, cowpunchers and even Hawaiian royalty. 6 x 9, 164 pages, $12.95, paperback.

*MAUI, THE ROMANTIC ISLAND* and *KAUAI, THE UNCONQUERABLE* by K.C. Publications. These books present full color photographs depicting the most magnificent sights on each island. Brief descriptive text adds perspective. Highly recommended. 9 x 12, 48 pages, $4.95 each, paperback.

*WHALES, DOLPHINS, PORPOISES OF THE PACIFIC*, from K.C. Publications. Enjoy the antics and of these beautiful aquatic creatures through full color photographs and descriptive text. 9 x 12, 48 pages, $4.95, paperback.

*HALEAKALA* and *HAWAII VOLCANOES* by K.C. Publications. Each offers dramatically distinctive scenery. Great as a memento or gift. Informative text accompanies these vivid photographs. 9 x 12, 48 pages, $4.95 each, paperback.

*MY TRAVELS IN HAWAII*, by Steve and Paul Roth, offers 56 delightful pages for the young traveler. A unique activity book for use on vacation or at home. Recommended ages K - 6. 8 1/2 x 11, 56 pages, $2.95, paperback.

*HAWAIIAN HIKING TRAILS*, by Craig Chisholm. This very attractive and accurate guide details 49 of Hawaii's best hiking trails. Each trail description includes photography, a topographical map, a statistical summary, and detailed directions. A color section in the forward part of the books tempts the hiker with the delights which await. 6 x 9, 152 pages, $12.95, paperback.

*COOKING WITH ALOHA*, by Elvira Monroe and Irish Margah. Discover the flavors, smells and tastes of the Hawaiian islands in your own kitchen with this beautifully illustrated and easy-to-follow cookbook. Delicacies range from exotic pickled Japanese seaweed or taro cakes to flavorful papaya sherbet or chicken 'ono niu. Drinks, appetizers, main courses and desserts are covered. 9 x 12, paperback, 184 pages, $7.95.

**SHIPPING**: Add $2 per book title, maximum of $4.00 to same address. A gift? Just supply us with the name and address! Orders promptly shipped first class mail or UPS.

**PARADISE PUBLICATIONS**      **(503) 246-1555**
**8110 S.W. Wareham, Suite 100**
**Portland, OR 97223**